# THE
# OFFALY
# WAR DEAD

# THE
# OFFALY
# WAR DEAD

## TOM BURNELL

Many thanks to Miss Rosemary Edwards of the County Library in Tullamore,
Ciarán Reilly, Edenderry Historical Society, and my daughter Kathleen Burnell
for all her typing skills and tolerance of this doddery old codger.

First published 2010

The History Press, Ireland
119 Lower Baggot Street,
Dublin 2, Ireland
www.thehistorypress.ie

British Library Cataloguing in Publication Data.
A catalogue record for this book is available from the British Library.

ISBN 978 184588 974 6

Typesetting and origination by The History Press
Printed in Great Britain
Manufacturing managed by Jellyfish Print Solutions Ltd

# CONTENTS

# FOREWORD

For too long a taboo subject within Irish historical studies, and indeed the mind-set of the general public, Irish involvement in the Great War, 1914-1918, is finally being recognised and understood. Such an understanding is only possible when one considers the events and climate of the time, without the hindsight of the war's outcome or subsequent events in Irish history. With the centenary of the out-break of the war fast approaching, local historical studies will enlighten further our knowledge of this momentous event in history. Tom Burnell's lists of the Great War dead of various counties, and which now includes Offaly (formerly King's County), leads the way in that field. From every village and town throughout Co. Offaly, men enlisted to serve the war effort. Some of these men had previous army experience or connections to previous military campaigns, especially the Boer War. For others a sense of adventure or curiosity led them to battle fields of Europe. In 1917, it was reported that as many as 452 from the county town of Tullamore had heard 'the call of the bugle' since 1914. The village of Ballycumber sent seventy-two men of whom they were extremely proud; their names were erected at the nearby railway station throughout the course of the war. The imposing military barracks at Crinkill, near Birr, ensured that enlistment in that area, where the Prince of Wales' Leinster Regiment (Royal Canadians) were stationed, was also strong. For the people of Birr, the enlistment of the fifth Earl of Rosse (who later died from injuries sustained in the war) was an encouraging and inspirational gesture.

Less than a month before the 1916 Easter Rising in Dublin, T.R. Dixon, British Army Recruiting Officer for Offaly, attended a meeting of the Edenderry Town Commissioners, at which Denis Fay presided over as chairman. After hearing Dixon's request for more troops, the town council decided to form themselves into a committee to stimulate recruiting in that part of the King's County. Many questions remain unanswered as to why certain individuals decided to enlist. It may not be so simple as to suggest that economic necessity was the sole reason why many decided to go to war. Why did twenty-seven-year-old Patrick Behan, of Edenderry, a chair maker, secure in a thriving employment, enlist to fight for the 'rights of small nations'? His friend and neighbour, an unemployed grocer's assistant, Michael Foley, then aged twenty-two, threw his lot in with the Irish volunteers on Easter Monday 1916 in the G.P.O.

The enduring horrors of the war were everyday lived by the people back home. Anxious parents, wives, and children waited nervously on news of loved ones. In

July 1918, a Mrs Connell of Edenderry received word that her son, Patrick, might be alive, and that he was being held prisoner. However, weeks later, news arrived that Connell was nearly a year dead and was buried at Cambrai. The people of Offaly were also quick to lend a hand to those who were suffering and displaced because of the war. A committee was formed to raise funds to house Belgian refugees, and in late 1914, Mrs Nesbitt of Tubberdaly House, Rhode, took in a family of four. After several fundraising events in Edenderry, the sum of £37 was raised for the refugees of the war, while Aylesbury Mills employed two Belgian workers in June 1915. The Great War also accelerated the decline of the gentry around Ireland as the sons of the Irish Big House failed to return home. Such men from Offaly included the aforementioned earl of Rosse, Wilfred Beaumont Nesbitt, Assheton Biddulph, and Frederick Charles Bloomfield.

Today the memorials in Tullamore's O'Connor Square, the stained glass window at St Brendan's church in Birr, and the memorial at Castro Petre at Edenderry offer everyday reminders of the sacrifices, and perhaps futility of these deaths. Tom Burnell's list of Offaly's War Dead will give names to the men from Offaly who gave the supreme sacrifice in the 'war to end all wars'. It will also act as a guide for genealogical studies, and will provide others with a template of useful sources for undertaking further research. If it achieves either or both of these aims it will surely have been a worthwhile venture.

Ciarán J. Reilly,
Secretary, Edenderry Historical Society

This photo was taken in front of the memorial in O'Connor Square, Tullamore. Courtesy of the Offaly Historical & Archaeological Society, Tullamore Co. Offaly.

# TERMINOLOGY

**Killed in action:** The soldier was killed during engagement with the enemy.

**Died of wounds:** The soldier was not killed outright and may have made it back to the Regiments Aid post or Casualty Clearing Station before he eventually died of his wounds.

**Died at home:** Death by drowning, suicide, accident, or illness in the UK. Home in these cases means in the UK or Ireland and not necessarily where he lived. Many times I have come across this and it turned out to be that the soldier died in a UK hospital.

**Died of wounds at home:** The soldier was not killed outright and may have made it back to the Regiments Aid post or Casualty Clearing Station before he eventually died of his wounds back in the UK or Ireland.

**Died:** Can mean death by drowning, suicide, accident, or illness.

**Sources**: The Commonwealth War Graves Commission, 'Soldiers died in the Great War'. Soldiers of the Great War, The New Library, and Archives Canada. The National Archives of Australia. Nominal Rolls of the New Zealand Expeditionary Force. *King's County Independent, King's County Chronicle, Midland Tribune, Tipperary Sentinel* and *King's County Vindicator*. De Ruvigny's Roll of Honour. The Public Records Office in Kew, UK. The National Roll of the Great War, London, The War Graves of the British Empire, Commonwealth War Graves Commission registers for the Irish Free State, and 'Ireland's Memorial Records'.

# A

**ABBOT/ABBOTT, Frederick James:** Rank: Lance Corporal. Regiment or Service: Queens Own Cameron Highlanders. Unit: 1ˢᵗ Battalion. Date of death: 25 September 1914. Service no: 8598. Formerly he was a Lance Corporal with the Royal Scots Fusiliers where his number was 8186. Born in Birr, Co. Offaly. Enlisted in Dublin. Killed in action. He has no known grave but is listed on the La Ferte-Sous-Jouarre Memorial in France.

**ACRES, William:** Rank: Pte. Regiment or Service: Irish Guards. Date of death: 19 December 1914. Age at death: 17. Service no: 6236.

*Supplementary information:* Son of Henry and Eva Acres, of Ballybeg, Brosna, Co. Offaly. He is not listed in 'Soldiers died in the Great War'. Grave or Memorial Reference: D.29. Cemetery: Caterham and Warlingham (Caterham) Burial Ground, UK.

**ADAMS, John Goold:** Rank: Captain. Regiment or Service: Leinster Regiment. Unit: 1ˢᵗ Battalion. Date of death: 5 May 1915. Killed in action. From the *Midland Tribune*, *Tipperary Sentinel* and *King's County Vindicator*, 1915:

John Goold Adams.

DEATH OF CAPTAIN JOHN GOOLD ADAMS.

The Ven, J M Goold-Adams, Archdeacon of Derry, has received intimation that his only son, Captain John Goold-Adams, of the First Leinster Regiment, was killed in action near Ypres on the 4ᵗʰ inst. The news arrived on Sunday morning as the Archdeacon was preparing to conduct Services in Clonleigh Parish Church. Though only 32 years of age, Captain Goold-Adams had seen much service. After passing through Sandhurst, he received his commission in the First Leinsters.

Subsequently he was accepted for service in Nigeria, where he remained for several years. In the autumn of 1913 he was married to Miss Irene Biddulph, second daughter of Mr and Mrs Assheton-Biddulph, Moneyguineen, Kinnitty. Afterwards he went to India on duty, returning home on the outbreak of hostilities to serve in his regiment at the front. A couple of months ago he was slightly wounded but soon recovered in an hospital at Le Harve, and rejoined his regiment.

## Leinster's Roll of Honour:

TUESDAY'S CASUALTY LIST.

Captain Goold Adams, who was the only son of the Ven J.M. Goold Adams, Archdeacon of Derry, was married in the autumn of 1913 to Miss Irene Biddulph, second daughter of Mr Assheton Biddulph, MFH, Moneyguyneen, Kinnitty. He was 32 years of age and had seen much service in Nigeria and India, from where he returned on the outbreak of the war to serve in his regiment at the front. A couple of months ago he was slightly wounded, but on May 4 he fell in action near Ypres. The young officer was as popular in his regiment as are his young widow and her parents in the King's and adjoining counties, and much sympathy is extended to them in their mourning.

## From De Ruvigny's Roll of Honour:

*Adams, John Goold*. Capt., 1ˢᵗ battn, Prince of Wales Leinster Regiment (Royal Canadians). Son of the Ven. John Michael Goold Adams, Rector of Clonleigh, County Donegal, and Archdeacon of Derry, by his wife, Emma, daughter of Robert McClintock, of Dunmore, County Donegal, D.L. Born in Rosdowney Vicarage, Londonderry, 10 Oct, 1883. Educated at Bilton Grange Preparatory School, Rigby, and Sandhurst; gazetted 2ⁿᵈ Lieut. Leinster regt. 22 April, 1903, becoming Lieut, 15 Dec, 1904, and Capt, 21 Sept, 1912; served at Pretoria, 1903-4, with the Mounted Infantry at Harrysmith, 1904-5, and in the Mauritius, 1905-6, and was employed with the West African Frontier Force in Northern Nigeria, 1908 to Nov, 1913. After the outbreak of war in Aug, 1914, he accompanied his regiment to France (Dec, 23), was wounded in Feb, 1915, and was killed in action at Hill 60, near Ypres, 4 May following. He married ay Moneyguineen, Birr, King's County, 5 Aug, 1913, Irene Grace, daughter of Assheton Biddulph, M.F.H., of Moneyguineen aforesaid.

Has no known grave but is commemorated on Panel 44 on the Ypres (Menin Gate) Memorial in Belgium.

**AHERN/AHERNE/AHEARN, Patrick Joseph:** Rank: Lieutenant (Quartermaster). Regiment or Service: Leinster Regiment. Unit: 7ᵗʰ Bn. Age at death: 41. Date of death: 9 September 1916.

*Supplementary information:* Son of Mrs M. Ahern, of Thurles, Co.

Tipperary. Husband of Mary Ellen Ahern, of 2 Townsend Street House, Birr, Co Offaly. Won the South African War medal. From a Tipperary newspaper article:

Patrick Joseph Ahern.

A GUILLEMONT HERO. HOW LIEUTNANT, P.J. AHEARN FELL.

Mrs Edward Murphy, The Mall, Thurles, has received the following letter from the colonel commanding the 7th Leinsters; "27th September, 1916. Dear Mrs Murphy, As soon as possible after your poor brother met his death in action I write you to convey the sympathy of all ranks in this battalion, and to give such particulars as I am able. Your brother was killed while gallantly leading the attack east of Guillemont on the 9th September. Although his duty was Lieutenant and Quartermaster he was always anxious to be in it when fighting was going on. He had obtained promotion as Captain. His death is also a very sad loss to us. He was killed, I believe, instantly. His orderly was with him at the time, but he himself was wounded and taken back, so I cannot question him for further information at present.

We were all under a very heavy fire for a long time, and we with difficulty, managed to get our wounded away. It was a thrilling sight to see on that morning officers and all men at Holy Communion. It will be an ease of mind to you to know that your gallant brother died a hero for God and his country. I have written to his sorrowing mother. I hope some further information may come to you at a later date. With deepest sympathy with you in your great sorrow. Believe me, yours very truly. Colonel, Credy, 7th Leinster Regiment".

From the *Midland Tribune*, *Tipperary Sentinel* and *King's County Vindicator*, September 1916:

Major Gaye, of the 7th Leinsters, has written to Mrs Ahearne conveying deep regret and sympathy on the death of her husband on behalf of himself and all ranks. "When there was fighting to be done" Major Gaye wrote, "he always insisted on being to the fore, and died whilst gallantly leading his men in an attack about 300 yards of Guillemont.

From the *King's County Chronicle*, November 1915:

THE LEINSTERS IN BATTLE.
(BY A REGIMENTAL POET.)

Lieut P.J. Ahearne, of the 7th Leinsters, has very kindly sent for the benefit of the readers of the "King's County Chronicle" the following lines composed by a signaller of the regiment, whose home is not many miles from the 'Model Town," and we gladly give the post a welcome to our columns. We hope that his stirring verses will not only be read with interest by his gallant comrades in a dug-out in France, but will also awake the patriotic feelings of those who, though in more comfortable surroundings now, should give the lively Leinsters a helping hand.

THE 27TH DIVISION.

We sailed from Bombay more than
   ten months ago,
And formed up at Winchester
   under Genral Snow.
He said "Now, my lads, I suppose
   you all know,
You're the 27th Division."

The first trenches we saw were at
   Dickebush,
Where the Huns tried hard to give
   us the push,
But they got cannoned right off
   the cush,
By the 27th Division

On the 14th of February the
   Germans came round,
And tried to take from us a place
   called the mound;

They had to postpone it, because
   they found,
The 27th Division.

Not the Kaiser got wild, he raved,
   and he swore.
He said to Von Kluck, "I'll send one
   army corps",
Von Kluck said, "Dear Kaiser, send
   three or four,
It's the 27th Division."

At St. Eloi the Huns tried once
   more in vain,
They came a few yards, but were
   pushed back again,
Von Kluck said "Dear Kaiser, I am
   not to blame,
It's the 27th Division."

We shifted once more round Ypres
   way,
When the Germans saw us some
   started to pray,
And others packed up and shouted
   good day,
To the 27th Division.

They tell the Kaiser is going quite
   daft,
He's nearly done, you can see it,
   not 'arf,
And all he does now is to say, "Gott
   strafe
The 27th Division."

Although by this time our ranks
   got thin,
We'll fight and wear the same
   cheerful grin.
And amongst the first troops to
   enter Berlin
Will be the 27th Division.

[Not wishing to leave the boys of the 16th Division out in the cold, Lieut. Ahearne adds the following "reinforcing" verse:]

To back up the 27th, we can only say
Soon our comrades to help we
    earnestly pray,
And we'll shorten the war by a year
    and a day,
Will the 16th [Irish] Division.

Has no known grave but is commemorated on Pier and Face 16.C. Memorial:
Theipval Memorial in France.

**ALLEN, Thomas William:** Rank:
Quartermaster Sergeant. Regiment
or Service: 1st County of London
Yeomanry (Middlesex Yeomanry).
Age at death: 27. Date of death: 29
March 1919. Service no: 260041.

*Supplementary information:* Son of
Edward and Janet M. Allen. Husband
of Daisy Evelyn Allen, of 100
Elphinstone Road, Hastings. Grave or
Memorial Reference: 46. Cemetery:
Birr Military Cemetery, Co. Offaly.

**ALLCOCK, Louis:** Rank: Pte.
Regiment or Service: Durham Light
Infantry. Unit: 2nd Battalion. Date of
death: 21 September 1914. Service no:
8421. Born in Goldenbridge, Dublin.
Enlisted in Nottingham while living
in Birr. Killed in action. He has no
known grave but is listed on the La
Ferte-Sous-Jouarre-Memorial in
France.

**ARMSTRONG, Martin:** Rank:
Pte. Regiment or Service: Leinster
Regiment. Unit: 2nd Battalion. Date of
death: 24 June 1916. Service no: 3602.
Born in Clara, Co. Offaly. Enlisted
in Athlone, Co Westmeath. Killed in
action in Kemmel. Age at death: 28.
Awarded the Mons Star. Grave or
Memorial Reference: L.3. Cemetery:
Kemmel Chateau Military Cemetery
in Belgium.

# B

**BAILEY, Abraham:** Rank: Sergeant. Regiment or Service: Irish Guards. Unit: 1st Battalion. Date of death: 6 November 1914. Service no: 1627. Born in Rynagh, Co. Offaly. Enlisted in Birr, Co. Offaly. Killed in action. From an Offaly newspaper, '1627, Sergeant A. Bailey, 1st Battalion, Irish Guards, reported missing, 6 November 1914. His relations would be glad of any news concerning him. He was the youngest son of the late Joseph Bailey, Park, Banagher.' Grave or Memorial Reference: Has no known grave but is commemorated on Panel 11. Memorial: Ypres (Menin Gate) Memorial in Belgium.

**BARKER, Arthur Samuel:** Rank: Regimental Sergeant Major. Regiment or Service: Royal Field Artillery and Royal Horse Artillery. Unit: 86th Brigade Headquarters. Date of death: 26 July 1916. Age at death: 33. Service no: 37147. Born in Dublin. Enlisted in Dublin. Died of wounds.

*Supplementary information:* Won the Distinguished Conduct Medal. Son of Samuel and Alice Barker. Native of Dublin. From the *King's County Chronicle*, July 1915, 'Regimental Sergeant Major Arthur S Barker, R.F.A. who as a schoolboy lived with his aunt Miss Barker, of John's Place, Birr, was presented last week with the D.C.M. by the King at Buckingham Palace.' From the *King's County Chronicle*, September 1916:

Details are just to hand of the death from wounds on July, 26th of R.S.M. Arthur S. Barker, Royal Field Artillery, late of Birr. A winner of the Distinguished Conduct Medal and the Cross of St George (the Russian equivalent of the Victoria Cross). Barker had also been wounded three times in the Great War. The manner of his death was befitting a hero. Although suffering from fatal hurts himself he gallantly assisted his wounded comrades into safety, and was engaged in this noble work when he collapsed from weakness due to loss of blood. Deceased was a nephew of Miss Barker, formerly of John's Place, Birr and he was educated at Birr Model School.

Grave or Memorial Reference: II.E.15. Cemetery: Heilly Station Cemetery, Mericourt-L'Abbe in France.

**BARRETT, Henry:** Rank: Drummer. Regiment or Service: Leinster Regiment. Unit: 2nd Battalion. Date of death: 12 August 1915. Service No 9334. Born in Birr, Co. Offaly. Enlisted in Aldershot, Hants. Killed in action.

*Supplementary information:* Grave or Memorial Reference: IID25. Cemetery, Birr Cross Roads Cemetery in Belgium.

**BARRY, Albert:** Rank: Pte. Regiment or Service: Yorkshire Regiment. Unit: 4$^{th}$ and 1$^{st}$/4$^{th}$ Battalion. Date of death: 14 May 1915. Service no: 3020. Born in Bishop Middleham, Durham. Enlisted in Northallerton while living in Oakhill in Bath. Died of wounds.

*Supplementary information:* He is listed on the Tullamore Roll of Honour. Grave or Memorial Reference: VC.36. Cemetery: Boulogne Eastern Cemetery in France.

Note: I do not see the Offaly connection but include him for your reference. It also says he was killed in September 1915. You can see how the dates do not tally and he was the only Albert Barry that died while in service with the Yorkshire Regiment.

**BARRY, William:** Rank: Sergeant. Regiment or Service: Royal Garrison Artillery. Unit: 66$^{th}$ Siege Bty. Age at death: 28. Date of death: 4 October 1917. Service no: 28881. Born in Ayems, Bally-Brittas, Co. Laois. Enlisted in Fort Westmoreland while living in Kileavan, Co. Offaly. Killed in action.

*Supplementary information:* Son of Stephen and Mary Barry, of Grange Cottage, Killeigh, Tullamore, Co. Offaly. Grave or Memorial Reference: II.B.12. Cemetery: White House Vemetery, St Jean-Les-Ypres in Belgium.

**BARTLEY, Patrick:** Rank: Pte. Regiment or Service: Connaught Rangers. Unit: 2$^{nd}$ Battalion. Date of death: 1 November 1914. Service no: 4084. Born in Birr, Co. Offaly. Enlisted in Ballinasloe, Co. Galway while living in Birr. Killed in action. Age at death: 20. Grave or Memorial Reference: He has no known grave but is listed on Panel 42 on the Ypres (Menin Gate) Memorial in Belgium.

*Supplementary information:* Son of Patrick and Jane Bartley, of Pound Street, Birr, Co. Offaly. From *King's County Chronicle*, April 1915:

SAFETY OF BIRR SOLDIER.

It has been truly said that strange things are happening in the present war, and not the least are the ways in which some people who have been mourned as dead have turned up again as if nothing had happened. A case in point. In November last Mrs Bartley, Pound Street, Birr, was officially notified that her son, Patrick, a private in the Connaught Rangers, had been killed in action, and she was the recipient of much sympathy. Yesterday morning, however, she received a field service post card from her son saying that he was quite well and was being sent down to the base. And with a touch of irony he expressed wonder that he had received no letters from her. But she is so glad now that he will have no complaint on this head in future.

Note: The question of whether this man died or survived is answered when the Commonwealth War Graves

Commission added the next of kin details to his readout. This information is only added after the war and has to be voluntarily supplied by the next of kin for inclusion. A quick check of the Connaught Rangers war diary for the 8th of November also shows that he was killed in action on 8 November.

**BEATTIE, Patrick:** Rank: Pte. Regiment or Service: East Lancashire Regiment. Unit: 1st Battalion. Date of death: 3 November 1914. Service no: 8625. Born in Tullamore, Co. Offaly. Enlisted in Tullamore. Killed in action.

*Supplementary information:* Brother of James Beattie, of 21 Davitt's Street, Tullamore, Offaly. Listed on the Tullamore Roll of Honour as **BEATTY.** Grave or Memorial Reference: Panel 5 and 6. Memorial: Ploegsteert Memorial in Belgium.

**BEAUMONT-NESBITT, Wilfrid Henry:** Rank: Captain, also listed as Lieutenant/Acting Captain. Regiment or Service: Grenadier Guards. Unit: No. 2 Coy. 2nd Bn. Age at death: 23. Date of death: 27 November 1917. Awarded the Military Cross and listed in the *London Gazette*. Killed in action.

*Supplementary information:* Son of Edward and Helen Beaumont-Nesbitt, of Tubberdaly, Edenderry, Co. Offaly. From *The Times* 4 December 1917:

Capt W.H. Beaumont Nesbitt Grenedier Guards killed on November 27 2nd son of E.J. and Mrs Nesbitt of Tubberdaly. He was educated for the navy at Osborne and Dartmouth, joined the Grenadier guards in 1915. Went to the front that year. Sept 1916 wounded at Les Boeufs in the Battle of the Somme, where he was the M.C.

Appointed instruction to the household brigade officer cadet Battalion the year before rejoining the front.

From De Ruvigny's Roll of Honour:

Beaumont-Nesbitt, Wilfred Henry, M.C., Capt., Grenadier Guards; 2nd son of Edward John Beaumont-Nesbitt, of Tubberdaly, Edenderry, King's County, by his wife, Helen, daughter of Frederick Freeman-Thomas. Born Eastbourne, Co. Sussex, 2 Sept, 1894. Educated at Ludgrove, Osbourne; Dartmouth Naval Colleges, and Trinity College, Cambridge. Gazetted Midshipman, and was invalided out of the Navy in 1912. Gazetted 2nd Lieut, in the Grenadier Guards in Feb, 1915. Promoted Lieut, 1916, and Capt, the same year. Served with the Expeditionary Force in France and Flanders from June, 1915, was wounded at Les Boeufs during the Somme Battle in Sept, 1916. On recovery, was appointed instructor to the Household Brigade Officers Cadet Battn. Returned to France in Aug, 1917, and was killed in action at Fontaine, near Bourlon Wood, 27 Nov, following. He was awarded the Military Cross for gallant and distinguished service in the field.

Grave or Memorial Reference: Panel 2. Memorial: Cambrai Memorial, Louveral in France.

**BEEHAN/BEHAN, Patrick:** Rank: Pte. Regiment or Service: Middlesex Regiment. Unit: 13th Battalion. Secondary Regiment: 5th (Royal Irish) Lancers. Date of death: 6 April 1917. Service no: G/41910. Born in Edenderry, Co. Offaly. Enlisted in Dublin while living in Offaly. Died of wounds. Age at death: 36.

*Supplementary information:* Son of the late Edward and Mary Behan, of Edenderry, Co. Offaly. From the *Leinster Leader* 5 May 1917, 'Mrs Behan of New Row has received official confirmation of the death of her son Patrick on Good Friday. Known as Parky he was in the fifth Irish Lancers.' Grave or Memorial Reference: I.B.10. Cemetery: Fosse No. 10 Communal Cemetery Extension, Sains-En-Gohelle in France.

**BEGLEY, Henry Frederick:** Rank: Pte. Regiment or Service: Connaught Rangers. Unit: 1st Battalion. Date of death: 27 July 1919. Service no: 11027. Born in Birr, Co. Offaly. Enlisted in Maryboro while living in Dublin. Killed in action in North Russia. Age at death: 27.

*Supplementary information:* Son of William and Agnes Begley, of 23 Upper Dorset Street, Dublin. He has no known grave but is listed on the Special Memorial, B8. Cemetery: Archangel Allied Cemetery in the Russian Federation.

**BEHAN, P.:** Rank: Pte. Regiment or Service: Middlesex Regiment. Unit: 13th Battalion. Date of death: 6 April 1917. Age at death: 36 (Commonwealth War Graves Commission) 34 ('Ireland's Memorial Records'). Service no: 41910. Killed in action at Vimy Ridge.

*Supplementary information:* Son of the late Edward and Mary Behan, of Edenderry, Co. Offaly. He is not listed in 'Soldiers died in the Great War'. Grave or Memorial Reference: I.B.10. Cemetery: Fosse, No 10, Communal Cemetery Extension, Sains-En-Gohelle in France.

**BENSON, Arthur George:** Rank: Corporal. Regiment or Service: Royal Dublin Fusiliers. Unit: 2nd Bn. Date of death: 18 November 1918. Service no: 13097. Age at death: 19. Born in Shinrone, Co. Offaly. Enlisted in Dublin while living in Shinrone. Died of wounds seven days after the war ended.

*Supplementary information:* Son of James and Catherine Benson, of 4 Sutton Villas, Dargle Road, Bray, Co. Wicklow. Native of Bellevue, Shimroe, Offaly. From *King's County Chronicle*, January 1915:

THREE BRAVE SONS
FROM SHINRONE.

It will be read with pleasure and a sense of congratulation to their respected father, Mr Jas, Benson, Shinrone, that his three sons have promptly responded to the call to arms. James, the eldest who was until recently an assistant Master in Bishop Cotton School, Bangalore, and formerly of Rathmines College, Dublin, has received a commission in the 101$^{st}$ Grenadiers (Indian Army). He expects to be sent on active service to German East Africa, where it may be remembered the Regiment was badly cut up in November last. Mr Benson's other son, Harry, who emigrated to Melbourne only last July and was doing extremely well has, with true gallantry joined the Australian Contingent. Another son, Arthur, is in training at the Curragh with the Royal Dublin Fusiliers. He has been offered Lance Corporal, stripe but modestly declined, on the ground of his youth, he being only 16 years of age. Their many friends wish them a victorious career.

## From *King's County Chronicle*, July 1917:

MILITARY MEDAL.

Lance Corporal Henry Benson, of the 12$^{th}$ Australian Field Ambulance, has received the Military Medal for conspicuous gallantry in stretcher bearing under heavy shell fire at Messines on the 7$^{th}$ June, 1917. He was decorated specially by the General of his Division. This gallant young man is a son of Mr James Benson, of Bellvue, Shinrone, who received notification of the honour conferred on his son from the Australian Headquarters in London. Some years ago, Lance Corporal Benson was employed in Messrs, Rhodes and Son, drapers, Roscrea.

He went to Australia in July, 1914, and joined the Australian Furces in January, 1915. he was sent to Egypt and did hospital work there for some time. More than a year ago he went to France, where he has since been engaged in the Field Ambulance. A brother of his, Captain H. W. Benson, is at present in Palestine and has been recommended for a high distinction. Another brother, Arthur, was in the 6$^{th}$ Dublins, and went through the Gallipoli campaign. He has been invalided home.

## From *King's County Chronicle*, November 1918:

Another of our brave lads has fallen, practically when peace is at hand. We refer to Corporal A. G. Benson, who died of wounds received in action and bronchial pneumonia, at the 5$^{th}$ General Hospital, Rouen, on 18$^{th}$ inst. He was the third serving son of Mr James Benson, Bellvue, Shinrone. On the outbreak of war he joined the Royal Dublin Fusiliers. He was at the landing of Suvla Bay. Later he was sent to Salonika, and served in operations against the Bulgarians in November, 1915, and early in March 1918, he was sent to Egypt. In the recent fighting he took part in the capture of Le Chateau, etc. In an extract from his last letter he stated: 'I am going over the top in a couple of hours. If I am killed you will know that I died trusting the Lord, and died defending my country.'

## Grave or Memorial Reference: S.III.J.6. Cemetery: St Sever Cemetery Extension, Rouen in France.

**BENSON, William John:** Rank: Rifleman. Regiment or Service: Royal Irish Rifles. Unit: 2nd Battalion. Date of death: 8 July 1916. Service no: 4412. Born in Shinrone, Co. Offaly. Enlisted in Dublin while living in Shinrone. Killed in action. From *King's County Chronicle*, September 1915:

> FOUR KING'S COUNTY, BROTHERS.
> It is a matter for pride to their friends at home that so many young King's County men are doing their full share at the front. Some parents have one son, some a couple, and some even more. My James Benson, Belview, Shinrone can take this superior place. One son is Sec. Lieut J W Benson, 101st Grenadiers, who was sent to East Africa last month in charge of reinforcements. Another, Henry, of the R.A.M.C., is in the Australian General Hospital, Egypt. William, No. 3, is in the trenches "somewhere in France." And Arthur, No. 4, is in the Dardanelles where the fighting has been exceptionally fierce and long.

From De Ruvigny's Roll of Honour:

> *Benson, William John,* Private, 2nd Battn. (86th Foot), The Royal Irish Rifles, 5th son of James Benson, of Bellevue, Shinrone, King's County, Schoolmaster, by his wife, Catherine, daughter of James Wilson; born, Shinrone afore-said, 15 Nov. 1894. Educated at the Scriptural School there; was a grocers assistant; enlisted in March, 1915; served with the Expeditionary Force in France and Flanders from the fol-lowing June; was reported wounded and missing after the fighting on 8 July 1916, and is assumed to have been killed in action on that date.

Grave or Memorial Reference: He has no known grave but is listed on Pier and Face 15A and 15B on the Theipval Memorial in France.

**BERGIN, Edward:** Rank: Pte. Regiment or Service: Leinster Regiment. Unit: 2nd Battalion. Date of death: 25 April 1916. Service no: 3168 and 3/3168. Born in Shinrone, Co. Offaly. Enlisted in Birr, Co. Offaly. Died. Grave or Memorial Reference: VIII.A.98. Cemetery: Boulogne Eastern Cemetery in France.

**BERGIN, Denis Patrick:** Rank: Pte. Regiment or Service: Royal Inniskilling Fusiliers. Unit: B Company, 1st Battalion. Date of death: 2 May 1915. Service no: 8922. Born in Birr, Co. Offaly. Enlisted in Manchester. Died at sea. Age at death: 24.

*Supplementary information:* Son of John and Norah Bergin, of 31 Clare Street, Temple Street, Chorlton-on-Medlock, Manchester. Grave or Memorial Reference: He has no known grave but is listed on Panel 97 to 101 on the Helles Memorial in Turkey.

**BERRY, Edward Fleetwood:** Rank: Captain. Regiment or Service: 9th Gurkha Rifles. Indian Army. Unit: Adjt. 2nd Bn. attd. 1st Bn. Date of death: 17 April 1916. Age at death: 27. Born: 23 May 1889. He won the Military Cross and is listed in the *London Gazette*.

*Supplementary information:* Son of Mary Fleetwood Berry (*née* Chatterton), of Kilgarran, Enniskerry, Co. Wicklow, and the late Ven. James Fleetwood Berry, B.D, Archdeacon of Tuam. Date of birth: 23 May 1888 in Sligo. Died of wounds received in Mesopotamia (modern Iraq) on 17 April 1916. He left school in 1906 and passed into Sandhurst; 2nd Lt. Wiltshire Regiment 1907. He was transferred to the Indian Army Goorka Rifles in 1909 and Burma Rifles in 1914 and was A.D.C. to Lord Carmichael, Governor of Bengal; also served in the Great War in France and Mesopotamia. Awarded the Military Cross for 'brilliant dash and leadership' at Neuve Chapelle on 10 March 1915. He has no known grave but is listed on Panel 51 of the Basra memorial in Iraq. He is also listed on the Great War memorial Cross in St Nicholas Collegiate Church of Ireland, Church Lane in Galway.

**BIDDULPH, Robert Assheton:** Rank: Second Lieutenant. Regiment or Service; 2nd Dragoon Guards (Queen's Bays). Age at death: 25. Date of death: 19 November 1916. *Supplementary information:* Son of Assheton and Florence C. Biddulph, of Pan's Garden, Warnham, Sussex. From *King's County Chronicle*, 1916:

LIEUT. R. BIDDULPH.

Much regret over his death.

Very great regret was felt in Kinnitty and district on Monday when it was known that Lieut. Robert A. Biddulph had passed away in an hospital in England. Deceased was only son of the late Assheton Biddulph, M.F.H., and much sympathy is felt with the family at his early demise. It was only in January of the present year the sad news was published of the death of Mr Assheton Biddulph, of Moneyguyneen, Kinnitty, aged 65 years. We hope in our next issue to publish further particulars of the sad demise of Second-Lieutenant, Robert A. Biddulph.

From *King's County Chronicle*, January 1916:

DEATH OF MR ASSHETON BIDDULPH, M.F.H.

It has been heard with much regret in Birr and throughout the King's County that Mr Assheton Biddulph, of Moneyguyneen, the popular master of the King's County Hunt, had passed away on Monday at Bath.

Although it was known locally that Mr Biddulph was unwell in England, and on that account was unable to hunt in King's County this season, very few people realised that his illness was of a serious nature, and the unexpected news which reached Birr on Tuesday that he had succumbed to heart failure, as the result of blood poisoning, came as a shock to his large circle of friends, and well-wishers, and to many others who had looked upon the late M.F.H. as a gentleman who, by his unfailing kindness and courtesy, had deserved earned universal esteem and respect.

In August last Mr Biddulph had the misfortune of getting a wasp's sting on his ankle, for which he was carefully treated by Dr Morton. About a month afterwards he was well enough to undertake a journey to England to visit his son, who is an officer in the Queen's Bays. Some days later Mr Biddulph again felt unwell, and had once more to undergo medical treatment. Every hope was entertained that he would be speedily restored to perfect health, and that he would be able to return to Ireland to resume his duties as M.F.H., which for over thirty years, he had discharged so satisfactorily. But these fervent hopes were destined to be unrealised, and by his death King's County has lost one of the best known and most highly respected of its local gentry.

In 1884 Mr Assheton Biddulph put together, at his own expense, and entirely new pack of hounds, and hunted the whole reunited Ormond and King's County territory till the 1896-1897 season. The Ormond and King's County was the oldest hunt in Ireland, and from time to time the country had been divided and reunited again. In 1898 the country underwent another division, Mr Biddulph continuing as Master of the King's County, and hunted this territory until the present season. The North Tipperary Hounds were out on Tuesday, but on hearing of the death of Mr Biddulph the members did not proceed with the day's engagement. The greatest sympathy is felt for Mrs Biddulph and the other members of the family in their bereavement.

The funeral will take place at Killoughey Church at 12.30pm on Friday. A memorial service will be held at Kinnitty at the same hour.

Grave or Memorial Reference: South-west of entrance. Cemetery: Killoughy Church of Ireland Churchyard, Co. Offaly. See also **ADAMS, John Goold.**

**BLANC, John:** Rank: Pte. Regiment or Service: Royal Dublin Fusiliers. Unit: 1st Battalion. Date of death: 14 October 1918. Service no: 22754. Born in Edenderry, Co. Offaly. Enlisted in Bolton while living in Manchester. Killed in action. Age at death: 29.

*Supplementary information:* Son of John and Elizabeth Blanc, of 7 Queen Street, Hulme, Manchester. Native of Edenderry, Leix. Grave or Memorial Reference: V.D.II. Cemetery: Dadizeele New British Cemetery in Belgium.

**BLANC, Peter:** Rank: Pte. Regiment or Service: Royal Dublin Fusiliers. Unit: 2nd Battalion. Date of death: 5 November 1918. Service no: 27710. Born in Edenderry, Co. Offaly. Enlisted in Bolton while living in Old Trafford. Died of wounds. Grave or Memorial Reference: III.A.II. Cemetery: Premont British Cemetery in France.

**BLOOMFIELD, Frederick Charles:** (Served under the alias, **TRENCH**). Rank: Private. Regiment or Service: London Regiment (London Scottish). Unit: 1st/14th Bn, also listed as 14th Bn. Age at death: 38. Date of death: 1 July 1916. Service no: 5746. Enlisted in London while living in Tipperary. Killed in action.

*Supplementary information:* Son of Henry Bloomfield Trench, of Huntington, Portarlington, Co. Offaly. Husband of Catherine Anne Swetenham MacManaway (formerly Trench), M.B.E., of Greystone Hall, Limavady, Co. Londonderry. He has no known grave but is listed on Pier and Face 9C and 13C on the Thiepval Memorial in France.

**BOLAND, Patrick:** Rank: Pte. Regiment or Service: Royal Inniskilling Fusiliers. Unit: 5th Battalion. Date of death: 8 November 1918. Service no: 27067. Born in Tullamore, Co. Offaly. Enlisted in Tullamore. Killed in action. This man is listed as **BOLAND, Patrick** in 'Soldiers died in the Great War' and 'Ireland's Memorial Records' and **Boland, D.** in the Commonwealth War Graves Commission. From *King's County Chronicle*, November 1918:

> Two days before the "cease fire" Corporal P. Boland, Royal Inniskilling Fusiliers, 2nd Batt.,

youngest son of Mr Pat. Boland, Tullamore, was killed in action in France. His father, with whom the boy was a great favourite, and the other members of the family were greatly distressed by the sad news which came from Sec-Lieut, Gibson, who stated that he fell gallantly. Deceased soldier and his chum, an Ulster chap, named McKenna changed home address prior to going into action with the promise that should one survive the other survivor would correspond with the parents. McKenna survived and kept his promise, his letter arriving by the same post as Lieut Gibson's.

The late Corporal Boland joined the Inniskilling Fusiliers about three years ago during Major O'Connor's recruiting tour in the King's County. He visited his parents on a short furlough in August last and was then in robust health. He took part in several engagements, both in Palestine, and Servia, and never received a scratch in any of them. His death when peace had practically been proclaimed is particularly tragic. Deep sympathy is felt for his parents in their sad bereavement.

Grave or Memorial Reference: D.16. Cemetery: Avesnes-Le Sec Communal Cemetery Extension in France. See **WALSH, Luke,** his brother-in-law who was also killed.

**BOLGER, George:** Rank: Private. Regiment or Service: Royal Irish Regiment. Unit: 5th Bn. Age at death:

33. Date of death: 20 September 1916. Service no: 1117. Born in Birr and enlisted in Birr. Died in Salonika.

*Supplementary information:* Son of William and Winifred Bolger, of Nenagh. Husband of Ellen Bolger, of Birr Road, Nenagh, Co. Tipperary. Grave or Memorial Reference: III.H.15. Cemetery: Struma Military Cemetery in Greece.

**BOLGER, James:** Rank: Sergeant. Regiment or Service: Royal Munster Fusiliers. Unit: 1st Bn. Age at death: 37. Date of death: 28 November 1915. Service no: 5851. Awards: DCM. Born in Tipperary Town, enlisted in London while living in Nenagh. He won the Distinguished Conduct Medal before he died in Gallipoli.

*Supplementary information:* Son of Mrs Winifred Bolger, of Birr Road, Nenagh, Co. Tipperary. Has no known grave but is commemorated on Panel 185 to 190. Memorial: Helles Memorial in Turkey.

**BOND, Samuel Thomas:** Rank: Gunner. Regiment or Service: Royal Field Artillery. Unit: 'A' Bty. 320th Bde. Age at death: 19. Date of death: 23 January 1918. Service no: 119903. Born in Rahan in Co. Offaly and enlisted in Birr. Died at home.

*Supplementary information:* Son of Samuel T. Bond (late of Royal Irish Constabulary), and Margaret Frances Bond, of Parochial Hall, Mary Street, Clonmel, Co. Tipperary. From the *King's County Chronicle*, February 1918:

The headstone of Samuel Thomas Bond in Norfolk.

OBITUARY. CORPORAL SAMUEL T. BOND, R.F.A.

It is with much regret we have to record the accidental death on January 24th, at Aylsham, Norfolk, of Gunner S.T. Bond, R.F.A., son of Const. Bond R.I.C., Ferbane. The deceased's battery, under the command of Major C.H. Levenson, was drilling in Blickling Park, near

Aylsham, on that date, and Gunner Bond as riding on the rear side of gun limber, being No. 2 of the sub-section. He dismounted about 20 yards before the position was reached for the battery to come into action, while the gun team was still moving and attempted to unlimber the guns.

He apparently lost his footing, and before his comrade could get the team to stop, the near gun wheel had passed over his body. A motor ambulance soon arrived, and he was carried in an unconscious state to Norfolk Military Hospital, where he died the same evening from asphyxiation, due to injuries caused to his ribs and lungs. On January 28th the remains were conveyed on a gun-carriage from Norfolk to Aylsham by a team of the battery and were interred with full military honours at Aylsham cemetery, the Rev. L. Bickswell, Church of England Chaplain to the Forces at Aylsham, officiating. Three volleys having been fired and the Last Post sounded, a beautiful wreath from all ranks of the battery was placed on the grave.

His late clergyman, the Rev. J.T. Webster, Frankford, received a very touching letter from the command-ing officer stating that the deceased was so highly esteemed by all ranks arrangements are being made by the officers and men to have a Royal Artillery Military Cross erected over his grave at their own expense. The late Corporal Bond was 19 years of age, and much sympathy is felt for his friends in their great loss.

Grave or Memorial Reference: G.72. Cemetery: Aylsham Cemetery in Norfolk, UK.

**BOOTH, Charles:** Rank: Driver. Regiment or Service: Royal Army Service Corps. Unit: 124th Company. Date of death: 8 October 1914. Service no:T1/4333. Born in Birr, Co. Offaly. Enlisted in Cardiff while living in Shrewsbury. Died at home.

*Supplementary information:* Son of Capt. J. Booth (Royal Army Pay Dept.). Grave or Memorial Reference: AF.1727. Cemetery: Aldershot Military Cemetery, UK.

**BORROWS/BURROWES, Luke:** Rank: Gunner. Regiment or Service: Royal Garrison Artillery. Unit, 116th Siege Battery. Date of death: 21 April 1917. Service no: 28023. Born in Clara, Co. Offaly. Enlisted in Tullamore, Co. Offaly while living in Clara, Co. Offaly. Awarded the Mons Star and Victory Medal. Killed in action. Grave or Memorial Reference: IV.C.24. Cemetery: Tilloy British Cemetery, Tilloy-Les-Mofflaines in France.

**BOWE, Michael:** Rank: Lance Corporal. Regiment or Service: Leinster Regiment. Unit: 2nd Battalion. Date of death: 27 March 1915. Service no: 7947. Born in Malta. Enlisted in Birr, Co. Offaly. Died of wounds at home ('Soldiers died in the Great War'), Died of wounds in Christ Church Hospital in England, won the 1914 star ('Ireland's Memorial Records'). Age at death: 26.

Michael Bowe.

*Supplementary information*: Son of Michael Bowe. Husband of Maria Wrafter (formerly Bowe), of Castle Lodge, Birr, Co. Offaly. The image above is taken *King's County Chronicle*, 1916. Grave or Memorial Reference: Screen Wall. 1.C.B.1209. Cemetery: Greenwich Cemetery, UK.

**BOWLER, Edward** (Eddie) **St Kentigern:** Rank: Pte. Regiment or Service: Machine Gun Corps. Unit: Infantry, 72nd Company. Date of death: 12 August 1916. Service no: 27747. Formerly he was with the Royal Irish Rifles where his number was 10728. Born in Keswick ('Soldiers died in the Great War'), 'Ireland's Memorial Records' state he was born in Co. Offaly. Enlisted in Cork. Died of wounds at the Casualty Clearing Station based in Corbie, France. Age at death: 22/23.

*Supplementary information:* Son of Staff. Q.M.S. Bowler (Royal Army Service Corps) and Mrs W.J. Bowler, of Bough, Rathvilly, Co. Carlow. Grave or Memorial Reference: Plot 2 Row A Grave 90. Cemetery: Corbie Communal Cemetery Extension in France.

**BOYD, Allan:** Rank: Pte. Regiment or Service: Royal Irish Fusiliers. Unit: 9th Battalion. Date of death: 25 May 1917. Service no: 23897. Born in Tullamore, Co. Offaly. Enlisted in Monaghan while living in Emyvale. Died of wounds. Age at death: 21. This man is listed as **BOYD, Allan** in 'Soldiers died in the Great War' and 'Ireland's Memorial Records' and **BOYD, William Allan Nesbit** in the Commonwealth War Graves Commission.

*Supplementary information:* Son of Thomas Henry and M.A. Boyd, of Carrigans, Emyvale, Co. Monaghan. Grave or Memorial Reference: N 9. Cemetery: Pond Farm Cemetery in Belgium.

**BOYER, Joseph:** Rank: Corporal. Regiment or Service: Leinster Regiment. Unit: 2nd Battalion. Date of death: 31 July 1917. Service no: 9443. Born in Birr, Co. Offaly. Enlisted in Jullundur in India. Killed in action. He has no known grave but is listed on Panel 44 on the Ypres (Menin Gate) Memorial in Belgium.

**BOYLAN, James:** Rank: Pte. Regiment or Service: Northumberland

Fusiliers. Unit: 1st/6th Battalion (Territorial). Date of death: 16 April 1917. Service no: 267246. Formerly he was with the Sherwood Foresters where his number was 32514. Born in Clonminch Co. Offaly. Enlisted in Derby. Died. He has no known grave but is listed in Bay 2 and 3 on the Arras Memorial in France

**BRACKEN, Samuel:** Rank: Pte. Regiment or Service: Irish Guards. Unit: B Company, 1st Battalion. Date of death: 22 October 1914. Service no: 4596. Born in Clara, Co. Offaly. Enlisted in Tullamore. Killed in action. Age at death: 22.

*Supplementary information:* Awarded the Mons Star. Son of Samuel and Annie Bracken, of Lisaniskey, Clara, Co. Offaly. From De Ruvigny's Roll of Honour:

> *Bracken, Samuel,* Private, No 4596, 2st battn, Irish Guards, eldest son of Samuel Bracken, of Lisansikey, Clara, King's County, Farmer, by his wife, Annie, daughter of Bernard Duffy; born Clara, King's County, 3rd Dec, 1891. Educated at the Franciscan Brothers Monastery School there. Enlisted 10 Nov, 1913, went to France 12 Aug, 1914. Took part in the retreat from Mons, and subsequent engagements and was killed in action at Bethune 22 Oct, following. Buried at Bethune. He was mentioned in Despatches (London gazette, 19 Oct, 1914), for gallant and distinguished service in the field.

He has no known grave but is listed on Panel 11 on the Ypres (Menin Gate) Memorial in Belgium.

**BRADLEY, John McDonald:** Rank: Lieutenant. Regiment or Service: Royal Dublin Fusiliers .Unit: 17th Bn. Age at death: 27. Date of death: 30 September 1918. Age at death: 27. Died of wounds.

*Supplementary information:* Son of Donald Alexander and Alice Elizabeth Bradley, of Tullamore. Grave or Memorial Reference: XV.A.14. Cemetery: Grevilliers British Cemetery in Pas-De-Calais, France.

**BRENNAN, Joseph:** Rank: Pte. Regiment or Service: Royal Dublin Fusiliers. Unit: 2nd Battalion. Date of death: 15 February 1915. Service no: 5350. Born in Edenderry, Co. Offaly. Enlisted in Naas while living in Edenderry. Killed in action. Age at death: 23.

*Supplementary information:* Son of Anne Walker (formerly Brennan), of Blundell Street, Edenderry, Co. Offaly, and the late James Brennan. Grave or Memorial Reference: I.E.4. Cemetery: Prowse Point Military Cemetery in Belgium.

**BRENNAN, Thomas:** Rank: Pte. Regiment or Service: Royal Irish Regiment. Unit: 2nd Battalion. Date of death: 21 March 1918. Service no: 11058. Born in Philipstown, Co. Offaly. Enlisted in Tullamore while living in Philipstown, Co. Offaly. Killed in action. Age at death: 24.

*Supplementary information:* Son of Thomas and Margaret Brennan, of Kilclonfert, Daingean, Co. Offaly. *King's County Independent*, July 1917:

ON LEAVE.

After spending eighteen months in the firing zone, and being twice wounded, one rather seriously, Private Thomas Brennan, of Kilclonfert, was allowed a short furlough to see his friends during the week. After such a trying time, his experiences, needless to say, were eventful, and would make 'good copy' as his regiment (Royal Irish Fusiliers) bore the brunt of the fighting in many a hard fought battle. He was very cheerful and was full of hope for a speedy victory.

Grave or Memorial Reference: Panel 30 and 31. Memorial: Pozieres Memorial in France.

**BRENNAN, Thomas:** Rank: Private. Regiment or Service: Leinster Regiment. Unit: 2nd Bn. Date of death: 20 October 1914. Service no: 6395. Born in Templemore. Enlisted in Birr. Killed in action. From *King's County Chronicle*, March 1916, 'Private Thomas Brennan, of the 2nd Leinsters, a fine specimen of an Irish soldier, gave his life in France in the service of King and Country. His brother, Co Sergt-Major Cornelius, of the 18th Royal Irish, was wounded at Mons. Their father is Mr Patrick Brennan, ex-Sergt. Of the R.I.C., an esteemed resident of Green Street.' He has no known grave but is listed on Panel 10 on the Ploegsteert Memorial in Belgium.

**BRIEN P.:** Rank: Gunner. Regiment or Service: Royal Garrison Artillery. Age at death: 36. Date of death: 4 April 1919. Service no: 21900. Grave or Memorial Reference: North of ruin. Cemetery: Killoughy Old Graveyard, Co. Offaly.

**BRIEN, Thomas:** Rank: Pte. Regiment or Service: Leinster Regiment. Unit: 2nd Battalion. Date of death: 9 August 1918. Service no: 4530. Born in Birr, Co. Offaly. Enlisted in Birr while living in Birr. Killed in action. Age at death: 18.

*Supplementary information:* Son of Mr and Mrs James Brien, of Birr, Co. Offaly. From *King's County Chronicle*, September 1918:

We regret to announce the death in action, of Private Thomas Brien, Leinster Regiment, son of the late Mr Jas. Brien, baker, Birr. The deceased, who was only in his 18th year, was a young fellow of bright and happy disposition, extremely popular and beloved by his comrades. The manner of his death was conveyed to the deceased's sister in a sympathetic letter from Lieut. Frank Kilpatrick, officer commanding D. Company, in the course of which he stated that her brother was killed when on patrol with the writer and a few others on the 9th August.

"We were just returning," he continued, "when a hostile machine-gun opened fire and a bullet hit your poor brother in the eye, and before I got to him he passed away. We carried his body in and sent it down the line for burial. Your brother was a good and gallant lad and most popular in the company, and I greatly mourn his loss. Please accept my very deepest sympathy in you great trouble, and may God give you strength to bear your great loss."

Grave or Memorial Reference: II.G.14. Cemetery: Borre British Cemetery in France.

**BRISLAND, Walter Frederick:** Rank: Lance Corporal. Regiment or Service: Kings Yorkshire Light Infantry. Unit: 2nd Battalion. Date of death: 7 May 1915. Service no: 8885. Born in Birr, Co. Offaly. Enlisted in London. Died of wounds. Grave or Memorial Reference: II.A128. Cemetery: Bailleu Communal Cemetery (Nord) in France

**BROPHY, Peter:** Rank: Lance Corporal. Regiment or Service: Leinster Regiment. Unit: 2nd Battalion. Date of death: 16 June 1917. Service no: 1345. Born in Shinrone, Co. Offaly. Enlisted in Birr, Co. Offaly while living in Shinrone. Killed in action. Age at death: 17.

*Supplementary information:* Son of the late Kyran and Margaret Brophy, of Shamboe, Borris-in-Ossory, Ballybrophy, Co. Laois. He has no known grave but is listed on Panel 44 on the Ypres (Menin Gate) Memorial in Belgium.

**BROPHY, Timothy:** Rank: Pte. Regiment or Service: Leinster

Regiment. Unit: 2nd Battalion. Date of death: 25 September 1915. Service no: 10363. Born in Tullamore, Co. Offaly. Enlisted in Tullamore. Killed in action. Age at death: 24.

*Supplementary information:* Son of Patrick and Kate Brophy, of Pensioners Row, Tullamore, Co. Offaly. Listed on the Tullamore Roll of Honour as **BROPHY Thomas, Jnr**. Grave or Memorial Reference: I.o.9. Cemetery: Essex Farm Cemetery in Belgium.

**BROUGHAL, Lawrence:** Rank: Pte. Regiment or Service: Royal Munster Fusiliers. Unit: 6th Battalion. Date of death: 9 August 1915. Service no: 5006. Formerly he was with the Royal Dublin Fusiliers where his number was 16586. Born in Edenderry, Co. Offaly. Enlisted in Naas, County Kildare while living in Edenderry. Died of wounds in Gallipoli. In a snippet in the *Co. Offaly Chronicle* in September 1915 it states that his brother, Private Michael Broughall was missing in action at that time. Michael is not in any war dead databases. Grave or Memorial Reference: He has no known grave but is listed on Panel 185 to 190 on the Helles Memorial in Turkey.

**BROWNE, John:** Rank: Pte. Regiment or Service: Royal Irish Regiment. Unit: 2nd Battalion. Date of death: 5 September 1918. Service no: 16457. Formerly he was with the Royal Dublin Fusiliers where his number was 22152. Born in Clara, Co.

Offaly. Enlisted in Tullamore while living in Clara. Died of wounds. Grave or Memorial Reference: III.F.40. Cemetery: Bac-Du-Sud British Cametery, Bailleulval in France.

**BROWNE, Llewellyn Albert:** Rank: Gunner. Regiment or Service: Royal Horse Artillery and Royal Field Artillery. Unit: $3^{rd}$-$7^{th}$ Trench Mortar Battery. Date of death: 8 May 1916. Service no: 64785. Born in Ballyshane, Co. Offaly. Enlisted in Nenagh. Killed in action. Age at death: 23.

*Supplementary information:* Son of James Browne, of 4 Zetland Street, Belfast. Born in Co. Offaly. Grave or Memorial Reference: V.B.I. Cemetery: Citadel New Military Cemetery, Fricourt in France.

**BRUDER, Michael:** Rank: Lance Corporal. Regiment or Service: Connaught Rangers. Unit: $6^{th}$ Battalion. Date of death: 3 September 1916. Service no: 743. Born in Birr, Co. Offaly. Enlisted in Athlone while living in Athlone, Co. Westmeath. Killed in action. He has no known grave but is commemorated on Pier and Face 15 A on the Theipval Memorial in France.

**BRUMFITT, Thomas Rawl:** Rank: Sergeant. Regiment or Service: Seaforth Highlanders. Unit: $2^{nd}$ Battalion. Date of death: 1 September 1916. Service no: 9379. Born in Birr, Co. Offaly. Enlisted in Edinburgh, Midlothian. Died of wounds. Age at death: 27.

*Supplementary information:* Son of Joseph and Emma Brumfitt. Born at Birr. Grave or Memorial Reference: I.Q.1. Cemetery: Wimereux Communal Cemetery, Pas de Calais, in France.

**BRYAN, Patrick:** Rank: Pte. Regiment or Service: Leinster Regiment. Unit: $2^{nd}$ Battalion. Date of death: 1 August 1917. Service no: 5100. Born in Edenderry, Co. Offaly. Enlisted in Edenderry, Co. Offaly while living in Edenderry. Died of wounds. Age at death: 25.

*Supplementary information:* Son of Patrick and Anne Bryan, of Edenderry, Co. Offaly. Grave or Memorial Reference: Cemetery: III.C.20. Mendingham Military Cemetery in Belgium.

**BURKE, Joseph:** Rank: Pte. Regiment or Service: Royal Irish Regiment. Unit: $2^{nd}$ Battalion. Date of death: 10 June 1917. Service no: 3349. Born in Banagher, Co. Offaly. Enlisted in Birr, Co. Offaly. Died of wounds. Grave or Memorial Reference: VI.F.9. Cemetery: Wytschaete Military Cemetery in Belgium.

**BURKE, Joseph:** Rank: Pte. Regiment or Service: Leinster Regiment. Date of death: 14 September 1914. Service no: 1629. Born in Co. Offaly. Killed in action in France. Age at death: 29. This man is a bit of a mystery. He only appears in 'Ireland's Memorial Records'. He is not listed in 'Soldiers died in the Great War' nor is he listed with the Commonwealth War Graves Commission. A quick check with the National Archives in Kew shows that there is no Medal Index Card for No 1629 Joseph Burke.

**BURNELL, William Ivor:** Rank: Pte. Regiment or Service: Royal Dublin Fusiliers. Date of death: 20 November 1919. Age at death: 27. Service no: 25989. Date of birth: 20 May 1892. Died after discharge from the army. Discharged with Pulmonary T.B. in November 1916. He was entitled to the British War Medal, Victory Medal, and Silver War Badge. Grave or Memorial Reference: Carrick Graveyard, Edenderry, Co. Offaly.

**BURROWS, Frank:** Rank: Pte. Regiment or Service: Connaught Rangers. Unit: 2nd Battalion. Date of death: 26 August 1914. Service no: 7168. Born in Clara, Co. Offaly also recorded as Kilbride. Enlisted in Tullamore while living in Cork. Killed in action. He has no known grave but is listed on the La Ferte-Sous-Jouarre-Memorial in France.

**BURROWS/BURROWES, George:** Rank: Sergeant. Regiment or Service: Lincolnshire Regiment. Unit: 1st Battalion. Date of death: 4 February 1916. Service no: 7813. Born in St Paul's, Dublin ('Ireland's Memorial Records' state he was born in Co. Offaly). Enlisted in Gainsborough while living in Leicester. Died of wounds. Age at death: 34.

*Supplementary information:* Husband of Agnes Cooley (formerly Burrowes), of 44 Northampton Street, Leicester. Grave or Memorial Reference: H.10. Cemetery: Bailleul Communal Cemetery (Nord) in France.

**BURROWES/BORROWS, Luke:** Rank: Gunner. Regiment or Service: Royal Garrison Artillery. Unit: 116th Siege Battery. Date of death: 21 April 1917. Service no: 28023. Born in Clara, Co. Offaly. Enlisted in Tullamore, Co. Offaly while living in Clara. Awarded the Mons Star and Victory Medal. Killed in action. Grave or Memorial Reference: IV.C.24. Cemetery: Tilloy British Cemetery, Tilloy-Les-Mofflaines in France.

**BUTLER, Hugh:** Rank: Private. Regiment or Service: Labour Corps. Unit: 89th Coy. Date of death: 9 June 1918. Service no: 478180. Formerly he was with the Leinster Regiment where his number was 3197. Born in Rathcabbin, Birr. Enlisted in Birr. Killed in action. Son of Mrs Butler, Ballay, Rathcabbin. Grave or Memorial Reference: III.C.2. Cemetery: Hershin Communal Cemetery Extension in France.

**BUTLER, James:** Rank: Pte. Regiment or Service: Royal Irish Regiment. Unit: 2nd Battalion. Date of death: 8 May 1915. Service no: 6482. Born in Frankford, Co. Offaly. Enlisted in Clonmel while living in Frankford, Co. Offaly. Killed in action. He has no known grave but is listed on Panel 33 on the Ypres (Menin Gate) Memorial in Belgium.

**BUTLER, Martin:** Rank: Pte. Regiment or Service: Royal Irish Regiment. Unit: 6th Battalion. Date of death: 4 June 1916. Service no: 7973. Born in Shinrone, Co. Offaly. Enlisted in Cloughjordan, Co Tipperary. Killed in action. Age at death: 21. Son of Edward and Margaret Butler, of Knocknacree, Cloughjordan, Co. Tipperary. 'Ireland's Memorial Records' and the 'Commonwealth War Graves Commission' give his Date of death as 4 June 1916. 'Soldiers died in the Great War' states he died on 4 June 1917. Grave or Memorial Reference: I.K.18. Cemetery: Dud Corner Cemetery, Loos in France.

**BYRNE, George Johnston:** Rank: Lance Corporal. Regiment or Service: Auckland Regiment, N.Z.E.F. Unit: 1st Bn. Age at death: 32. Date of death: 29 September 1918. Service no: 30729.
*Supplementary information:* Son of John and Mary Byrne. Husband of the late Janie Byrne. Born at Portland, Birr. Grave or Memorial Reference: II.C.7. Cemetery: Fifteen Ravine British Cemetery, Villers-Plouich, Nord, in France.

**BYRNE, Thomas:** Rank: Pte. Regiment or Service: Leinster Regiment. Unit: 2nd Battalion. Date of death: 30 December 1917. Age at death: 36. Service no: 4182. Born in Thomastown, County Kilkenny. Enlisted in Maryborough. Died at sea. Son of Thomas and Bridget Byrne. Husband of Margaret Kennedy (formerly Byrne), of New Road, Birr, Co. Offaly. From the *Midland Tribune*, January 1918, 'It is announced that Private T Byrnes [*sic*], Burkes Hill, Birr, has been drowned at sea.' From the *King's County Chronicle*, 1918:

BIRR SOLDIER DROWNED.

On Sunday last the sad news was received by Mrs Byrnes [*sic*], Burke's Hill, that her husband, Pte Thomas Byrnes, Leinster Regiment, had been drowned on a voyage to Egypt, the ship being torpedoed. The official news stated that his body had been recovered. The late Private Byrne had about two years service, and was a fine stamp of a soldier. Much sympathy is felt with the bereaved wife and four children.

Grave or Memorial Reference: C.47. Cemetery: Alexandria (Hadra) War Memorial Cemetery in Egypt.

# C

**CADELL, Assheton Biddulph:**
2nd Lieutenant. Regiment or Service: Queen's Own (Royal West Kent Regiment). Unit: 8th Battalion. Date of death: 19 December 1916. Age at death: 21. Died of wounds. Son of Nevil Pottow Cadell and Gertrude Louisa Cadell, of 'Foxlease' Camberley, Surrey. From De Ruvigny's Roll of Honour:

*Cadell, Assheton Biddulph*, 2nd Lieut., 10th (Reserve) Battn, The Devonshire Regiment, attached to the 8th (Service) Battn, The Queen's Own (Royal West Kent Regt), only child of Dr Nevil Pottow Cadell, of Foxlease, Camberley, by his wife, Gertrude Louisa, daughter of the late Francis Wellesley Marsh Biddulph, of Rathrobin, King's County, J.P. Born in Tiverton, North Devon, 18 March, 1894. Educated at Woodcote, Co. Oxon (Rev J. H. Wilkinson), and Lancing College. Obtained a commission in the Devonshire Regiment, 17 March, 1915. Served with the Expeditionary Force in France and Flanders from 6 Oct, following, where he was attached to the 8th West Kent Regt., and died in the ambulance on his way to hospital three hours after having been wounded in action at Chateau Belge, near Ypres, 19 Feb [*sic*] 1916. Buried in Lyssenthoek Soldiers Cemetery, near Poperinghe.

Grave or Memorial Reference: II.A.36. Cemetery: Lijssenthoek Military Cemetery in Belgium.

**CAHILL, Michael:** Rank: Pte. Regiment or Service: Connaught Rangers. Unit: 1st Battalion. Date of death: 23 October 1918. Service no: 8553. Born in Tullamore, Co. Offaly. Enlisted in Galway while living in Tullamore. Died in Egypt.

*Supplementary information:* 'Ireland's Memorial Records' and 'Soldiers died in the Great War' gives his name as **CAHILL, Michael** whereas the Commonwealth War Graves Commission gives it as **CAHILL, H**. Grave or Memorial Reference: A. 88. Cemetery: Haifa War Cemetery in Israel.

**CALLAGHAN, Joseph:** Rank: Pte. Regiment or Service: Leinster Regiment. Unit: 3rd Battalion. Date of death: 6 January 1916. Service no: 10495. Born in Clara, Co. Offaly. Enlisted in Mullingar. Died at home. Grave or Memorial Reference: Alternative Commemoration: buried in Cork Military Cemetery. He is commemorated on the Special Memorial on the Grangegorman (Cork) Memorial Headstones.

**CALLAGHAN, William:** Rank: Pte. Regiment or Service: Royal Irish Regiment. Unit: 5<sup>th</sup> Battalion. Date of death: 16 August 1915. Service no: 17. Born in Tullamore, Co. Offaly. Enlisted in Clonmel. Killed in action in Gallipoli. He has no known grave but is listed on Panel 55 on the Helles Memorial in Turkey.

**CALLAGHAN, William:** Rank: Pte. Regiment or Service: Royal Irish Regiment. Unit: 2<sup>nd</sup> Battalion. Date of death: 25 August 1918. Service no: 6669. Born in Birr, Co. Offaly. Enlisted in Limerick while living in Birr. Killed in action. Age at death: 26.

*Supplementary information:* Son of the late John Callaghan. He has no known grave but is listed on Panel 5 on the Vis-En-Artois Memorial in France.

**CAMPBELL, Stephen:** Rank: Pte. Regiment or Service: Leinster Regiment. Unit: 1<sup>st</sup> Battalion. Date of death: 10 March 1915. Service no: 3479. Born in Clara, Co. Offaly. Enlisted in Maryborough. Died of wounds. Age at death: 19.

*Supplementary information:* Brother of Christopher Campbell, of Harbour Street, Mountmellick, Co. Offaly. Grave or Memorial Reference: J.21. Cemetery: Bailleul Communal Cemetery (Nord) in France.

**CARPENTER, James:** Alias, true name is **MAXWELL, James.** Rank: Pte. Regiment or Service: Leinster Regiment. Unit: 1<sup>st</sup> Battalion. Date of death: 12 May 1915. Service no:

9437. Born in Tullamore, Co. Offaly. Enlisted in Tullamore, Co. Offaly. Died of wounds.

*Supplementary information:* Son of James and Mary Maxwell, of Tullamore, Co. Offaly. He is also listed on the Tullamore Roll of Honour. Grave or Memorial Reference: 1.A.9. Cemetery: Brandhoek New Military Cemetery in Belgium.

**CARROLL, Charles:** Rank: Pte. Regiment or Service: Royal Irish Fusiliers. Unit: 1<sup>st</sup> Garrison Battalion. Date of death: 23 April 1916. Service no: 907 and G/907. Formerly he was with the Leinster Regiment where his number was 4971. Born in Tullamore, Co. Offaly. Enlisted in Athlone while living in Tullamore. Died in India. He has no known grave but is listed on Face E of the Kirkee 1914-18 Memorial in India.

**CARROLL, Edward:** Rank: Pte. Regiment or Service: Irish Guards. Unit: 2<sup>nd</sup> Battalion. Date of death: 1 October 1916. Service no: 7178. Born in Ballyboy, Co. Offaly. Enlisted in Tullamore, Co. Offaly. Died of wounds. Age at death: 21.

*Supplementary information:* Son of Edward and Julia Carroll, of Kilnagall, Kilcormac, Co. Offaly. From the *County Offaly Chronicle*, 1916, 'Daniel and Edward Carroll, of Kilnagall, joined the 6<sup>th</sup> Leinster Regiment and the Irish Guards respectively. Dan is in Greece and Edward is in France.' Grave or Memorial Reference: B.15.3. Cemetery: St Sever Cemetery Extension, Rouen in France.

James Carroll.

**CARROLL, James:** Rank: Pte. Regiment or Service: Royal Dublin Fusiliers. Unit: 2nd Battalion, 'Ireland's Memorial Records' give 3rd Battalion. Date of death: 24 February 1916. Service no: 3405. Born in Edenderry, Co. Offaly. Enlisted in Carlow while living in Edenderry, Co. Offaly. Died of wounds in King George VI Hospital, Dublin. Grave or Memorial Reference: North-east of ruin. Cemetery: Monasteroris Old Graveyard, Co. Offaly.

**CARROLL, Patrick:** Rank: Second Lieutenant. Regiment or Service: Royal Dublin Fusiliers. Unit: 10th Battalion. Date of death: 8 February 1917. Killed in action. Age at death:

22. From *Midland Tribune, Tipperary Sentinel* and *County Offaly Vindicator* December 1916:

Sec-Lieut. Patrick Carroll, son of Mr T. Carroll, Cumberland Street, Birr, and recently of the Birr Union Office staff, has come home during the week for the first time since obtaining his commission. He has been in several of the important Somme engagements, and returns to the firing line this Saturday evening.

From *King's County Chronicle*, September 1915:

Sergeant James Carroll, 3rd Battalion Dublin Fusiliers, son of Mr Thomas Carroll, is now home on furlough. He was clerk in the office of Mr J. J. Kennedy, solicitor, and was a very respectable and popular young fellow. As he enlisted only four months ago his promotion to the rank of Sergeant has been very rapid, and we are sure has been equally well deserved, for he is a clever and well set-up young soldier. He comes now from training at Sittingbourne, and no doubt finds that his comrades in Birr has not waned in his absence, as everyone here is glad to see him again.

From *King's County Chronicle*, January 1918:

Corporal Myles Carroll, S.I.H., has also been home for Christmas. He had been some four months in hospital as a result of an ugly shrapnel wound in the forehead, and, judging by the deep scar, he had an extremely narrow escape. Pieces of the same shell also wounded him in the hand. He is now quite recovered, and a large circle of friends vied with each other in making his short stay as enjoyable as possible.

Grave or Memorial Reference: VII.C.29. Cemetery: Ancre British Cemetery, Beaumont-Hamel in France.

**CARROLL, Thomas:** Rank: Pte. Regiment or Service: Connaught Rangers. Unit: 6th Bn. Age at death: 35. Date of death: 2 April 1916. Service no: 2873. Age at death: 35. Born in Tullamore. Enlisted in Athlone, Co. Westmeath while living in Tuam, Co. Galway.

*Supplementary information:* Son of James and Mary Carroll, of Herald House, Dublin Road, Tuam, Co. Galway. Native of Cappincier, Tullamore, Co. Offaly. Grave or Memorial Reference: I.H.29. Cemetery: Noeux-Les-Mines Communal Cemetery in France.

**CARROLL, William:** Rank: Pte. Regiment or Service: Royal Dublin Fusiliers. Unit: 1st Battalion. Date of death: 10 May 1916. Service no: 9486. Born in Edenderry, Co. Offaly. Enlisted in Naas, Co Kildare while living in Edenderry, Co. Offaly. Died of wounds. Age at death: 35.

*Supplementary information:* Son of Con Carroll. Born at Edenderry, Co.

Offaly. Grave or Memorial Reference: 6.R.C.27A. Cemetery: Birkenhead (Flatbrick Hill) Cemetery, Wirral, UK.

**CASSIDY, James:** Rank: Pte. Regiment or Service: South Lancashire Regiment. Unit: 2nd Battalion. Date of death: 24 October 1914. Service no: 6916. Born in Dissarn, Co. Offaly. Enlisted in Birr, Co. Offaly while living in Belmont, Co. Offaly. Killed in action. Grave or Memorial Reference: He has no known grave but is listed on Panel 23 on the Le Touret Memorial in France.

**CASSIDY, James:** Rank: Pte. Regiment or Service: Royal Dublin Fusiliers. Unit: 6th Battalion. Date of death: 3 October 1916 ('Ireland's Memorial Records' and 'Soldiers died in the Great War') 2 October 1916 (Commonwealth War Graves Commission). Service no: 15557. Born in Edenderry, Co. Offaly. Enlisted in Naas while living in Edenderry. Killed in action in the Balkans. Age at death: 23.

*Supplementary information:* Son of Mrs B. Connell (formerly Cassidy), of Blundell Street, Edenderry, Co. Offaly. Grave or Memorial Reference: III.J.11. Cemetery: Struma Military Cemetery in Greece.

**CAWLEY, Patrick:** Rank: Pte. Regiment or Service: Irish Guards. Unit: 2nd Battalion. Date of death: 31 July 1917. Service no: 9708. Born in Knockearl, Co. Offaly. Enlisted in Borrisokane, Co Tipperary. Killed in action. Has no known grave but is commemorated on Panel 11. Memorial: Ypres (Menin Gate) Memorial in Belgium.

**CHANDLER, George Henry:** Rank: Pte. Regiment or Service: Canadian Infantry (Quebec Regiment). Unit: 16th Battalion. Date of death: 4 March 1918. Service no: 1001260. Age at death: 31.

*Supplementary information:* Son of Edward and Jane Chandler, of Clonsast, Rathangan, Co. Offaly. Data from enlistment documents: Address: Shoal Lake, Man. Next of kin: Edward Chandler (father) of Clonsist, Rathangan, Co. Offaly. Date of birth: 25 June 1886. Trade: Farmer or Policeman. Single. Six years with Royal Irish Constabulary. Height: 5ft 11in. Girth: 40in. Range of expansion: 40in. Complexion: fair. Eyes: brown. Hair: brown. Grave or Memorial Reference: II. E. 6. Cemetery. Barlin Communal Cemetery Extension in France.

**CLAFFEY, Patrick Joseph:** Rank: Pte. Regiment or Service: Wellington Regiment, New Zealand Expeditionary Force. Unit: 2nd Battalion. Date of death: 4 October 1917. Service no: 28323. Killed in action. Age at death: 33.

*Supplementary information:* Son of Patrick and Anne Claffey, of Connaught Street, Birr, Co. Offaly. Information taken from the Nominal Ross of the New Zealand Expeditionary Force:

Patrick Joseph Surname: Claffey War: Serial No: 28323. First Known Rank: Private Occupation before Enlistment: Labourer. Next of Kin: Mrs Anne Claffey-Ryan (mother), Connaught Street, Birr, King's County, Ireland. Body on Embarkation: New Zealand Expeditionary Force Embarkation Unit: 18th Reinforcements Auckland Infantry Battalion, A Company Embarkation Date: 11 October 1916. Place of Embarkation: Wellington, New Zealand. Transport: HMNZT 67 Vessel: *Tofua* Destination: Plymouth, England Nominal Roll Number: 43 Page on Nominal Roll: 3 Last Unit Served: Wellington Infantry Regiment. Place of Death: Ypres, Belgium. Date of death: 4 October 1917 Year of Death: 1917 Cause of Death: Killed in action.

Grave or Memorial Reference: N.Z. Apse, Panel 6. Memorial: Tyne Cot Memorial in Belgium.

**CLARKE, Daniel:** Rank: Pte and Drummer. Regiment or Service: Leinster Regiment. Unit: 2nd Bn. Date of death: 7 November 1914. Service no: 9305. Born in Templemore. Enlisted in Dublin. Died of wounds. Grave or Memorial Reference: III.L.9. Cemetery: Trois Arbres Cemetery, Steenerck in France.

**CLARKE, John:** Rank: Lance Corporal. Regiment or Service: Leinster Regiment. Unit: B Company, 2nd Battalion. Date of death: 13 August 1917. Service no: 10223.

Born in Portarlington, Co. Offaly, (Portarlington, Co Laois in 'Ireland's Memorial Records'). Enlisted in Mareyborough. Killed in action in France. Age at death: 18.

*Supplementary information:* Son of Luke Clarke, of Bishopswood, Portarlington, Co. Laois. Has no known grave but is commemorated on Panel 44. Memorial: Ypres (Menin Gate) Memorial in Belgium.

**CLARKE, John Thomas:** Rank: Lance Corporal. Regiment or Service: Royal Dublin Fusiliers. Unit: B Company, 2nd Battalion. Date of death: 21 March 1918. Service no: 25822. Born in Inchicore, Dublin. Enlisted in Dublin while living in Banagher, Co. Offaly. Killed in action. Age at death: 22.

*Supplementary information:* Son of James and Mary Anne Clarke, of Harbour Street, Banagher, Co. Offaly. Grave or Memorial Reference: He has no known grave but is listed on Panels 79 and 80 on the Pozieres Memorial in France.

**CLARKE, Norman:** Rank: Lance Corporal. Regiment or Service: Royal Dublin Fusiliers. Unit: 1st Battalion, the Commonwealth war Graves Commission gives his Unit as 10th Battalion. Date of death: 19 September 1917. Service no: 40322. Formerly he was with the Connaught Rangers where his number was 7353. Born in Cloghan, Co. Offaly. Enlisted in Ballinasloe while living in Manchester. Killed in action.

Grave or Memorial Reference: I.G.25. Cemetery: Croisilles British Cemetery in France.

**CLARKE, Peter Paul:** Rank: Cadet. Regiment or Service: Leinster Regiment. Unit: 7th Battalion. Date of death: 1 July 1916. This man is not in any other war dead database. He is listed on the Tullamore Roll of Honour only. I do not see the Offaly connection but include him for your reference.

**CLARKE, Peter:** Rank: Pte. Regiment or Service: Leinster Regiment. Unit: 7th Battalion. Date of death: 6 September 1916. Service no: 2863. Born in Boheroe, Co Limerick. Enlisted in London while living in Tullamore. Died of wounds. Age at death: 26.

*Supplementary information:* Son of James Clarke and Honora Ryan (his wife), of Dromkeen, Pallasgreen, Limerick. Native of Dromkeen. Grave or Memorial Reference: X.C.3A. Cemetery: Etaples Military Cemetery in France.

**CLARKE, Richard:** Rank: Pte. Regiment or Service: Leinster Regiment. Unit: D Company, 2nd Battalion. Date of death: 31 July 1917. Service no: 6456. Born in Birr, Co. Offaly. Enlisted in Birr, Co. Offaly while living in Birr, Co. Offaly. Killed in action. Age at death: 29/30.

*Supplementary information:* Awarded the Mons Star. Son of Mrs Mary Clarke, of Cornmarket Street, Birr, Co.

Offaly. Husband of Honora Clarke, of 34 Cloheen Road, Clonakilty, Co. Cork. From the *King's County Chronicle*, February 1916, 'Three sons of Mrs Clarke, Church Street are with the colours – Privates Richard, home wounded; Patrick, still on active service, and Daniel, killed in action in France, all of the 2nd Leinsters.' Has no known grave but is commemorated on Panel 44. Memorial: Ypres (Menin Gate) Memorial in Belgium.

**CLAVIN, Patrick:** Rank: Pte. Regiment or Service: Royal Inniskilling Fusiliers. Unit: 7th/8th Battalion. Date of death: November 1918. Service no: 44175. Formerly he was with the Leinster Regiment where his number was 3112. Born in Kilbride, Co. Offaly. Enlisted in Birr. Died of wounds.

*Supplementary information:* VI.F.43. Cemetery: Terlincthun British Cemetery, Wimille, in France

**CLAVIN, Patrick:** Rank: Pte. Regiment or Service: Leinster Regiment. Date of death: 21 October 1918. Service no: 3112. Born in Co. Offaly. Died of gas poisoning. Age at death: 39. This man is a bit of a mystery. He only appears in 'Ireland's Memorial Records'. He is not listed in 'Soldiers died in the Great War' and he is not listed with the Commonwealth War Graves Commission. A quick check with the National Archives in Kew shows that there is no Medal Index Card for No. 3112 Patrick Clavin.

**CLEARY, James F.:** Rank: Pte. Regiment or Service: Irish Guards. Unit: Reserve Battalion also listed as 3rd Battalion. Date of death: 28 July 1917. Service no: 1579. Born in Rinay, Co. Offaly. Also listed in 'Ireland's Memorial Records' as born in Banagher and date of death as 27 July 1917. Enlisted in Manchester, Lancs while living in Chelsea, Middlesex. Died at home. Age at death: 38.

*Supplementary information:* In 'Soldiers died in the Great War' he is listed as winner of a Military Medal, and in 'Ireland's Memorial Records' he is listed as winner of a D.C.M., and in another listing for him in 'Ireland's Memorial Records' ( there are 2) it states he won the Military Medal and died of wounds in France. The Commonwealth War Graves Commission state he won the Military Medal. From the *Midland Tribune*, 1918, 'It is announced that Private J Cleary, D. C. M., Irish Guards, late of Banagher, has died in a London hospital after having an arm amputated.' Privates Patrick and Thomas Cleary, 3rd Leinsters, and two brothers Private Bernard, Irish Guards, and Private William Cleary, 3rd Leinsters from Banagher are briefly mentioned the *King's County Chronicle*, April 1916. They may be related. Grave or Memorial Reference: L 44. Cemetery: Great Warley (Christ Church) Cemetery, UK.

**CLEARY, Patrick Joseph:** Rank: Pte. Regiment or Service: Auckland Regiment, New Zealand Expeditionary Force. Unit: 1st

Battalion. Date of death: 5 May 1917. Service no: 10999. Age at death: 36. Killed in action.

*Supplementary information*: Son of Patrick Joseph and Mary Anne Cleary, of Main Street, Birr, Co. Offaly. Educated Presentation School, Birr and Rockwell College, Cashel. Information taken from the Nominal Roll of the New Zealand Expeditionary Force: Patrick Joseph. Surname: Cleary. Serial No: 10999 First Known Rank: Private. Occupation before Enlistment: Bushman. Next of Kin: Mrs M. Cleary (mother), Birr, Co. Offaly. Body on Embarkation: New Zealand Expeditionary Force Embarkation. Unit: 12th Reinforcements Wellington Infantry Battalion, J Company. Embarkation Date: 6 May 1916. Place of Embarkation: Wellington, New Zealand. Vessel: Mokoia or Navua Destination: Suez, Egypt. Nominal Roll Number: 31. Page on Nominal Roll: 9. Last Unit Served: Auckland Infantry Regiment. Place of Death: Messines, Belgium. Date of death: 5 May 1917 Year of Death: 1917 Cause of Death: Killed in action. From the *King's County Chronicle*, August 1915:

> The intelligence has reached their relatives in Birr that two of the local men who joined the 6th Leinsters of the formation of that Battalion were wounded in recent fighting in the Dardanelles. One is Corporal William Cleary, eldest son of Mr Patrick Cleary, of Main Street … both are now in hospital in Hampshire, from which the news comes from the men themselves by postcard. No further particulars are given, but we tender our sympathy to their relatives, and wish the brave fellows speedy recovery.

From the *King's County Chronicle*, September 1915:

> But that it would be unfair to particularise where all have been doing their share, we might lay stress upon the part taken in this gigantic war by a large portion of the manly muscle of the King's County, and more especially our own Birr, for, from the commanding officer down to the private, the 'Model Town' is represented. Moreover some of her sons have been put out of action, not a few being in the death roll. Amongst the latest hit, but fortunately not fatally, is Corporal William Cleary, 6th Battalion Leinsters, eldest son of Mrs Patrick Cleary, victualler, Main Street. This brave young non-commissioned officer, while in a fierce encounter in the Dardanelles, sustained a wound in the leg from grape shot. That his escape with his life was almost miraculous will be admitted when it is known that his helmet was blown off his head, so that his being able to return home on leave is simply a marvel in this war of marvellous incidents. We understand the head gear in question got such a wrecking that the commanding officer has secured it as a regimental memento of what the brave 6th Leinsters have already

passed through. We regret to have to add that it suffered heavily both in killed and wounded.

## From the *King's County Chronicle*, May 1917:

PRIVATE PATRICK JOSEPH CLEARY.
An official War Office telegram on Monday to Mrs Patrick Cleary, Main Street, Birr, contained the sad intelligence that her second son, Patrick Joseph, had been killed in action of May 5. The deceased young soldier, who went to Australia some years ago, joined the 1st Auckland Infantry Brigade, and accompanied it to France, where he had only been a few months when he lost his life. Writing to his bereaved mother, the Rev R. Richard, R.C. Chaplain gave further news that the deceased was killed in the trenches by shell-fire and was buried by the rev. gentleman in a military cemetery near the front line. Concluding, he said: "I write to assure you of the deep sympathy of all his officers and comrades in your grievous loss. He had my earnest prayers in Holy Mass." We extend our sincere sympathy to Mrs Cleary and family in their great bereavement.

Grave or Memorial Reference: II.E.4. Cemetery: St Quentin Cabaret Military Cemetery in Belgium.

## CLIBBORN, Cecil Hamilton:
Rank: Captain. Regiment or Service: Royal Irish Regiment. Unit: 92nd Punjabis. Date of death: 7 April 1916. Age at death: 29.

*Supplementary information:* Son of Col. and Mrs Clibborn, of 87 Victoria Street, London. From the *King's County Chronicle*, April 1916:

King's County officer killed. Captain Cecil Hamilton Clibborn, 92nd Punjabis, died of wounds on 10th April. He was the youngest and only surviving son of Lieut-Col. Clibborn, C.I.E., of Moorock, Ballycumber, and grandson of G. Butler Hamilton, R.A.M.C.

He was born in 1886, and was educated at St Colomb's College and Westward Ho; the young officer entered Woolwich, and passed into Royal Garrison Artillery in 1905. He served in West Indies, Jamaica, and India, and after transferring to the Indian Army in Burmah. He went to Egypt with the Indian Expeditionary Force, and was in the battle of Serapeum and through operations in Egypt. Was first wounded 6th January, 1915 and returned to duty end of that month in charge of a machine gun section.

Captain Clibborn was a good all-round sportsman and polo player. He was an excellent linguist, having qualified in many Eastern languages, including Chinese, Arabic, Persian, and Burmese. His only brother, Captain C.J.H. Clibborn, was killed in France last December.

Grave or Memorial Reference: He has no known grave but is listed on Panel 50 of the Basra memorial in Iraq.

**CLIBBORN, Cuthbert John Hamilton:** Rank: Captain. Regiment or Service: Royal Horse Artillery. Unit: 'D' Bty. Age at death: 32. Date of death: 14 December 1915. Awards: Mentioned in Despatches. Killed in action.

*Supplementary information:* Son of Lt. Col. I. Clibborn, C.I.E., and Mrs Clibborn, of Moorock, Ballycumber, Co. Offaly. Grave or Memorial Reference: I.G.7. Cemetery: Erquinghem-Lys Churchyard Extension in France.

**COGHLAN, Michael:** Rank: Sergeant. Regiment or Service: Irish Guards. Unit: 1st Battalion. Date of death: 17 September 1916. Service no: 3663. Born in Frankfort, Co. Offaly. Enlisted in Athlone, Co Westmeath. Killed in action. Age at death: 25. He has no known grave but is listed on Pier and Face 7 D on the Theipval Memorial in France.

**COLBOURNE, Michael:** Rank: Pte. Regiment or Service: South Lancashire Regiment. Unit: 2nd Battalion. Date of death: 24 October 1914. Service no: 7448. Born in Birr, Co. Offaly. Enlisted in Birr. Killed in action. Age at death: 25.

*Supplementary information:* Son of John and Esther Colbourne, of Moorpark Street, Birr, Co. Offaly. He has no known grave but is listed on Panel 23 of the Le Touret Memorial in France. Note: Pte Michael Colbourne 7448 South Lancashire Regiment and Pte Michael Collum 7448 South Lancashire Regiment both enlisted in the same place and died on the same day in the same regiment in the same Battalion with the same service number. Both are listed in 'Ireland's Memorial Records'. Colbourne only is listed in 'Soldiers died in the Great War' and the Commonwealth War Graves Commission. They appear to be the same man.

**COLBURN, Michael:** Rank: Pte. Regiment or Service: Leinster Regiment. Unit: 2nd Battalion. Date of death: 27 March 1918. Service no: 5666. Born in Banagher, Co. Offaly. Enlisted in Birr, Co. Offaly while living in Banagher, Co. Offaly. Killed in action. Age at death: 20.

*Supplementary information:* Son of John and Elizabeth Colburn, of Banagher, Co. Offaly. He has no known grave but is listed on Panel 78 on the Pozieres Memorial in France.

**COLE, Robert:** Rank: Lance Corporal. Regiment or Service: Leinster Regiment. Unit: 2nd Battalion. Date of death: 10 November 1914. Service no: 6591. Born in Birr, Co. Offaly. Enlisted in Birr, Co. Offaly. Killed in action in Armentieres. Age at death: 32.

*Supplementary information:* Son of Joseph Cole, of Glebe Street, Birr, Co. Offaly. From the *King's County Chronicle*, November 1914:

> When the present war is over Birr may well be proud of the many gallant sons she sent to the front in the

defence of freedom against the "might is right" policy of Germany. Amongst them is Private T Cole of the 1st Connaught Rangers, who came from India with the first Expeditionary Force from that Country, and arrived in France in time for the retreat of the Germans from near Paris. He was wounded by a bayonet in the hand in a charge on the 2nd September, and as he was getting back into his trench a piece of shrapnel struck him on the back. Seeing a dying comrade near he tried to give him a drink from his bottle, and while doing so was wounded in the leg by a rifle bullet.

After being in hospital in France for some time he was brought to Bristol from where he came to Birr on sick leave. He is full of praise for the Gurkhas who, he says, strike terror into the Germans. He did not see any instances of the Red Cross being fired upon by the enemy, but in hospital with him was a child which was held over a fire by the Germans while its mother got them something to eat. He is in the best of spirits and is anxious to be 'in it' again.

From the *King's County Chronicle*, November 1914:

Mr Joseph Cole, Birr, has received notification of the death in action of his son, Lance Corporal Robert, of the 2nd Leinsters, which occurred about the 18th or 20th October. Another son, Corporal Joseph, is at the front in the 1st Leinsters, and the youngest son, Pte Thomas, who was home on sick leave having been wounded, has gone back to his regiment. Mr John Howard, Moorpark Street, and ex-Sergt, 3rd Leinsters, who served in the South African War, received a similar sad letter s to his son Tom, also a Corporal in the same Battalion. These are only a couple of the many mourned over in the King's County and Tipperary. Son of Mr Joseph Cole, Tailor, Glebe Street.

Has no known grave but is commemorated on Panel 10. Memorial: Ploegsteert Memorial in Belgium.

**COLEMAN, Richard:** Rank: Guardsman. Regiment or Service: Guards Machine Gun, Machine Gun Guards. Unit: 4th Battalion. Date of death: 28 March 1918. Service no: 1046. Formerly he was with the Irish Guards where his number was 8920. Born in Rochford Bridge, Tyrrellspass. Enlisted in Tullamore, Co. Offaly while living in Fathingstown, Co Westmeath. Killed in action. Grave or Memorial Reference: VI.A.2. Cemetery: Bucquoy Road Cemetery, Ficheux in France

**COLGAN, Thomas:** Rank: Pte. Regiment or Service: The Loyal North Lancashire Regiment. Unit: 9th Bn. Age at death: 34. Date of death: 19 June 1917. Service no: 14941. Born in Bolton. Enlisted in Bolton while living in Great Harwood, Lancashire. Killed in action.
*Supplementary information:* Son of Thomas and Bridget Colgan, of Castle House, Sragh, Tullamore, Co. Offaly. Grave or Memorial Reference: Panel 41 and 43. Memorial: Ypres (Menin Gate) Memorial in Belgium.

**COLLINS, Richard:** Rank: Pte. Regiment or Service: (King's Royal Irish) Hussars. Unit: 8th Battalion. Date of death: 31 March 1918. Service no: 13933. Born in Mountrath, Queen's County. Enlisted in Birr while living in Shinrone, Co. Offaly. Died of wounds. Age at death: 29.

*Supplementary information:* Son of Mr and Mrs James Collins, of Shinrone, Co. Offaly. From the *Midland Tribune*, April 1918, 'Private R Collins, Shinrone, who volunteered at the outbreak of the war, has died of wounds received in action. He served two and a half years in France, and had seen some heavy fighting.' Grave or Memorial Reference: II.H.10. Cemetery: Gezaincourt Communal Cemetery Extension in France.

**COLLIS, John:** Rank: Pte. Regiment or Service: Irish Guards. Unit: 2nd Battalion. Date of death: 22 September 1916. Service no: 7885. Born in Birr, Co. Offaly. Enlisted in Birr. Died of wounds. Age at death: 19.

*Supplementary information:* Son of James and Bridget Collis, of Killeen Farm, Birr, Co. Offaly. A parody in the *King's County Chronicle*, April 1915:

> A Sergeant in the Royal Irish Fusiliers serving at the front composed this parody of the popular song "My Little Wet Home in the West" and sent it home to a relative.

> I've a little wet home in the trench,
> Where the rain storms continually drench,
> There's a dead cow close by,
> With her hoofs towards the sky,
> And she gives off a beautiful stench.
> Underneath in place of a floor,
> There's a mass of wet wood and some straw,
> Oh, the "Jack Johnson's" tear,
> Through the rain sodden air,
> O'er my little Wet Home in the Trench.

> There are snipers who keep on the go
> So you must keep your napper down low,
> For their star shells at night.
> Make a deuce of a light.
> And it causes the language to flow,
> Then bully and biscuits we chew,
> For its days since we tasted a stew,
> But with shells dropping there,
> There's no place to compare,
> With My Little Wet Home in the Trench.

From the *King's County Chronicle*, March 1916, 'Mr John Collis, Killeen, a valued employee of the Earl of Rosse, has two sons serving in the Irish Guards. Private Richard, who belonged to the R.I.C., and patriotically volunteered, and Private John, both of whom are in France.' Grave or Memorial Reference: XVI.C.9A. Cemetery: Etaples Military Cemetery in France.

**COLLUM, Michael:** Rank: Pte. Regiment or Service: South Lancashire Regiment. Unit: 2nd Battalion. Date of death: 24 October 1914. Service no: 7448. Born in Birr, Co. Offaly. Enlisted in Birr. Killed in action. Age at death: 25.

*Supplementary information:* Son of John and Esther Colbourne, of Moorpark Street, Birr, Co. Offaly. Grave or Memorial Reference: He has no known grave but is listed on Panel 23 of the Le Touret Memorial in France.

Note: Pte Michael Colbourne 7448 South Lancashire Regiment and Pte Michael Collum 7448 South Lancashire Regiment both enlisted in the same place and died on the same day in the same regiment in the same Battalion with the same service number. Both are listed in 'Ireland's Memorial Records', Colbourne only is listed in 'Soldiers died in the Great War' and with the Commonwealth War Graves Commission. They appear to be the same man.

## COLTON, Frederick William:

Rank: Pte. Regiment or Service: Royal Irish Regiment. Unit: 27th Battalion. Date of death: 22 February 1918. Service no: 25157. Formerly he was with the South Irish Horse where his number was 2455. Born in Tullamore, Co. Offaly. Enlisted in Dublin while living in Tullamore, Co. Offaly. Killed in action. Age at death: 21.

*Supplementary information:* Son of Abraham C. and Margret Anne Colton, of Charleville Square, Tullamore, Co. Offaly. Volunteered in 1916. From the *King's County Chronicle*, March 1918:

Private Frederick William Colton, of the South Irish Horse, transferred to the Royal Irish Regiment, son of Mr Abraham Colton, of Charleville Square, Tullamore, and Oldtown House, Croghan, has been killed in action in France. He was a bright, handsome, athletic and gentlemanly youth, only 21 years of age, and had eight months service in France. He was educated at Wesley College, Dublin, and was intended to take up farming as a profession, by his father, who is extensively engaged in it.

Like many other youths he was filled with patriotic fervour to fight for his country, and asked permission of his father to join the army. This was promised if again claimed after the lapse of a year; and on the expiry of the period it was again sought and obtained. The deceased soldier was of a gallant type, and if spared had doubtless a brilliant career. His commanding officer in the sad epistle to his parents, conveying intelligence of his death, says he was a favourite with all the officers and men of his battalion, and narrates that he was killed instantaneously by an enemy shell on the road moving to an advanced position of attack, and is buried behind British lines.

He was about to return home for six months special training with the view to a commission – a brave, modest, high-spirited, and chivalrous youth, he will be long remembered by Tullamore people, who feel with his bereaved parents in their sorrow.

From De Ruvigny's Roll of Honour:

Colton, Frederick William, Private, No 25157, 7<sup>th</sup> Battn, The Royal Irish Regiment. Second son of Abraham Colton of Charleville Square, Tullamore, Farmer, by his wife, Margaret Anne, daughter of the late Richard Odlum; born, Croghan, King's County, 16<sup>th</sup> March, 1895. Educated at Wesley College, Dublin; was a Farmer; enlisted in the Royal Irish Regiment, 26 Dec, 1916; served with the Expeditionary Force in France and Flanders from April, 1917 and was killed in action at Epehy, 22 Feb, 1918. Buried in Villers Faucon Communal Cemetery, north east of Peronne.

Grave or Memorial Reference: I.B.17. Cemetery: Villiers-Faucon Communal Cemetery Extension in France.

**COMER, Patrick:** Rank: Pte. Regiment or Service: Leinster Regiment. Unit: 7<sup>th</sup> Battalion. Date of death: 12 April 1916. Service no: 3177. Born in Clonfert, Co. Galway. Enlisted in Birr, Co. Offaly while living in Ferbane, Co. Offaly. Killed in action. From the *King's County Chronicle,* June 1916:

> From Rosfarahart ... also poor Paddy Comber [sic], so well known and liked, joined the Leinsters, and was killed in France only a few weeks ago. He was employed as underkeeper by Mr H.L. King, D.L., whose two other gamekeepers, George and Edward Fitzgerald, also joined. They are now being trained in the South Irish Horse.

Grave or Memorial Reference: F.27. Cemetery: Bois-Carre Military Cemetery, Haisnes in France.

**CONLON, Edward:** Rank: Pte. Regiment or Service: Leinster Regiment. Unit: 3<sup>rd</sup> Battalion. Date of death: 10 October 1918. Service no: 35039. Born in Brackna, Co. Offaly. Enlisted in Mullingar, Co. Westmeath. Died at sea.

*Supplementary information:* Son of Mr P. Conlon, of Ballynoland Brackna, Rathagan, Co. Kildare. Grave or Memorial Reference: RC.599. Cemetery: Grangegorman Military Cemetery in Dublin.

**CONNELL, Patrick:** Rank: Pte. Regiment or Service: Machine Gun Corps. Unit: Infantry, 235<sup>th</sup> Company. Date of death: 30 November 1917. Service no: 36409. Formerly he was with the Royal Irish Regiment where his number was 9891. Born in Edenderry, Co. Offaly. Enlisted in Dublin while living in Edenderry. Killed in action. Age at death: 19.

*Supplementary information:* Son of John and Mary Connell, of New Row, Edenderry. From the *Leinster Leader,* 13 July 1918, 'Mrs Connell New Row has received word that her son Private Patrick, Leinster Regiment might be alive. It was stated he was getting treatment for a wound when the Germans captured the camp.' He has no known grave but is commemorated on Panel 12 and 13. Memorial: Cambrai Memorial, Louveral in France.

**CONNOLE, John J.:** Rank: Sergeant. Regiment or Service: York and Lancashire Regiment. Unit: 11th Battalion. Date of death: 23 February 1916. Service no: 4480. Born in Co. Offaly. Died of Pneumonia in Stafford. Age at death: 42.

*Supplementary information:* Husband of Julia Connole, of Crinkle, Birr. Won the South African Medal. He is listed under **CONNOLE, J.** in the Commonwealth War Graves Commission. From the *Midland Tribune, Tipperary Sentinel* and *King's County Vindicator,* April 1916:

DEATH OF SERGEANT JOHN JOSEPH CONNOLE.

His many friends have heard with deep regret of the death of Sergeant John Joseph Connole. Serving in the Boer War, he was invalided from the service, and for fourteen years had been in the clerical department at Hadfield, Ltd, Sheffield. When the present war broke out he re-enlisted, and engaged in training men of the York and Lancaster Regiment at Rugely, Cannock Chase, Staffs.

The funeral took place on Sunday (February 27th) with full military honours. The chief mourners were–Mrs J Connole and Mr J. Connole, widow and son; Mrs B. McRedmond, sister-in-law; Mr R. Connole, brother, Mrs R. Connole, sister-in-law; Miss M. Connole, niece; Mr and Mrs Moran, Mr and Mrs Holland, Mr and Mrs Edmondson, Mr and Mrs Allop, Mr and Mrs West, Mr Brown, Corporal Brown, M Burden, Mr Foster, Mrs Wownend (?), Miss Hunday, Mr and Mrs Morley.

Grave or Memorial Reference: 27 (northwest Part). Cemetery: Handsworth (St Joseph) Roman Catholic Graveyard, UK.

**CONNOLLY, John:** Rank: Pte. Regiment or Service: Leinster Regiment. Unit: 2nd ( SDGW and CWGC) also listed as 4th ('Ireland's Memorial Records'), Battalion. Date of death: 20 October 1918. Service no: 4679. Born in Birr, Co. Offaly. Age at death: 19. Enlisted in Birr, while living in Birr. Killed in action or missing. Was in the employ of Lord Rosse before enlistment. From the *King's County Chronicle,* April 1916, 'Two sons of the late Mr Michael Connolly, of Killeen, Birr, volunteered on the outbreak of war. They are: Private Thomas, of the 2nd Gloucesters, in Salonika; and Private John, of the A.S.C. serving in France.' Grave or Memorial Reference: VII.B.13. Cemetery: Harlebeke New British Cemetery in Belgium.

**CONNOLLY, Thomas:** Rank: Pte. Regiment or Service: Leinster Regiment. Unit: 2nd Battalion. Date of death: 20 May 1918. Service no: 4679. Born in Birr, Co. Offaly. Age at death: 20. Born in Birr. This man is not listed with the Commonwealth War Graves commission nor is he in 'Soldiers died in the Great War'. He is only listed in 'Ireland's Memorial Records'. He may be **CONNOLLY, JOHN,** No 4679 above.

**CONNOR, Daniel:** Rank: Pte. Regiment or Service: Royal Dublin Fusiliers. Unit: 2nd Battalion. Date of death: 1 July 1916. Service no: 22271. Born in Portarlington, Co. Offaly. Enlisted in Maryborough while living in Portarlington. Killed in action. Age at death: 30.

*Supplementary information:* Husband of Ann Murphy (formerly Connor), of Kilmalogue, Portarlington, Co. Offaly. Grave or Memorial Reference: I.D.36. Cemetery: Sucrerie Military Cemetery, Colinclamps in France.

**CONNOR, Michael:** Rank: Pte. Regiment or Service: Leinster Regiment. Unit: 2nd Battalion. Date of death: 31 August 1916. Service no: 3206. Born in Tubber, Co. Offaly. Enlisted in Tullamore, Co. Offaly. Killed in action. He is also listed on the Tullamore Roll of Honour. Grave or Memorial Reference: He has no known grave but is listed on Pier and Face 16C on the Theipval Memorial in France.

**CONNORS, Michael:** Rank: Private. Regiment or Service: Leinster Regiment. Unit: 2nd Bn. Date of death: 4 September 1918. Service no: 5664. Born in Roscrea. Enlisted in Roscrea while living in Brosna, Co. Offaly. Killed in action. Age at death: 20.

*Supplementary information:* Son of Michael and Mary Connors, of Brosna, Roscrea, Co. Offaly. Grave or Memorial Reference: Bristol. Castle Cem Mem 3. Messines Ridge British Cemetery in Belgium.

**CONROY, Bernard:** Rank: Pte. Regiment or Service: Leinster Regiment. Unit: 2nd Battalion. Date of death: 16 August 1915. Service no: 9701. Born in Kilbridge, Co. Offaly. Enlisted in Tullamore, Co. Offaly. Killed in action. He is also listed on the Tullamore Roll of Honour. Grave or Memorial Reference: Union Street Graveyard No. 1 Cem. Mem. 12. Cemetery: Birr Cross Roads Cemetery in Belgium.

**CONROY, Patrick:** Rank: Pte. Regiment or Service: Connaught Rangers. Unit: 2nd Battalion. Date of death: 19 September 1914. Service no: 6595. Born in Philipstown, Co. Offaly. Enlisted in Cork while living in Tullamore, Co. Offaly. Killed in action. He is also listed on the Tullamore Roll of Honour. He has no known grave but is listed on the La Ferte-Sous-Jouarre-Memorial in France.

**CONROY, Thomas:** Rank: Pte. Regiment or Service: Leinster Regiment. Unit: 2nd Battalion. Date of death: 2 August 1918. Service no: 3615. Born in Tullamore, Co. Offaly. Enlisted in Tullamore while living in Tullamore. Killed in action.

*Supplementary information:* Brother of Patrick Conroy, of 35 Herbertshire Street, Denny, Stirlingshire. Grave or Memorial Reference: Special Memorial, 18. Cemetery: New Irish Farm Cemetery in Belgium.

**CONVY, Michael:** Rank: Sergeant. Regiment or Service: King's Liverpool Regiment. Unit: 4th Bn. Date of death:

26 September 1917. Service no: 8646. Born in Clara, Co. Offaly. Enlisted in Warrington while living in Clara. Killed in action. Age at death: 42. Supplementary information: Son of Patrick and Mary Ann Convy. Husband of Elizabeth Convy, of 9 Abbeyview, Bray, Co. Wicklow. From the *King's County Independent*, January 1915, 'Clara's Roll of Honour, Patrick Convey, Dublin Fusiliers – Prisoner of war.' Grave or Memorial Reference: He has no known grave but is listed on Panel 31 to 34 and 162 and 162A and 163A the Tyne Cot Memorial in Belgium.

**CONWAY, Richard:** Rank: Pte. Regiment or Service: Lancashire Fusiliers. Unit: 16th Battalion. Date of death: 22 November 1916. Service no: 12475. Born in Birr, Co. Offaly. Enlisted in Salford. Killed in action. Grave or Memorial Reference: II.A.16. Cemetery: Mailly Wood Cemetery, Mailly-Maillet in France.

**COOKE, Joseph:** Rank: Corporal. Regiment or Service: Leinster Regiment. Unit: 1st Battalion. Date of death: 10 March 1917. Age at death: 24. Born in Ballinasloe. Enlisted in Birr, Co. Offaly. Died in Salonika.

*Supplementary information:* Son of Kate Cooke, of Limerick Street, Roscrea. From the *King's County Chronicle*, March 1917:

CORPORAL JOSEPH COOKE.

The death took place on 10th March, following an operation for appendicitis, of Corporal Joseph Cooke,

Leinster Regiment, aged 23. He joined the army at the early age of 15, and had five years service in India. Early in 1914 he went with his regiment to France, and took part in the battles of Neuve Chapelle and Ypres, being wounded at the latter place. At "Hill 60" he was "gassed" and after recovering was given a short furlough to his native Birr. Later he went to Salonika and underwent at Malta an operation, which ended fatally. He was fine young soldier, a great favourite with all ranks, and much sympathy is felt with his mother in her great loss.

Grave or Memorial Reference: VIII.E.3. Cemetery: Struma Military Cemetery in Greece.

**COONE, James:** Rank: Pte. Regiment or Service: Leinster Regiment. Unit: 2nd Battalion. Date of death: 14 November 1915. Service no: 7171. Born in Frankfort, Co. Offaly. Enlisted in Birr. Killed in action. There is a Pte Joseph Coone, 2nd Leinsters listed in the *King's County Chronicle* in 1916 with a photograph and adds, 'served in France and Salonika, also went through the Boer War. He is a relative of Mr Patrick Walsh, Master Tailor, Birr Union.' From the *King's County Chronicle*, 1916:

William Coone, Leinster Regiment, contracted disease while serving with the Mediterranean Expeditionary Force, was invalided home, and is now in Cork. He had four brothers also in the army. Three were called up on the Reserve, one (James) was killed in action in France. Thomas who joined voluntarily, is in Greece, as are also Patrick and Joseph. All belong to the Leinster Regiment.

Grave or Memorial Reference: He has no known grave but is listed on Panel 44 on the Ypres (Menin Gate) Memorial in Belgium.

**COONEY, Joseph:** Rank: Pte. Regiment or Service: Royal Irish Regiment. Unit: 'D' Company, 2$^{nd}$ Battalion. Date of death: 3 September 1916. Service no: 10928. Born in St Mary's, Clara, Co. Offaly. Enlisted in Athlone while living in Clara. Killed in action. Age at death: 21.
*Supplementary information:* The Commonwealth Wargraves Commission gave his name as **COONEY, John Joseph**. Son of Matthew and Ellen Cooney, of 2 St Mary's Terrace, Scotch Parade, Athlone, Co. Westmeath. He has no known grave but is listed on Pier and Face 3A on the Theipval Memorial in France.

**CORNALLY, Edward:** Rank: Pte. Regiment or Service: Royal Munster Fusiliers. Unit: 2$^{nd}$ Battalion. Date of death: 10 November 1917. Service no: 6573. Born in Ferbane, Co. Offaly. Enlisted in Neath, Glamorgan while living in Glyn Neath, Glamorgan. Killed in action. Age at death: 30.
*Supplementary information:* Son of John and Teresa Cornally, of Loughbrown, Newbridge, Co.

Kildare. He has no known grave but is listed on Panels 143 to 144 on the Tyne Cot Memorial in Belgium.

**CORNALLY, Joseph:** Rank: Pte. Regiment or Service: Irish Guards. Unit: No. 2 Coy. 1$^{st}$ Bn. Age at death: 31. Date of death: 1 February 1915 Service no: 2696. Born in Drumkeaney, Co. Westmeath. Enlisted in Tullamore. Killed in action.
*Supplementary information:* Son of James and Kate Cornally, Killaghantober, Ballycumber, Co. Offaly. Grave or Memorial Reference: II.B.13. Cemetery: Cuinchy Communal Cemetery in France.

**CORNALLY, Michael:** Rank: Pte. Regiment or Service: Machine Gun Corps. Unit: Infantry. Date of death: 1 April 1918. Service no: 115271. Formerly he was with the Hereford Regiment where his number was 238693. Enlisted in Birkenhead. Killed in action. Grave or Memorial Reference: III.M.6. Cemetery: Peronne Communal Cemetery Extension in France.

**CORNALLY, Patrick:** Rank: Pte. Regiment or Service: Irish Guards. Unit: 1$^{st}$ Battalion. Date of death: 12 September 1917. Service no: 10729. Born in Ballinahound, Co. Offaly. Enlisted in Naas, Co Kildare. Killed in action. Grave or Memorial Reference: V.D.1. Cemetery: Artillery Wood Cemetery in Belgium.

**CORRIGAN, John:** Rank: Private First Class (Private Second Class in Commonwealth War Graves Commission). Regiment or Service: Royal Air Force. Date of death: 10 October 1918. Service no: 292310. Born in Birr. Age at death: 18.

*Supplementary information:* Son of Thomas and Norah Corrigan, of Tinahelly, Riverstown, Birr, Co. Offaly. 'Ireland's Memorial Records' state that he was drowned on the SS *Leinster* on 10 October 1918. SS *Leinster* was torpedoed and sunk by German Submarine U-123 on 12 October 1918. He has no known grave but is listed on the Hollybrook Memorial, Southampton, UK

**CORRIGAN, Patrick:** Rank: Pte. Regiment or Service: Leinster Regiment. Unit: 2nd Battalion. Date of death: 21 October 1918. Service no: 10348. Born in Coolderry, Co. Offaly. Enlisted in Birr. Died. Age at death: 23.

*Supplementary information:* Son of Thomas Corrigan, of Tinneykelly, Corrig, Co. Offaly. Grave or Memorial Reference: II.D.24. Cemetery: Delsaux Farm Cemetery, Beugny in France.

**COSTELLO, Edward William:** Rank: Lieutenant. Regiment or Service: Royal Inniskilling Fusiliers. Unit: 3rd Battalion. Secondary Regiment, Machine Gun Corps, Infantry attached to the 3rd Battalion attached to the 87th Company. Date of death: 1 July 1916. Age at death: 19. Killed in action.

*Supplementary information:* Son of Mr and Mrs T.D. Costello, of 55 Pembroke Road, Ballsbridge, Dublin. From the *King's County Independent*, July 1916:

YOUNG TULLAMORE MAN KILLED.

Mr T.D. Costello, Manager of the Hibernian Bank, Tullamore, received intelligence during the week that his son Lieut. E. Costello, Inniskillings, was killed in action in France in the Big Push, which commenced on July the 1st. Lieutenant Costello was at home in Tullamore a few weeks ago, and since he obtained his Commission has been on active service at the Dardanelles, and in Egypt. Deep sympathy is felt for Mr and Mrs Costello in their bereavement. Lieut Bull, son of Mr Richard Bull, Sub-Sheriff of King's County, was wounded in the same battle. He is at present in hospital in England.

From the *King's County Chronicle*, September 1917:

Lieut.Col. E.W. Costello, V.C. of the Indian Army, who has been awarded the Order for Distinguished Service in the war in Mesopotamia, is a cousin of Mr T.D. Costello, whose gallant son, Lieut. T.D. Costello, was killed at the battle of the Somme, in 1st July, 1916. Colonel Costello won his V.C. some years ago in the Malakand Pass in the North West Provinces.

There seems to be some mix-up of information in the above article with names. He has no known grave but is listed on Pier and Face 4D and 5B on the Thiepval Memorial in France.

**COUGHLAN P.:** Rank: Pte. Regiment or Service: Connaught

Rangers. Unit: 3rd Bn. Date of death: 13 October 1916. Service no: 8435. This man is only listed in the Commonwealth War Graves Commission. I include him because of this even though he was discharged as an invalid the army at the time. The following is a shortened version of the inquest, From the *King's County Independent*, October 1916:

SAD ACCIDENT.

Brave Connaught Ranger who fought at Mons and Marne.

Killed in his native Town. Victim of a motor collision.

No blame to anyone. Details disclosed at inquest.

A sad and tragic occurrence took place in Tullamore on Friday night last by which a labourer and a discharged soldier, named Patrick Coughlan, who resided with his parents at Rapp, near the town, on the Tyrrellspass road, met his death. The deceased who was about 40 years of age, was going home from town and when approaching Kilbeggan Bridge, where the gradient is very steep he was knocked down by a motor belonging to Mr R.H. Poole, which was returning from Ballymore, County Westmeath with Mr Patrick Frayne, a commercial traveller in the employment of Messrs D.E. Williams. The deceased, according to the evidence given at the inquest, had been in Mr James Brazel's public house, some few minutes before the accident, and asked to be served with a pint of porter, which was not supplied to him, the publican who was familiar with his demeanour which was rather eccentric, advising him to go home. When about 90 yards from Mr Brazel's door, a motor car throwing out a long beam of light suddenly topped the bridge. The car, according to Mr Frayne, who was sitting in the front beside the driver, a young man named Robert Curham, was descending the bridge at a pace of about 4 to 6 miles an hour. The head-lights revealed a man, who afterwards turned out to be deceased, approaching on the centre of the road, and on his swerving the car he suddenly darted towards the wall, which abuts Mr Conroy's premises, being struck and knocked down, the wheels of the car passing over his body.

A young man named O'Dowd who was coming down the bridge and who witnessed the occurrence ran to pick up the man whom he found in an unconscious condition. The driver of the motor car which was brought up suddenly and Mr Frayne, came to his assistance; and lifting the injured man into the car conveyed him to the King's County Infirmary. Priest and doctor were hastily summoned and both Father McCormack and Dr. Kennedy were soon in attendance, but the unfortunate man only survived a few minutes after the arrival of the doctor, who found him in a state of collapse and beyond human aid.

The deceased had been in the army for a number of years; served in India, where like many soldiers he got sun-stroke. Being a reserve man he was called up on mobilisation order at the outbreak of the war in 1914. He was in several of the fierce engagements of the first year of the war, being present at the retreat from Mons and the battle of the Marne, where he was wounded. He was invalided from the army in July, 1915, and subsequently discharged owing to ill health and a slight eccentricity of habit due in all probability to the many hardships endured during the campaign of the winter of 1914-15. Deceased belonged to the second battalion of the Connaught Rangers, a corps which has distinguished itself all through the campaign and which comprises many Tullamore men.

He is also listed on the Tullamore Roll of Honour. Grave or Memorial Reference: 2.23. Cemetery: Clonminch Catholic Cemetery, Co. Offaly.

**COUGHLAN, Robert:** Rank: Pte. Regiment or Service: Royal Dublin Fusiliers. Unit: 2nd Battalion. Date of death: 1 July 1916. Service no: 21179. Born in Ferbane, Co. Offaly. Enlisted in Birr. Died of wounds. Grave or Memorial Reference: Special Memorial 3. Cemetery: Sucrerie Military Cemetery, Colinclamps in France.

**COUGHLAN, William:** Rank: Pte. Regiment or Service: Machine Gun Corps. Unit: Infantry. Date of death: 9 June 1917. Service no: 66777. Formerly he was with the Leinster Regiment where his number was 4594. Born in Birr, Co. Offaly. Enlisted in Birr. Killed in action. Age at death: 25.

*Supplementary information:* Son of Michael Coughlan, of 3 Church Street, Dublin. Has no known grave but is commemorated on Panel 56. Memorial: Ypres (Menin Gate) Memorial in Belgium.

**COULTER, Michael:** Rank: Pte. Regiment or Service: Royal Dublin Fusiliers. Unit: 3rd Bn. Date of death: 14 August 1914. Service no: 8434. Born in Dublin and enlisted in Dublin. Died at home.

*Supplementary information:* Son of Mrs M. Coulter, of Ballyhair, Fahy, Co. Offaly. Grave or Memorial Reference: In southeast part. Cemetery: Upper Aghada Cemetery, Co. Offaly.

**COWEY, Thomas:** Rank: Company Sergeant Major. Regiment or Service: Royal Garrison Artillery. Unit: Attached to the Permanent Staff (Royal Jersey Artillery). Date of death: 17 June 1918. Service no: 279110. Born in Newart Hall, Lanarkshire. Enlisted in Guernsey. Died at home. From the *King's County Chronicle*, July 1918:

OBITUARY.
Sergt Major T. Cowey.
Amidst many tokens of regret the remains of the late Sergt. – Major T. Cowey, of the 110 Company, R.G.A. were laid to rest at Almorah cemetery. The late Sergeant-Major

was the father of Captain Cowey, at present on active service, and of Cuba House, Banagher. A Requiem Mass was offered for the repose of his soul at S. S. Mary and Peters Church previous to the funeral, which was a military one. It consisted of a firing party of 25 men and the band of the Regiment, flaying the funeral march. The cortege was followed by 50 men of the R.G.A. and staff. The grave was covered with floral tributes from his children, the officer commanding, and the officers, R.G.A., non-commissioned officers, etc., etc.

Amongst those present were; H. E. Major-General Sir A. Wilson, K.C.B. Lieut-Governor, Lieut-Colonel A.C. Hall, R.A. ; Lieut-Colonel L.T. Bowles, O. C. Jersey Garrison Battalion; Lieut-Colonel J.R. Yourdi and P.B. Bentlif, R.A.M.C; Major H.S. Le Rossignol, Major H Randall 110th Coy, R.G.A. ; Captain G.J. Robin, A.D.C; Captain L. L'Hogier, Adjutant Jersey (8) Batt; Lieuts. Blampied, Binet, Rossitet and Romerie. Detachments of the R. A., Jersey (G) Battalion, and R.A. M.C. and Departmental Corps. Rev. Father Bitot officiated at the graveside.

Grave or Memorial Reference: I.12.B. Cemetery: St Hellier (Almorah) Cemetery, Jersey.

**COWLEY, Patrick:** Rank: Pte. Regiment or Service: Connaught Rangers. Unit: 2nd Battalion. Date of death: 14 September 1914. Service no: 3451 in 'Soldiers died in the Great War'

and No. 6451 in 'Ireland's Memorial Records' and the Commonwealth War Graves Commission. Born in Tullamore, Co. Offaly (also down as born in Kilbride). Enlisted in Tullamore while living in Tullamore. Killed in action. He is also listed on the Tullamore Roll of Honour. Grave or Memorial Reference: Special Memorial 9. Vailly British Cemetery in France.

**COX, James:** Rank: Pte. Regiment or Service: Royal Dublin Fusiliers. Unit: 1st Battalion. Date of death: 27 March 1916. Service no: 21553. Born in Rhode, Co. Offaly. Enlisted in Coatbridge while living in Rhode. Died. Grave or Memorial Reference: III.B.18. Cemetery: Mazargues War Cemetery, Marseilles in France.

**COX, John James:** Rank: Pte. Regiment or Service: Royal Munster Fusiliers. Unit: 1st Battalion. Date of death: 21 August 1915. Service no: 5500. Born in Banagher, Co. Offaly. Enlisted in Glasgow while living in Banagher. Killed in action in Gallipoli. Age at death: 28.

*Supplementary information:* Son of Joseph and Kate Cox (*née* Foley), of Queen Street, Banagher, Co. Offaly. Privates Patrick Snr, Patrick Jnr, Christopher and Timothy Cox, (father and three sons from Banagher). 3rd Battalion, Leinster Regiment are briefly mentioned the *King's County Chronicle*, April 1916. They may be related. He has no known grave but is listed on Panel 185 t o 190 on the Helles Memorial in Turkey

**CRONIN, James:** Rank: Pte. Regiment or Service: Royal Welsh Fusiliers. Unit: 5th/6th Battalion. Date of death: 21 October 1918. Service no: 74010. Formerly he was with the Royal Dublin Fusiliers where his number was 10327. Born in Edenderry, Co. Offaly. Enlisted in Naas, Co Kildare while living in Edenderry. Died in Egypt. Age at death: 28. Grave or Memorial Reference: F.83. Cemetery: Kantara War Memorial Cemetery in Egypt.

**CRONLEY/CRONLY, Thomas:** Rank: Pte. Regiment or Service: Royal Irish Fusiliers. Unit: 5th Battalion. Date of death: 3 October 1918. Service no: 30137. Formerly he was with the Royal Dublin Fusiliers where his number was 21538. Born in Ballyboy, Co. Offaly. Enlisted in Kilcormac, Co. Offaly. Died of wounds. Age at death: 21.

*Supplementary information:* Brother of William Cronly, of Cappagolan, Kilcormac, Tullamore, Co. Offaly. Grave or Memorial Reference: III.C.9. Cemetery: Houchin British Cemetery in France.

**CROSBY, Hugh (Eugene):** Rank: Pte. Regiment or Service: (King's) Liverpool Regiment. Unit: 5th Battalion also listed as ( 5478) 1st/8th Battalion. Date of death: 8 August 1916. Age at death: 34. Service no: 307584. Born in Trim, Co. Meath. Enlisted in Liverpool while living in Liverpool. Killed in action.

*Supplementary information:* Son of John Crosby, of Chapel Street, Tullamore, Co. Offaly. He is listed on the Tullamore Roll of Honour, however, I do not see the Offaly connection but include him for your reference. He has no known grave but is listed on Pier and Face 1D 8B and 8 C on the Thiepval Memorial in France.

**CULLEN, James:** Rank: Pte. Regiment or Service: Royal Dublin Fusiliers. Unit: 6th Battalion. Date of death: 8 December 1915. Service no: 13032. Born in Edenderry, Co. Offaly. Enlisted in Paisley while living in Edenderry. Killed in action in the Balkans.

*Supplementary information:* Son of Patrick and Catherine Cullen, of Ballykillen, Edenderry, Co. Offaly. He has no known grave but is listed on the Doiran Memorial in Greece.

**CULLINAN, Edward Patrick:** Rank: Sergeant. Regiment or Service: Lord Strathcona's Horse (Royal Canadians). Date of death: 30 March 1918. Age at death: 30. Service no: 6168. Born in Ennis, Co. Clare. Enlisted in Sewell, Manitoba on 23 June 1915. Date of birth: 15 March 1885. Next of kin: Listed on his enlistment documents as father, this indicates that he got married after enlistment as there is a line struck through that entry. Father's name and address: Thomas Cullinan, Fountain House, Ennis, Co. Clare. Occupation on Enlistment: Rancher. Previous military experience: Seven years in the 6th Dragoon Guards.

*Supplementary information:* Son of Thomas and Angela P. Cullinan, of 16 Victoria Avenue, Cork. Husband of Alice Anastasia Cullinan, of Cumberland Terrace, Birr, Co. Offaly. He has no known grave but is listed on the Vimy Memorial in France.

**CUNNINGHAM, Thomas:** Rank: Pte. Regiment or Service: Leinster Regiment. Unit: 1st Battalion. Date of death: 19 September 1918. Service no: 4175. Born in Kilbride, Co. Offaly. Enlisted in Tullamore, Co. Offaly. Killed in action in Egypt. Grave or Memorial Reference: T.24. Cemetery: Ramleh War Cemetery in Israel.

**CURNANE, Christopher:** Rank: Pte. Regiment or Service: Royal Irish Regiment. Unit: 2nd Battalion. Date of death: 30 September 1918. Service no: 6946 and 4/6946. Born in Kilbride, Co. Offaly. Enlisted in Tullamore, Co. Offaly. Died of wounds. Grave or Memorial Reference: III.F.10. Cemetery: Sunken Road Cemetery, Boiusleux-St. Marc in France.

**CURRAN, James:** Rank: Pte. Regiment or Service: Leinster Regiment ('Ireland's Memorial Records') and the Royal Irish Regiment (Commonwealth War Graves Commission). Unit: 1st Garrison Battalion, (Commonwealth War Graves Commission) 2nd Battalion ('Ireland's Memorial Records'). Date of death: 30 November 1918. Service no: 11286. Born in Birr. Died of wounds in Alexandria.

James Curran.

*Supplementary information:* Brother of Patrick Curran, of Moorpark Street, Birr, Co. Offaly He is not listed in 'Soldiers died in the Great War'. From the *King's County Chronicle*, February 1916:

> Five sons of the late Andrew Curran, High Street, who was in the 3rd Leinsters, served through the South African War, and was out on pension when he died, are on active service, viz: Private Patrick, who formerly belonged to the 1st Batt, Leinsters, is now serving with the Irish Guards; Privates Andrew, James (wounded at the Aisne), Joseph (14 months in the trenches and wounded at Ypres); and Richard, who is at present in training.

From the *King's County Chronicle*, June/July 1918:

Twice Torpedoed and Three Times Wounded.

A letter recently received by Mrs Curran, Moorpark Street, Birr, from her son, Private James Curran, of the 18th Royal Irish, contains a thrilling account of his experiences on the *Aragon*, which, it will be remembered, was sunk in the Mediterranean on December 30, with the loss of 610 lives. Private Curran was an officer's servant on the ill-fated vessel, and was engaged in packing valises when the ship was struck by the torpedo. He relates how he immediately fell in at his post, and stood there until 160 nursing sisters on board were taken safely off. As the vessel went down sooner than was expected, the order was given "Every man for himself." Escorting destroyers then came up, and Private Curran, who had just time to get his boots off, jumped into the sea and swam to a destroyer, on to which he helped the officer, to whom he was a servant. "I was just shaking hands with him," he said, "When the destroyer was torpedoed, so that in less than 25 minutes I was torpedoed twice."

He managed to keep afloat for over three hours by holding on to a piece of wreckage, when a small boat came on the scene, which picked him up and brought him to a trawler which took him aboard and landed him at Alexandria. Private Curran was on the Western front for two years, where he was wounded three times and it was while on his way to the Far East that he underwent the thrilling experiences narrated above. When war broke out he was on the reserve of the Leinster Regiment, and was afterwards transferred to the 18th Royal Irish. There were four other brothers in the army, one of them, Private Joseph, of the Leinsters, being killed in France by a German sniper. Another brother, Private Patrick, formerly of the Leinsters, who was on pension, patriotically offered his services, again in the present war, and served in France with the Irish Guards. He was invalided out, and is now on pension.

While in the Leinsters he served throughout the Boer War. The other two brothers are Corporal Andrew, of the Leinsters, presently stationed in Tipperary after being for a long period in France, and Private Richard, of the Machine Gun Corps, now in Egypt. A brother-in-law, Private Cushing, of the Leinster Regiment, was killed early in the war.

Grave or Memorial Reference: C.133. Cemetery: Alexandria (Hadra), War Memorial Cemetery in Egypt.

**CURRAN, Joseph:** Rank: Pte. Regiment or Service: Leinster Regiment. Unit: B Company, 2nd Battalion. Date of death: 4 April 1916. Service no: 9700. Born in Birr, Co. Offaly. Enlisted in Birr. Died of wounds. Age at death: 22.

Joseph
Curran.

*Supplementary information:* Awarded the Mons Star. Son of Andrew Curran, of Birr, Co. Offaly. From the *King's County Chronicle*, October 1915:

LOCAL VETERAN'S "LAST POST."

On Wednesday, 27th October, Mr Andrew Curran, Moorpark Street, Birr, at the age of 68, answered the "last roll call." A week before he was quite well, but what was apparently a cold developed into pneumonia. About 50 years ago he joined the Shropshire Light Infantry in London, and took part in the Zulu War. He afterwards joined the 3rd Leinsters (then the King's County Militia) and went with them to the South African war, and was twice wounded. He received the Queen's and King's medals, and a life pension. His eldest son, Patrick, late of the 1st Leinsters, was also wounded in the same campaign, invalided home, and afterwards discharged on pension.

There are four other sons at present in the 2nd Leinsters – Corp, Andrew, wounded twice in Flanders; Pte James, wounded at Armentieres, and now at the Dardanelles; Pte Joseph, twelve months in the trenches, and wounded at Ypres, and Prt Richard, now at the Curragh. His son-in-law, Pte Charles Cushing, was killed at Armentieres. Owing to the absence of the Leinster Depot Band on recruiting it was impossible to have a military funeral, but a party of the Leinsters, in charge of Sergeant Joseph O'Hara, formed pall-bearers. All the sons, except one, had the melancholy satisfaction of following the remains, with many sympathisers, to Clonoghill Cemetery.

From the *King's County Chronicle*, May 1916:

PTE. J. CURRAN'S "GOOD-BYE."

Writing to Mrs Curran, High Street, Birr, on the death of her son, Pte, Joseph, who died in hospital on 4th April from a wound in the head received on the previous day, the Rev. denis Doyle R.C. Chaplain to the 2nd Leinster Regt, in the course of a letter says: "Surely God wanted him, for it was quite a stray bullet that hit him when it was dark. It was the night his company was coming from the trenches. He was very happy and for fun said "I'll take a last look and say good-bye to the Germans." He raised his head above the parapet and got a bullet through the forehead. With much sympathy, Yours sincerely, Denis Doyle."

The deceased young soldier was 15 months in the trenches and was wounded. After recovering he was about three months in the trenches when he was killed. He was a brother of Private James Curran.

Grave or Memorial Reference: II.D.226. Cemetery: Bailleul Communal Cemetery Extension (Nord) in France.

**CUSHEN, Patrick:** Rank: Pte. Regiment or Service: Leinster Regiment. Unit: 2<sup>nd</sup> Battalion. Date of death: 20 October 1918. Service no: 10031. Born in Killoughey, Co. Offaly. Enlisted in Birr, Co. Offaly. Died of wounds.

*Supplementary information:* Son of Ellen Cushen, of Mount Bolus, Co. Offaly. Grave or Memorial Reference: IV.H.31. Cemetery: Duhallow A.D.S. Cemetery in Belgium.

**CUSHING, Charles:** Rank: Private. Regiment or Service: Leinster Regiment. Unit: 2<sup>nd</sup> Bn. Date of death: 3 May 1915. Service no: 7957. Born in Chelsea, London. Enlisted in London. Killed in action.

Charles Cushing.

*Supplementary information:* Husband of Mrs E. Cushing, of Moorpark Street, Birr, Co. Offaly. See the articles attached to Joseph and James Curran. There is also an article in the *King's County Chronicle* in 1916 that shows pictures of his brothers-in-law who were also serving who were Pte Andrew Curran, and Pte Richard Curran of the 2<sup>nd</sup> Leinsters. Grave or Memorial Reference: C.6. Cemetery: Ferme Buterne Military Cemetery, Houplines in France.

# D

**DALTON, Daniel:** Rank: Pte. Regiment or Service: Royal Irish Regiment. Unit: 2ⁿᵈ Battalion. Date of death: 24 August 1918. Service no: 4999. Born in Castleisland, Co. Kerry. Enlisted in Cahir, Co. Tipperary while living in Tullamore, Co. Offaly. Killed in action. Age at death: 39.

*Supplementary information:* Son of John and Elizabeth Dalton, of Charleville Parade, Tullamore, Co. Offaly. Grave or Memorial Reference: Special Memorial 3. Grave reference II.B.18. Cemetery: St Symphrien Military Cemetery in Belgium.

**DALY, James:** Rank: Pte. Regiment or Service: Irish Guards. Unit: 1ˢᵗ Battalion. Date of death: 10 October 1917. Service no: 4701. Born in Ferbane, Co. Offaly. Enlisted in Dublin. Killed in action. Grave or Memorial Reference: XV.F.19. Cemetery: Cement House Cemetery in Belgium.

**DALY, Thomas:** Rank: Pte. Regiment or Service: Royal Dublin Fusiliers. Unit: 1ˢᵗ Battalion. Date of death: 22 December 1915. Service no: 21794. Born in Kilbride, Co. Offaly. Enlisted in Tullamore. Killed in action in Gallipoli. Age at death: 19.

*Supplementary information:* Son of Michael and Anne Daly, of Pensioners Row, Tullamore, Co. Offaly. He is also listed on the Tullamore Roll of Honour. Grave or Memorial Reference: II.E.6. Cemetery: Twelve Tree Copse Cemetery in Turkey.

**DARCY, John:** Rank: Lance Corporal. Regiment or Service: Leinster Regiment. Unit: 1ˢᵗ Battalion. Date of death: 4 March 1915. Service no: 9177. Born in Birr, Co. Offaly. Enlisted in Birr. Died of wounds. Age at death: 21.

*Supplementary information:* Son of Michael and Bridget Darcy, of Fortal, Birr. Grave or Memorial Reference: III.C.76. Cemetery: Boulogne Eastern Cemetery in France.

John Darcy. Photo from *King's County Chronicle*, 1916.

**DAVIDSON, Ernest J.:** Rank: Lance Corporal. Regiment or Service: Argyll and Southerland Highlanders. Unit: 14ᵗʰ Battalion. Date of death: 21 March 1918. Service no: S/14267. Born in Toberdaly, Co. Offaly. Enlisted in Dundee, Forfars. Killed in action. Grave or Memorial Reference: Bay 9. Memorial: Arras Memorial in France.

Joseph Davis.

**DAVIS/DAVIES, Joseph:** Rank: Pte. Regiment or Service: East Lancashire Regiment. Unit: 1ˢᵗ Battalion. Date of death: 3 November 1914. Service no: 8608. Born in Birr, Co. Offaly. Enlisted in Birr. Killed in action. Age at death: 28. Supplementary information: Son of Henry and Margaret Davis, of Newbridge Street, Birr. From the *King's County Chronicle*, December 1914:

> Another brave young Birrman who has given his life for the cause of freedom is Mr Joseph, of the 1ˢᵗ East Lancashires, third son of Mrs Davis, Newbridge Street, and brother of Mr Patrick Davis of the 'King's County Chronicle' staff. The sad news was received in an official intimation on Thursday last, and the meagre information it contained stated that he was killed in action on 3ʳᵈ November, the locality not being known. Much sympathy is felt with the bereaved mother and family.

Grave or Memorial Reference: Panel 5 and 6 on the Ploegsteert Memorial in Belgium.

**DAVIS, Michael:** Rank: Pte. Regiment or Service: Leinster Regiment. Unit: 2ⁿᵈ Battalion. Date of death: 27 March 1918. Service no: 5347. Born in Cadamstown, Co. Offaly. Enlisted in Blackburn, Lancashire. Died of wounds. He has no known grave but is listed on Panel 78 on the Pozieres Memorial in France.

**DAVIS, The Revd William Henry:** Rank: Chaplain 4ᵗʰ Class. Regiment or Service: Canadian Army Chaplains Department. Secondary Regiment: 4ᵗʰ Canadian Mounted Rifles Battalion. Date of death: 9 August 1918. Enlisted on 6 March 1916 in Edmonton, Alberta, Canada. Won the Military Cross and is listed in the *London Gazette*. Age at death: 34. Data from Officers Declaration Paper. Born: Co. Offaly. Date of birth: 21 January 1883. Next of kin: James Davis (father) of Tullamore. Occupation: Clerk in Holy Orders. Religion: Church of Ireland.

*Supplementary information*: Son of James and Anne Davis, of Davistown, Co. Offaly. Hon. Capt. Chaplain Davis

The Revd William Henry Davis.

is represented on the In Memoriam page by the people of the Parish of St Peter's Anglican church, in Edmondton, Alberta, where a picture of him and a plaque dedicated to his life and service hangs. Revd Davis transferred from the 138th BN, and served as Chaplain with the 4CMR from 15 February. 1917 to his loss on 18 August. 1918. From research generously provided by Duff Crerar:

Chaplain Davis was the Anglican rector of St. Peter's church in Bonnie Doon when he joined the 138th battalion, but went to the front with the 4th CMRs. At the battle of Paschendaele, waving a Red Cross flag, Davis took out a large party of stretcher-bearers under fire to search for wounded in No Man's Land. His fearlessness may have triggered a spontaneous truce, as the Germans ceased fired.

For his part in this strange interlude, Davis was awarded the Military Cross. In 1918 at the Battle of Amiens he was directing stretcher-bearers with wounded men when a shell killed him.

Davis had previously turned down his bishop's request to return to Edmonton, in order to stay with his men. "He came from Western Canada but he had retained his Irish heart and Celtic charm. If he knew what fear was he never showed it.

No officer was more loved for his character or admired for his bravery than Padre Davis.

From *The 4th Canadian Mounted Rifles, 1914-1919*:

There was another Davis attached to the Battalion Captain W.H. Davis, Chaplain, recently joined, who at once became endeared to the men. The first glimpse they had of their beloved Padre in action was seeing him in the twilight on the crest of the Ridge, his steel helmet hung over his arm, prayer-book in hand, burying the dead, regardless of shells dropping around him …

There were many others who did more than their mere duty, but none would begrudge another mention of the Chaplain, Captain W.H. Davis at Vimy and every other action, so at Passchendaele this Padre exceeded his duty by exposing himself unnecessarily. He went forward with the men, mustering and organizing a party of stretcher-bearers, gaining the admiration of all the combatants by walking about in the open looking for wounded, apparently oblivious of his danger. It was a miracle that he lived to enter another action. His coolness and unselfish thoughtfulness for the welfare of others gained for him a very warm spot in the hearts of all the men. One officer, "who saw the Padre laboriously coming toward him through a downpour of "crumps" asked him what he was doing walking around in the open; his reply had its usual candour: "I was getting anxious about you." During the afternoon of the 26th he so successfully controlled the stretcher-bearers and set such a wonderful example that practically all the wounded were collected.

One incident which illustrates the curious turn of events of that day is not recorded in the Diary, but has been gleaned from witnesses. It shows how rapidly a situation could alter and throws some light on the curious psychology of the real combatants. Late in the after-noon by common, uncommunicated consent, without notification or sanction, both sides suddenly decided on a temporary armistice to look after their wounded and dead.

It was one of those spontaneous things, arranged without agreement. It just happened. It suited both sides. Some think that the Germans were probably awed by the unusual sight of Padre Davis with such a large party nonchalantly walking about and as soon as they realized what he was doing, decided to do likewise. Suddenly large numbers of Germans got out of their trenches and commenced to search for their wounded. The idea was mutual.

When the Germans found a wounded Canadian they would mark his position by sticking his rifle in the mud and placing his helmet on it or carry him to a pill-box which soon became a clearing station where the troops of both sides foregathered and exchanged the wounded. Since sunrise the fighting had been bitter, each side trying to create as much havoc as possible among the men whom they were now trying to succour. It was a rational paradox for the men in the line. But the unofficial truce did not last long. Some young, enthusiastic forward-observing officer of the gunners could not resist reporting the existence of so many targets and soon the guns opened on the weary missionaries who had to postpone their rescuing.

Lyrics from the song 'The Padre' by Jon Brooks, Canadian published essayist and singer/songwriter:

I was William Henry Davis
from Edmonton's parish of Bonnie
    Doon.
I followed St Paul to Calvary,
my flock, the 8th Canada Brigade.
Compassion I felt and bravery I
    feigned;
and 'The Padre' was my name.

And it's a good life if we forgive it.
And when we forgive it's a good
    life, it's a good life.

I buried Lieutenant Jack Campbell,
said a prayer for Captain Johnny
    Woods.
I tripped on a skull in the
    Paschendaele spring
rain-washed of dignity's muddy grave.
The tag was missing but I knew by
    the teeth
the remains of Smilin' Jaf Eaton.
I gave a service for Sergeant-Major
    Dunlop
and by whom I saw God's Son's cry.
Shot in the stomach at Abraham's
    Heights,
my dying God mouthed to the
    black wind, 'why?'
A stretcher-bearer offered up a
    'Woodbine;'
and for that last grace Death will
    wait a while.

My bones lie in Quesnel beside my
    men.
My Atonement, the Battle of Amiens.
Cleansed of my big and dark Irish
    heart
by the good shrapnel through
    which I came.
I was William Henry Davis
ah, but 'The Padre' was my name. "

From the *King's County Chronicle*,
August 1918:

THE LATE REV. W.H. DAVIS.
Officer's Letter of Sympathy.
Our last issue contained the sad
news of the death, in action, on 9th
August, of Hon. Capt and Chaplain
William Henry Davis, attached
to the Canadian Mounted Rifles;
and the following letter, received
by the deceased Rev, gentleman's
mother, Mrs James Davis, Manor
House, Acontha, Tullamore, gives
further details of her gallant son's
death.

"Dear Madam,
As you have doubtless by now
received the sad news of the Padre's
death, some particulars from his
comrade, though imperfectly
expressed, may perhaps bring some
comfort to you, his relatives and
friends. The Padre lived with this
company, and was a member of our
mess for many months, as he and
our former company commander,
Major Hart, were always together;
and all members of this battalion
held him in the highest regard,
both as an unfearing comrade and
adviser, and respected him for his
conscientious energy in looking
after the comfort of the men. None
of those who saw his work in the
mire and swamps of Passchendale
will ever forget.
    On the afternoon of the 9th
August just before the battalion
was jumping off for the assault,
the Padre was leading a party of
stretcher-bearers through the
village, which was then under
very heavy bombardment, as the
enemy had a short time before
been driven out. He was mortally wounded by a shell, and died
almost instantly.
In company with Lieut. Col.

McGreer, head of the chaplain service of the Canadian Forces, and a long number of Padre's of all denominations, and the officers and men of his battalion, we reverently placed his body to rest in the vine-clad country of Le Quesnel, near the main road from Amiens to Royl [sic]. His grave in the French communal burying ground under overhanging trees, and we erected a cross with the name and full particulars carved thereon as best we could. The men strewed the place with wild flowers. The funeral took place in advance of the guns, when the corps was again going over to the assault, but even in these circumstances there were few dry eyes amongst the rough and stern-faced soldiery as Colonel McGreer, in broken voice, recited the burial service. If there is anything that any of us can do, we would be glad if you would command us. This company sends you and the Padre's friends and relatives their heartfelt condolence"

Faithfully yours,

E. V. MacMillan, Lieut.,

B Company, 4<sup>th</sup> C. M. R. Bn.

From the *King's County Chronicle*, August 1918:

ROLL OF HONOUR.

Hon Capt and Chaplain W. H. Davis. We regret to announce the death of Honorary Captain and Chaplain William Henry Davis, M.C., attached to the Canadian Mounted Rifles, who was killed in action on 9<sup>th</sup> August. The deceased Revd gentleman, who left Ireland at an early age, was the only son of Mr James Davis, Manor House, Acontha, Tullamore, formerly of Davistown, Frankford, and was beloved, not only by his parishioners in Canada, but by the many friends and acquaintances at home who were quick to perceive in the young Rev. gentleman the attributes that go to make up the true Christian minister and perfect gentleman.

During a visit home he preached in Ballyboy Church, and the congregation were much impressed by the fervour of his discourse. On Sunday last the Rev. F.R.M. Hitchcock, Rector of Kinnitty, paid an eloquent and feeling tribute to the deceased clergyman's memory. To the bereaved parents and other relatives we offer our sincere sympathy in their great sorrow.

Grave or Memorial Reference: 1. Cemetery. Le Quesnel Communal Cemetery in France.

**DAY/DEA, John:** Rank: Pte. Regiment or Service: Leinster Regiment. Unit: 2<sup>nd</sup> Battalion. Date of death: 19 May 1916. Service no: 7941. Born in Birr, Co. Offaly. Enlisted in Birr. Killed in action.

*Supplementary information:* Son of Mrs M. Dea, of Bridge Street, Birr. From the *King's County Chronicle*, June 1916:

Another brave young soldier has given his life for King and Country in the person of Drummer John Dea, of the Leinsters, son of Mrs Dea, Mill Lane, Birr, who died from a wound received in action in May last. The deceased soldier was stationed in India for some years, afterwards coming to Birr. He was a first-rate musician, his services in the Depot Brass and Reed Band being greatly valued. He went with the first Expeditionary Force to France, was home on leave last autumn and escaped until he met his death as stated above. There are two other brothers serving, viz; Private Michael, of the Connaught Rangers, who was wounded in France, was invalided home and is at present in Co. Cork. The other, Private Wm., 2nd Leinsters, was home on leave from France some weeks ago, after a long spell in the trenches, looking first-rate, and has gone back again. A brother-in-law, Sergt Quirke, is with the Leinsters at Salonika.

Mrs Dea, has received from the Rev. Denis Doyle, Chaplain of the Leinsters, a sympathetic letter in reference to the death of their son. It appears, writes the Chaplain, he was alone when he was hit in the leg by a shell and evidently died from loss of blood.

"It is sad," he continued "how our poor boys get knocked out, and my heart breaks for them. It is worse for you poor mothers and wives. But God will bless you for your sacrifice and will give you the comfort that no man can give you."

Further details are given in a letter to Mrs Dea from C. Saunderson, who writes, "He was taking a message from the front to the reserve trenches when he was shot in both legs. He was found after by some of his comrades, who did all in their power, but it was of no use. He died from loss of blood before they got him to the dressing station. Believe me I am very sorry for you in your trouble. You have lost a good son and I have lost a friend. His comrades will miss him. He was a great little man; his company officer never moved a yard but he had Jacky with him. I was speaking to him only an hour before he met with his end; he was in good spirits and I don't believe I ever saw him otherwise. He was to have leave soon, but God disposed otherwise for him. He fell in a good cause and the Great God takes his children to himself. "

I have not been able to locate William Day/Dea in any war dead database available to me. Grave or Memorial Reference: II.B.21. Cemetery: Ration Farm (La Plus Douve) Annexe in Belgium.

**DEEGAN, James:** Rank: Pte. Regiment or Service: Royal Munster Fusiliers. Date of death: 26 September 1914. Service no: None given. Born in Co. Offaly. Killed in action in France. Age at death: 25. Awarded the Mons Star.

*Supplementary information:* He is only in 'Ireland's Memorial Records' with the above information. This man exists in no other database.

**DEEGAN, James:** Rank: Pte. Regiment or Service: Royal Munster Fusiliers. Unit: 2nd Battalion. Date of death: 9 May 1915. Service no: 5935. Born in Frankford, Co. Offaly. Enlisted in Athlone, Co. Westmeath while living in Banagher, Co. Offaly. Killed in action. Grave or Memorial Reference: He has no known grave but is listed on Panels 11 and 12 on the Le Touret Memorial in France.

**DEEHAN, Thomas:** Rank: Gunner. Regiment or Service: Royal Garrison Artillery. Date of death: 30 July 1916. Service no: 62520. Born in Durrow, Co. Offaly. Enlisted in Tullamore while living in Durrow. Killed in action. Grave or Memorial Reference: I.U.14. Cemetery: Becourt Military Cemetery, Becordel-Becourt in France.

**DELAHUNTY, William:** Rank: Pte. Regiment or Service: Leinster Regiment. Unit: 1st Battalion. Date of death: 1 May 1916. Service no: 61. Born in Frankford, Co. Offaly (also listed as born in Ballyboy). Enlisted in Falkirk, Stirlingshire. Died. Grave or Memorial Reference: 123. Cemetery: Salonika (Lembet Road) Military Cemetery in Greece.

**DELANEY, Martin:** Rank: Pte. Regiment or Service: Leinster Regiment. Date of death: 15 March 1915. Service no: 2679. Born in Banagher, Co. Offaly. Enlisted in Mullingar. Killed in action in France. Age at death: 42. He only appears in 'Ireland's Memorial Records' under this number. He is not listed in 'Soldiers died in the Great War' under the number 2679 but is listed as 3685 and he is listed with the Commonwealth War Graves Commission under the same number where the date of death is given as 12 April 1915 and his age at death as forty. A quick check with the National Archives in Kew shows that there is no Medal Index Card for No 2679 Martin Delaney.

*Supplementary information:* Son of Martin Delaney, of Banagher, Co. Offaly. Husband of Kate Delaney, of Clara Road, Moate, Co. Westmeath. Privates William Delaney, Irish Guards, and Private Thomas Delaney, 3rd Leinsters from Banagher are briefly mentioned the *King's County Chronicle*, April 1916. They may be related. Grave or Memorial Reference: II.C.2. Cemetery: Hazebrouck Communal Cemetery, Nord, in France.

**DELANEY, William:** Rank: Corporal. Regiment or Service: Royal Irish Regiment. Unit: 2nd Battalion. Date of death: 20 November 1917. Service no: 10999. He won the Military Medal and is listed in the *London Gazette*. Born in Oldtown, Co. Offaly. Enlisted in Kilkenny while living in Oldtown, Co. Offaly.

Died of wounds. Grave or Memorial Reference: G.3. Cemetery: St Leger British Cemetery in France.

**DEMPSEY, Christopher:** Rank: Acting Bombardier. Regiment or Service: Royal Horse Artillery and Royal Field Artillery. Unit: 48th Battery, 36th Brigade. Date of death: 19 October 1917. Service no: 60859. Born in Clonbrown, Clonbologue, Co. Offaly. Enlisted in Dublin. Died of wounds. Age at death: 29.

*Supplementary information:* Son of Lawrence and Marcell Dempsey, of Clonbrown, Co. Offaly. Grave or Memorial Reference: I.E.32. Cemetery: Duhallow A.D.S. Cemetery in Belgium.

**DEMPSEY, Patrick:** Rank: Sergeant. Regiment or Service: Yorkshire Regiment. Unit: 6th Battalion. Date of death: 30 September 1916. Service no: 7766. He won the Distinguished Conduct Medal. Born in Edgeworthstown, Co. Longford. Enlisted in Newry while living in Birr. Killed in action. Age at death: 30. Awarded the D.C.M.

*Supplementary information*: Son of Patrick and Mary Dempsey, of Edgeworthstown, Co. Longford. Husband of Mary Dempsey, of Newbridge Street, Birr, Co. Offaly. From *King's County Chronicle*, February 1915:

Amongst the recipients of the distinguished Conduct Medal announced in Saturday's daily papers appears the

Patrick Dempsey.

name of Patrick Dempsey, postmaster, of Brosna, who, was a couple of years ago as postman in the Birr rural districts. He had been on the reserve and has been fighting since August with the Yorkshire Regiment, which left England over a thousand strong, and is now reduced to three hundred. He has also been promoted Corporal in the field, and we rejoice to add he has so far escaped without even the proverbial scratch.

From the *King's County Chronicle*, June 1915:

D.C.M. PRESENTED TO AN IRISHMAN. At a ceremonial parade on the Chester Castle Square of an imposing character on Wednesday morning in the presence of Regulars and Territorials, General Sir H. Mackinnon presented the coveted Distinguished Conduct Medal to a gallant soldier. The recipient was Corporal Patrick Dempsey, of the 2nd Yorkshire Regiment a patient at the Hoole Bank Red

Cross Hospital, where he has been cared for tenderly since April 3rd. The Corporal had the distinction of being thrice recommended for the honour, which was awarded for conspicuous gallantry in the carrying of despatches under heavy fire. He also is a crack shot, and all the time he was at the front rendered excellent service.

It was the first presentation of the sort in that city. On parade were about 150 of the Depot, also men of the 3rd Line of the 5th Cheshires, the Cheshire Brigade, R.F.A. (T. F.), and the Territorial R.A.M.C. Interested spectators were four brake-loads of Corporal Dempsey's comrades from the Red Cross Hospital and a number of Red Cross nurses who gave a picturesque touch to the proceedings. The military formed three sides of a square, and after making the presentation the General chatted with the recipient, also two other winners of the D.C.M. The parade was addressed by the General, who spoke encouragingly to the men of the example set by such gallant conduct, which would help affairs in France to go on as well as they were doing.

The band of the Depot Cheshire Regiment, played selections during the morning. Corporal Dempsey, who is brother-in-law to Mr P. Davis, of the "*King's County Chronicle*" staff, is at present at home in Brosna, King's County, on a short leave. He looks remarkably well considering

that he went to France with the first Expeditionary Force and endured the hardships of the terrible winter campaign.

From the *King's County Chronicle*, 1916:

IN MEMORIAM.
Sergeant Patrick Dempsey, D.C.M., York and Lancashire Regiment, killed in action, 30th, September, in France. A native of Edgeworthtown, Co. Longford.
Lines composed by Miss Mary Browne, Newbridge Street, Birr, in which town the deceased soldier was employed in the Post Office.

Another, yet another, of our bravest
    and our best,
Has gone to feed the rancour of
    hate's unwise behest,
Has gone and left us poorer, the
    rich blood in his veins,
That nerved his heart has placed him
    mid Erin's honoured names.

A few more hearts in mourning, a
    hearth-fire quenched in woe,
'Till late with all the brightness of
    Christian love aglow;
A few more orphans wailing, one
    heart too sad for tears,
From darkling vistas looming of
    coming lonely years.

Sprung from her toiling legion; her
    fine old fighting race,
As husband, father, he nobly filled
    each place;
With more than manhood's cour-

age, and all a warrior's flame,
He gave you back the sword you
    gave, aglow with hero fame.
O victim for small nations, how shall
    our fate be told?

As dross or stubble or held as bur-
    nished gold;
My masters treat her wisely, her
    steel is clean and true,
Or when 'tis false you've hacked
    the blade with treason and with
    rue.
Oh mother Queen, you're speaking –
    My sons where'er you fall;

In France or on my bosom, I'll bear
    your dying call;
Your last words from the trenches
    are; Mother gal Mo Chroide
We died for God's great glory, for
    freedom and for them.

Marie Ní Bruin.

From the *King's County Chronicle*,
October 1916:

### SERGEANT PATRICK DEMPSEY, D.C.M.

Killed in action in France.

On Friday last the sad news was received of the death of Sergeant Patrick Dempsey, D. C. M., 6th Yorkshire Regiment, who was killed by a sniper on 30th September. The deceased soldier, who was on the reserve, rejoined on the outbreak of war, and had seen much active service. He was wounded at the battle of Neuve Chapelle, and after recovery he was sent to Egypt, but was afterwards sent to France again, where he met his death. After being three times recommended for the D. C. M. he was awarded it for conspicuous gallantry in carrying despatches under heavy fire, the presentation being made by General Sir H. Mackinnon at a Red Cross Hospital at Chester. In civil life he was a postal employee at Birr, his duties bringing him into contact with a great number of people who one and all entertained for him the greatest regard.

After his transfer to Brosna, he was appointed instructor of the Volunteers in Shinrone and district, and received great praise for the splendid results showed by the young men under his charge. He comes of a military family, his father, who is still alive, having been in the same regiment; and there were also two more brothers of deceased serving in the present war, one of whom was also killed, and the other is missing. Another brother lost his life in the South African War. The deceased was a native of Edgeworthstown, Co Longford, was brother-in-law to Mr P. Davis, of the staff of this paper, and leaves a wife and four children to mourn his untimely end. In a letter appraising the deceased's widow of the sad news Capt C. Downay, 6th Yorkshires, writes:

"Dear Madam,

It is with mingled feelings of deep regret and pride that I have to inform you of the passing of your husband and regret that we lost so good and popular a N. C. O., and pride in the way he did his duty to the end. On 30th Sept, 'Paddy' as his chums called him, was well to the fore, and was shot by a sniper and suffered no pain.

But that sniper did not live to shoot another round. Sergt Dempsey is sadly missed by all ranks, both in his own platoon and the rest of the company. So, dear madam, your sorrow will be tempered by the knowledge that he died in the execution of his duty and without pain."

He has no known grave but is listed on Pier and Face 3A and 3D on the Thiepval Memorial in France.

**DENNEHY, Patrick James:** Rank: Lance Corporal. Regiment or Service: Royal Berkshire Regiment. Unit: 8th Battalion. Date of death: 21 March 1918. Service no: 18274. Born in Tullamore. Enlisted in Reading while living in Dublin. Killed in action. Age at death: 25.

*Supplementary information*: Son of James and Anna M. Dennehy, of 32 John Street, Kilkenny. Has no known grave but is commemorated on Panel 56 and 57. Memorial: Pozieres Memorial in France.

**DENNIGAN, Michael:** Rank: Pte. Regiment or Service: Leinster Regiment. Unit: 2nd Battalion. Date of death: 19 June 1915. Service no: 3480. Born in Tullamore, Co. Offaly. Enlisted in Mullingar. Died of wounds.

*Supplementary information:* Nephew of M. Hayden, of Military Road, Mullingar, Co. Westmeath. Grave or Memorial Reference: B.7. Cemetery: La Brique Military Cemetery, No 1 in Belgium.

**DEVOY, Henry:** Rank: Pte. Regiment or Service: Leinster Regiment. Unit: 2nd Battalion. Date of death: 1 June 1918. Service no: 4832. Born in Birr, Co. Offaly. Enlisted in Birr. Killed in action. Age at death: 36.

*Supplementary information:* Son of Thomas and Mary Anne Devoy. Grave or Memorial Reference: F. 15. Cemetery: Cinq Rues British Cemetery, Hazebrouck in France.

**DEWAN, Michael:** Rank: Pte. Regiment or Service: Leinster Regiment. Unit: 2nd Battalion. Date of death: 6 August 1918. Service no: 4667. Born in Birr, Co. Offaly. Enlisted in Birr, while living in Birr. Killed in action. Grave or Memorial Reference: II.G.1. Cemetery: Borre British Cemetery in France.

**DEWANE, Robert:** Rank: Pte. Regiment or Service: Leinster Regiment. Unit: 2nd Battalion. Date of death: 2 May 1915. Service no: 3311. Born in Birr, Co. Offaly. Enlisted in Maryborough, Co. Laois. Killed in action. Age at death: 25.

*Supplementary information:* Son

of Christy and Mary Dewane, of Upper Coote, Mountrath, Leix. Grave or Memorial Reference: I.C.13. Cemetery: Erquinghem-Lys Churchyard Extension in France.

**DICKSON, Martin:** Rank: Pte. Regiment or Service: Machine Gun Corps (Infantry). Unit: 19<sup>th</sup> Bn. Age at death: 20. Date of death: 20 November 1918. Service no: 53679. Born in Limerick. Enlisted in Birr, Co. Offaly. Died. Formerly he was with the Leinster Regiment where his number was 10570.

*Supplementary information*: Son of Mrs M. Long, of Newbridge Street, Birr, Co. Offaly. From *King's County Chronicle*, February 1918:

PROMOTION FOR BIRR OFFICER.

The many friends of his respected father, Mr John Dickson, Newbridge Street, Birr, will be pleased to hear that his son, John, who was formerly Sergt-Major in the Leinster Regiment, has been promoted Captain. He served through the Boer War, and was on pension when the present war broke out, but imbued with the patriotic desire to further serve his country he volunteered for active service, and for over two years went through severe fighting in France. Unfortunately, the arduous campaigning and severe weather brought on rheumatism which compelled him to relinquish active service, and some months afterwards he was adjudged by a medical board to be fit only for home service. He is presently in the Depot at Preston, attached to the 16<sup>th</sup> South Lancashires. Although the gallant subject of this notice has over 30 years service he is still in the prime of life, and it is the earnest wish of his numerous friends that he may long be spared to enjoy his well-earned promotion and rest.

Grave or Memorial Reference: III.A.12. Cemetery: Poznan Old Garrison Cemetery in Poland.

**DICKSON, Samuel James:** Rank: Able Seaman. Regiment or Service: Royal Navy. Unit: HMS *Monmouth*. Age at death: 20. Date of death: 1 November 1914. Service no: J/8265.

*Supplementary information:* Son of Matilda Dickson, of 31 Rosebank Street, Belfast, and the late Robert Dickson. Native of Edenderry, Co. Offaly. On this day HMS *Monmouth* received an 8.2-inch shell from the SMS *Gneisenau,* which almost blew her to pieces. She limped away and later that day was sent to the bottom by SS *Nurnberg.* There were no survivors. Grave or Memorial Reference: 1. Memorial: Plymouth Naval Memorial, UK.

**DIGAN, Edward:** Rank: Pte. Regiment or Service: Irish Guards. Unit: 1<sup>st</sup> Battalion. Date of death: 6 January 1919. Service no: 10102. Born in Clara, Co. Offaly. Enlisted in Dundee, Forfar while living in Upton, Co. Offaly. Died of wounds in Rouen. Age at death: 24.

*Supplementary information*: Son

of Thomas and Catherine Digan, of Clara. Husband of Nellie C. Corcoran Digan, of Upton, Clara, Co. Offaly. Grave or Memorial Reference: P.V.J.9B. Cemetery: St Sever Cemetery Extension, Rouen in France.

**DIGAN/DIGNAN, Michael:** Rank: Pte. Regiment or Service: Connaught Rangers. Unit: 5th Battalion. Date of death: 7 December 1915. Service no: 5297. Born in Kilbride, Co. Offaly. Enlisted in Ballinasloe, Co. Galway while living in Tullamore, Co. Offaly. Killed in action in Salonika. Age at death: 24.

*Supplementary information*: Son of Dennis and Nannie Digan, of 77 Harold Cross Cottages, Dublin. Born at Tullamore, Co. Offaly. He is also listed on the Tullamore Roll of Honour. Grave or Memorial Reference: Doiran Memorial in Greece.

**DIGAN, Thomas:** Rank: Pte. Regiment or Service: Leinster Regiment. Unit: 2nd Battalion. Date of death: 27 June 1916. Service no: 2038. Born in Frankford, Co. Offaly. Enlisted in Birr, Co. Offaly. Killed in action. Grave or Memorial Reference: Y.3. Cemetery: Kemmel Chateau Military Cemetery in Belgium.

**DIGBY, Lionel Kenelm:** Rank: Pte. Regiment or Service: Norfolk Regiment. Unit: 7th Bn. Age at death: 34. Date of death: 18 October 1918. Service no: 38456. Born in Bramley in Surrey. Enlisted in Northwich in Norfolk. Died of wounds.

*Supplementary information*: Son of Reginald and Caroline Grace Digby, of Geashill Castle, Co. Offaly. Rector of Tittleshall, Norfolk. Grave or Memorial Reference: Near south-east corner of church. Cemetery: Raimbeaucourt Churchyard in France.

**DOHERTY, James:** Rank: Lance Corporal. Regiment or Service: Royal Munster Fusiliers. Unit: 1st Battalion. Date of death: 21 August 1915. Service no: 8695. Born in St Mels, Longford. Enlisted in Athlone, Co Westmeath while living in Clara, Co. Offaly. Killed in action in Gallipoli. From the *King's County Chronicle*, September 1915:

ONE OF THE IRISH.

Late in the afternoon the weary doctors sensed a slackening in the flowing tide of casualties. They were still coming in, being attended to, and passed out in a steady stream, but somehow there seemed less rush, less urgency, less haste on the part of the bearers to be back from a fresh load. And – ominous sign – there were many more of the bearers themselves coming back as casualties. The reason for these things took a little finding. The fighting line was now well advanced, and every yard of advance meant additional time and risk in the bearing back of the wounded. One of the regimental stretcher-bearers put the facts bluntly and briefly to the doctors; "The open ground as' the communication trenches is a fair hummin' wi' shells and' bullets. We're just about losin' two bearers for every one casualty we bring out. Now we're leavin' 'em lie there snug as we can till dark." A chaplain came in and asked permission to stay there. "One of my regiments has gone up," he said, "and they'll bring the casualties in here. I won't get in your way, and I may be able to help a little. Here is one of my men now." A stretcher was carried in and laid with its burden under the doctor's hands. The man was covered with wounds from head to foot. He lay still while wounds from head to foot. He lay still while the doctors cut the clothing off and adjusted bandages, but just before they gave him morphine he spoke. "Don't let me die, doctor," he said; don't let me die. Don't say I'm going to die." His eyes met the chaplain's and the grey head stooped near to the dying one. "I'm the only one left, padre," he said. "My old mother" But the lad was past saving.

He died there on the table under their hands. "God help his mother!" said the chaplain softly. "It was her the boy was thinking of – not himself. His father was killed yesterday – old Jim Doherty, twenty-three years service."

He has no known grave but is listed on Panel 185 to 190 on the Helles Memorial in Turkey.

**DOHERTY, Thomas:** Rank: Corporal. Regiment or Service: Leinster Regiment. Date of death: 9 March 1917. Service no: 16308. Born in Co. Offaly. Killed in action in France. Age at death: 25. This man is a bit of a mystery. He only appears in 'Ireland's Memorial Records'. He is not listed in 'Soldiers died in the Great War' nor is he listed with the Commonwealth War Graves Commission.

**DOLAN, Edward Aloysius:** Rank: Pte. Regiment or Service: Irish Guards. Unit: 1st Battalion. Date of death: 26 October 1914. Service no: 2199. Born in Kilbride (also spelled Kilbridge in the records), Co. Offaly. Enlisted in Tullamore, Co. Offaly. Killed in action. Age at death: 36.

*Supplementary information*: Son of the late James and Ellen Dolan, of Canal Bank, Tullamore, Co. Offaly. Served in the South African Campaign. He is also listed on the Tullamore Roll of Honour. Grave or Memorial Reference: Panel 11. Memorial: Ypres (Menin Gate) Memorial in Belgium.

**DONLEN, Owen Joseph:** Rank: Pte. Regiment or Service: Australian Infantry, A.I.F. Unit: 49th Bn. Age at death: 28. Date of death: 22 December 1918. Service no: 3377. Trade: Labourer. Next of kin: Mrs Mary Donlen, (mother) P.O. Mareeba,

North Queensland. Age on enlistment: 24 years, 6 months. Height: 5ft 9in. Weight: 140lbs. Complexion: Dark. Eyes: Grey. Hair: dark. Date: 14 October 1916. Place: Cairns, Queensland. From the report of the Court of Enquiry:

1st Witness: A Private. On the morning I was of a party sent to find the body of a man drowned in the MEUSE. We dragged a lock on the left ban, near BOUVIGNES, and the body was found in the lock. I did not see any marks of violence on the body.

2nd Witness: A Private. This morning I was one of a party which dragged a lock on the left bank of the MEUSE near BOUVIGNES. We found the body of Pte Donlen in the lock and carried it to the Battalion H.Q.

3rd Witness: A Captain. Today I examined the body of a man at Battalion H.Q. at 11.30p.m. I found no marks of violence on the body, and in my opinion the cause of death was drowning.

4th Witness: Captain (Adjutant). Battalion routine orders have been issued forbidding the use of the footbridge over the weir about 500 yards below the Battalion Headquarters. A sentry is posted at the end of the weir on the right bank of the MEUSE.

5th Witness: A Lieutenant. Today I was Officer in charge of a party to search for Pte. O.J. Donlen, who was reported to have been drowned last

night. His body was found in the lock opposite the Cloth Mills, LEFFE, DINANT, and on the left bank of the river. He had in his pockets sixty francs, the amount paid yesterday. There were no marks of violence on his body.

6th Witness: A Private. About 9pm. on the night of 22nd / 23rd inst Pte Donlen and I were coming along the river bank to our barracks at LEFFE. We were on the left bank near BOUVIGNES. When level with the weir opposite the Cloth Mill, Donlen stumbled into the lock. The water was within 3 or 4 feet of the coping. I lay flat on the path and grasped Donlen. I held him about a minute calling for assistance. No one answered so he decided to try to swim to the end. I lost sight of him in the dark and he failed to answer me when I called to him. I took off my boots and dived in after him, but could not locate him. I had some difficulty in getting out. The water was exceptionally cold. I reported the occurrence to my Coy orderly Sgt on my return, which took half an hour as I had to go up to the PONT DES ALLIES to cross the MEUSE. Neither of us had anything to drink. When Donlen fell in we were just going to look at the footbridge crossing. We went by the sound of the rushing water, and did not think that we were near the stream, not knowing anything about the lock. So it came that Donlen, who was on my left fell in before he knew he was near the brink. But for the accident we would have been back at our quarters in proper time, Donlen being very anxious to get back.

The Court then proceeded to examine the river bank at the scene of the accident, and find it very easy for an accident to happen so. In conversation with Belgian civilians the Court hears that several accidents have happened at that spot. A pair of wet puttees left by Pte - are recovered corroborating his statement as to his attempt to save his comrade.

The Finding

That No. 3370. Pte Donlen, O.J. was drowned in the river MEUSE, at BOUVIGNES, DINANT on the night o 22$^{nd}$/23$^{rd}$ Dec, 1916.

That he met his death by accident and that no one was to blame for his death. That No. 3452. Private 49$^{th}$ Battalion made a fine attempt at rescue, the water being cold, the night dark, and the stream dangerous and not knowing whether he could get out of the lock, again or not.

That at the time of his death Pte Donlen was "in bounds" and so may considered as being in performance of his military duty.

Dated 23 December 1916.

*Supplementary information*: Son of Owen and Mary Donlen of Mareeba, Queensland. Native of Ferbane. Grave or Memorial Reference: In southeast part. Cemetery: Dinant Communal Cemetery in Belgium.

**DONOGHUE, Laurence:** Rank: Pte. Regiment or Service: Royal Scots Fusiliers. Unit: 1$^{st}$ Battalion. Date of death: 11 May 1917. Service no: 3 3498. Born in Crochin, Co. Offaly. Enlisted in Perth while living in Cloghan. Died of wounds.

*Supplementary information*: Son of James Donoghue, of Clonagh, Crogham, Philipstown, Co. Offaly. Grave or Memorial Reference: III.M.48. Cemetery: Duisans British Cemetery, Etrun in France.

**DONOHOE, Patrick:** Rank: Pte. Regiment or Service: Royal Irish Rifles. Unit: 2$^{nd}$ Battalion. Date of death: 3 January 1917. Service no: 2666. Born in Tullamore, Co. Offaly. Enlisted in Cavan while living in Cootehill, Co. Cavan. Died in Salonika. He is listed in the Commonwealth War Graves Commission as **DONOHOE, E.** and in 'Ireland's Memorial Records' and 'Soldiers died in the Great War' under **DONOHOE, Patrick.** Grave or Memorial Reference: III.G.15. Cemetery: Struma Military Cemetery in Greece.

**DOOLAN, Patrick:** Rank: Pte. Regiment or Service: Leinster Regiment. Date of death: 28 March 1917. Service no: 2653. Born in Co. Offaly. Died of wounds in France. Age at death: 40. This man is a bit of a mystery. He only appears in 'Ireland's Memorial Records'. He is not listed in 'Soldiers died in the Great War' and he is not listed with the Commonwealth War

Graves Commission. A quick check with the National Archives in Kew shows that there is no Medal Index Card for No. 2653 Patrick Doolan.

**DOOLAN, Patrick:** Rank: Pte. Regiment or Service: Leinster Regiment. Unit: 2nd Battalion. Date of death: 4 September 1918. Service no: 2851. Born in Ferbane, Co. Offaly. Enlisted in Birr, Co. Offaly while living in Banagher, Co. Offaly. Killed in action. Grave or Memorial Reference: IV.F.11. Cemetery: Wulverghem-Lindenhoek Road Military Cemetery in Belgium

**DOOLEY, James Joseph:** Rank: Gunner. Regiment or Service: Royal Field Artillery and Royal Horse Artillery. Date of death: 12 November 1916. Service no: 36989. Born in Frankford, Co. Offaly. Enlisted in London. Died of wounds. Grave or Memorial Reference: II.H.16. Grove Town Cemetery, Meaulte in France.

**DOOLEY/DOONLEY, John:** Rank: Pte. Regiment or Service: Leinster Regiment. Unit: 7th Battalion. Date of death: 19 August 1916. Service no: 5305. Born in Banagher, Co. Offaly. Enlisted in Birr, Co. Offaly while living in Cloghan, Co. Offaly. Killed in action. Age at death: 38. Listed in the Commonwealth War Graves Commission as **DOOLEY, T.**, 'Soldiers died in the Great War' as **DOOLEY, John** and in 'Ireland's Memorial Records' as **DOONLEY, John** (From Cloghan) and **DOOLEY**

**John** (from Banagher).

*Supplementary information*: Husband of S. Dooley, of Cloghan, Co. Offaly. Grave or Memorial Reference: I. H. 39. Cemetery: Philosophe British Cemetery, Mazingarbe in France.

**DOOLEY, John:** Rank: Pte. Regiment or Service: Irish Guards. Unit: 2nd Battalion. Date of death: 31 July 1917. Service no: 10479. Born in Bragmore, Co. Offaly. Enlisted in Dublin. Killed in action in France. He has no known grave but is listed on Panel 11 on the Ypres (Menin Gate) Memorial in Belgium.

**DOONAN, J.:** Rank: Private. Regiment or Service: Middlesex Regiment. Unit: 13th Bn. Date of death: 13 December 1917. Service no: G/41885. Born in Kilbeggan, Co. Westmeath. Enlisted in Waterford while living in Co. Westmeath. Formerly he was with the Lancers where his number was 24247.

*Supplementary information*: Son of Mr J. Doonan, of Spellanstown, Tullamore. Grave or Memorial Reference: I.J.9. Cemetery: Hargicourt British Cemetery, Aisne in France.

**DOWD, John Charles:** Rank: Pte. Regiment or Service: Canadian Infantry (Manitoba Regiment). Unit: 27th Battalion. Date of death: 5 August 1917. Service no: 72398. Age at death: 31.

*Supplementary information*: Son of John Charles and Mary Evaline Dowd, of 255 Simcoe Street, Winnipeg. Born at Dromakeenan, Co. Offaly. Data from enlistment documents: Born: Dublin. Next of kin: John Charles Dowd (father) of 644 Furby Street, Winnipeg. Man. Date of birth: 12 December 1885. Trade: Engineers Assistant. Height: 5ft 5in. Girth: 36in. Complexion: Medium. Eyes: Grey. Hair: Brown. Grave or Memorial Reference: AN. 119. Cemetery: Windsor Cemetery, Berkshire, UK.

**DOWNEY, Edward:** Rank: Lance Corporal. Regiment or Service: Royal West Surrey Regiment. Unit: 7th Battalion. Date of death: 10 August 1917. Service no: L/11445. Formerly he was with the 5th Lancers where his number was 3867. Born in Crinkle, Co. Offaly. Enlisted in Birr while living in Inchigula, Co. Offaly. Killed in action. Age at death: 22.

*Supplementary information:* Son of John and Fanny Downey, of Crinkle, Birr, Co. Offaly. Husband of Mary Downey, of 5 Queen's Terrace, Great Brunswick Street, Dublin. Grave or Memorial Reference: Has no known grave but is commemorated on Panel 11-13 and 14 on the Ypres (Menin Gate) Memorial in Belgium.

**DOYLE, John:** Rank: Corporal. Regiment or Service: Connaught Rangers. Unit: 2nd Battalion. Date of death: 30 October 1914. Service no: 2804 also lised as 2864. Born in Athlone, Co Westmeath. Enlisted in Oranmore, Co Galway while living in Tullamore, Co. Offaly. Killed in action. He is also listed on the Tullamore Roll of Honour. Grave or Memorial

Reference: Has no known grave but is commemorated on Panel 42 on the Ypres (Menin Gate) Memorial in Belgium.

**DOYLE, Michael:** Rank: Sapper. Regiment or Service: Corps of Royal Engineers. Unit: 61st Field Company. Date of death: 25 July 1915. Service no: 40060. Born in Clara, Co. Offaly. Enlisted in Kilkenny while living in Clara, Co. Offaly. Killed in action. Grave or Memorial Reference: Has no known grave but is commemorated on Panel 9 on the Ypres (Menin Gate) Memorial in Belgium.

**DRENNAN, James:** Rank: Pte. Regiment or Service: Leinster Regiment. Unit: Depot. Date of death: 20 September 1917. Service no: 2711. Age at death: 26. Born in Kilbride, Co. Offaly. Enlisted in Birr, Co. Offaly. Died at home.

*Supplementary information:* Son of John Drennan, of Wellington Barracks, Coleman Street, Tullamore. Grave or Memorial Reference: Free ground 287. Cemetery: Clonminch Catholic Cemetery, Co. Offaly.

**DUDLEY, Harry** (Also listed as Henry) **Pemberton:** Rank: 2nd Lieutenant. Regiment or Service: Leinster Regiment attached to the 2nd Battalion Royal Irish Regiment. Date of death: 3 September 1916. Age at death: 36. From De Ruvigny's Roll of Honour:

2nd Lieut, 3rd Reserve Battalion, The

Prince of Wales Leinster Regiment, (Royal Canadians), 3<sup>rd</sup> son of the late Henry, N.Dudley, M. D., formerly of Kinnitty, King's County, and afterwards of Durrow, Queen's County by his wife, Mary Elizabeth (2 Burdett Ave, Sandycove) dau of John Pemberton, of Blackrock, Dublin; b. Kinnitty, 8 May, 1880; educ by private tuition; Lanly School, and Dublin. On the outbreak of war he returned home from Singapore, and joined the 7<sup>th</sup> (Service) Battalion, of the Royal Dublin Fusiliers; went to the Dardinelles, and was severely wounded at Suvla Bay, August 1915; on his recovery was gazetted, 2<sup>nd</sup> Lieut, 3<sup>rd</sup> Leinster Regiment, Nov, 1915; proceeded to France, July, 1916, where he was attached to the 2<sup>nd</sup> Royal Irish Regiment, and was killed in action near Guillemont, 3<sup>rd</sup> Sept, 1916. Supplementary information: Son of Henry N. Dudley, M. D., and Mary E. Dudley (*née* Pemberton), of Durrow, Queen's Co. Previously wounded when serving as Lce. Cpl. with the 7<sup>th</sup> Bn. Royal Dublin Fusiliers, in Gallipoli, Aug., 1915.

Grave or Memorial Reference: XIV.K.6. Cemetery: Delville Wood Cemetery, Longueval in France.

**DUFFY, James:** Rank: Pte. Regiment or Service: Border Regiment. Unit: 6<sup>th</sup> Battalion. Date of death: 19 August 1917. Service no: 16610. Formerly he was with the Leinster Regiment where his number was 217. Born in Philipstown,

Co. Offaly. Enlisted in Manchester while living in Clonirore, Co. Offaly. Killed in action. Grave or Memorial Reference: XIII.F.8. Cemetery: New Irish Farm Cemetery in Belgium.

**DUFFY, Thomas:** Rank: Pte. Regiment or Service: Royal Irish Fusiliers. Unit: 7<sup>th</sup>/8<sup>th</sup> Battalion. Date of death: 7 June 1917. Service no: 15949. Formerly he was with the Leinster Regiment where his number was 217. Born in Clara, Co. Offaly. Enlisted in Tullamore. Killed in action. Age at death: 39.

*Supplementary information:* Son of James and Mary Duffy. Husband of Mary Duffy, of Wheelright Lane, Tullamore, Co. Offaly. Has no known grave but is commemorated on Panel 42 on the Ypres (Menin Gate) Memorial in Belgium.

**DUFFY/DUFLY, William:** Rank: Pte. Regiment or Service: Border Regiment. Unit: 1<sup>st</sup> Battalion. Date of death: 21 August 1915. Service no: 6345. Born in Tullamore, Co. Offaly. Enlisted in Manchester while living in Tullamore. Killed in action in Gallipoli. Grave or Memorial Reference: II.D.17. Buried in Green Hill Cemetery in Turkey.

**DUGGAN, George Grant:** Rank: Captain. Regiment or Service: Royal Irish Fusiliers. Unit: 5<sup>th</sup> Bn. Date of death: 16 August 1915. Age at death: 29.

*Supplementary information:* Son of George and Emilie Duggan, of Ferney, Greystones, Co. Wicklow. Husband of Dorothy Duggan, of Glenvar, St Kevin's Park, Rathgar, Dublin. B.A. Trinity College, Dublin. Member of the Dublin University Athletic Union; also an Irish International cross country runner. As part of the 10th Irish Division in Gallipoli he died of wounds during the fight for Kislagh Dagh and is mentioned in the book *The Irish at the Front* by Michael McDonagh. His brother Lt J.R. Duggan 5th Bn, Royal Irish Regiment died (age at death 20) the same day in the Dardinelles. His son Dermot Harry Tuthill died during the Second World War on HMS *Ardent* where he was a surgeon. From De Ruvigny's Roll of Honour.

DUGGAN, George GRANT, Capt, 5th (Service) Batt. Royal Irish Fusiliers, 3rd s. of George Duggan, of 5 College Street, Dublin & Ferney, Greystones, Co. Wicklow, Manager, Provincial Bank of Ireland, Ltd, Dublin, by his wife, Emilie Asenath, dau. of Col. Charles Coote Grant, late Bedfordshire Regt. (died 23 Aug. 1914) b. Birr, Kings Co, 12 April, 1886 educ. High School, and Trinity College, Dublin, where he graduated BA. in 1908; and on leaving there entered the service of the Irish Lights Commissioners. He was one of the original members of the Dublin University O.T.C. and was one of the first N.C.O. to be appointed, being promoted Corpl. 1910, and the following year was one of small body of N.C.O. and Cadets specially selected for exceptional efficiency and smartness, to attend the coronation. He subsequently (27 Jan. 1912) received a commission on the unattached list (T.F.) for service with the D. U. O. T. C, and was promoted Lieut. 8 Feb. 1913. He qualified at the School of Musketry, Hythe, in March, 1914, and was appointed to the command of a platoon in the School of Instruction for officers of the new Armies established in Trinity College in Sept. of the same year.

On the temporary closing of this school, about the middle of the following month, he joined the 5th Battn. Royal Irish Fusiliers as Lieut. and was at once promoted to the command of a company, with the rank of temporary Capt, 28 Oct. 1914. He left with his regt. for the Dardanelles, early in July, 1915; took part in the landing at Sulva Bay, 6 Aug. 1915, and in the severe fighting there during the following ten days was severely wounded on the 16th on the Ridge over the Bay, and died the same day on board H.M. hospital ship Gloucester Castle. Buried that night in the Egean Sea. His yst. brother fell in action there the same day (see following notice). Capt. Duggan, of a bright and genial disposition, was one of the finest long-distance runners that Trinity College has ever possessed, and it would be no light task to compile a list of his many triumphs in the College Park, with the D.U. Harriers, in inter- University and in International contests. For several years he organised the College Races, and managed the affairs of the Dublin University Athletic Union with conspicuous success. But his greatest work was, undoubtedly, the inauguration of

Trinity Week, an enterprise to which he devoted himself heart and soul, and of the original Committee of which he was the foremost member. He was also a former Scoutmaster of the 6th South County Dublin (Lesson Park) troop; a member of the Executive of the County Dublin Association and an active member of the Sea Scout Committee, in whose interests he worked until the outbreak of war. He m. at Christ Church, Leeson Park, Dublin, 24 Aug. 1910, Dorothy Isabella Tuthill (12 St. Reven's Park, Rathgar, Dublin), only child of the late Henry Johnson, of Oaklands, Upper Assam, and had two sons: George Villiers Grant, b. 31 5 May, 1911; and Dermot Harry Tuthill, b. 5 July. 1912.

From *King's County Chronicle*, September 1915:

TWO BIRR BROTHERS KILLED.

The death is announced on August 17th of Captain George Grant Duggan, aged 29, Royal Irish Fusiliers, as the result of wounds received at the Dardanelles on August 16th. He was buried at sea. He was the third son of Mr George Duggan, 5 College Street, Dublin, formerly in the Birr branch of the Provincial Bank. Lieut John Rowswell Duggan, 5th Royal Irish Regiment, killed in action at the Dardanelles on August 16th, aged 20, was the fifth son. Their parents were very popular in Birr and their friends here, including Mr and Miss St. George, deeply sympathise in their bereavement.

Grave or Memorial Reference: He has no known grave but is listed on Panel 178 to 180 on the Helles Memorial in Turkey and he is also commemorated on a marble plaque on the walls of the reading room in Trinity College, Dublin.

**DUGGAN, John Roswell:** Rank: Lieutenant. Regiment or Service: The Royal Irish Regt. 5th Bn. Unit: 5th Battn. (Pioneers.) Brother of George Grant Duggan above. From De Ruvigny's Roll of Honour:

Son of George Duggan, of 5 College Street. Dublin and Fernay Greystones, Co. Wicklow. Manager Provincial Bank of Ireland, Ltd, Dublin, by his wife, Emilie Asenath, dau. of Col. Charles Coote Grant, late Bedfordshire Regt. b. Dublin, 31 Oct. 1894; educ. The High School, Dublin, where he won a 1st Class Scholarship, and passed into Trinity College, Dublin, in 1912. There he joined the Medical School and became, like his brother, a prominent Member of the O. T. C. On the out-break of war he relinquished his medical studies and was gazetted 2nd Lieut, 5th Royal Irish Regt, 15 Aug. 1914, and promoted Lieut, 28 Jan. 1915. He left with his regt. for the Dardanelles early in July 1915, as part of the 10th Division, and was killed in action on the Karakol Dagh Spur. above Sulva Bay, 16 Aug. 1915; unm. He was at first reported wounded and missing and no officer saw him fall, but the Medical Officer of the

John Roswell Duggan.

Dressing Station at Sulva Bay, to whom Lieut. Duggan went when shot through his left wrist and with shrapnel injury to face and side, told him he should go to the Hospital Ship. He said his men were without an officer so he rejoined them in the firing line, and the subsequent story is briefly told by his Sergt. P. J. Nolan (on whose testimony his death was officially reported). "He left the firing line, had his wounds dressed and returned shortly afterwards, where he was hit in the face with an explosive bullet and killed." To his father, Sergt.

Nolan wrote: "Your son could have saved his own life, but he was always good to his men and he died encouraging them to fight till the last"; and his Col, Earl of Granard, wrote "I am sorry to tell you that your son has been missing since 10

Aug. He went with his company into action our that date, and we have not seen him since. I have enquired from several of the men of his company and they all tell me that he was wounded whilst gallantly leading his men. I sincerely hope that he is a prisoner, and it is always a consolation to know that the Turks treat their prisoners with the greatest consideration. I have now soldiered for a great many years and can honestly say that I never came across a better subaltern; and as regards his social qualifications, he was beloved by all ranks of the regt. Lieut. Duggan was a noted rifle shot and won many medals and prizes, including Daily Express and Lord Roberts Medals; Adjutants cup of Trinity College, O. T.C, and he was presented with a rifle for the highest aggregate score in Leinster Schools, 1912.

Lieutenant J. R. Duggan was killed on August 16th in Gallipoli, aged 30. He was educated at the High School, Dublin, where he won a first class scholarship and entered Trinity College in 1912. There he joined the Medical School, but on the outbreak of war he decided to relinquish his medical studies and was gazetted second Lieutenant in the 5th Royal Irish Regiment. Two brothers of these officers, Mr Duggan's second and fourth sons, are in the Naval Service, one being in the Transport Department at Whitehall and the other an assistant paymaster in a battleship.

Grave or Memorial Reference: He has no known grave but is commemorated on special memorial 9 in AZMAK Cemetery in Suvla, Turkey and he is also commemorated on a marble plaque on the walls of the reading room in Trinity College, Dublin.

**DUNCAN, Kiernan:** Rank: Pte. Regiment or Service: Irish Guards. Unit: 2nd Battalion. Date of death: 20 June 1917. Service no: 8329. Born in Ferbane. Enlisted in Birr, Co. Offaly. Died of wounds. Age at death: 32. From *King's County Chronicle*, June 1916:

> From Ferbane. Kieran Duncan has joined the Irish Guards, and is now holding up the Kaiser somewhere in France. His brother, Bill, has joined recently, and is in training to give Kieran a hand. Coming of a stock that served in previous wars – well if King George had enough such men the result would not be long in doubt.'

There is an article on his wife and six children in the *King's County Independent*, July 1917 under the heading Ferbane Court. Grave or Memorial Reference: Plot 3, Row E, Grave 12. Cemetery: Ferme-Olivier Cemetery in Belgium.

**DUNCAN, William:** Rank: Pte. Regiment or Service: Irish Guards. Unit: 1st Battalion. Date of death: 1 August 1917. Service no: 11239. Born in Ferbane, Co. Offaly. Enlisted in Athlone, County Westmeath. Killed in action. 'Ireland's Memorial Records' states he died of a bullet wound received at Ypres. From *King's County Chronicle*, August 1917:

FERBANE SOLDIER KILLED.

On Monday week the sad news reached Mr Peter Duncan, Ferbane, that his son William Duncan, Irish Guards, was killed by a shell in France. The Chaplain, Fr Foxe, in writing to the father said the fallen solder was most attentive to his religion, and received communion previous to his death. Much sympathy is felt for his bereaved father, who only one month from this date received the news that his eldest son, Kieran, also of the Irish Guards, was killed in action.

Grave or Memorial Reference: I.B.5. Cemetery: Bleuet Farm Cemetery in Belgium.

**DUNFORD, Michael:** Rank: Pte. Regiment or Service: Leinster Regiment. Unit: 2nd Battalion. Date of death: 24 January 1917. Service no: 5098. Born in Duagh, Co. Kerry. Enlisted in Edenderry, Co. Offaly while living in Edenderry. Killed in action. Age at death: 34.

*Supplementary information:* Son of Timothy and Kate Dunford, of Duane, Co. Kerry. Husband of Margaret Dunford of 15 Thomas Street, Dublin. Grave or Memorial Reference: I.M.35. Cemetery: Maroc British Cemetery, Grenay in France.

**DUNN, John:** Rank: Donkeyman. Regiment or Service: Mercantile Marine. Unit: SS *Thracia* (Liverpool). Age at death: 35. Date of death: 27 March 1917.

*Supplementary information*: Son of the late Joseph and Brigid Dunn (*née* Barry). Husband of Theresa Dunn (*née* Byrne) of 5 Hill Court, Sylvester Street, Liverpool. Born at Tullamore. The Steamship *Thracia* was on a voyage from Bilbao to Ardrossan stuffed with a cargo of iron ore when she was torpedoed by German Submarine UC69 in the Bay of Biscay 12 miles north of Belle Isle. 36 of the crew died, the only survivor of the sinking being fifteen and a half-year old Cadet Douglas V Duff. The submarine was a Type UCII coastal minelayer which later sank after it collided with German submarine (U96) in 1917. Grave or Memorial Reference: He has no known grave but is listed on the Tower Hill Memorial, UK.

**DUNNE, Francis Xavier**, also listed as **DUNNE, Patrick Francis:** Rank: Pte. Regiment or Service: Australian Machine Gun Corps. Unit: 1st Company also listed as H Company, 1st Battalion. Date of death: 18/19 August 1916. Age at death: 41. Service no: 930. Born in Edenderry. Enlisted in Randwick, New South Wales on 29 September 1914 while living in Raymond Terrace, New South Wales. Educated privately. Occupation on enlistment: Labourer. Martial status: single. Previous military experience: 7 years with the Connaught Rangers and 3 years with the Rhodesian Horse. Time expired. Age at embarkation: 38. Age on enlistment: 38 years, 2 months. Height 6ft 1in. Complexion: Dark.

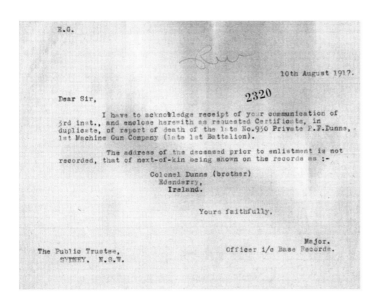

Francis Xavier Dunne.

Eyes: Blue. Hair: Brown/Grey. Served in Mudros, Alexandria, Tel-el-Kabir, Sereapeum, Ebblingham, Muspatha, Anzac, and Marseilles. Also served in Gallipoli where he was wounded in the left arm in April 1915 and sent to No. 15 General Hospital where he was treated and sent back to duty a week later. Next of kin listed as his brother: Colonel W. Dunne, Army Service Corps in Jonestown, Edenderry. Col Dunne was also a Magistrate for Queen's County and Secretary to the Department of Defence and he is mentioned in *The Time History of the War in South Africa 1899-1902* where he served with Supply and Transport 367. Killed in action.

KILLED IN ACTION.

The death is announced in action in France of Francis Xavier Dunne, 1st Australian Machine Gun Company. Deceased was the youngest brother of Colonel. W. Dunne, J.P., C.B., Joanstown [*sic*] Edenderry, and of Dr T.A. Dunne, J.P., Castletown, Queen's County. He served throughout the war since its very commencement in the various fields, including Egypt, Dardanelles (where he was wounded), and in France (where he met his death). Another brother of his is serving with the South African Infantry.

He has no known grave but is listed on the Villers-Bretonneux Memorial in France.

**DUNNE, John:** Rank: Pte. Regiment or Service: Royal Dublin Fusiliers. Unit: 2nd Battalion. Date of death: 25 April 1915. Service no: 5554. Born in Kilbride, Co. Offaly. Enlisted in Dublin. Killed in action.

*Supplementary information:* Brother of Mrs B. Murphy, of 3 Grove Avenue, Harold's Cross, Dublin. He has no known grave but is listed on Panel 44 and 46 on the Ypres (Menin Gate) Memorial in Belgium.

**DUNNE, Joseph:** Rank: Lance Corporal. Regiment or Service: Scottish Rifles. Unit: 9th Battalion. Date of death: 9 April 1917. Service no: 16308. Born in Frankford, Co. Offaly. Enlisted in Hamilton while living in Motherwell. Killed in action. Grave or Memorial Reference: He has no known grave but is listed in Bay 6 on the Arras Memorial in France.

**DUNNE, Thomas:** Rank: Corporal. Regiment or Service: Canadian Infantry (Quebec Regiment). Unit: 'C' Company, 24th Battalion. Date of death: 29 September 1916. Service no: 65294. Age at death: 21.

*Supplementary information*: Son of Denis and D. Dunne, of Monevaul, Portarlington, Co. Offaly. Data from enlistment documents. Date of birth: 12 April 1885. Trade or calling: Hotel Waiter. Age: 19. Height: 5ft8¼in. Complexion: Fair. Eyes: Blue. Hair: Brown. He has no known grave but is listed on the Vimy Memorial in France.

Thomas Dunne. Image courtesy of Michael Crawford.

**DUNNE, William P.:** Rank: Pte. Regiment or Service: Irish Guards. Unit: 1st Battalion. Date of death: 18 May 1915. Service no: 1053. Born in Birr, Co. Offaly. Enlisted in Whitehall, Middlesex while living in Birr, Co. Offaly. Killed in action.

*Supplementary information:* Brother of John Dunne, of Mill Street, Birr, Co. Offaly Awarded the Mons Star. From the *King's County Chronicle*, June 1915:

A BIRR MAN'S BATTLE EXPERIENCE.

A friend of his in Birr has sent the following interesting extract from a letter which he has just received from Private Wm. Cleary, 1st Battalion, Irish Guards, son of the late Mr Patrick Cleary, of Castle Street, and in which we are sure many readers of the "King's County Chronicle" will take a lively interest:

"I had some narrow escapes since I saw you last Christmas, having come out of three big battles without a scratch, the last being on 18th May, at Reichburg. Out of 1,100 men we only had 464 left at the roll call, and 4 officers out of 19 were left to take charge that night. Bob Sheppeard, of Cree, and Willie Dunne, of Mill Street were killed, and Lord Rosse was severely wounded. He went into action a brave man, and I hope he will pull through. The men on my right and left were killed, so I am lucky. The "Jack Johnsons" were flying all over the place, but in spite of everything we took the German trenches and a farm-house. What do you think of the Huns using gas? I was knocked out yesterday, but I am alright again. It's not bad when a fellow wants to sleep (moryah)!"

Grave or Memorial Reference: Has no known grave but is commemorated on Panel 4. Memorial: Le Touret Memorial in France.

**DUNPHY, K. P.:** Rank: Lieutenant. Regiment or Service: Leinster Regiment. Unit: 2nd Battalion. Date of death: 19 May 1920. He won the Military Medal and is listed in the *London Gazette*. Grave or Memorial Reference: In the South West part. Cemetery: Durrow Catholic Churchyard, UK.

**DURNIN, Denis:** Rank: Pte. Regiment or Service: Royal Dublin Fusiliers. Unit: 9th Battalion. Date of death: 6 March 1917. Service no: 26440. Born in Birr, Co. Offaly. Enlisted in Dublin while living in Birr. Died of wounds. Age at death: 27.

*Supplementary information:* Son of the late Denis Durnin and Bridget Flanagan Durnin, of Bridge Street, Birr. Husband of Mary Durnin, of Moorpark Street, Birr. From *Midland Tribune*, *Tipperary Sentinel* and *King's County Vindicator*, November 1916, 'Private Denis Durnin, of the Royal Dublin Fusiliers, has been wounded at the front. He was only five months in the army when he volunteered for active service. His stepfather, Mr Flanagan, the well known Birr tailor, resides at Moorpark Street, Birr. Private Dunrin, is expected home for a few days at Xmas.' Grave or Memorial Reference: 14 (Screen Wall). Cemetery: Kensal Green (St Mary's) Roman Catholic Cemetery, UK.

# E

**EADES, John:** Rank: Lance Sergeant. Regiment or Service: Royal Inniskilling Fusiliers. Unit: 9th Battalion. Date of death: 6 December 1916. Service no: 27331. Born in Birr, Co. Offaly. Enlisted in Birr. Died of wounds at home. Age at death: 27 ('Ireland's Memorial Records') and 20 (Commonwealth War Graves Commission).

*Supplementary information:* Son of William and Annie Eades, of Cappaneale, Birr. From *King's County Chronicle*, November 1915:

VOLUNTEERS FROM BIRR.

It is gratifying to know that Lord Wimbourne's appeal has not been altogether without effect, and the readers of the "King's County Chronicle" will be glad to know that the following young men have patriotically answered the country's call: Mr Thomas Eades, of Messrs Fayle, 10th Dublins; Mr John Eades, Cappaneale, Inniskillings; Mr Joseph Pennefeather, Inniskillings; Mr William Vickery, aged 17, Messrs Davis, 3rd Leinsters; Mr William Henderson, Highlanders; Mr Thomas Breen, Gas Works, 3rd Leinsters; Mr Owen Cahill, Seffin.

On the whole it cannot be said that the response has been of an encouraging nature. Both in Birr and in Roscrea, military recruiters found it most difficult to persuade eligible young men to come forward freely now. One more spurt – the final – will be made this week, and then the Department of Recruiting will receive reports from all over Ireland. It is the opinion of men who are in touch with the authorities that if those, who should volunteer, continue to shirk their responsibilities, they will only have themselves to blame if the next Government move on a mild form of compulsory enlistment.

Grave or Memorial Reference: III.A.180. Cemetery: Bailleul Communal Cemetery Extension (Nord) in France.

**EADES, Robert:** Rank: Pte. Regiment or Service: Canadian Infantry. Unit: 73rd Battalion. Date of death: 6/5 April 1917. Service no: 1332081. Born in Birr, Co. Offaly. Died of wounds. Age at death: 23/24.

*Supplementary information*: Son of William and Annie Eades, of Cappaneale, Birr, Co. Offaly. Data from enlistment documents. Present address: 400 Gordon Avenue, Verdun. Date of birth: 17 September 1893. Trade or calling: C.P.B. Policeman.

Age: 22. Height: 5ft 10½in.
Complexion: Fair. Eyes: Grey. Hair:
Brown. Distinctive marks: mole on
back. Grave or Memorial Reference:
I.G.58. Barlin Communal Cemetery
Extension in France.

**EAGLETON, Michael:** Rank:
Pte. Regiment or Service: Leinster
Regiment. Unit: 2nd Battalion. Date
of death: 4 July 1916. Service no: 3442.
Born in Birr, Co. Offaly. Enlisted in
Birr, Co. Offaly. Killed in action. From
the *King's County Chronicle*, 1916, 'Mr
John Eagleton, Wood Lane, gave two
sons, namely, Private Edward, of the 6th
Leinsters, who had been frost bitten and
is now at the other extreme of tempera-
ture in Egypt, and Private Michael, who
had also been frost bitten, and is now
at the base in France.' From the *King's
County Chronicle*, July 1916:

BIRR SOLDIER KILLED IN ACTION.

The sad news reached his sister, Mrs
Donoghue from Rev Denis Doyle,
Chaplain, 2nd Leinster Regiment,
that her brother, Pte Michael
Eagleton, of the 2nd Leinsters, had
been killed in action on 5th July.
Deceased, who was only 19 years of
age, was a fine type of a young fellow,
and of a bright and cheery disposition. He had been at the front for
over a year, and was frost-bitten last
winter. There is another brother, Pte
Edward in France, and a brother-
in-law, Corpl, Thomas Donoghue,
2nd Leinsters, is at present in Netley
Hospital suffering from a fractured
shin sustained in action in France

Michael
Eagleton.

on 29th June. Much sympathy is felt
for the bereaved relatives in their sad
affliction. The following is the letter
received from the Chaplain:

"Dear Mrs Donoghue
I am sorry to have to tell you the
sad news in this letter. Your brother,
Michael Eagleton, was killed on 5th
July. I was not with him, as he died
outright. He was a very good fellow,
much loved by his platoon commander, and he was always so bright
and cheerful. That he was quite
ready to die I know, for he was
regular at the sacraments, and was
living a food Catholic life. This must
be your only consolation. Yet it is
a great one to know that he is so
happy and out of this dreadful war,
which is breaking people's hearts. I
said Mass for the repose of his soul,
and laid him to rest yesterday near
some of his comrades.
God bless you,
Yours in sympathy.
Denis Doyle."

The deceased young soldier's father
is Mr John Eagleton, Wood Lane, a
respected inhabitant of Birr.

Grave or Memorial Reference: Y.1. Cemetery: Kemmel Chateau Military Cemetery in Belgium.

**EAGLETON/EGLETON, Thomas:** Rank: Lance Corporal. Regiment or Service: Irish Guards. Unit: 2nd Battalion. Date of death: 5 December 1917. 'Ireland's Memorial Records' give his Date of death as 17 December 1917. Service no: 6379. Born in Birr, Co. Offaly. Enlisted in Birr, Co. Offaly. Died of wounds. Age at death: 23. Eagleton, Thomas, M.M. Corporal. Service Number; 6379. Irish Guards. 2nd Battalion. From De Ruvigny's Roll of Honour:

Thomas Eagleton. The image above is taken from the *King's County Chronicle*, 1916 and includes the following information, 'Irish Guards, was gassed in France, and is now in England. His father, Mr Michael Eagleton resides at Newbridge Street, Birr.'

Son of Michael Eagleton, Newbridge Street, Birr, King's County by his wife Bridget, daughter of Thomas McGuinness of County Kilkenny. Born 26th April 1894. Educated Presentation Brothers School, Birr, was a shop assistant, enlisted 2nd Jan, 1915. Served with the Expeditionary Force in France and Flanders from 1st May following and was killed in action on the Somme 5th December, 1917. Buried 5 and a half miles North East of Combles. His Captain wrote; "He was deeply regretted by the NCOs and men of No 1 Coy. He was awarded the Military Medal in November 1917, for bravery in discharge of duty.

From the *King's County Chronicle*, December 1917:

Sincere sympathy is felt with the bereaved parents, Mr and Mrs Michael Eagleton, Newbridge Street, Birr, who last week received the sad news that their son had died of wounds received in action. Although not more than a boy in years, he was physically a splendid type of soldier, and his death is much regretted. He joined the army about three years ago, and had been previously gassed, but recovered, and was again sent to France, where he met his death.

From the *King's County Chronicle*, December 1915:

In Memory of Lance Corporal Tom Eagleton. Irish Guards. Died of wounds in France, Dec. 5th, 1917.

At home in Ireland is grief, deep grief,
The mother's wailing is keen and
    loud,
And the hard-won stripe brings
    scant relief,
If its threads are sewn in a crimson
    shroud.

O! Lord, look down on the old
    green land,
Where homes are telling this tale
    of woe;
A loved one dead, on a foreign
    strand,
His blood small price for the ruby's
    glow.

O! Tom, alanna, with heart of
    mirth,
And quizzical face full of Irish fun;
Your clay now gathered to stranger
    earth,
And neighbours weep for the neigh-
    bour's son.

Full brave, my boy, have you played
    your part;
A host of valour is Ireland's fame,
Your soul of humour cheered ev'ry
    heart,
And comrades brighten'd to hear
    your name.

No more the hearth-fire's flame
    shall light,
To laughter sweet at your song and
    jokes,
And with mother's eyes grow glad
    and bright
With love and pride at each note you
    woke

But swiftly passes the evening dream,
The mem'ry sweet of those mirth-
    ful hours;
Yet to fond hearts they will ever
    seem,
Scant-laden with love's choicest flowers.

But, oh, the carnage and the strife
That took you from our midst, mó
    croidhe;
The God who gave your spirit life,
May hold you in love's mystery.

Maire Ní Bruin
10, Newbridge Street, Birr.

Grave or Memorial Reference:V.D.17.
Cemetery: Rocquigny-Equancourt
Road British Cemetery, Equancourt
in France.

**EGAN, John:** Rank: Pte. Regiment
or Service: Leinster Regiment.
Unit: 2$^{nd}$ Battalion. Date of death:
2 April 1917. Service no: 3621.
Born in Birr, Co. Offaly. 'Ireland's
Memorial Records' say he was born
at St Brendan, Birr. Enlisted in Birr,
Co. Offaly. Killed in action. Grave
or Memorial Reference: IV.A.16.
Cemetery: Lievin Communal
Cemetery Extension in France.

**EGAN, Patrick:** Rank: Pte.
Regiment or Service: Connaught
Rangers. Unit: 2$^{nd}$ Battalion. Date of
death: 14 September 1914. Service no:
8358. Born in Banagher, Co. Offaly.
Enlisted in Birr, Co. Offaly while
living in Banagher, Co. Offaly. Killed
in action. Age at death: 30.

*Supplementary information:* Brother of Michael Egan, of Banagher, Co. Offaly. Served in the South African Campaign. From *Midland Tribune, Tipperary Sentinel* and *King's County Vindicator* February 1917, 'Private Patrick Egan (Connaught Rangers), of the firm of Egan and Son, painters and decorators, Banagher, who is missing since October 1914, has now been presumed to have been killed.' Grave or Memorial Reference: He has no known grave but is listed on the La Ferte-Sous-Jouarre-Memorial in France.

**EGAN, William:** Rank: Pte. Regiment or Service: Irish Guards. Unit: 2nd Battalion. Date of death: 21 October 1915. Service no: 7884. Born in Drumcullen, Co. Offaly. 'Ireland's Memorial Records' list his birth as Birr. Enlisted in Birr. Died of wounds. Age at death: 18/19.

*Supplementary information:* Son of Daniel and Bridget Egan, of Ballinree, Killyon, Birr, Co. Offaly. Grave or Memorial Reference: IV.F.58. Cemetery: Bethune Town Cemetery in France.

**ELCOATE, Thomas:** Rank: Pte Regiment or Service: Australian Machine Gun Corps. Unit Text: 4th Battalion. Secondary Regiment: Australian Army Service Corps Secondary. Unit: late (Driver) 2nd Light Horse Bde. Date of death: 9 August 1918. Service no: 1023.

*Supplementary information*: Son of William and Agnes Elcoate, of Ballinasragh, Co. Offaly. Husband of Katharine M.S. Elcoate, of 56 Bartholomew Road, London, N.W.S. Data from enlistment documents. Born in Belfast. Age: 20 years. Trade: Farmer. Next of kin: William Elcoate (father) 137 Stanmillis Road, Belfast. Height: 5ft 11in. Complexion: Medium. Eyes: Grey. Hair: Brown. Distinctive marks: Birth mark left upper arm. Date: 19 September 1914. Place: The Warren, Marrickville, N.S.W. The following is a letter sent to his wife:

"Dear Madam,
With reference to the report of the regrettable loss of your husband, the late No 1023, Private T Elcoate, 4th Machine Gun Battalion, I am now in receipt of advice, which shows he was wounded in action (Gunshot wound groin) on 8 August 1918, and admitted to 13th Australian Field Ambulance, transferred to 20th Casualty Clearing Station, where he died on 9 August 1918. He was buried at Vignacourt, Chaplain the Rev L.T. Causton, attached to the 20th Casualty Clearing Station officiating. The utmost care and attention is being devoted, where possible, to the graves of our fallen soldiers. It is understood photographs are being taken as soon as practicable for transmission to next of kin. These additional details are furnished by direction, it being the policy of the Department to forward all information received in connection with the deaths of members of the Australian Imperial Force. Yours faithfully, Officer I.C. Base records.

"This man died at 2p.m. on 9 August 1918 from shell wound of groin. He was buried in Vignacourt Cemetery, France. (1. 4000. Sheet 53E, w22, B. 4. 7) by the Rev L.J. Causton, C.F. He was only semi-conscious whilst here and nothing further can now be said about this case.

J. F. Ritchie, Lt Col, Commanding Officer."

His death plaque and memorial scroll does not seem to have been sent to his wife. Written where her name should be is 'missing in England'. Grave or Memorial Reference: V.B.8. Vignacourt British Cemetery in France.

**ENGLISH, George:** Rank: Pte. Regiment or Service: Royal Dublin Fusiliers. Unit: 8<sup>th</sup> Bn. Date of death: 6 September 1916. Service no: 16771. Born in Roscrea, Co. Offaly. Enlisted in Manchester. Killed in action. He has no known grave but is listed on Pier and Face 16C on the Thiepval Memorial in France.

# F

**FAGAN, James:** Rank: Pte. Regiment or Service: Household Cavalry and Cavalry of the line including the Yeomanry and Imperial Camel Corps. Unit: 4th (Queens Own) Hussars, D Squadron. Date of death: 5 November 1914. Service no: 13246. Born in Mountjoy, Dublin. Enlisted in Birr, Co. Offaly while living in Birr. Killed in action. Age at death: 29.

*Supplementary information*: Husband of Ellen Fagan, of Ross Row, Birr, Co. Offaly. Grave or Memorial Reference: Panel 5. Memorial: Ypres (Menin Gate) Memorial in Belgium.

**FALLON, Joseph:** Rank: Lance Corporal. Regiment or Service: Royal Dublin Fusiliers. Unit: 9th Battalion. Date of death: 30 April 1916. Service no: 21236. Born in Birr, Co. Offaly. Enlisted in Birr. Died of wounds.

*Supplementary information*: Son of the late Mr and Mrs B. Fallon. From *Midland Tribune, Tipperary Sentinel* and *King's County Vindicator*, 1916, 'Official notification was received in Birr on Friday, by his mother, of the death on 30 April from wounds received in France, of Corporal Joseph Fallon, Royal Dublin Fusiliers. He was only 20 years of age, and enlisted about a year ago. Much regret is felt by all who knew him.' From the *King's County Chronicle*, May 1916:

Death of Corporal J. Fallon. Corporal Joseph Fallon, 9th Dublin Fusiliers, died on April 30, from wounds received in action in France. The news was conveyed to his mother in an official announcement last week. He was employed at Miss Kilmartin's, Main Street, Birr, and joined the army some months after the outbreak of the war. He was a very intelligent young man and, did much to improve his education at the Birr Technical School, winning for himself the high opinion of the Principal (Mr Flynn) and of his fellow pupils. He was a member of the Young Men's Society Band, and was greatly esteemed by all the members of the society.

Speaking at the Technical School on Monday night the Principal (Mr Flynn) referred to the death of a former student, Corporal Fallon. For four years he had been a regular attendee at the classes, and he was known to many of those present that night. No-one was more enthusiastic nor more anxious to improve his education, nor was he happy if he had not his comrades with him. Should one be missing from his anointed place Joe would not feel satisfied till he had looked him up, ad unless the cause of his absence was unavoidable Joe would bring him along.

Before his departure for France he called to bid good-bye. Cheerful and large hearted as ever, he went to do his duty. But though he lies in a far away country he is not forgotten, and on behalf of his fellow-students and himself, the Principal wished to tender to his relatives their deepest sympathy.

Grave or Memorial Reference: III.H.75. Cemetery: Bethune Town Cemetery in France.

**FEEHAN, Martin:** Rank: Pte. Regiment or Service: Leinster Regiment. Unit: 1st Bn. Age at death: 30. Date of death: 12 May 1915. Service no: 2926. Born in Birr, Co. Offaly and enlisted in Dublin. Killed in action.

*Supplementary information*: Husband of Julia Feehan, of Cloughjordan, Co. Tipperary. From the *Midland Tribune*, *Tipperary Sentinel* and *King's County Vindicator*, 1915:

> Motored to jail. The well known soldier Feehan was hauled up by the police the other day to expiate a "seven days" item which had been investigated at a recent court. As the train fare and motor fare to Tullamore represent about the same thing, the soldier was prepared for his seclusion by the exhilarating experience of being "chauffeured" to jail. When a delinquent like the soldier can, with economy, have a motor in preference to a train, one would think

a "move" expedient on the part of the railway company.

Has no known grave but is commemorated on Panel 44. Memorial: Ypres (Menin Gate) Memorial in Belgium.

**FEENEY, Frank:** Rank: Pte. Regiment or Service: Leinster Regiment. Unit: 1st Battalion. Date of death: 24 February 1915. Service no: 9231. Born in Killeigh, Co. Offaly. Enlisted in Tullamore. Killed in action. Has no known grave but is commemorated on Panel 44. Memorial: Ypres (Menin Gate) Memorial in Belgium.

**FEERY, Joseph:** Rank: Pte. Regiment or Service: Royal Irish Regiment. Unit: 2nd Battalion. Date of death: 14 July 1916. Service no: 11064. Born in Philipstown, Co. Offaly. Enlisted in Tullamore, Co. Offaly while living in Philipstown. Killed in action. Age at death: 24.

*Supplementary information:* Son of Bernard and Elizabeth Feery, of Rathdrum, Ballycommon, Daingean, Offaly. From the *King's County Independent*, June 1917:

> REPORTED MISSING.
>
> Being reported as 'Missing' since the 14th July, 1916, the congregation at Mass I Philipstown Catholic Church on Sunday last were requested to pray for the repose of the soul of Private Joseph Feery, 3rd Leinster Regiment, who belonged to Ballycommon, and who fell in action on the date mentioned but whose death could not be definitely ascertained until recently.

Grave or Memorial Reference: Pier and Face 3A. Memorial: Thiepval Memorial in France.

**FEERY, Patrick:** Rank: Pte. Regiment or Service: Leinster Regiment. Unit: 2nd Battalion. Date of death: 31 July 1917. Service no: 2007. Born in Kilbride, Co. Offaly. Enlisted in Birr, Co. Offaly. Killed in action.

*Supplementary information:* Brother of Mrs Kate Kelley, of Thomas Street, Tullamore, Offaly. From the *King's County Chronicle*, 1916:

> Sergeant Feery, 2nd East Lancs., who was decorated with the Military Cross, and promoted on the field for gallantry in action on the Somme, has been spending a short leave with his sisters, and brother in Tullamore. Another brother of the Sergeant's was recently reported wounded in France.
>
> The Sergeant is a young soldier, apparently just in his prime, compact, well knit and muscular, and ideal Irish infantryman, and proud of his distinction. He had some years' service before the war.

Grave or Memorial Reference: Panel 44. Memorial: Ypres (Menin Gate) Memorial in Belgium.

**FFRENCH, George Edward:** Rank: Lieutenant. Regiment or Service: Royal Air Force. Unit: 27th Squadron. Date of death: 23 May 1918. Age at death: 18.

*Supplementary information*: Son of the Revd Le B. Edward and Violet S. Ffrench, of Kilconnell Rectory, Ballinasloe, Co. Galway. Born at Shinrone, Co. Offaly. Formerly of O.T.C., Trent College, Derbyshire. From the *King's County Chronicle*, July 1918:

THE LATE LIEUT. FFRENCH.

A Perfect Chum and Loved by All. The last issue of the Killaloe Diocesan Magazine, in recording the death of the above gallant young flying officer, together with details of his career, gives the following extract from the deceased's last letter home: "Last Friday I went over the lines with a formation of our machines. About 15 miles over the lines my engine gave out almost together, so I had to leave my formation and make the best of my way back by myself. As the engine was scarcely working, I was losing height all the way back. I hardly left our formation at twelve thousand feet when I was dived on by five Hun scouts. As the engine was no good, and we were heading for the lines, we could only put up a running fight. However, we shot down one of the Huns, and the others soon lost heart and left us."

A fellow pilot writes: "He was a perfect chum, and loved by us all, especially those who knew him intimately and it is awful to think that he is gone." The Major of his squadron wrote: "Although he had not been very long with us, he was most popular with us all, and was doing extremely well as a pilot. He was just a delightful fellow, and, alas! It always seems that the best ones are taken."

"Nothing is here for tears; nothing
   to wail,
Or knock the breast; no weakness,
   no contempt,
Dispraise, or blame; nothing but
   well and fair,
And what may quiet us in a death
   so noble."

The late Lieutenant Ffrench was the
eldest son of the Rev. Le B.E. Ffrench,
rector of Kilconnell, and formerly of
Shinrone, where the deceased was
born in 1899. He was educated at
Chesterfield School, Birr, and Trent
College, Derbyshire. At the latter
school he became Head of his House,
and was a member of the cricket XI.
and Rugby XV. He was also one of
the best shots in the Rifle Corps,
which had previously won Lord
Roberts Cuo, offered for shooting
in competition with all the Public
Schools in England. He joined the
Royal Flying Corps in August, 1917,
was trained at Hastings and Oxford,
and received his commission, after
examination, last December. He subsequently completed his training at
Wyton and Marske, obtaining his
"Wings" in March. He was immediately ordered to France, and in the
short period of his active service had
been in several engagements, was
mentioned in the confidential report
of the Air Force as having brought
down a German machine and was
killed in action as stated in out issue at
the time, on May 23rd.

From 'Airmen Died in the Great War':

2nd Lt George Edward Ffrench
(aged 18 and from Shinrone, Co.
Offaly, Eire) was killed on 23rd May
1918 and was buried at Pernes in
France. From Henshaw's "The Sky
Their Battlefield" He was piloting
his DH9 No: D5616 with Cpl F Y
McLauchlan as his observer when
the engine fell off at about 6:10am
near Maria Aeltre, having left the
aerodrome at Fourneuil, where
Number 27 squadron was based at
the time. His observer was also killed.
Trevor Henshaw mentions that there
was a claim made by Lt D. Collin of
Ja 56 in the same area and at about
the same time, but possibly for a
downed Bristol.

Grave or Memorial Reference:
II.C.45. Cemetery: Pernes British
Cemetery in France.

**FIELDS, John William:** Rank: Pte.
Regiment or Service: Royal Dublin
Fusiliers. Unit: 1st Bn. Date of death:
19 July 1917. Service no: 4093.
Formerly he was with the Leinster
Regiment where his number was
3530. Born in Mullalaghan, Co.
Monaghan. Enlisted in Belfast while
living in Moneygall, Co Tipperary.
Died of wounds. Age at death: 22.

*Supplementary information*: Son
of Patrick and Teresa Fields, of
Mullaloughan, Co. Monaghan.
Husband of Margaret Fields, of
Springfield, Moneygall. Grave
or Memorial Reference: II.F.3.
Cemetery: Mendingham Military
Cemetery in Belgium.

**FITZGERALD, James:** Rank: Shoeing Smith. Regiment or Service: Royal Horse Artillery and Royal Field Artillery. Unit: 73rd Battery, 5th Brigade. Date of death: 14 October 1918. Service no: 53101. Born in Shinrone, Co. Offaly also listed as born in Shinkowe, Co. Offaly. Killed in action. Age at death: 28.

*Supplementary information*: Son of James and Johanna Fitzgerald, of Garbally, Shinrone, Co. Offaly. Grave or Memorial Reference: V.A.21. Cemetery: Premont British Cemetery in France.

**FITZGIBBON, Michael Joseph:** Rank: Captain also listed as Lieutenant on the CWGC. Regiment or Service: Royal Dublin Fusiliers. Unit: 7th Battalion. Date of death: 15 August 1915. Killed in action. From the *King's County Independent*, 1915:

KILLED IN ACTION. CAPTAIN M. FITZGIBBON.

Mr John Fitzgibbon, M.P., and Mrs Fitzgibbon will have the heartfelt sympathy of the people of Connaught, and, more especially, of Roscommon and Mayo, on the death of their son, Capt. M.M. Fitzgibbon, 7th Dublin Fusiliers, who was killed in action at the Dardanelles on August 15th, which, by coincidence, was his 29th birthday. Captain Fitzgibbon was well known in his active district of Castlerea, and also in Tullamore, where, as a law student has spent some years as an apprentice to Messrs, Hoey and Denning, solicitors. He was probably the most popular member of his very popular family, and amongst his many acquaintances in Tullamore his death will be very sincerely mourned.

He was a young man of brilliant intellect, and he had before him a very successful career in the legal profession, but he surrendered this to answer the call. He was gazetted as Lieutenant in the Dublin Fusiliers, and before the departure of the Division for the Mediterranean, he was promoted to the rank of captain. He was just a week on Turkish soil when he was killed. We desire to join in the common expression of sympathy with his bereaved parents, and to his relatives in their great loss.

From the *King's County Independent*, September 1915:

Michael Joseph Fitzgibbon.

THE LATE CAPT. FITZGIBBON.

Tribute to his Bravery.

Lance-Corporal's Touching Letter.
The following letter has been received by Mr John Fitzgibbon, M.P., from Lance-Corporal P.J. Madden, 5th Royal Irish Fusiliers. No. 17527, Queen's F.I. Ward, 5th Royal Irish Fusiliers, Graylingwell, War Hospital, Chichester, Sussex, September 1st, 1915:

"Dear Mr Fitzgibbon,
You may feel surprised to get a letter from the above address, but I wish to send my sincere sympathy to your-self, Mrs Fitzgibbon and you family on the death of your son, and I assure the loss of such a gallant Captain will not alone be felt among the Dublin Fusiliers, but in the whole 10th Irish Division. The shelling was so severe and the fighting so incessant, we lost most of our officers in the landing. Captain Fitzgibbon was one of the few left to head the Irish Troops, and he set a fine example of pluck and courage to his junior officers and men, and cheered us on to victory when we captured Chocolate Hill and a line of trenches on the evening of August 6th at the point of the bay-onet. After that charge we were all exhausted, and as the fighting grew quieter the inclination to sleep was almost irresistible, yet owing to the nearness of the enemy it was danger-ous, and every man was ordered to "stand to arms".

All night long Captain Fitzgibbon kept sending messages to Headquarters and receiving replies. I heard after his idea was to keep passing messages down the lines, so that no man could sleep. He was successful. No man slept. On August 10th, the night I was wounded, the Connaught Rangers and Inniskillings relieved the Dublin and Irish Fusiliers who had slept four days in the firing line, and were allowed to base for a rest. Captain Fitzgibbon and Captain Lennon were all right then, and were not due back in the firing line till Sunday morning, so it must be in the now famous charge of the 16th August the gallant Captain fell. It was a pity, but a still greater loss, as the losing of such men as Captain Fitzgibbon will not hasten the end of this dreadful war, which I am sure you can never forget.

When the history of this war comes before the public that land-ing and taking of Suvla Bay will be mentioned, and a tribute of recog-nition will be paid to the two brave Captains from Castlerea, who took the lion's share of the work in pull-ing their men through. Captain Fitzgibbon did not fall into the hands of the Turks alive. He met with a hero's death, leading his men to victory, envied by most soldiers and regretted by all. Trusting you will accept my deepest sympathy. – I remain, yours very sincerely,
P.J. Madden, Lance Corporal,
J. Fitzgibbon, Esq., M.P."

From the *Castlerea Guardian*:

SYMPATHY.

Mr P. Conry presided at the weekly meeting of the Castlerea Board of Guardians on Saturday. The other members present were: Messrs. M.G. Sweeney and Mr M.H. Grogan. Mr P.A. Flanagan, Clerk was also in attendance.

The minutes of last meeting having been read and signed, Mr M.H. Grogan said: Mr Chairman and gentlemen, we have all heard with regret of the death of our townsman, Captain Fitzgibbon. Indeed, it is very sad that at the very first engagement of his active military life he met his death. I am sure had it been his fate to live through this horrible war, he was one who would reach a very high rank in military circles, for he possessed all the qualities that make a brave soldier. This meeting is very small. I know that every member of our Board was aware that this day's meeting would be adjourned in respect to the memory of the late Captain Fitzgibbon. Our colleague's absence from the meeting today is due to sharing with us in our sympathy with the Chairman and his family. I propose: That we, the Castlerea Board of Guardians, have heard with deep regret of the death of Captain Michael Fitzgibbon, who was killed in action in the Dardanelles. That we tender to his father, Mr John Fitzgibbon, M.P. and the other members of his family, our sincere sympathy in their sad affliction, and as a mark of respect to the deceased soldier, we do adjourn the Board meeting without transacting any business. Copy of this resolution to be forwarded to Mr Fitzgibbon.

Mr M.G. Sweeney: I second that resolution. It is with deep regret we learn of the early death of Captain Michael Fitzgibbon. He was a promising young gentleman studying for the law, and had he been spared there was a splendid career before him. It was with deep regret we all heard of his death.

Chairman: We all sincerely regret his early death. He was a brave young man, who wished to serve his country by joining the army when he considered it his duty.

He is also listed on the Tullamore Roll of Honour. Grave or Memorial Reference: He has no known grave but is listed on Panel 190 to 196 on the Helles Memorial in Turkey.

**FITZNOLAN, Michael Joseph:** Rank: Company Quartermaster Sergeant. Regiment or Service: Kings Liverpool Regiment. Unit: 1st Battalion. Date of death: 16 May 1915. Service no: 9485. Born in Birr, Co. Offaly. Enlisted in Dublin while living in Birr. Killed in action. He has no known grave but is listed on Panels 6 to 8 on the Le Touret Memorial in France.

**FITZPATRICK, Thomas:** (Also listed as **PATRICK Thomas**). Rank: Pte. Regiment or Service: Leinster Regiment. Unit: B Company, 2nd Battalion. Date of death: 22 August 1918. Service no: 3262. Born in

Crinkle, Birr, Co. Offaly. Enlisted in Birr. Killed in action by Shellfire. Age at death: 23.

*Supplementary information*: Son of William and Mary Fitzpatrick, of Crinkle, Birr, Co. Offaly. Eight years service, wounded three times and gassed once. Listed in 'Ireland's Memorial Records' and 'Soldiers died in the Great War' as Fitzpatrick, Thomas and in the Commonwealth War Graves Commission as Fitzpatrick, Patrick Thomas. From the *King's County Chronicle*, May 1915:

Thomas Fitzpatrick.

THE BARBARIC "GAS" DEATH.

An officer sends the following harrowing description of what he saw:

"Yesterday and the day before I went to see some of the men in hospital who were "gassed" and the day before on Hill 60. The whole of England and the civilised world ought to have the truth fully brought before them in vivid detail, and not wrapped up as at present. When we go to the hospital we had no difficulty in finding out in which ward the men were, as the noise was sufficient to direct us. There were about 20 of the worst cases in the ward on mattresses all more or less in a sitting position, propped up against the walls. Their faces, arms, hands were of a shiny, grey-black colour, with mouths open, and lead glazed eyes, all swaying backwards and forwards trying to get breath. It was the most appalling sight, all those poor black faces, struggling for life, what with the groaning and noise of the efforts for breath. Colonel _____, who, as everyone knows, has had as wide an experience as any, one all over the savage parts of Africa, told me to-day that he never felt so sick as he did after the scene in these cases. There is practically nothing to be done for them, except to give them salt and water to try and make them sick.

The effect of gas is to fill the lungs with a watery, frothy matter, which gradually increases and rises till it fills up the whole lungs, and comes up to the mouth; then they die; its is suffocation; slow drowning taking in some cases one or two days. Eight died last night out of twenty I saw, and most of the others I saw will die; whilst those who get over the gas invariably develop acute pneumonia. It is without the most awful form of scientific torture. Not one of the men I saw in hospital had a scratch or wound. The nurses and doctors were all working their utmost against this terror; but one could see from the tension of their nerves that it as like fighting a hidden danger which was overtaking everyone. The gas is in a cylinder, from which when they sent it out, it is propelled a distance of 100 yards. It there spreads. The Germans have given out that it is a rapid, painless death. The liars."

From the *King's County Chronicle*, August 1918:

PRIVATE THOMAS FITZPATRICK.
Leinster Regiment.
The news of the death in action of the above fine young soldier was heard with much regret. He was only 23 years of age, and was home on his last leave in February. When war broke out he was on the reserve, and had been through numerous engagements. He was very popular, and in civil life was an industrious employee of the District Council. Sincere sympathy is felt with his bereaved parents, Mr and Mrs Wm. Fitzpatrick, Crinkle. The official notice of his death was accompanied with a message of sympathy from their Majesties the King and the Queen.

Grave or Memorial Reference: II.F.24. Cemetery: La Kreule Military Cemetery, Hazebrouck in France.

**FLAHERTY, Thomas:** Rank: Sergeant. Regiment or Service: Leinster Regiment. Unit: 2nd Battalion. Date of death: 28 January 1916. Service no: 9247 (listed in 'Ireland's Memorial Records' as 9347). Born in Clara, Co. Offaly. Enlisted in Birr. Died.
*Supplementary information*: Son of Mary Flaherty, of Middle Street, Galway. Grave or Memorial Reference: II.B.37A. Cemetery: Lijssenthoek Military Cemetery in Belgium.

**FLANAGAN, John:** Rank: Pte. Regiment or Service: Leinster Regiment. Unit: 2nd Battalion. Date of death: 1 April 1917. Service no: 10234 ('Soldiers died in the Great War') 1234 ('Ireland's Memorial Records'). Born in Birr, Co. Offaly. Enlisted in Birr. Died of wounds.
*Supplementary information*: Awarded the 1914 Star. From the *Midland Tribune, Tipperary Sentinel* and *King's County Vindicator*. April 1917, 'Mrs Flanagan, Cornmarket Street, Birr, recently received official intimation of the death in action of her son, but she received a letter from him under a date five days later than that, on which the War Office stated he had been killed. It is sincerely hoped that the War Office has made a mistake.' From the *King's County Chronicle*, February 1916:

Rejoined for the war. Private Patrick Flanagan, Church Street, an old Leinster Regiment soldier, re-joined at the out break of the war, and was posted to the 6th Leinsters. He is at present serving in Egypt. His two sons, Private John and Private Thomas are on active service with the 2nd Batt. Of their fathers regiment. A brother of Private Patrick, senr, Private John, joined last May and is serving with the same regiment.

Grave or Memorial Reference: I.B.25. Cemetery: Fosse No 10 Communal Cemetery Extension, Sains-En-Gohelle in France.

**FLANAGAN, Michael:** Rank: Pte. Regiment or Service: Leinster

Regiment. Unit: 1ˢᵗ Battalion. Date of death: 1 October 1915. Service no: 9672. Born in Kilbride, Co. Offaly. Enlisted in Birr, Co. Offaly. Killed in action. Age at death: 19.

*Supplementary information:* Son of Joseph and Ellen Flanagan, of 3 Old Warders Quarters, Marlborough Lines, North Camp, Aldershot. Enlisted November 1910. Also served in India. Born at Tullamore, Co. Offaly. From the *King's County Independent*, April 1915:

"ROYAL IRISH REGIMENT.
COMMANDING OFFICER HIT TWICE.
Company Wiped out.
Germans Twenty to One.
Mrs Flanagan's four sons in the Battle Line.

(To the Editor)
Sir,
Kindly grant me space in your most esteemed paper for the enclosed letter from my son, Private Flanagan, 1ˢᵗ Royal Irish Regiment, who has recently been wounded at St Eloi. I also beg to state I have three more sons at the front, viz: Sergt. A. Flanagan, 2ⁿᵈ Royal Munster Fusiliers; Corporal C.I. Flanagan, 1ˢᵗ Leinster Regiment; and Private M. Flanagan, 1ˢᵗ Leinster Regiment. Wishing your esteemed paper every success.

Faithfully yours,
Ellen J. Flanagan (Mother)
Married Quarters.
Marlborough Barracks, Dublin"
22 April 1915.

Extract from letter from Private J. Flanagan, Tullamore, 1ˢᵗ Battalion, Royal Irish Regiment.
Grand Duchess George of Russia Hospital.
Harrogate, Leeds, England.

Dear Mother,
I have just arrived at this hospital last night; it is a lovely hospital to be in. It belongs to the Princess of Russia. Dear mother, I got wounded on the night of the big charge, and had to stop in a little broken-down house for shelter, so as the Germans would not see me, as I was useless. I was only 50 yards away from their trench. That was the one they took off us, and we had to take it again, which we did; so, I saw all the operations myself. Our Commanding Officer got hit twice and all my company was killed, as far as I could see; my Company was first to charge out of the whole Division. That will tell you we were very unlucky and my section was leading with fixed bayonets; I was the second man to use the bayonet on the Germans. But I was not long in position before I got knocked over, and it was God's will, because if I had gone any further I would have got cut up into pieces as the Germans were about 20 to our 1, and had about 6 machine guns playing on our company. I don't know how I came out of it alive. I am surprised to be here. So dear mother, I must come to a close. I saw my brother Michael, after getting hit;

he pulled me into his trench where the Leinsters were; I had a hearty shake hands with him on leaving hospital.

Your fond son,
John J. Flanagan

From the *King's County Independent*, January 1916:

FIVE SONS IN ARMY.
Letter from Tullamore Woman.
Kevin St, Tullamore. 19 January 1916.

"Sir

Kindly permit me to give the following particulars of my five sons in you most esteemed paper. I also beg to inform you that about 9 months ago they appeared in your issue, together with their photos and may add I think was the first family to appear in your most esteemed paper. I was then at Maryborough Barracks, Dublin, employed on the Bk. Department A.S. Corps, and resigned for the purpose of re-enlistment as an army pensioner as drill instructor. I regret to state I was medically unfit, owing to defective vision, by Doctor Kennedy, Tullamore. I am now employed as rural postman here in Rahan. The following I beg to state as regards my five sons, viz: Dvr, J.P. Flanagan, 1st Royal Irish Regiment, 7 years service, wounded at St Eloi, now at the front. Came from India in December, 1914; champion athletic of the said Battalion while in India; holds medals for same.

Corporal C.J. Flanagan, 1st Leinster Rgt., came from India in December, 1914, wounded, now at St Ann's Hill, Convalescent Home, Blarney. Pte Michael Flanagan, killed on Oct last; saved his brother, Dvr Flanagan, 5 years service, when wounded at St Eloi; shook hands and never seen each other afterwards.

Sergeant A. Flanagan, 2nd R. M. Fulisiers, 2½ years service; wounded, and now drill instructor at Aghada, Co. Cork; promoted from Lance Corporal to Sergeant on the battle field in France; has recently won cross country race at Aghada, and now about to run for Cork Championship. Pte Bertie, Flanagan, 4th Royal Dublin Fusiliers, formerly page boy Royal Marine Hotel, Kingstown, now serving at Sittingbourne, Kent, England. Mr Flanagan s 4 sons were serving in the Regular Army previous to the was and Mr Flanagan served formerly in the Leinster Regiment and Royal Munster Fusiliers, and left with the rank of Lance-Sergeant and served in the Boer War, and afterwards went to India to the Punjab with the 1st Batt, R. Munster Fusiliers. I appeal to you if you would kindly give particulars of my late son, Michael, 1st Leinsters, killed in action on your issue of last week, the gallantry of him saving his brother when wounded at St Eloi. Hoping I am not intruding.

I am, sir, your obedient servant.
Joe Flanagan, Army Pensioner,
Acting Postmaster, Rahan."

He is also listed on the Tullamore Roll of Honour. Grave or Memorial Reference: VII.C.9. Cemetery: Assevillers New British Cemetery in France.

**FLANNERY, Michael:** Rank: Pte. Regiment or Service: Connaught Rangers. Unit: 1st Bn. Date of death: 23 November 1914. Service no: 10125. Born in Nenagh. Enlisted in Birr while living in Birr. Killed in action. Supplementary information: Son of John and Margaret Flannery, of Pound St, Birr, Offaly. From the *King's County Chronicle*, February 1916, 'Mr John Flannery, formerly of Connaught Street, has four sons in the army: Privates Daniel, John and Christopher of the Leinsters, and Pte Michael, of the Connaughts, killed in France. Grave or Memorial Reference: He has no known grave but is listed on panel 43 on the Le Touret Memorial in France.

**FLANNERY, Patrick:** Rank: Pte. Regiment or Service: Leinster Regiment. Unit: 2nd Battalion. Date of death: 10 June 1917. Service no: 9456. Born in Ballycumber, Co. Offaly. Enlisted in Birr, Co. Offaly. Killed in action. Age at death: 24.

*Supplementary information*: Son of Mrs Mary Tighe (formerly Flannery), of Derries, Ferbane, Offaly. Grave or Memorial Reference: Panel 44. Memorial: Ypres (Menin Gate) Memorial in Belgium.

**FLEURY, William:** Rank: Pte. Regiment or Service: Auckland Regiment, New Zealand Expeditionary Force. Unit: 1st Battalion. Date of death: 4 October 1917. Service no: 28703. Killed in action.

*Supplementary information*: Information from his records: Occupation on enlistment: Boardinghouse keeper. Next of kin: Mrs William Fleury (wife), care of Pullen, Armitage, and Co., 99 Albert Street, Auckland, New Zealand. From the *King's County Chronicle*, December 1917:

ROLL OF HONOUR.

His many friends in Birr will hear with deep regret this week that Dr Fleury has received definite news from an officer at the front in France that his brother, William, has been killed in action on 4th October. He was wounded early in the attack and was sent to the rear. Not reporting at any of the local dressing stations he was posted as wounded and missing, but he was afterwards found dead, having been killed by a shell on his way to the dressing station. "He was a fine soldier," writes one officer. "and a man who was liked and respected by both officers and men of his company." In Birr and district William Fleury, or "Bill," as he was known, possessed of a genial and kindly disposition, was extremely popular. Interested in every form of sport, his fine appearance marked him out as a splendid specimen of manhood. Before the war he was in New Zealand, and joined the Anzac forces after the outbreak. The news of his death will be heard with profound regret.

Grave or Memorial Reference: VI.P.4. Cemetery: Dochy Farm New British Cemetery in Belgium.

**FLOOD, John:** Rank: Lance Corporal. Regiment or Service: Highland Light Infantry. Unit: 10th/11th Battalion. Date of death: 17 August 1918. Service no: 12811. Born in Clara, Co. Offaly. Enlisted in Glasgow. Died of wounds. Date of death is give in 'Ireland's Memorial Records' as 17 August 1917 and in 'Soldiers died in the Great War' and the Commonwealth War Graves Commission as above. Grave or Memorial Reference: Pier and Face 15C. Memorial: Theipval Memorial in France.

**FLYNN, Denis:** Rank: Aircraftman, 2nd Class. Regiment or Service: Royal Air Force. Unit: Fleet Aircraft Depot. Date of death: 17 April 1920. Age at death: 18. Service no: 332123.

*Supplementary information:* Husband of Bridget McDonald (formerly Tooher), of Dromakeenan, Brosna. Grave or Memorial Reference: In the southwest part. Cemetery: Durrow Catholic Churchyard, UK.

**FLYNN, Edward:** Rank: Pte. Regiment or Service: Royal Irish Regiment. Unit: 2nd Battalion. Date of death: 19 September 1914. Service no: 7335. Born in Dublin. Enlisted in Dublin while living in Tullamore, Co. Offaly. Killed in action. From the *King's County Independent*, December 1916:

TULLAMORE SOLDIER.

Prayers were offered up by the congregation at the Masses in the Church of the Assumption, Tullamore on Sunday, for the repose of the soul of Edward Flynn who was a Private in the second Battalion of the Connaught Rangers, and who was called up on the mobilisation at the outbreak of the war. The deceased had been reported as "Missing" since the early days of the campaign, and no definite information could be obtained by his father, Mr John Flynn, as to his whereabouts. It was, however, reported by some of his comrades that he had been killed but there was nothing official to that effect. There no longer seems to be any doubt as to the poor fellow's fate. Deceased was a company commander of the Tullamore Volunteers and was extremely popular. He has a brother still serving with the colours.

He is also listed on the Tullamore Roll of Honour. Grave or Memorial Reference: He has no known grave but is listed on the La Ferte-Sous-Jouarre-Memorial in France.

**FORAN, Patrick:** Rank: Pte. Regiment or Service: Leinster Regiment. Unit: 2nd Battalion. Date of death: 28 May 1915. Service no: 3235. Born in Kilbride, Co. Offaly. Enlisted in Maryborough, Co. Laois. Killed in action. Age at death: 24.

*Supplementary information:* Son of Lawrence and Maria Foran, of Davy's Alley, Kilmalogue, Portarlington, Co.

Offaly. Grave or Memorial Reference: C.16. Cemetery: Ferme Buterne Military Cemetery, Houplines in France.

**FOY, James:** Rank: Pte. Regiment or Service: Black Watch. Unit: 1st Battalion. Date of death: 23 October 1914. Service no: 9454. Born in Tullamore, Co. Offaly. Enlisted in Liverpool, Lancashire. Killed in action. Has no known grave but is commemorated on Panel 37. Memorial: Ypres (Menin Gate) Memorial in Belgium.

**FOY, Thomas:** Rank: Pte. Regiment or Service: Kings Own Scottish Borderers. Unit: 2nd Battalion. Date of death: 1 November 1914. Service no: 8786. Born in Tubberdaly, Co. Offaly. Enlisted in Hamilton, Lanark. Killed in action. Age at death: 28.

*Supplementary information*: Son of Martin and Esther Duffy Foy. Grave or Memorial Reference: He has no known grave but is listed on Panel 23 on the Le Touret Memorial in France.

**FOY, Thomas:** Rank: Pte. Regiment or Service: U.S. Army. Unit: 314th Field Artillery Regiment, 80th Division. Date of death: 13 October 1918. Enlisted from Torresdale, Pennsylvania, USA. Killed in action. From the *King's County Independent*, November 1918:

REGRETTED DEATH.
Much regret was occasioned by the news which was received in Philipstown on Monday of the death

Thomas Foy.

in action in France of Private Thomas Foy, of the United States Army. This young soldier who was a son of Mr Michael Foy. Of Walsh Island, went to America some five years ago, and was succeeding in the land of his adoption until the call went forth to do battle against the Germans. Of a winning disposition and courteous and affable by nature, the deceased possessed the gift of making friends everywhere, and so he is deeply and genuinely regretted by all. With such a promising career before him it is sad to see the young life cut off so suddenly. To his grief stricken parents and to his many friends we tender our deepest sympathy.

Grave or Memorial Reference: Plot H, Row 24, Grave 13. Cemetery: Meuse-Argonne Cemetery, Romagne in France.

**FULTON, James:** Rank: Pte. Regiment or Service: Royal Dublin Fusiliers. Unit: 3rd Battalion. Date of death: 2 February 1915. Service no: 5713. Born in Edenderry, Co. Offaly. Enlisted in Dublin. Died at home. Grave or Memorial Reference:

He is commemorated on the Grangegorman (Cork) Memorial Headstones Spec. Alternative Commemoration – He is buried in Cork Military Cemetery.

**FULTON, Thomas:** Rank: Pte. Regiment or Service: Royal Dublin Fusiliers. Unit: 1st Battalion. Date of death: 11 December 1915. Service no: 5721. Born in Edenderry, Co. Offaly. Enlisted in Stirling while living in Edenderry. Died in Gallipoli.

*Supplementary information*: Son of Thomas and Bridget Fulton, of Blundell Street, Edenderry, Co. Offaly. From the *Leinster Leader*, 22 July 1916:

Private Thomas Fulton Dublin Fusiliers spent a brief holiday with his family in Edenderry from the Tunnel Road. He fought in France and was on the landing group on Suvla Bay and fought against the Bulgarians. Said landing at Suvla Bay was the worst of his experiences and indescribable. A man named Thomas Connor was by his side and they bade each other goodbye when they saw what they were in. there parting was amusing. Connor – Goodbye old man, We'll never get out of this. Fulton – No Begor, Say I, were done for this time Tom. And they shook hands and parted. Connor – goodbye again. When the whole thing was over the 1st person he met was Connor and he said you were not killed then. Fulton replied No were you!

Fulton said that Private Galway a lad that used to work in Hopkins in Edenderry was killed in the landing. They met many Edenderry men at Salonika. He said that the Germans were great fighters and a crack shot.

Grave or Memorial Reference: V.D.168. Cemetery: Portianos Military Cemetry in Greece.

**FURLONG, Thomas:** Rank: Pte. Regiment or Service: Royal Dublin Fusiliers. Unit: 2nd Battalion. Date of death: 1 July 1916. Service no: 18737. Born in Kilbride, Co. Offaly. Enlisted in Dublin while living in Ballydrohid, Co. Offaly. Killed in action.

*Supplementary information:* He is buried beside Tipperary-man Patrick Delaney from Ballingarry who was also killed on the first day of the Battle of the Somme. Patrick was also in the 2nd Bn Royal Dublin Fusiliers, they may have fell side by side. He is also listed on the Tullamore Roll of Honour. Grave or Memorial Reference: I.D.95. Cemetery: Sucrerie Military Cemetery, Colinclamps in France.

# G

**GALWAY, Edward:** Rank: Corporal. Regiment or Service: Royal Dublin Fusiliers. Unit: 6th Battalion. Date of death: 15 August 1915. Service no: 12088. Born in Portarlington, Co. Offaly. Enlisted in Maryborough while living in Street, Co. Westmeath. Killed in action in Gallipoli. Age at death: 39. Supplementary information: Son of the late John and Elizabeth Ann Galway. Served in the South African War. See article in above under **FULTON, Thomas**. Grave or Memorial Reference: He has no known grave but is listed on Panel 190 to 196 on the Helles Memorial in Turkey.

Richard Maurice Brooks Gamble.

**GAMBLE, Richard Maurice Brooks:** Rank: Second Lieutenant. Regiment or Service: King's Liverpool Regiment. Unit: 7th Battalion (Territorial). Date of death: 16 May 1915. Age at death: 22. Killed in action.

*Supplementary information*: Son of Richard Keene Gamble, B.L., J.P., of 51 Fitzwilliam Square, Dublin. From the *King's County Chronicle*, May 1915:

> The death is announced from wounds of Second Lieut. R.M.B. Gamble, 7th King's Liverpool Regiment. He was the eldest son of Mr Richard K.

Gamble, J.P. Killooly, Co. Offaly, and 51 Fitzwilliam Square, President of the Dublin Chamber of Commerce. The young officer received his commission in September, 1914.

From De Ruvigny's Roll of Honour:

> Gamble, Richard Maurice Brooks, 2nd Lieut, 1/7th Battn, King's Liverpool Regt (T.F.). Eldest son of Richard Keene Gamble of 51 Fitzwilliam Square, Dublin, Carriglea, Greystones, Co Wicklow, and Derrinboy House, Kilcormac, Co. Offaly., B.L., J.P., President of the Chamber of

Commerce, Dublin, by his wife, Hannah Maria, daughter of Maurice Brooks, of Oaklawn, County Dublin, J.P., D.L., and godson of the late Richard William Gamble, of Killooly Hall, Co. Offaly, and 51 Fitzwilliam Square, Dublin, Q.C., County Court Judge, Ireland; born at Leeson Park, Dublin, 16 July, 1893. Educated at M. Le Penton's School, Dublin, afterwards at Tonbridge School, Kent, and Trinity College, Dublin, where he had matriculated in Arts and Medicine, and was about to take his degree when war broke out. He was a member of the O.T.C., and immediately volunteered and was gazetted to the Liverpool Regt, 5 Sept, 1914. He went with his regt. to the Front in March, 1915, and was killed in action, when leading his men in an attack on the German trenches at Richbourg, on the night of 15-16 May, 1915 and was buried at the Rue de Bois, half a mile south of Richbourg St. Vaast, with eight brother officers killed in the same attack; *unm.* His Commanding Officer described the circumstances; "We were ordered to take the German trenches. Under heavy fire he led his men with the greatest bravery, and had reached the parapet of the German trenches when he fell with two German under him, death being instantaneous." Lieut. Gamble obtained a silver medal for shooting when ar school in Dublin and was very keen on fishing and shooting.

Grave or Memorial Reference: VIII.B.30. Cemetery: Guards Cemetery, Windy Corner, Cuinchy in France.

**GANNON, John:** Rank: Pte. Regiment or Service: Leinster Regiment. Unit: A Company, 7th Battalion. Date of death: 3 September 1916. Service no: 5071. Born in Kilbride, Co. Offaly. Enlisted in Tullamore, Co. Offaly while living in Tullamore, Co. Offaly. Killed in action.

*Supplementary information*: Son of John and Mary Gannon, of Tullamore. Husband of Bridget Gannon, of Magazine, Tullamore. Grave or Memorial Reference: III.M.6. Cemetery: Delville Wood Cemetery, Longueval in France.

**GANNON, William:** Rank: Pte. Regiment or Service: Leinster Regiment. Unit: 2nd Battalion. Date of death: 1 September 1916. Service no: 10095. Born in Birr, Co. Offaly. Enlisted in Birr, Co. Offaly. Killed in action. From the *King's County Chronicle*, February 1916, 'The late Mr Philip Gannon, Pound Street, a former bus driver of Egan's Hotel, has two sons serving: Private James, 1st batt, Leinsters, who was out in India and came home with that battalion to proceed to France, where he was wounded. He is again on active service in the Near East. Private William, 2nd Battalion Leinsters, is on active service in France.' From the *King's County Chronicle*, November 1917, 'Private James Gannon, 2nd Leinsters, has arrived on a well earned furlough. This is his third leave from the front, and, although he has been in severe hardships, he looks in the pink of condition. A brother, Private William, of the same Regt., was killed over a year ago. Their father was the late Mr Philip Gannon, of Pound Street, Birr.' Grave or Memorial Reference: Pier and Face 16 C. on the Thiepval Memorial in France.

**GARRETT, Henry:** Rank: Pte. Regiment or Service: Leinster Regiment. Unit: 3rd Battalion. Date of death: 18 January 1915. Service no: 8282. Born in Clara, Co. Offaly. Enlisted in Tullamore, Co. Offaly. Died at Home. From the *King's County Chronicle*, January 1915: 'A verdict of death from heart failure was returned at an inquest on Monday on Private H. Garrett, 3rd Batt, Leinster Regiment, who was found unconscious on the floor of the dormitory at Cork Barracks, and died within an hour.' Grave or Memorial Reference: He is commemorated on the Grangegorman (Cork) Memorial Headstones Spec. Memorial. Alternative Commemoration – He is buried in Cork Military Cemetery.

**GEORGE, Frederick Ralph:** Rank: Lieutenant. Regiment or Service: Connaught Rangers. Unit: 1st Battalion. Date of death: 5 November 1914. Killed in action. From the *King's County Chronicle*, March 1915, 'Lieut F.R. George, Connaught Rangers, and formerly of Ballyburley, Co. Offaly, killed in action, left estate valued at £12,573. He bequeathed his swords and personal effects to his sister May. £500 each to Judge and Mrs R Wakely. £333 to each of their three daughters,

and all other property to his uncle, J.F. George, for life, with remainder equally between his sisters and brothers.' From De Ruvigny's Roll of Honour:

> *George, Frederick Ralph,* Lieut and Adjutant, 1st Battn. (88th Foot) The Connaught Rangers. Son of the late Barry George. Born Mountshannon House, Co. Clare, 9 September 1883. Educated at Abbey School, Tipperary and Trinity College, Dublin. Was gazetted 2nd Lieut, Connaught Rangers, 13 Jan, 1906, and promoted Lieut, 2 Jan, 1909 being appointed Adjutant in June, 1914. Served in the European War, and was killed in action 5 Nov, 1914, during a bayonet attack.

Grave or Memorial Reference: II.A.2. Cemetery: Rue-Du-Bacquerot No 1 Military Cemetery, Laventie in France.

**GERAGHTY, Columb:** Rank: Pte. Regiment or Service: Manchester Regiment. Unit: 7th Reserve Battalion. Date of death: 8 August 1918. Service no: 5435. Born in Daroll, Co. Offaly. Enlisted in Manchester while living in Dublin. Died at Home. Grave or Memorial Reference: 19. 4. Cemetery: St Peter-in-Thanet Churchyard, UK.

**GERAGHTY/GERAHTY, Denis:** Rank: Lance Corporal. Regiment or Service: Machine Gun Corps. Unit: Infantry. Date of death: 13 April 1918. Service no: 45282. Formerly he was with the Connaught Rangers where his number was 6996. Born in Tedmonagha, Co. Offaly. Killed in action.

*Supplementary information*: 'Ireland's Memorial Records' and 'Soldiers died in the Great War' gives name as **GERAGHTY, Denis** and the Commonwealth War Graves Commission as **GERAHTY, Denis.** Grave or Memorial Reference: III.H.780. Cemetery: Meteren Military Cemetery in France.

**GIBSON, David:** Rank: Pte. Regiment or Service: Royal Irish Regiment. Unit: 2ⁿᵈ Bn. Age at death: 35. Date of death: 16 August 1918. Service no: 9922. Born in Tipperary and enlisted in Roscrea. Died.

*Supplementary information*: Son of John and Selina Gibson, of Ballybritt, Roscrea, Co. Tipperary. From the *King's County Chronicle*, 1918:

AGHANCON.

It is with deep regret Aghancon learned the sad news of the death of Private David Gibson, of the Royal Irish Regiment, whilst a prisoner of war in Germany. The tidings came as a very great shock to his widowed mother, who, now that hostilities have ceased, was looking forward to her son's homecoming. We at Aghancon offer to Mrs Gibson our combined sympathy in her great sorrow.

Grave or Memorial Reference: V.F.25. Cemetery: Valenciennes (St Roch) Communal Cemetery in France.

**GIBSON, William:** Rank: Pte. Regiment or Service: Irish Guards. Unit: 1ˢᵗ Battalion. Date of death: 9 October 1917. Service no: 10013. Born in Killeigh, Co. Offaly. Enlisted in Portarlington, Co. Laois. Killed in action. Age at death: 22.

*Supplementary information:* Son of Michael Gibson, of Cloneyquin, Portarlington, Co. Offaly. Grave or Memorial Reference: Has no known grave but is commemorated on Panel 10 and 11. Memorial: Tyne Cot Memorial in Belgium.

**GILL, Thomas Patrick:** Rank: Pte. Regiment or Service: Royal Irish Regiment. Unit: 2ⁿᵈ Battalion. Date of death: 20 July 1918. Service no: 11511. Born in Edenderry, Co. Offaly. Enlisted in Tullamore, Co. Offaly while living in Edenderry, Co. Offaly. Killed in action. Age at death: 31.

*Supplementary information*: Son of James and Margaret Gill (*née* McCabe), of New Row, Edenderry, Co. Offaly. Grave or Memorial Reference: Has no known grave but is commemorated on Panel 30 and 31. Memorial: Pozieres Memorial in France.

**GILLIGAN, Patrick:** Rank: Pte. Regiment or Service: Royal Dublin Fusiliers. Unit: 8ᵗʰ Battalion. Date of death: 5 April 1916. Service no: 16593 and 8/16593. Born in Gallen, Ferbane, Co. Offaly. Enlisted in Birr, Co. Offaly while living in Gallen, Ferbane. Killed in action. Age at death: 34.

*Supplementary information*: Son of Owen Gilligan, J.P. and Kate Gilligan. From the *King's County Independent*, April 1916:

It was with deep regret his relatives and acquaintances became aware of the death of Patrick Gilligan, late of Galle, Ferbane, who was killed in action in France on the 5th Inst. Deceased was son of the Late Mr Owen Gilligan, J.P, Gallen, Ferbane. Some eighteen months ago he volunteered for service in the Dublin Fusiliers, and has been in the trenches since last December. He undoubtedly had a calling for "The Soldiers Life" as early in his youth he made "The Wild Boy's Escape" and joined the Irish Guards, from which regiment his father bought him out a year subsequently.

On the appearance of the Volunteers he was prominent being in charge of the Belmont Volunteers, then almost the largest contingent in the county. His popularity amongst all classes was unequalled as is the feeling of regret he leaves behind. The captain of his battalion writes thus to his brother; "I am able to say that his death was absolutely instantaneous, and he probably felt no pain. A cross was erected over his grave, and his friends put up a small memorial in the trench where he met his death. I knew your brother from the first day he joined, and always had a great admiration for him. His loss was deeply felt in the company, for he had many friends, and was popular with everybody. I wish there were more like him. He was a fine man, and met with a soldier's death."

Such was the impression of his captain, which shows that he was carried to his last end the cheerful, witty, good-natured disposition which made him so deeply regretted at home. His many comrades and acquaintances recognise the great blow which his brothers and sister have sustained, and tender their sincere sympathy.

Grave or Memorial Reference: He has no known grave but is listed on the Special Memorial 9 in Bois-Carre Military Cemetery in France.

**GILMORE, John:** Rank: Sapper. Regiment or Service: Corps of Royal Engineers. Date of death: 28 October 1918. Service no: 23458. Formerly he was with the Leinster Regiment (5th Div.Signal Coy, R. E.) where his number was 8660. Born in Birr, Co. Offaly. Enlisted in Birr, Co. Offaly. Died. Age at death: 30.

*Supplementary information:* Son of Andrew and Mary Gilmore, of 30 Stanley Street, Foleshill, Coventry. Native of Birr. Co. Offaly. From the *King's County Chronicle*, June 1915:

According to a letter which found its way through the enemy's lines, to a friend in Birr and sent by Private John Gilmore, of the Royal Engineers, the lot of captives, like himself, in Germany is far from being a happy one. This young soldier, who had the misfortune of falling into their hands, writes that the prisoners are insufficiently fed and are forced to work like convicts. His father was formerly in the employment of Dooly's Hotel, and he himself worked for a time in the "King's County Chronicle" Office.

Grave or Memorial Reference: IX.G.9. Cemetery: Cologne Southern Cemetery in Germany.

**GLEESON, Patrick:** Rank: Pte. Regiment or Service: Leinster Regiment. Unit: 1st Battalion. Date of death: 14 February 1915. Service no: 3487. Born in Birr, Co. Offaly. Enlisted in Birr, Co. Offaly. Killed in action. From the *King's County Chronicle*, March 1916, 'Private Patrick Gleeson, 1st Leinsters, son of the late Mr Philip Gleeson, High Street, was reported missing in February 1915. His mother would be grateful for any news concerning him.' Grave or Memorial Reference: He has no known grave but is listed on Panel 44 on the Ypres (Menin Gate) Memorial in Belgium.

**GLENNON, Patrick:** Rank: Pte. Regiment or Service: Royal Dublin Fusiliers. Unit: 2nd Battalion. Date of death: 21 March 1918. Service no: 19364. Born in Lucan, Co. Dublin. Enlisted in Maryborough while living in Kilcormack, Co. Offaly. Killed in action. Grave or Memorial Reference: II.B.2. Cemetery: Unicorn Cemetery, Vend'huile in France.

**GOLDING, James:** Rank: Pte. Regiment or Service: 1st County of London Yeomanry (Middlesex Yeomanry). Date of death: 2 November 1918. Enlisted in Shoreditch while living in Finsbury. Service no: 260927. Died at Home. From the *King's County Chronicle*,

November 1918, 'Birr. Private Golding, of the Middlesex Yeomanry, who had been ailing for some weeks, died in the Military Hospital, and was buried in the cemetery at Crinkle with full military honours on Tuesday.' Grave or Memorial Reference: 45. Cemetery: Birr Military Cemetery, Co. Offaly.

**GORMAN, Daniel:** Rank: Gunner. Regiment or Service: Royal Garrison Artillery. Unit: 19th Siege Battery. Date of death: 28 March 1918. Service no: 177326. Born in Shinrone, Co. Offaly. Enlisted in Coalville while living in Nuneaton. Killed in action. Grave or Memorial Reference: Has no known grave but is commemorated on Panel 10. Memorial: Pozieres Memorial in France.

**GORMAN, James:** Rank: Pte. Regiment or Service: Leinster Regiment. Unit: 7th Battalion. Date of death: 3 September 1916. Service no: 5081. Born in Tullamore, Co. Offaly. Enlisted in Dundee, Forfar while living in Dundee. Killed in action.

*Supplementary information*: Listed as John in 'Ireland's Memorial Records' and James in 'Soldiers died in the Great War' and the Commonwealth war Graves Commission. From the *King's County Chronicle*, June 1916:

The Gorman family is one of the many in Tullamore which maintains a fine military record for sending men to the fighting line – Private James Gorman, Royal Irish Regiment, is the eldest son of Mrs Ellen Gorman, Kevin Street, Tullamore, who has three sons, two brothers, two sons-in-law, and cousins and other relatives now serving in the army. James was on the Reserve at the commencement of the war; he was wounded and taken prisoner at the battle of Mons. Private John Gorman, 1st Leinsters, was stationed in India, returned to England with the Indian contingent, and was sent to the front in France, where he was frost-bitten in the foot. He was allowed home on leave, and afterwards returned to France from which he was sent to Salonika.

He is serving in the machine-gun section. Piper Patrick Gorman, 2nd Connaughts, served 14 months in the trenches in France, was wounded in the leg and invalided home. He is 22 years of age, and prior to enlistment in August, 1914, was a member of the Trade and Labour Band. He is now a Piper in the band of his regiment at Kinsale, Co Cork. Private Joseph Hickey, 3rd Leinsters, and Private Michael Hickey, 4th Leinsters, are Mrs Gorman's brothers. The former has had 19 years service in the regiment; and the latter had seven years service in the militia. Both are serving at the front. Sergt. Alfred Smith and Private Jack Sweeney, 5th Lancers, are both sons-in-law of this worthy Irish matron, and have been gallantly serving their King and Country in France.

The former, and Englishman, has been wounded and is now at home in hospital. Mrs Gorman was the daughter of a brave soldier, who served 21 years with the colours, and she is proud of her gallant sons, and also to have so many of her kith and kin each manfully bearing his part in the great war.

Private J. Gorman, 3rd Leinsters, would rank with the veterans. Grey-haired, and too old now for service he is reminiscent, and smiles as he passes – a friendly smile – over the heroes names. Amongst them are those of his own brave boys in whom he feels paternal pride. But are his own few words not worthy of notice now? They are; they refer no doubt to a time now long passed away in the hurry and tragedy of the great war now on; but they are valuable all the same as showing how one generation after another has played a signal part in the wars of the Empire. In 1874, a force in which was numbered, 30,000 strong, was mobilised in Portsmouth, Gosport, and Chatham – ex-Private Gorman says they were all Irish soldiers.

Those were the days of the "Eastern Question" and Lord Beaconsfield was attending the Berlin Conference and striving to "Peace with Honour", The Duke of Cambridge, Commander-in-Chief, inspected the men, and asked whether any of them had any grievance of which to complain, or any objection to leave on active service, some of them being presumably volunteers from Militia battalions. Not a single man demurred – all were ready.

"We were a fine body of men", said ex- Private Gorman, with a gleam of honest pride in remembrance of his comrades, "I was 5 feet 7½ inches, and the smallest man on parade; the Duke declared he was proud of us and that he had never seen a finer lot of men together before; forty of us were from this town of Tullamore that day, and now all are passed away except one who remains here still – and myself.

He is also listed on the Tullamore Roll of Honour. Grave or Memorial Reference: He has no known grave but is listed in Pier and Face 16C on the Thiepval Memorial in France.

**GORRY, Michael:** Rank: Pte. Regiment or Service: Leinster Regiment. Unit: 2nd Battalion. Date of death: 30 September 1916. Service no: 4379. Born in Tullamore, Co. Offaly. Enlisted in Birr, Co. Offaly. Killed in action.

*Supplementary information:* Son of Michael Francis Gorry, of Harbour Street, Tullamore. From the *King's County Independent*, September 1916:

KILLED IN ACTION.

Mr M.F. Gorry, Newsagent, Tullamore received intelligence during the week that his son, Private M. Gorry, of the Leinster Regiment, had been killed in action in France on the 30th September. The late Private Gorry, whose elder brother is in the R.A.M.C., joined the Leinsters in January, 1915, and took part in the severe fighting during the winter of that year, and the spring of the present year, when he became a victim to shell shock, and was for several weeks in hospital. Having recovered he was granted a short furlough in April, to see his parents of whom he was a favourite. Shortly after his return to his unit he was sent back to the front. He had been all through the heavy fighting which took place during the months of July, August and September and on the 30th of the last named month was mortally wounded. Deep sympathy is felt for Mr Gorry in his bereavement for his son, who was only 19.

From the *King's County Chronicle*, September 1917:

Private Joseph Gorry, R.A.M.C., son of Mr Michael Gorry, newsagent, Church Street, Tullamore, is spending a few days leave at his home and finds his popularity in his native town in pre-war days has not waned. He is a very smart young soldier, of whom his parents are justly proud, and is a favourite with everyone of his acquaintance. His younger brother, Michael, joined the Leinster Regiment, and was killed in action a year ago.

From the *King's County Chronicle*, October 1917:

IN MEMORIUM.

In remembrance of Michael Gorry, Jnr, Tullamore, killed in action in France on 30th Sept, 1916, aged 19 years.

If we were near to raise your head.

Or hear his last farewell,

The blow would not have been so hard

To those he loved so well

Inserted by his loving father, Michael F. Gorry.

He is also listed on the Tullamore Roll of Honour. Grave or Memorial Reference: IV.A.3. Cemetery: Villers Station Cemetery, Villers-Au-Bois, Pas-De-Calais, in France.

**GRAVES, Gordon:** Rank: Sergeant. Regiment or Service: Royal Dublin Fusiliers. Unit: 2nd Battalion. Date of death: 21 March 1918. Service no: 27012. Born in Killdeas, County Fermanagh. Enlisted in Dublin while living in Birr, Co. Offaly. Killed in action. Age at death: 35.

*Supplementary information*: Son of Francis Graves, of Enniskillen, Co. Fermanagh. Husband of Annie Turner (formerly Graves), of Mill Cottages, Kilmaine, Fortel, Birr. Enlisted in 1916 from R.I.C. Grave or Memorial Reference: Panel 79 and 80. Memorial: Pozieres Memorial in France.

**GREENE, Patrick:** Rank: Pte. Regiment or Service: Royal Inniskilling Fusiliers. Unit: 8th Battalion. Date of death: 29 April 1916. Age at death: 19. Service no: 26171. Formerly he was with the Royal Dublin Fusiliers where his number was 15069. Born in Limerick, Co. Limerick. Enlisted in Tullamore, Co. Offaly. Died of wounds.

*Supplementary information:* Son of Thomas and Mary Greene, of Charleville Road, Tullamore, Co. Offaly. Grave or Memorial Reference: He has no known grave but is listed on Panel 60 on the Loos Memorial in France.

**GRENNAN/GREENAN, Samuel:** Rank: Pte. Regiment or Service: Royal Inniskilling Fusiliers. Unit: 1st Battalion. Date of death: 22 August 1915. Service no: 9763. Born in Tubber, Co. Offaly. Enlisted in Athlone. Killed in action in Gallipoli.

*Supplementary information:* Brother of Edward Grennan, of Sheeane, Cloughabanny, Clara, Co. Offaly. Grave or Memorial Reference: He has no known grave but is listed on the Helles Memorial on Panel 97 to 101.

**GRESSON, John Edward:** Rank: Second Lieutenant. Regiment or Service: Cheshire Regiment. Unit: 3rd Battalion attached to the 2nd Battalion. Date of death: 24 May 1915. Killed in action. From the *King's County Chronicle*, June 1915:

Another Birr man has laid down his life in this unparalleled war, the heroic victim being Lieut John. E. Gresson, 2nd Batt, Cheshire Regt, youngest son of the late Major W. H. Gresson, who, afetr his service in the old 65th regiment, resided for a number of years in Woodville, Birr, the house now in the possession of Mr T. Roberts Garvey, and where the deceased was born 34 years ago. His widowed mother, who mourns the sad loss, has been living in Fernleigh, Cheltenham, and it is the merest truth to add that deep sympathy is felt by all her friends in our community.

Grave or Memorial Reference: Has no known grave but is commemorated on Panel 19-22 on the Ypres (Menin Gate) Memorial in Belgium.

**GUINAN, Michael:** Rank: Pte. Regiment or Service: Leinster Regiment. Unit: 2nd Battalion. Date of death: 2 September 1916. Service no: 7817. Born in Ballinadown, Co. Offaly. Enlisted in Birr. Killed in action. From the *King's County Chronicle*, February 1916, 'Three sons of the late Mr Michael Guinan, of Woodville, Birr, are now serving with the colours – Privates Terence, Michael and Jack, all of the 2nd Leinsters, are now on active service.' Grave or Memorial Reference: Has no known grave but is commemorated on Pier and Face 16 C. Memorial: Thiepval Memorial in France.

# H

**HACKETT, Eric Adrian Nethercote:** Rank: Second Lieutenant. Regiment or Service: Royal Irish Regiment. Unit: 6th Battalion. Formerly he was with the Munster Fusiliers. He won the Military Cross and is listed in the *London Gazette*. Date of death: 24 April 1918. Age at death: 21.

*Supplementary information:* Born in Molbrooke, Clonmel, Co. Tipperary, 6 August 1895. Killed in action at Ginchy. Son of Edward A. and Emilie Elliott Hackett, of Castletown Park, Ballycumber. Educated at All Hallows School, Honiton, Devon. (O.T.C.). Killed in action. From the *King's County Chronicle*, September 1916, 'Sec-Lieut. Eric Adrian Nethercote Hackett, Royal Irish Regiment, aged twenty one years, who has been killed in action, was the second son of Mr E.A. Hackett, M.E., M. Inst. C.E., of Clonmel, and grandson of the late Mr Thomas Hackett, J.P., Castletown, Ballycumber, Co. Offaly.' From the *King's County Chronicle*, October 1916, 'On September 9, Sec Lt. Eric Adrian Nethercote Hackett, aged 21 years, second son of Edward H. and Emily Hackett, Poulavanogue, Clonmel, and grandson of the late Thomas Hackett, Esq., J.P., Castletown, Ballycumber, King's County, was killed in action.'

Grave or Memorial Reference: Has no known grave but is commemorated on Pier and Face 3A. Memorial: Theipval Memorial in France. He also has a memorial inscription with the family graves in Liss Cemetery.

**HACKETT, Learo Aylmer Henry:** Rank: Captain (TP). Regiment or Service: Royal Irish Rifles. Unit: 10th Battalion. Formerly he was with the Munster Fusiliers. He won the Military Cross and is listed in the *London Gazette*. Date of death: 24 April 1918. Killed in action.

*Supplementary information:* Born in Estcourt, Natal, South Africa on 22 June 1884. Son of Edward A. and Emilie Elliott Hackett of Castletown, Ballycumber, Co. Offaly. Killed in action. From the *King's County Chronicle*, May 1918, 'Captain L.A.H. Hackett, M.C.R.I. Rifles, was killed in action on 24th April. He was the eldest and only surviving son of Mr E.A. Hackett, C.S., Clonmel, and grandson of the late Mr Thomas Hackett, J.P., Castle Armstrong, King's County. His brother, Lieutenant Eric Hackett, was killed in action in Sept, 1916.' Grave reference: III.A.7. Buried in Minty Farm Cemetery in Belgium. He also has a memorial inscription with the family graves in Liss Cemetery.

**HACKETT, Venice Clementine Henrietta:** Rank: (Miss) Nurse. Regiment or Service: Voluntary Aid Detachment attached to the British Red Cross Society. Date of death: 13 October 1918. Died. This is one of the very few occasions when a woman is recorded in 'Officers died in the Great War'. It gives her name as **HACKETT, Venice Clementina**.

*Supplementary information:* Daughter of Edward A. Hackett and Emilie Hackett, of Castletown Park, Ballycumber. Venice Hackett was a member of the Voluntary Aid Detachment and was one of the victims on the M.V. *Leinster*. This mail boat was torpedoed and sunk by a German submarine. She is also recorded as having died of pneumonia in London, returning from France. 'Ireland's Memorial Records' gives her place of birth as Scotland. She had three brothers who were also killed in the First World War. As far as I can ascertain only two of her brothers were killed in First World War the other brother, who died in 1915 in Clonmel was Edward Fawcett Hackett and was sixteen years old when he died. She is listed in Officers Died in the Great War. Grave or Memorial Reference: In southwest part. Cemetery: Ballycumber (Liss) Churchyard, Co. Offaly.

**HARPUR, Edward Percival H.:** Rank: Lieutenant. Regiment or Service: Royal Irish Rifles. Unit: 7th Battalion. Officers died in the Great War and 'Ireland's Memorial Records' give his unit as Royal Irish Rifles and the Commonwealth War Graves Commission gives his unit as the Royal Irish Fusiliers. Date of death: 11 September 1916. Born in Tullamore. Fell in Action ('Ireland's Memorial Records'). Died of Wounds (Officers Died in the Great War). Age at death: 24/25.

*Supplementary information*: Son of the Revd William and Mrs Harpur, of 'Wavecrest', Vico Road, Dalkey. Husband of Eileen Harpur, of 3 Idrone Terrace, Blackrock, Co. Dublin. Grave or Memorial Reference: II.C.70. Cemetery: La-Neuville British Cemetery, Corbie in France.

**HARTE, William:** Rank: Pte. Regiment or Service: Loyal North Lancashire Regiment. Unit: 2/4th Battalion (Territorial Force). Date of death: 8 October 1918. Service no: 31040. Formerly he was with the East Lancashire Regiment where his number was 40497. Born in Clonavoe, Co. Offaly. Enlisted in Fleetwood, Lancashire while living in Clonavoe. Died of wounds. Age at death: 37. Grave or Memorial Reference: XIII.E.5. Cemetery: Cologne Southern Cemetery in Germany.

**HARTE, William:** Rank: Pte. Regiment or Service: Leinster Regiment. Unit: 6th Battalion. Date of death: 31 December 1915. Service no: 3133. Born in Philipstown, Co. Offaly. Enlisted in Maryborough, Co. Laois. Died of wounds at home. From the *King's County Independent*, September 1915:

WOUNDED.

Much regret was felt in Philipstown when the news was received there during the week that Private William Hart, of the Leinsters (nephew of Mr P.J. Hart, R.D.C.), was seriously wounded during an engagement in the Dardanelles, and is at present in an hospital in England. Before the war started Private Hart was making a good living at his trade as a tailor, but he threw all up to fight for the Empire.

Although the writer of the following newspaper article was not from Offaly, I include it for your reference simply because as was in the 6th Battalion Leinster Regiment. The information would be relevant to the experiences Pte Harte/Hart who was in the same unit. From the *Midland Tribune*, *Tipperary Sentinel* and *King's County Vindicator* quoting an article in the *Westmeath Examiner* September 1915:

In Gallipoli: Sixth Leinsters Officers vivid story.

In the course of a lengthy letter, dated September 2nd, an officer of the Sixth Leinsters, 10th Division, native of Mullingar, at present invalided at Lady Strangford Hospital, Port Said, says: "I was sent here four days ago, and I am still here trying to get right again. I got ill, and was taken on board the hospital ship, had a four days run to Alexandria, and then an eight hours run here by train. I am now in bed, and feeling anything but well, I wonder have you seen the losses in the papers? Our Colonel was wounded also major Stannds [?], Captain Parke and Little. Those killed included Captain Darcy, Lieutenant Goff, Figgis and Griffiths who lived next to me in the Curragh, and Hickson. Before we got reinforced there were only two officers left to each company, and those losses all occurred practically in the one day.

The 10th Hampshire Regiment (which was in Mullingar last winter and spring) had only one officer left, and the Irish Rifles only three officers left. We went through the devils own time, but I came through safely. Griffiths was killed beside me with shrapnel just as he and I had finished tea. I escaped with a piece being taken out of the rim of my helmet by a bomb whilst making an attack at night. The man beside me had his head taken off. We proceeded to take him in, but he just asked to be "left there to die." Two sergeants I had were wounded. Young Gill was hit, I think pretty badly, and poor Nicholas Smyth was killed by the same shell that killed Griffiths. Nicholas and Alec Little were lying together in the same dug-out. Alec told me that Nicholas said "I am hit" and lay still. Alec Little is a member of the Lynn family and was at school at St Mary's with me. I was transferred to – Company, as all the officers in it had been killed. I made particular enquiries about young Dan Flood, and learned that he got hit in the arm and leg, but that neither wound was serious. He is in some hospital now.

There is always work to be done, and then you never can escape from the eternal noise of shrapnel and high explosives. You are always under fire, but you soon get used to that. I asked a sergeant who had received seven wounds in France whilst serving with our first Battalion what he thought of Anzac. He told me France was only child's play to this. He found it so, poor chap, for he was killed that night. I often thank God that I am a Catholic. One night I met an Australian Priest on the hillside. He came and sat beside me, and heard my confession and asked the Little Flower to take me under her protection. I have somehow felt that I could come through all right. I heard the Turks jabbering as hard as they could before we came up with them. I told you it fairly make one ill to hear their shout as they approach "Allah, Allah!" the sound of their voices increasing as they came nearer and prepare to charge. The effect at night is very weird. I often wished I were seated again by the fireside, with my feet on the fender, and friends around me. However you get used to everything in time, and you become surprised that you can keep so cool when you want to keep your men well in hand. You forget yourself altogether, and walk about as if it were an everyday occurrence.

I suppose all our training would be of very little use if the result were not like that. I may as well confess I was fearful as to how I would stick under fire for the first time. I am glad the result has been satisfactory. It is wonderful careless and indifferent one is inclined to become even after a very short time. Looking back now, it seems brutally callous. You see sights and, I was going to say smell sights-that if I had seen at home at one time would have made me sick. But out here you can't help getting used to all these things. The biggest fright and the most awful, I hope, I will ever get, was when, one night, hurrying into the darkness, I tripped and fell over a dead Turk! He was about the size of three men, for he had been there over a week, and I can assure you he was "ripe." I came down bash on him; my fingers disappeared –ugh! I can't tell you anymore, except that I fled, and I think I hadn't a bit of skin left on my fingers for two whole days. I felt myself 'high' also. The night poor Griffiths was killed he and I asked a New Zealand Captain to tea. The Captain kindly consented, and brought some condensed milk with him. We were grateful for the milk, as we hadn't any since we landed. After tea Griffiths stood up, and the New Zealander was writing some notes. I was between the two, finishing a dog biscuit, when a shell burst, and the fingers of the New Zealander's hands were taken off, his blood sprinkling my trousers.

The shell went over me and hit Griffith, killing him. If Little Flower ever saved anyone she saved me. Just before that shell came the New Zealander officer and I found that we were both Catholics. He was after coming down the hill and we were going up. He said to me, "I am not religious, but I have an aunt in a convent and she prays for me. She asked me before I left home to always say – "My Jesus mercy." I have said it all day, otherwise I would not have been alive now. I saw men being killed all round me. The white patch on my knee is a man's brain; my tunic is covered with the blood of another." While being carried down to the beach the captain called me and asked me not to forget the little prayer he had spoken to me about. He also said that if he had not said it the shell would have killed him. As the stretcher bearers carried him away he told me to keep the condensed milk as he would not require it. If it hadn't been for the tin of milk we probably would not have asked him to tea. You see how even a tin of milk may be responsible for one man's life, and may put an end to another soldier's career.

I mention these few little incidents, thinking that they may interest you. Sometimes, too, even amid all the horrors of war, one sees humorous things. I was in the trench one day when a tall young Irish boy was having a doze. As I came along someone must have nudged him, for he stood up to yawn. At the same time a shrapnel burst over him, and the young fellow was so frightened that he could not close his mouth. I had to send him off to the doctor to get his mouth shut. Where we are now is a very nice place. There is a very large window opening on a veranda, and then about twenty yards of sand to the sea. I think if people could only realise how many thousands of somebody's boys are lying on the hard ground through-out the night listening to the thud of the machine guns and the angry bark of the snipers rifle, they would oftener pray to God for the dying and the dead, and those whose tomorrow may be to-day. I heard one fellow talk in admiration of a tiny revolver which another fellow showed him. They were privates. The owner of the revolver tapped the butt of it insignificantly saying, perhaps the stretcher-bearers may leave him wounded and without water. He put the revolver back carefully into its holster. Two things struck me about that remark.

The first was, how utterly inca-pable the majority of religions are of teaching their followers that we are not masters of our own lives, and that we cannot take away what does not belong to us. The second thought was how wonderfully fear-less of death some men are and that as long as a country has such men she can dare anything. One ques-tion I would like answered, and it is this: at the supreme moment do men of this type not fear, and again, if they do kill themselves are they not mad with pain? The incident set me thinking, and I wondered at the complexity of man's nature. On the other hand, I have seen men, hundreds of them, with their rosaries around their necks, for the majority here go in "glad-neck" style, no coat, or collar, just a shirt, trousers, rifle and ammunition, not forgetting the most important of all, the water bottle. Those who wear their brown rosary are every bit as brave and as dauntless as those who carry the revolver to get rid of the pain – I should have said a million times more so, for the one is a coward and fears the pain, although in his ignorance he may believe he is doing his best. The other hangs on his rosary, and although in torture, he clings to it all the while. You see a poor broken form pass by on a stretcher. I have seen the poor sufferer's hands flutter feebly towards his neck, and I know that he is looking to what is stronger than pain and death, and that is the faith in his Rosary.

It was only the night before I was sent down to the beach that a poor chap who was up with me in the trenches was shot dead. I had just left my spot in the trenches and had come out of my dug-out, when I was sent for. The poor fellow had leaned back in the very spot I had left. A bullet had gone through his temple passing out behind his ear. I can see the lantern glimmering as the doctor bends over him; and then, turning to me tells me death has been instantaneous. It was my duty to get the dead man's pay book and anything else that was in his possession. Around the poor fellow's neck was his scapulars, and beads, which I also took charge of, thinking that perhaps some day I might meet his poor mother and have the satisfaction of handing them to her. Ah me! When I think of the hundred and one little things that have happened, I think God has been very good to me, and I have a lot to thank the 'Little Flower' for. Don't fret for me, as I will turn up all right. The doctor has just been in – he is an Irishman – from Tipperary. He asked me if I thought I would able to 'stand a winter in Gallipoli'."

From the *Midland Tribune*, *Tipperary Sentinel* and *King's County Vindicator* quoting an article in the *Westmeath Examiner* written by a Private, September 1915:

THE DARDANELLES:-EXPERIENCES WITH THE SIXTH LEINSTERS.
Private Joseph Kelly of the Sixth Leinsters, who has just returned from the Dardanelles, interviewed by a "Westmeath Examiner" correspondent, told a thrilling story of the life-and-death struggle that is being waged at the Dardanelles. He spoke of the bravery and heroism of the Irish soldiers with modesty, but he is warm in his praise of the Irish Catholic Chaplains attached to the Brigade.

Private Kelly joined the army on the 17th August, 1914, a few weeks after the outbreak of the war. The Leinsters, with the Munsters and the Dublins, which go to make up part of the 10th and 29th Division of the Irish Brigade, were landed at the Dardanelles in June. Private Speaks of the landing with pride and wonder, as they had to fight their way from the very waters edge. His Battalion did not suffer so severely as the Munsters, Dublins, and Australians, as these three whole Battalions were cut to pieces while landing.

The first thing that struck the soldier, was the nature of the country. "It is all covered with sandy hills." Immediately on landing they got into the firing, and into action at once. The Turks, he said, are all big men, and when about to charge they roar like lions, but once faced with cold steel they became quiet enough, and all of them who do not "bite the earth" steal back like mice.

"I was eleven weeks" says Kelly "in the firing line before I was knocked out. It was fighting most of the time, but out there you get used to it." "We were very lucky at landing, as we only lost two men. We may thank the big guns on the battleships for that, as they completely dominate the Turkish Artillery. But once we landed the enemy had the range on us, and our only chance was to start work at once. The attacks out there last day and night. I was in an engagement that lasted 36 hours; my shoulder was stiff at the end, but I did not mind. We had no trenches to take cover in, only as we entrenched ourselves, or succeeded in putting the Turks out of theirs. The only protection we had was a piece of head-covering. The gullies and trenches that we capture always conceal snipers; one gully in particular was lined with them. On the first Sunday in harvest I was at the capture of a woman sniper. The Turkish women are better snipers than the men."

"We had some terrible fighting in Shroudray Valley and at the taking of Chocolate Hill. We advanced from 'Dead Man's Drop,' and carried the position across 'Dead Man's Ridge.' We were in the advanced lines, and were supported by the Irish Rifles, the East Lancashires and the Hants, as well as by the Australians and Gurkas. You can tell that all those regiments showed great bravery and are wonderful fighters, but I think it is no harm to say that when a position has been won the Irish regiments are depended on as the men and the hardest fighters certainly."

"The Gurkas are terrible fighters. They simply know no fear, and are as swift as greyhounds. They always want to fight alongside the Leinsters or some other Irish Regiment. In the capture of one of the hills the Gurkas outdistanced the Australians by 150 yards. The Australians are great fighters, but not so terrible as the swift and silent Gurkas. The Australians like to get the honour of winning a position, but always look to the Irish to maintain it."

"The Germans are doing very little of the hard fighting out there. The Turks have to do more of the 'spade work.' And the Germans try to come in for the 'rakings'.

The Turks are not at all satisfied, and many of them captured as prisoners say; 'England very good; Germany no good'."

"I would like to say as to the great heroism displayed by the Catholic chaplain, father Fahy, of Castlecomer, who was attached to the 29 Division. He was everywhere almost in the thick of the fight, encouraging and succouring the wounded and dying. It was in the taking of hill 971 the Irish regiments advanced with a wild cheer at 5 o clock in the morning, that I met Father Fahy, and he was singing – 'Here again, we're Irishmen, I'm from Castlecomer'."

"The officers, as well as all the men, held this brave priest in the greatest admiration. This heroic priest was cut in two while administering the last sacrament to a dying soldier. Our Battalion consisted of 1, 150 men, and about 600 of us were knocked out. I was wounded in the hip, shoulder and breast with bullets on the 10th of August."

"On the same day, our officer, Colonel Craske, was wounded, while Lieutenant Figgis was killed, also Lieut Hickson. We were holding Hill 793 against overwhelming odds. We held the position until we were reinforced by the Connaughts and other regiments. I was after being removed as the Connaught Rangers were going up singing."

From the *Midland Tribune*, *Tipperary Sentinel* and *King's County Vindicator*, November 1915:

Experiences in the Dardanelles – Lance Corporal B. Gill of the Sixth Leinster Regiment, writing from Bombay General Hospital, Alexandria where he is wounded, says; "I was wounded in the hip. The wound was caused by what is known as an explosive bullet. It took a piece right out of my hip, having exploded inside. It is not very painful, except when getting dressed." He continues: "There is very heavy fighting going on in this place – the Dardanelles – but, please God and His Blessed Mother I will come though safely, and, with her help, see you all again.

I feel I have someone's prayers to come through so well as I have. Bad as I am, I could be worse. On the night I was wounded all our Battalion went into action. The Turks are fairly beaten now; they can't last much longer. Lieutenant Brophil called me to him the night before I was wounded. He said; "How do you feel, Gill?" I replied: "alright". He told me to say my prayers, and that he had been speaking to an Australian officer, who was telling him he had a sister in a convent who had always enjoined on him to say the short prayer – "Sweet Jesus have mercy on me." This Australian officer had hardly said the words when his hands were blown off with shrapnel."

From the *King's County Independent*, January 1916:

PHILIPSTOWN. DEATH OF A HERO.

Much regret was felt in Philipstown on last Saturday evening, when the news was circulated of the death in the Royal Victoria Hospital, Netley, at the early age of 24 years, of Private William Hart (nephew of Mr Patrick. J. Hart, R.D.C.), who belonged to the 6th Battalion Leinster Regiment. The deceased was a tailor by trade, and was working away steadily until shortly after the outbreak of hostilities when, like many more of his countrymen, he was filled with a desire for fight for the Empire, and so gave up his work to become a soldier of the king. Being well set up and naturally smart too, took kindly to military training, and it was not long until, with the rest of his regiment, he was en-route for the Dardanelles, which has proved such a death-trap for so many gallant Irishmen. The deceased was reengaged in the landing at Suvla Bay in August, and, although only a mere youth, he fought with great bravery and coolness until laid prostrate by a bullet in the right knee, the wound proving so serious that the leg had to be afterwards amputated.

His wound could not, of course, be initially attended to until he was brought home to a place of safety. In his home life "Willie" Hart was very popular amongst his fellows, and he possessed a very wide circle of friends. He was very kind and considerate by nature and was of a most obliging disposition, and with a real "sport" from his very youth.

He was captain of the local football team, and he led his men to victory on more than one occasion. He knew now the meaning of fear, but was brave even to recklessness. We are sure that when the full account of the manner in which Private Hart received his death wound, comes to be generally know, it will be seen that he fought as an Irish hero should, and that he did credit to his country and race. May the foreign soil rest lightly o'er his brave heart.

For more information about this man see **STUDHOLME, Lancelot Joseph Moore.** Grave or Memorial Reference: RC. 868. Cemetery: Netley Military Cemetery, Hampshire, UK.

**HARTY, Daniel J.:** Rank: None given. Regiment or Service: Royal Army Medical Corps. Date of death: None given. Service no: None given. Killed at Sea. Born in Tullamore. This man is a bit of a mystery. He only appears in 'Ireland's Memorial Records'. It does not give rank, number, or Date of death. He is not listed in 'Soldiers died in the Great War', 'Officers died in the Great War' and he is not listed with the Commonwealth War Graves Commission. A quick check with the National Archives in Kew shows that there is no Medal Index Card for Daniel J. Harty of the RAMC, there is however a medal index card for Harte Daniel, No 30619, Royal Army Medical Corps but this man is not in the Commonwealth War Graves Commission or 'Soldiers died in the Great War' either which may indicate that he survived the war.

**HAYES, John:** Rank: Corporal. Regiment or Service: Connaught Rangers. Unit: 6th Battalion. Date of death: 21 March 1918. Service no: 1407. Born in Leomonaghan, Ballycomber, Co. Offaly. Enlisted in Galway while living in Preston. Killed in action. Grave or Memorial Reference: He has no known grave but is listed on Panel 77 on the Pozieres Memorial in France.

**HAYES, Patrick:** Rank: Pte. Regiment or Service: Irish Guards. Unit: 1st Battalion. Date of death: 25 July 1917. Service no: 4505. Born in Birr, Co. Offaly. Enlisted in Accrington, Lancs. Died of wounds. Grave or Memorial Reference: III.E.14. Cemetery: Niederzwehren Cemetery in Germany.

**HEENAN, Timothy:** Rank: Shoeing Smith Corporal. Regiment or Service: Royal Irish Regiment. Unit: 7th (South Irish Horse) Bn. Age at death: 25. Date of death: 10 October 1918. Service no: 73173. Born in Limerick. Enlisted in Limerick while living in Clareen. Died at sea.

*Supplementary information:* Son of Patrick and Sarah Heenan, of Clareen, Co. Offaly. Served in France. From the *King's County Chronicle*, November 1918:

THE SINKING OF THE LEINSTER.

"To the Editor.

Dear Sir,

I am shocked to learn that my nephew, T. Heenan, of the South Irish Horse, was on board the Leinster, and met an untimely death at the hands of the bloody Huns! It is barely three weeks since this brave young man paid me a visit in London, he was then looking the picture of perfect Irish manhood, standing well over six feet in height, and built in proportion, reminding me of his cousin, the late "Benecia Boy." I understand from a survivor that some of the S.I.H., "after rendering assistance to the women and children got into one of the boats only to be blown to atoms by a second torpedo from the murderous submarine"! Well, sir, I feel so wrath against those Prussian brutes that I fail in finding a word bad enough to describe them by; let "Prussian" suffice. Prussian signifies everything loathsome, cruel and filthy. There is one ray of satisfaction left to Irishmen here, that is, American, Australian, Canadian, and New Zealand. Irishmen will avenge this last dastardly outrage. They at least understand the "Mad dogs of Europe," and are helping to destroy them and save the world.

I beg to remain, yours sincerely.
J.C. Heenan,
"Clareen" South Park, Essex,
October 25th, 1918."

There is no middle course. Your
    crimes are Rank;
You chose the path of homicidal
    mania,
And signed your own damnation
    when you sank,
The Leinster and Lusitania.

To your devil's triumph seemed to
    complete,
The shrieks of murdered women
    roused your laughter;
You did not see the fate on limping
    feet
That followed after.

You proudly set yourself above all law,
Divine or human, Cruel, mean, and
    spiteful,
It seemed to you the world must
    stand in awe
Of one so frightful.

You laughed to scorn those warnings
From the West,
Nor ever thought the cloud would
    burst in thunder.
Too late, too late, your panic has
    confest
That fatal blunder.

Grave or Memorial Reference:
Memorial: Hollybrook Memorial, in
Southampton, UK.

**HEGARTY, James:** Rank: Corporal.
Regiment or Service: Leinster
Regiment. Unit: 1ˢᵗ Battalion. Date of
death: 4 May 1915. Service no: 6968.
Born in Birr, Co. Offaly. Enlisted in
Birr, Co. Offaly. Killed in action. Age
at death: 33.

*Supplementary information*: Son of
John and Maria Hegarty, of Eden
Road, Birr, Co. Offaly From the
*King's County Chronicle*, February
1918, 'Private Michael Hegarty, Irish
Guards, who was wounded a few
months ago, has come home on a

well-earned leave for fourteen days
to his home in Eden, Birr. Another
brother is in the same regiment.'
Has no known grave but is commemorated on Panel 44 on the Ypres
(Menin Gate) Memorial in Belgium.

**HEGARTY, Patrick:** Rank: Pte.
Regiment or Service: Royal Army
Ordnance Corps. Formerly he was
with the Leinster Regiment. Date of
death: 21 July 1919. Service no: S/9485.
Born in Roscrea, Co Tipperary.
Enlisted in Whitehall, London while
living in Birr, Co. Offaly. Died in
North Russia. Grave or Memorial
Reference: Buried in Maselskaya
Burial Ground and Commemorated
on the Archangel Memorial in the
Russian Federation.

**HEMPHILL, Richard Patrick:**
Rank: 2ⁿᵈ Lieut. Regiment or
Service: The Prince of Wales Leinster
Regiment ( Royal Canadians), attd,
RFC. Unit: 6ᵗʰ (Service) Battalion.
From *King's County Chronicle*,
December 1914, 'Although it is but a
short time since he joined the Cadet
Corps attached to the 7ᵗʰ Leinsters,
Mr Launcelot J. Studholme, J.P.,
Ballyeighan, Birr, has, we under-
stand, received a commission in the
Battalion.' From De Ruvigny's Roll
of Honour:

2ⁿᵈ Surv, son. of the Rev. Samuel
Hemphill, of Hamilton, Ailesbury
Road, Dublin, D. D., Litt, D., Chaplain
of the Magdalen Asylum there, and
of All Saints Church, Rouen, France,

Richard Patrick Hemphill.

and Examining Chaplain to the Archbishop of Dublin, by his wife Flora Margaret, eldest dau. of the late Rev. Canon Alexander Delap, Rector of Valencia, Co Kerry. b, the Rectory, Birr, Co. Offaly, 17 March, 1894, educ. Chesterfield School there; St Columba's College, Rathfarnham, Dublin; Campbell's College, Belfast, where he was a member of the O.T.C., and the University of Dublin, where also he was a member of the O.T.C., and was a medical student at Trinity College, Dublin.

He was an active member of the Student Volunteer Missionary Union, serving on the Irish Committee, and in April, 1914, volunteered for missionary work, being Superintendent of Fishamble Street Mission, Dublin; was gazetted 2nd Lieut, 6th Battalion, Leinster Regiment, 10 December, 1914; served with the Expeditionary Force in France and Flanders from 19th May to November, 1915, being attached to the 1st Battalion, Leinster Regiment; and with the Salonika Army from Nov, 1915, when he was a Machine Gun Officer and for a short time in command of a Company; became attached to the R. F. C. in Egypt in Feb, 1917, and was accidentally killed at Heliopolis, Cairo 24 March following, by falling of his aeroplane [sic]. Buried in old Cairo Cemetery (No 203, Section, F). Lieut-Col, H. W. Weldon, 1st Battalion, The Leinster Regiment, now (1918) commanding 4th Battalion, Royal Berkshire Regiment, wrote: "For nearly a year he was under me – during 1915 – when I was Adjutant, and for a short time his Company Commander, and I can honestly say I never knew a more conscientious, capable or pluckier soldier.

He was loved by his men, and had he been spared, I feel sure he would have made a great name for himself, if opportunity occurred. I think he was one of the nicest boys I ever met, and one I shall never forget. And Major T.R.A. Stannus, D.S.O., 6th Battalion, The Leinster Regiment (since died of wounds); "My recollections of your boy Pat are most vivid. He was a great favourite with us all, and was deservedly loved. His fine example stood out, and you have reason to be proud of your son. He was a fine man in every sense, and was, in addition, not afraid to conform to his high principals," Capt. T.D.

Murray, 1st Battalion, The Leinster Regiment, also wrote; "Your sorrow is shared by all of us out here. There was no one better liked in the Battalion.

The men in 'A' used to let him into their confidence, and they will all be sorry today. While in Dublin University he won a junior exhibition in 1912, a prize in classics in 1913, first prize in Natural Science in 1914, and Class Certificate of Merit in Anatomy in the same year. Died. 24 March 1917. Age at death: 23.

From the *King's County Chronicle*, 1917:

Particulars have now been ascertained of the accident in which Second Lieutenant R.P. Hemphill, the Leinster regiment and R.C. lost his life. He was flying as passenger with one of the instructors, when, through some unknown cause, the machine nose-dived to earth. The senior officer was terribly injured, but hopes are entertained of his recovery; but Lieut Hemphill survived less than two hours, having never regained consciousness.

From the *King's County Chronicle*, March 1916:

Rev. Dr. Hemphill's third boy, Alick, is now commissioned in the R.F.A., having passed through Woolwich. Dr. Hemphill's other sons, Cpt. Robert, R.A.M.C., and Lieut. Patrick, Leinster Regiment, are at the front, the former since the war began. Miss Hemphill is working in a Mediterranean hospital.

From the *King's County Chronicle*, March 1917:

LIEUT HEMPHILL DEAD.

Popular Young Birr Flying Officer Killed.

The sad news which reached Birr during the week, of the death from injuries received in a flying accident, of Sec. Lieut. Richard Patrick Hemphill, was heard with profound regret in Birr. And district. For over twenty years his father, the Rev. Dr. Hemphill, was Rector of Birr parish, and the deceased young officer was born here. The news is all the sadder by reason of the fact that it is only a few months ago since a younger brother, who was in the Artillery, lost his leg in action. An elder brother, Captain Hemphill, is still serving with his Majesty's forces. His sisters are also engaged at nursing and other war work. To this family that has done so much for King and Country, now comes the severe blow, caused by the death of a gallant young officer. Sec. Lieut. Hemphill, who died on the 24th of March, was only 23 years of age, and had a brilliant career.

He was attached to the Leinster regiment and Royal Flying Corps, and he saw foreign service continuously from May 17th, 1915, when he was transferred to the Leinsters, then at Ypres. He spent six months at Armentieres, and the Somme, after which he went to Salonika, where he continued for a year and two months and had command of a company as acting Captain on the Struma. He was transferred to Egypt on joining the Royal Flying Corps two months before the end of his career. He was a great favourite at St Columba's College, at Campbell College, and at Trinity College, Dublin. He was for four years in the O.T.C.s of Campbell College and Dublin University. His University course began with Classical Honours, First Honours in Natural Science, and very high marks at the end of his first and only year at the Medical School. He worked for a time at the Fishamble Street Mission, Dublin, and was active on the Committee of the Fuh-Kien Mission.

To his father; the Rev. Samuel, Hemphill, D.D. at present Chaplain of the Magdalen Church and Asylum, as well as to the members of his bereaved family, we tender our respectful sympathy as well as that of the people of Birr and surrounding districts.

From the *King's County Chronicle*, April 1917:

LATE LIEUT HEMPHILL.

In connection with the lamented death of sec. Lieut Richard Patrick Hemphill, the young Birr airman, who was killed in a flying accident, the following further particulars about a young career so tragically cut short, possess melancholy interest to the wide circle of friends of the deceased in Birr and district. Before the war young Mr Hemphill

was becoming a very good half in the 2nd NV, Rugby Dublin Team. When the war broke out, however, he took part in the larger game and became deeply interested in all the phases of the campaign. He wrote home a delightful description of his sensations as a flying man. He was happy and bright and never grumbled. At Le Touchet, near Armentieres, and at Dompierre, on the Somme, he was becoming a first-rate hand at trench raids and listening posts.

When he went to Salonika he said he was qualifying to be a County Surveyor's man, as he had an immense lot of road making to do. He sometimes commanded a company, and was beloved by his men. He was the life and soul of the party during the two Christmas seasons he spent at Salonika. By his brother officers, by his men, and by his relatives and friends at home his loss is deeply deplored.

Grave or Memorial Reference: F.203. Cemetery: Cairo War Memorial Cemetery in Egypt.

**HEMSWORTH, William, Christopher:** Rank: Pte. Regiment or Service: Royal Dublin Fusiliers. Unit: 8th Battalion. Date of death: 21 May 1917. Service no: 15122. Born in Birr, Co. Offaly. Enlisted in Birr. Killed in action. Age at death: 25.

*Supplementary information*: Son of George and Bridget Hemsworth (*née* Maher) of High Street, Birr, Co. Offaly.

*Supplementary information*: Born in 1892. From the *King's County Chronicle*, February 1916, 'Private Wm. Hemsworth, 8th Dublins, who joined at the outbreak of the war, went to France with the 16th Division. He is son of Mr George Hemsworth, High Street, himself an old soldier, who is well known as the civil and obliging postman of Crinkle district.' From the *King's County Chronicle*, July 1916, 'Birr young soldier killed. Another Birr soldier, Private William Hemsworth, Dublin Fusiliers, who was wounded in the neck, had a very narrow escape, the bullet missing the windpipe.' From the *King's County Chronicle*, June 1917:

KILLED IN ACTION.

Private Hemsworth.

As briefly reported in a previous issue the sad news had been confirmed of the death in action of Private William Christopher Hemsworth, of the Royal Dublin Fusiliers, which he joined in September, 1914. Previous to his enlistment he was employed as clerk by Mr P.V. Loughrey, solicitor, Birr. After his training he was sent to France with the 16th (Irish) Division on 19th December, 1915. He was seriously wounded on 6th April, 1916. He was again sent out on 14th December last, and was killed on 21st May, 1917. His father, George Henry Hemsworth, also served in India in the 1st Battalion, Leinster Regiment as N.C.O., and after leaving the army he served 21 years as postman in the Birr Post Office. His grandfather was Mr W. Baker Hemsworth, Barrister-at-Law, formerly of Abbeyville Park,

Lorrha, Co, Tipperary. His uncle was John Massey Dawson Hemsworth, Inspector of Police in Kimberley, South Africa. His aunt was Mrs Janet Carew, wife of Surgeon-Major R. H. Carew, Indian Army Medical Staff.

Grave or Memorial Reference: N. 79. Cemetery: Kemmel Chateau Military Cemetery in Belgium.

**HENNESSY, A P.:** (Also listed as **Patrick**). Rank: Lance Corporal. Regiment or Service: Leinster Regiment. Unit: 'C' Coy. 2nd Bn. Age at death: 19. Date of death: 31 July 1917. Born in Navan. Enlisted in Dublin. Killed in action. Service no: 9959.

*Supplementary information:* Son of Mrs E. Ryan, of Seffin, Birr, Co. Offaly. From the *King's County Chronicle,* August 1918: 'In Memoriam First Anniversary. – In sad and loving memory of Corps. Patrick Hennessy, Leinster Regiment, killed in action, 31 July 1917, second son of Mrs Ryan, Seffin, Birr, aged 19 years. Deeply regretted.' Grave or Memorial Reference: Has no known grave but is commemorated on Panel 44 on the Ypres (Menin Gate) Memorial in Belgium.

**HENNESSY, Christopher:** Rank: Pte. Regiment or Service: Royal Dublin Fusiliers. Unit: 7th Battalion. Date of death: 19 November 1915. Service no: 19370. Born in Tullamore, Co. Offaly. Enlisted in Dublin while living in Tullamore. Died at sea. Note: See the article that accompanies **Martin Hensey**. Hennessy may be Hensey. He is also listed on the Tullamore Roll of Honour as **HENSEY**, and states that Martin Hensey and Christopher Hensey are brothers. It also says that Martin died in Salonika. Grave or Memorial Reference: III.D.97. Cemetery: East Mudros Military Cemetery in Greece.

**HENNESSY, Herbert William:** Rank: Sergeant. Regiment or Service: Royal Fusiliers (City of London Regiment). Unit: 22nd Battalion. Date of death: 17 February 1917. Service no: 1233. Born in Birr, Co. Offaly. Enlisted in London while living in London, E. C. Killed in action. Age at death: 32. Won the Military Medal and is listed in the *London Gazette*.

*Supplementary information*: Son of John and Elizabeth Hennessy, of Birr, Co. Offaly. Grave or Memorial Reference: Pier and Face 8 C 9 A and 16 A. Memorial: Thiepval Memorial in France.

**HENRY, M.:** Rank: Pte. Regiment or Service: Leinster Regiment. Unit: 4th Bn. Age at death: 49. Date of death: 28 June 1918. Service no: 4036. He is not listed in 'Ireland's Memorial Records' or 'Soldiers died in the Great War'.

*Supplementary information:* Husband of Annie Henry, of Mount Sally, Birr. From the *King's County Chronicle*, July 1918:

LOCAL MILITARY FUNERAL.

With full military honours the remains were interred in Eglish graveyard on Saturday of Mr Michael Henry, aged 49 years, who died on 28th June at his residence, Mount Sally, Birr. He served with the Leinster Regiment in the South African and present war, and his death may to some extent, be attributed to these campaigns. He was attended in his last illness by Dr Fleury and the Rev. J.J. O'Meara, C.C., ministered to his spiritual needs. The remains were brought to St Brendan's R.C. Church on Friday evening. The band of the depot Leinster regiment and a firing party attended, and although it was market day there was a very representative attendance at the funeral. The chief mourners were – Annie, wife; Mrs McGrath, daughter; Annie Joe, and Bridie McGrath, granddaughters; Edward and Peter Henry, brothers, Mrs E. Henry, sister-in-law; Mrs Bridget Kelly, sister; Denis Murphy, brother-in-law, and Mrs Kenny, niece.

In the same issue:

On Saturday last a military funeral took place through the streets of Birr. The deceased was Michael Henry, of Mount Sally, an old soldier, retired. He was buried in Eglish. The band of the Leinster Depot, preceded by a detachment with rifles reversed, walked in front of the hearse.

Grave or Memorial Reference: About two yards south of main path. Cemetery: Eglish (Holy Trinity) Church of Ireland Churchyard, Co. Offaly.

**HENSEY, Martin:** Rank: Pte. Regiment or Service: Leinster Regiment. Unit: 2nd Battalion. Date of death: 15 March 1916. Service no: 3272. Born in Tullamore, Co. Offaly. Enlisted in Maryborough, Co. Laois. Killed in action. From the *King's County Chronicle*, June 1916:

Mr Peter Hensey, of Davit Street, TulLamore, has proved himself "a soldier and a man." He served in the 1st Leinsters in India, and throughout the South African campaign; and, still zealous for his country's honour, he offered himself for service again at the outbreak of the present deadly conflict of the great European Nations. But his day for the active campaign had passed, and though the offer showed the intrepid spirit of a brave soldier which the military authorities appreciated, the services were not accepted. Mr Hensey's martial feelings have been inherited by his sons, three of whom entered the army, of whom two have been killed. Martin Hensey, served in the 2nd Leinsters, and was killed in action in France.

Michael Hensey was also serving in France, but the afflicting news was received from the Protestant Chaplain of a Battalion by the respected father a few days ago that he had been dangerously wounded at Loos; Christopher, Dublin Fusiliers, joined the Battalion at the outbreak of the war, though only sixteen years of age. He had about twelve months service in France, when he was invalided at Salonika, died on the passage home, and was buried at sea. Thus, does war work havoc with men, and cover them with glory.

Note: Christopher Hensey does not appear in any of the war dead bases. He is also listed on the Tullamore Roll of Honour. Grave or Memorial Reference: I.K.4. Cemetery: Menin Road South Military Cemetery in Belgium.

**HERNON, Edward:** Rank: Pte. Regiment or Service: Royal Dublin Fusiliers. Unit: 2nd Battalion. Date of death: 21 March 1918. Service no: 28683. Born in Banagher, Co. Offaly. Enlisted in Manchester while living in West Ealing. Killed in action.

*Supplementary information*: Born at Banagher, Co. Offaly. Grave or Memorial Reference: Panel 79 and 80. Memorial: Pozieres Memorial in France.

**HERNON, Kieran:** Rank: Pte. Regiment or Service: Black Watch. Date of death: 28 July 1917. Service no: 2919. Born in Banagher, Co. Offaly. Killed in action. The above information only appears in 'Ireland's Memorial Records'. Kieran Hernon and Kieran Heron appear to be the same man even though their dates of death and service numbers are different. Neither of them are listed in the Commonwealth War Graves Commission or 'Soldiers Died in the Great War'.

**HERNON, Patrick:** Rank: Pte. Regiment or Service: South Wales Borderers. Unit: 12th Battalion. Date of death: 14 September 1916. Service no: 24238. Born in Birr. Enlisted in Mullingar, Co. Westmeath. Died of wounds. From the *King's County Chronicle*, 29 October 1914:

BIRR SOLDIERS EXPERIENCE.

Private Patrick Hernon, of the 2$^{nd}$ Batt, South Lancashire Regiment, and brother of Miss Hernon, Main Street, Birr, has come home from the front on a fortnight's sick furlough. He told "Chronicle" reporter thrilling tales of the field and particularly of the daring of our soldiers in the face of terrific artillery fire. He was in the withdrawal from Mons and saw the Germans shelling a Red Cross Hospital. In the battle of the Aisne while going into a bayonet charge to reinforce the Royal Irish Rifles he was struck by a bullet in the heel and was brought to a hospital in St Nazaire where he met another Birr man, Pte George Roe of the Royal Army Medical Corps, son of Mr Thomas Roe, Cumberland Street. From there he went to Central School, Aberdeen, and he gives the highest praise to the nurses there. On the expiration of his leave he is to report himself at Warrington, and says he will go back to the fighting line with a light heart. One of the bravest deeds he saw was by Private Healy, of Roscrea, who, under heavy fire carried wounded Major Ewart into safety.

From the *Midland Tribune, Tipperary Sentinel* and *King's County Vindicator*, 1914:

BIRR MEN AT THE FRONT.

Private Hernon, Second Battalion, South Lancashire Regiment, has returned to Birr on sick leave. He took part in the battle of Mons, and in the famous retreat from there. He was also at the battle of the Aisne, in which encounter he was wounded, a bullet entering his head. He gives graphic descriptions of his experiences while there. When retreating he says; "You could hear bullets going by your ear with a whiz, while shrapnel was flying in all directions." He describes the sight just before dusk as being "a hundred times worse than hell," with his comrades dropping on every side, heads, arms, or legs being blown off. On one occasion, while with a party of outpost duty, they came to a farmhouse which was brightly lit.

The officers went to the house for accommodation, while the soldiers went to an orchard close by. Suddenly all the lights in the house went out, and a volley was poured into them. In the morning, he says, it was dreadful to see the number of dead and wounded from the effects of one volley. The bravest act he saw, he says, was that of a soldier in his own company in charge of a machine gun, who had kept firing although three of his fingers had been shot off. The last he saw of this man was when they were just retreating over a hill. He was still coolly firing the gun, while they marched by.

From the *King's County Chronicle*, August 1916:

Mrs McNamara, Mill Street, Birr, has received a letter from the Rev. M. Ryan, R.C. Chaplain, stating that Pte Hernon, South Wales Borderers, a native of this town, had died in France from wounds. He was one month at the front when he received his fatal wound. He was of a quiet and inoffensive disposition, and was a steady, hard-working young man. In the course of his letter the chaplain stated – "The deceased asked me to write to tell you how ill he was. Unfortunately he died on 14ᵗʰ August, but was quite happy, and he wished you to have all."

Grave or Memorial Reference: I.J.59. Cemetery: Chocques Military Cemetery in France.

## HERON/HERNON, Kieran:
Rank: Pte. Regiment or Service: Black Watch (Royal Highlanders). Unit: 6ᵗʰ (Perthshire) Battalion (Territorial). Date of death: 30 July 1916. Service no: 265937. Born in Banagher, Co. Offaly. Enlisted in Perth. Killed in action. Grave or Memorial Reference: IX. E. 33. Cemetery: Caterpiller Valley Cemetery in France.

## HEWITT, James: Rank: Pte.
Regiment or Service: Leinster Regiment. Unit: 2ⁿᵈ Battalion. Date of death: 19 October 1914. Service no: 8398. Born in Kilbride, Co. Offaly. Enlisted in Athlone, County Westmeath. Killed in action. Age at death: 30.

*Supplementary information:* Son of James Hewitt, of Clara Road, Tullamore, Offaly.

*King's County Chronicle*, May 1916:

Mr James Hewitt, a fine sturdy type of Irishman, aged 65, and a widower; lives on the Clara Road, Tullamore; and he enjoys the distinction of having given four sons to his country. All have served in the Leinster Regiment, and the eldest son, James, has died in action in France. He had served seven years – six in India – and was retired, on the Reserve, at the outbreak of war, when he was called to the colours and went on active service with the British Expeditionary Force. He fell fighting on the 19ᵗʰ October, 1914. The brothers, William and Timothy, belonging to the 1ˢᵗ Leinsters, the same Battalion as James, and were serving at the outbreak of the War. The three brothers went into action together. The fourth son, Peter, was in the militia reserve, and on being called up rejoined the 2ⁿᵈ Leinsters. He was gassed in action in France, and now lies seriously ill in Netley Hospital. Peter was the old man's favourite son, living with him, and in steady employment when called away. It is the father's wish to see his son in hospital. May he soon be able to accomplish the realisation of the desire.

From the *King's County Chronicle*, September 1916, 'Private Hewitt, of the Leinsters, son of Mr James Hewitt, Clara Road, is home on seven days leave. He was wounded about two months ago in France, and has since been in hospital. On expiry of leave he will return to active service with his battalion.' Grave or Memorial

Reference: Panel 10. Memorial: Ploegsteert Memorial in Belgium.

**HICKEY, Francis:** Rank: Sergeant. Regiment or Service: Leinster Regiment. Unit: 2nd Battalion. Date of death: 11 August 1916. Service no: 9704. Born in Birr, Co. Offaly. Enlisted in Birr, Co. Offaly. Killed in action. Age at death: 22.

*Supplementary information*: Son of Mrs Bridget Hickey, of Glebe Street, Birr. Husband of Sarah Brophy (formerly Hickey), of 73 Burke's Hill, Birr, Co. Offaly. From the *King's County Chronicle*, August 1916:

KILLED IN ACTION. A GALLANT BIRR SERGEANT.

News reached Birr this week that on 13th August Sergt. Frank Hickey, a native of this town, had been killed in action in France. He was attached to the 2nd Leinsters and was only married in January. He was a son of Mrs Bridget Hickey, or Burke's Hill. In a letter to the deceased's wife, Captain Laville wrote informing her of her husband's death, and adding; "Hickey was a gallant fellow, and by his death I have lost my best platoon sergeant and a personal friend of mine and the whole company." The Rev. Denis Doyle, Chaplain, in another letter, wrote; "His loss will be felt severely by officers and men, for he was a fine brave soldier. He was with a working party and they were just finished work when two shells burst killing eight of our boys and wounded ten. Thank God they were all prepared to go."

Grave or Memorial Reference: III.J.7. Cemetery: Quarry Cemetery, Montauban in France.

**HILL, Joseph L.F.:** Rank: Lance Sergeant. Regiment or Service: Irish Guards. Unit: 2nd Battalion. Date of death: 13 April 1918. Service no: 7780. Born in Birr, Co. Offaly. Enlisted in Galway while living in Acton, Middlesex. Died of wounds. From the *King's County Chronicle*, April 1918:

SERGEANT FRED HILL.

Irish Guards.

Profound regret and deep sympathy with the grief stricken parents was the prevailing feeling in Birr and district when the sad news became known that the above named fine young soldier had been killed in action on 13th April, at the early age of 22 years. These feelings were also accentuated by the fact that only a very short time ago he was home for a brief holiday, when his fine appearance was very favourably commented on; and, certainly, he was a credit to his country, as well as to the flag he so nobly fought and died for. Tall and of fine physique, we was every inch a soldier and a man. Of a quiet unassuming disposition and cheery nature, he was beloved by all, and his comrades of the trenches, as well as his acquaintances in civil life, found him a loyal, true-hearted friend.

Before joining the army he held a fine position in Messrs. Burgess's furniture establishment in Athlone, but answering the call of duty he joined up in April, 1915. He was twice wounded – first, at the battle of Ypres, April, 1916, and secondly, at the battle of Boullion Wood in November, 1917. He was the youngest son of Mr and Mrs John Hill, Cumberland Street, Birr, and the sad news was conveyed in a letter from another son (James) of the same regiment. We tender to the afflicted parents our sincere sympathy in this their hour of trial, and venture to hope that their grief will be softened somewhat by the knowledge that their gallant son laid down his young life in the scared cause of liberty, in company with many thousands of other brave men, whose names will live in the ages to come.

Joseph L.F. Hill. This photo appears with that of his three brothers and is accompanied by the following information: 'Corporal Irish Guards, arrived home last week after being severely wounded in France. He is almost fully recovered, and has left for the depot at Warley. He expects to be soon back at the front again.'

From the *King's County Chronicle*, April 1918: 'Roll of Honour. April, 13, killed in action, Sergeant, J.L.F. Hill, Irish Guards, dearly-loved youngest son of John and A. M. Hill, Cumberland Street, Birr, aged 2.' Grave or Memorial Reference: Has no known grave but is commemorated on Panel 10. Memorial: Ploegsteert Memorial in Belgium.

**HILL, Joseph:** Rank: Pte. Regiment or Service: Leinster Regiment. Unit: B Company, 2nd Battalion. Date of death: 20 October 1914. Age at death: 20. Service no: 9989. Born in Athlone, Co. Westmeath. Enlisted in Birr. Killed in action.

*Supplementary information*: Son of Mrs M. Hill, of Clawshaun, Clara, Co. Offaly. He is listed in the casualty list for Clara men in the *Midland Tribune, Tipperary Sentinel* and *King's County Vindicator*, November 1914.
Note: See the article attached to **McKEON/McKEOWN, Patrick** The Frank Hill mentioned in it may be a relation. Grave or Memorial Reference: Panel 10 on the Ploegsteert Memorial in Belgium.

**HILL, Michael:** Rank: Pte. Regiment or Service: Royal Inniskilling Fusiliers. Unit: 2nd Battalion. Date of death: 22 July 1915. Age at death: 33. Service no: 7185. Born in Widnes in Lancashire. Enlisted in Tullamore. Killed in action.

*Supplementary information*: Native of Widnes. Son of Patrick and Ellen Hill. He is listed on the Tullamore Roll of Honour, however, I do not see the Offaly connection but include him for your reference. Grave or Memorial Reference: IV.D.21. Cemetery: Bethune Town Cemetery in France.

**HILL, William J.:** Rank: Corporal. Regiment or Service: Machine Gun Corps. Date of death: None given. Service no: 49001. Born in Co. Offaly. Killed by Shellfire in France. Age at death: 29. He only appears in 'Ireland's Memorial Records'. He is not listed in 'Soldiers died in the Great War' and he is not listed with the Commonwealth War Graves Commission. A quick check with the National Archives in Kew shows that there is no Medal Index Card for Serial No 49001, Corporal Hill.

**HILL, William Joseph:** Rank: 2ⁿᵈ Corporal. Regiment or Service: Corps of Royal Engineers. Unit: 5ᵗʰ Field Company, formerly 59 Field Company. Royal Engineers. Date of death: 18 January 1915. Service no: 16873. Born in Birr, Co. Offaly. Enlisted in Birr, Co. Offaly. Killed in action. Age at death: 29.

*Supplementary information*: Son of the late William Hill, of Grove Street, Crinkle, Birr, Co. Offaly. From the *King's County Chronicle*, January 1915:

During this formidable war King's County and Tipperary, like the rest of the Emerald Isle, have supplied their share to the roll of honour. Amongst the latest who has laid down his valiant young life is Corporal William

Hill, Royal Engineers. His father, who lives at Grove Street, Crinkle, received the news in the course of last week from Captain Palmer, who wrote a most sympathetic letter, describing him as an ideal soldier. It appeared from the same correspondence that the deceased and four others were building a redoubt when a too well aimed shell burst among them killing them all instantaneously. He served his time with Mr Power, building contractor and was considered an intelligent and industrious young man.

Grave or Memorial Reference: He has no known grave but is listed on Panel 1 on the Le Touret Memorial in France

**HINKSMAN, Reginald James:** Rank: Corporal. Regiment or Service: Royal Irish Rifles. Unit: B Company, 1ˢᵗ Battalion. Date of death: 7 February 1916. Service no: 16802. Born in Sheffield. Enlisted in Birr, Co. Offaly while living in Edenderry, Co. Offaly. Killed in action. Age at death: 22.

Reginald James Hinksman.

*Supplementary information:* Son of James and Harriett Hinksman, of 'Harbour View' Edenderry, Co. Offaly. Grave or Memorial Reference: I.D.34. Cemetery: Rue-Du-Bois Military Cemetery, Fleurbaix in France.

**HODGES, Harold Henry:** (Also listed as **Henry Harold**). Rank: Second Lieutenant. Regiment or Service: Leinster Regiment. Unit: 7th Battalion. Date of death: 13 July 1916. Age at death: 21. Killed in action.

*Supplementary information*: Son of John George Hodges, B.D., and Anna Maria Gore Hodges, of Ardnurcher Rectory, Moate, Co. Westmeath. Native of Belmont, Co. Offaly. From the *Midland Tribune, Tipperary Sentinel* and *King's County Vindicator,* August 1916:

Harold Henry Hodges.

KILLED IN ACTION.

At the monthly meeting of Ferbane School, Attendance Committee held in Ferbane Courthouse on 7th August, with the chairman, Rev. M.J. Kennedy, P.P. Shannonbridge, presiding, vice-chairman, Rev. E. Brady, C.C. Ferbane, Rev. B. Columb, C.C. Ferbane, the following resolution of sympathy was proposed by Rev. Brady – That we desire to place on record our regret at the untimely death of Lieutenant Harold Hodges, and hereby offer our sympathy to his parents and friends: James Hamill, Secretary.

The same article was repeated in the *King's County Independent.* From the *King's County Chronicle,* July 1916:

YOUNG LEINSTER OFFICER KILLED.

On Saturday morning rev. J. C. Hodges, Tissaran Rectory, Belmont, received a letter informing him of the death of his eldest son, sec-Lieut. Henry Harold Hodges, Leinster Regiment, on 13th July. When volunteers were first called for Mr Hodges, who was in the Portumna Branch of the Hibernian Bank, joined the Leinsters Cadet Company, and soon obtained a commission. His Commanding Officer, Col. Buckley, in sending the news, says; "A rifle grenade landed in the trench just beside him. He suffered no pain whatsoever, and death was absolutely instantaneous. Only a few hours before I had gone to see him about something; he was asleep in his shelter in the front line.

Dear lad, he looked so weary and exhausted as he lay in his wet clothes and muddy boots, but such a sweet happy smile was on his face. It seemed to me as if he was dreaming of home. I hadn't the heart to wake him, and passed on my rounds. A few hours later I heard of his death. He was a dear lad, and I was very fond of him – a brave lad too, with the heart of a lion. We will bury him at Vermelles Cemetery to-morrow night." Mr Hodges brother, Rev. R. J. Hodges, M.A., Rector of Youghal, has just heard that his son, Eric, in the Royal Irish, has been killed in action.

Grave or Memorial Reference: IV.A.1. Cemetery: Vermelles British Cemetery in France.

**HOEY, James:** Rank: Pte. Regiment or Service: Irish Guards. Unit: 1st Battalion. Date of death: 25 April 1916. Service no: 5045. Born in Wigan, Lancs. Enlisted in Wigan, Lancs while living in Clara, Co. Offaly. Killed in action. He is also listed on the Tullamore Roll of Honour. Grave or Memorial Reference: I.L.2. Cemetery: Menin Road South Military Cemetery in Belgium.

**HOGAN, Joseph:** Rank: Pte. Regiment or Service: Royal Irish Regiment. Unit: 5th Bn. Date of death: 18 September 1915. Service no: 4888. Born in Killen, Co. Tipperary. Enlisted in Naas while living in Birr. Died in Salonika. Age at death: 24.

*Supplementary information*: Son of Thomas and Mary Hogan, of Killimore, Co. Galway. Grave or Memorial Reference: He has no known grave but is listed on the Doiran Memorial in Greece.

**HOGAN, Peter:** Rank: Pte. Regiment or Service: Connaught Rangers. Unit: 5th Battalion. Date of death: 8 October 1918. Service no: 15299. Formerly he was with the Leinster where his number was 180. Born in Moate, Co. Westmeath. Enlisted in Tullamore, Co. Offaly while living in Clara, Co. Offaly. Killed in action. Grave or Memorial Reference: A.15. Cemetery: Serain Communal Cemetery Extension in France.

**HOGBEN, Henry Francis Thomas:** Rank: Lieutenant. Regiment or Service: Middlesex Regiment. Unit: 10th Battalion (Territorial). Date of death: 22 November 1915. Killed in action. From the *King's County Chronicle*, 1915, 'Lieutenant Henry Francis Thomas Hogben, 10th Middlesex, attached to the 2nd Norfolks, who was killed in action near Baghdad, between November 22 and 24, was the eldest son of Mr Fred Hogben, Cedars Park, Sunderland, formerly Headmaster of Chesterfield, Birr.' From the *King's County Chronicle*, December 1915:

Lieut. Henry Francis Thomas Hogben, 10th Middlesex Regiment, attached 2nd Norfolk Regiment, who was killed in Mesopotamia between November 22 and 24, was the eldest son of Mr F. Hogben, formerly of Chesterfield,

Birr. Born in 1890, he was educated at Bedford Grammar School, and entered the Medical School of Guy's Hospital. In 1909, winning the London University Open Scholarship. He was a member of the Bedford Grammar School Cadet Corps, 1905-1909, and of the Artist's Rifles Cadet Corps, 1909-1913, and obtained a commission in the 10th Middlesex Regiment in July, 1913. He went with his Regiment to India in October, 1914, and in April, 1915, was selected to take a draft from the 10th Middlesex Regiment to the Persian Gulf. He played football for Guy's, excelled in boxing, and was a powerful swimmer. In the years 1908-1914 he won many distinctions at Bisley. He was in the Bedford Grammar School Eight, and twice captained the London University Eight. He won the Open Championship of London University

Henry Francis Thomas Hogben.

Athletic Union Rifle Association and the All-Comers Aggregate in 1913, and was in the King's Hundred in 1913 and 1914.

## From De Ruvigny's Roll of Honour:

Hogben, Henry Francis Thomas, Lieut, 10th Battn, The Duke of Cambridge's Own (Middlesex regiment) T. F., attached to the 2nd Battn (9th Foot) The Norfolk regiment. Eldest son of Frederick Hogben, of 5 Cedars Park, Sunderland. Schoolmaster, by his wife, Emily, daughter of the late Dr Thomas Grace Geoghegan, of Dublin. Born in Galway, 18 April, 1890. Educated at Chesterfield School, Parsonstown (1898-1905); Bedford Grammar School (1905-9), and Guy's Hospital Medical School (1909-1914), winning the London University Scholarship; was a member of the Bedford Grammar School Cadet Corps from 1905 to 1909, and of the Artists Rifles from 1909 to 1913, obtaining a 2nd Lieutenancy in the 10th Middlesex Regt, 12th July, 1913, and was promoted Lieut, 26 Aug, 1914. Volunteered for foreign service of the outbreak of war, went to India with his regiment in Oct, 1914, and in April, 1915 was selected to take a draft from the 10th Middlesex Regt, to the Persian Gulf, when he was attached to the 2nd Norfolks, and was killed in a action at Chestiphon 22 Nov, following. Buried on the battlefield there. Col. C. Diamond wrote; "I was very reluctant to spare him, but he was very keen to go, and I knew that he would do the battalion credit in charge of our detachment." And his servant; "The battalion miss him, and especially my company, for Mr Hogben was very keen with the company in sports and a splendid soldier and a gentleman." He was a good all-round sportsman; won many distinctions at Bisley in the years 1908-1914; was in the Bedford Grammar School Eight, and twice captained the London University Eight; won the open Championship of London University Athletic Union Rifle Association and the All Comers Aggregate in 1913, in the King's Hundred in 1913 and 1914.

Grave or Memorial Reference: He has no known grave but is listed on Panels 30 and 64 the Basra Memorial in Iraq.

**HOLOHAN, Thomas:** Rank: Pte. Regiment or Service: Royal Dublin Fusiliers. Unit: 1st Battalion. Date of death: 12 July 1915. Service no: 16348. Born in Kilbride, Co. Offaly. Enlisted in Tullamore, Co. Offaly. Killed in action in Gallipoli. Age at death: 19.

*Supplementary information*: Son of Thomas and Elizabeth Holohan, of Clonminch Road, Tullamore, Co. Offaly. From *King's County Chronicle*, May 1916:

The call of duty. Private Thomas Holohan, 1st Royal Dublin Fusiliers, youngest son of Mr Thomas Holohan, Clerk of Petty Sessions, Tullamore, was wounded at Gallipoli on 12th July, 1915, and has since been missing. This brave young fellow was educated at Rockwell College, County

Tipperary; an Exhibitioner in the Intermediate course, and the winner of the first prize for an Irish essay at the Philadelphia Feis. He was only eighteen years of age, a bright and very popular young man, but very thoughtful and serious-minded. He was working for his father's office, and was moved by the strong conviction that one of the three brothers should serve his King and Country; but it was in his own ears that the trumpet call of duty was sounding; and with him to hear the call was to obey. In those early days of the war the local corps of volunteers gave many soldiers for the front, reservists and recruits. Young Private Holohan had six months training with the 1st Dublins before meeting the foe in the Near East.

He is also listed on the Tullamore Roll of Honour and says he was killed in Suvla Bay.

Grave or Memorial Reference: He has no known grave but is listed on Panel 190 to 196 on the Helles Memorial in Turkey

**HOMAN, Charles Gravers:** Rank: Pte. Regiment or Service: South African Motor Cyclist Corps. Unit: 2nd Battalion. Date of death: 21 February 1917. Service no: CM. 346. Age at death: 36.

*Supplementary information*: Son of the Revd Canon Homan and Mrs Mary Ethel Homan, of 6 Eglington Park, Kingstown. Also served in German South-West Africa. Born at Locheen Glebe, Offaly. Grave or

Memorial Reference: VIII.B.2. Iringa Cemetery in Tanzania.

**HOMAN, Henry Leslie:** Rank: Captain. Regiment or Service: Middlesex Regiment. Unit: 2nd Bn. Age at death: 36. Date of death: 10/March 1915. Killed in action.

*Supplementary information:* Son of the Rev. Canon and Mrs Mary Ethel Homan, of 6 Eglinton Park, Kingstown. Native of Lockeen Glebe, Birr, Co. Offaly. From the *King's County Chronicle*, March 1915:

The late Captain Homan. King's and Queen's sympathy.

The Rev. Canon Homan, on the death of his son, Captain H. Leslie. Homan, Middlesex Regiment, killed in action, at Neuve Chapelle, has received the following gracious message of sympathy from Buckingham Palace; "The King and Queen deeply regret the loss to you and the Army have sustained by the death of your son in the service of his country. Their Majesties truly sympathise with you in your sorrow." Private Secretary.

A LOWER ORMOND SOLDIER FALLEN.

Much sympathy has been evoked in Birr for the Rev Canon R.P. Homan and Mrs Homan, Kingstown, and formerly of Ballingarry and Lockheen parish, Barony of Lower Ormond, for the loss of their eldest son, Captain Henry Leslie Homan, Middlesex Regiment, killed in action on 10th March. He was born on January 21st, 1879, and entered the Army on May 23rd, 1900, gazetted Lieutenant on December 21st, 1901, and obtained his company on August 26th, 1909. Captain Homan, who was employed with the West African Frontier Force, from 1908 to 1912, took part in the Southern Nigeria Expedition in the former year, being mentioned in despatches and receiving the medal with clasp. In disposition his modesty and genial kindness were only equalled by his personal fearlessness in the face of danger.

It is sincerely hoped that this noble sacrifice in defence of his King and country and the freedom of his fellow-men will go some way to soften the parental grief; and all the more as their darling son was not alone a soldier but it is believed he was emphatically a Christian soldier living up to the high standard expressed in these lines;

I live for those that love me,
For those that know me true,
For the heaven that smiles above me,
And awaits my coming, too.
For the cause that needs assistance,
For the wrongs that need resistance,
For the future in the distance,
And the good that I can do.

Grave or Memorial Reference: III.K.6. Cemetery: Royal Irish Rifles Graveyard Laventie in France.

**HORAN, Thomas:** Rank: Pte. Regiment or Service: Lancashire

Fusiliers. Unit: 2<sup>nd</sup> Battalion. Date of death: 7 July 1915. Service no: 4620. Born in Co. Offaly. Enlisted in Bury, Lancs while living in Manchester. Killed in action. Age at death: 40.

*Supplementary information*: Son of Thomas and Catherine Horan, of Glebe Street, Birr, Co. Offaly. Husband of Mary Horan, of 16 Eltoft Street, Liverpool Road, Manchester. From the *Midland Tribune*, *Tipperary Sentinel* and *King's County Vindicator*, 1915:

### KILLED IN ACTION

News has been received in Birr by his brother, Mr James Horan, of the death of Corporal Horan, Lancashire Fusiliers, killed in action on the 7<sup>th</sup> July, last, from the wife of the deceased in England. The late Corporal Horan, who was a bricklayer, joined the army in the August of last year, soon after the outbreak of the war. He was a native of Glebe Street, Birr, but had been in England for a number of years. Regret is felt with his relatives at his demise.

Note: I also include the following interesting article purely for your reference. I am not sure if this is the same man. From the *Midland Tribune*, *Tipperary Sentinel* and *King's County Vindicator*, December 1914:

Private T. Horan, Irish Guards, in a letter to Mr Whelan Cloghan, says "I am looking forward to the day when I will be able to go home and have a good time, but that will be a good while yet. I got a very nasty wound; my thigh was broken by a dum-dum bullet. My leg was badly torn, portion of the bone (which was split in three parts) was blown away. I had some narrow, very narrow escapes. We were fighting a rearguard action at a place called Villers-Cotterets, on the retreat from Mons. We had one Brigade of Infantry, one Brigade of Artillery, and a Brigade of Cavalry, numbering in all about 5, 000. We were to hold the enemy in check while the other Division and Transport were retiring, and we did that for nine hours, although there were six Army Corps against us. We got surrounded in the evening, and would be all cut up only for the charge of the Scots Greys and the South Irish Horse. There were 167 of us wounded and taken prisoners besides the killed. All our officers, except two, were shot. The Commanding Officer was shot about ten yards from where I was lying. A piece of shell blew half his head away."

In a letter to his mother, Private Horan writes

"I am back again in England, in Cambridge Hospital. I am real strong now, and able to use ordinary food. I am sure you will be surprised to hear that I was a German prisoner for fourteen days. There were 300 of us taken by the Germans after the fight, and carried into a Chapel. I was shot after about six hours fighting. My Captain carried me away from where the hail of bullets and shells fell the thickest, and bandaged up my wounds. He then sent for the stretcher-bearers, but they were all shot, and he was knocked over an hour after. I was then out all that night, and next morning a German Officer came the way and saw me, and got me carried to an hospital. He also gave me a big bottle of wine, and I nearly drank it all in the first drink, as I was dying of thirst. For the fourteen days I could not eat the food the Germans gave us, but it was as good as they had for themselves. One potato, a piece of carrot and one rabbit among thirty six men, all boiled up in a boiler.

The French cavalry re-took us back from them on the 14th of September, and brought us to Lemans, where there was great care taken of us by our own doctors. My wounds were very bad for some time, but are now fairly well. Coming home shook me up a bit, and one of my wounds broke down, but it is now well again. I was in five bayonet charges, and came out all right, with the exception of a slight bayonet wound, but the doctor stitched it up, and it got better in no time. The battle-field is a ghastly sight after a big battle; French, English and Germans, all dead or dying. You would see all kinds of wounds. I often pitied a poor German, and gave him a drink of water. Burying the dead at night is another ugly job. It put me in mind of the burial of Sir John Moore, all put down in a coffinless grave, with only a stone to mark their lonely grave. I was told by a comrade that poor Paddy Sheehan fell at the battle of the Marne. I think I have related enough of history to you. I would have told all of this before now, but our letters had to be censored and if they seen anything like that in there they would be torn up."

From the *King's County Chronicle*, September 1915, 'Corporal Thomas Horan, Lancashire Fusiliers, aged 38, a son of the late Mr Thomas Horan, mason, Glebe Street, Birr, adds another to the list of brave King's County men in the roll of death with honour. He was killed at hill 60 on July 10, and leaves a wife and five children in Manchester.' Grave or Memorial Reference: Panel 33. Memorial: Ypres (Menin Gate) Memorial in Belgium.

**HOREY, John:** Rank: Pte. Regiment or Service: Household Cavalry and Cavalry of the line including the Yeomanry and Imperial Camel Corps. Unit: 4 Dragoon Guards (Royal Irish). Date of death: 3 November 1914. Service no: 7834. Born in Fallow, Co. Waterford. Enlisted in Athlone, Co. Westmeath while living in Birr, Co. Offaly. Killed in action. Age at death: 21.

*Supplementary information:* Son of Martin and Margaret Horey, of Whiteford, Birr, Co. Offaly. Grave or Memorial Reference: He has no known grave but is listed on Panel 3-5 on the Ypres (Menin Gate) Memorial in Belgium.

**HOULIHAN, Thomas:** Rank: Pte. Regiment or Service: Canterbury Regiment NZEF. Unit: 2$^{nd}$ Bn. Age at death: 27 Date of death: 5$^{th}$ October 1918. Service no: 62321. Brother of Patrick O'Houlihan who died with the Australians.

*Supplementary information:* Son of John Houlihan, of Abbeyville, Lorrha, Birr. From the *King's County Chronicle*, October 1918:

PTE T. HOULIHAN KILLED IN ACTION.

Mr John Houlihan, Abbey View, Lorrha, formerly of Connaught Street, Birr, has received official information of the death in action on 5$^{th}$ October of his gallant son, Private Thomas Houlihan, of the 2$^{nd}$ Batt. Canterbury (N.Z.) regiment. Deceased was 27 years of age, and his brother Patrick, aged 25, was also killed in September last year.

The Rev. Faher O'Flynn, C.I.B., New Zealand Expeditionary Force, writing to Mrs Houlihan, under date, 7$^{th}$ October, 1918, says: "It is with deepest regret I write you in connection with the death of your son, Private Thomas Houlihan, who was one of my flock, and a good one too. He was in the company of an officer and a sergeant, going towards a ridge, which faced the German line. Your son got on the ridge, and immediately the officer called on him to fall down, but it was too late, as a German gun had covered him. His death was instantaneous. It will be your consolation when you know that he was at Confession and Holy Communion just before going to the line; and no matter where Mass was celebrated, if he had the chance, he was sure to be present. I was speaking to his officer just after his death took place, and he spoke feelingly of his fearless spirit, and the good boy he was. The officer, who is going away to another unit, would like me to convey to you his sincere sympathy. I am sending you his personal belongings in a day or two, which I am getting together. His grave I shall have marked and taken care of. I shall remember him in my Mass as a personal friend; he, I am sure, is in a happier state. May he rest in peace."

Mrs Houlihan has received the following letter from Sec. Lieut J. Mitchell;

France, 14$^{th}$ October, 1918.
Dear Madam,
It is with deep regret that I have to write to you of the death of your son, who was killed in action on the afternoon of the 5$^{th}$ October. As he was a member of my platoon, perhaps the following facts from me would be appreciated by you. On the afternoon of the 5$^{th}$ this company was advancing when your son was hit by a sniper and killed instantly. I was only a few paces from him at the time and went to him at once. Life was then extinct. He could have suffered no pain. After dark the same evening

we recovered his body and buried him next day. I informed his Padre (father O'Flynn) and he had him removed to a cemetery. Your son was a favourite with us all, being both a soldier and a gentleman; and the whole company joins with me in extending their sympathy to you in your bereavement.

If I am able to give you any further particulars I am yours to command.

Remaining, faithfully yours,
J Mitchell, Second Lieut.
2nd Batt., C.I.B., N.Z.E.F, France.

Thomas's brother Patrick is listed under the name **O'HOULIHAN, Patrick.** Grave or Memorial Reference: I.B.30. Cemetery: Honnechy British Cemetery in the little village of Honnechy 8 kilometres south-west of Le Chateau, in France.

**HOWARD, Thomas:** Rank: Corporal. Regiment or Service: Leinster Regiment. Unit: 2nd Battalion. Date of death: 20 October 1914. Service no: 9416. Born in Birr, Co. Offaly. Enlisted in Birr, Co. Offaly. Killed in action. Age at death: 22.

*Supplementary information*: Son of John and Bridget Howard, of Moorpark Street, Birr, Co. Offaly. From the *Midland Tribune*, *Tipperary Sentinel* and *King's County Vindicator*, 1914, 'Birr deaths at the front. The War Office has notified Mr John Howard, Moorpark Street that his son, Signal Instructor Corporal Thos Howard, was killed in action on the 19th

October. Mr Howard himself as an old soldier, having served through the South African War. From the *King's County Chronicle*, November 1914:

Mr Joseph Cole, Birr, has received notification of the death in action of his son, Lance Corporal Robert, of the 2nd Leinsters, which occurred about the 18th or 20th October. Another son, Corporal Joseph, is at the front in the 1st Leinsters, and the youngest son, Pte Thomas, who was home on sick leave having been wounded, has gone back to his regiment. Mr John Howard, Moorpark Street, and ex-Sergt, 3rd Leinsters, who served in the South African War, received a similar sad letter as to his son Tom, also a Corporal in the same Battalion. These are only a couple of the many mourned over in the King's County and Tipperary.

From the *King's County Chronicle*, March 1916:

Ex-Sergeant John Howard, Moorpark Street, saw service with the Royal Irish Regiment in the Black Mountain Expedition in 1888; on the Indian Frontier and in the Mediterranean Stations. He afterwards joined the 3rd Leinsters and served throughout the South African campaign, at the termination of which he was granted a life pension. His eldest son, Corporal Thomas, of the 2nd Leinsters, went with the first Expeditionary Force to France and lost his life in the battle of Lille in October, 1914.

Grave or Memorial Reference: Panel 10. Memorial: Ploegsteert Memorial in Belgium.

**HOWES, Charles William:** Rank: Major, Temporary Captain and Acting Major. Regiment or Service: Durham Light Infantry. Unit: 19th Battalion. Date of death: 22 April 1918. Age at death: 31. Killed in action.

*Supplementary information*: Son of Maj. and Mrs W.R. Howes, of Anna Villa, Skerries, Co. Dublin. Husband of Mabel Howes, of 3 Mespil Road, Dublin. From the *King's County Chronicle*, May 1918:

> Captain C. W. Howes, Durham Light Infantry, who was killed in action on 22nd April, after three years service, was the eldest son of Major Howes, of Birr, and the husband of Mabel, eldest daughter of Rev A Gick, M.A., Rector of Ballymore Eustace. His colonel, writing about him, says; "He will be a great loss to me and the battalion. He died doing his duty nobly as a soldier should. He was a great favourite with us all, and his loss will be keenly felt by all ranks. He feared nothing, and was brave to a degree." The words of a comrade are: "All of us who knew him are nearly heartbroken, because he was in all our hearts, and officers and men loved and held him in the highest esteem and respect on account of his exemplary character and staunch devotion to duty." Previous to the war, the late Captain Howes was, for a time, teacher at Chesterfield school, Birr.

Grave or Memorial Reference: IV.A.20. Cemetery: Bouzincourt Communal Cemetery Extension in France.

**HUGHES, James:** Rank: Pte. Regiment or Service: Leinster Regiment. Unit: 2nd Battalion. Date of death: 29 January 1916. Service no: 4838. Born in Kilbride, Co. Offaly. Enlisted in Birr, Co. Offaly while living in Tullamore, Co. Offaly. Killed in action. Age at death: 36.

*Supplementary information*: Son of John Hughes, of William Street, Tullamore. Husband of Sarah Hughes, of Convent View, Tullamore, Co. Offaly From the *King's County Chronicle*, February 1916:

> TULLAMORE SOLDIER'S DEATH.
>
> News reached Tullamore of Friday last of the death of Private James Hughes, of the 3rd Leinsters. He was a son of the late Mr J. Hughes, for many years employed in a responsible position in the local distillery of the late Mr Bernard Daly, now Messrs Egan's and brother of the Rev. Fr. Daly, P.P., of Australia, and of Mr William Hughes, late clerk of Tullamore Rural Council, and now a member of the Council. Private Hughes enlisted in Birr in August last, and had only been on active service in France a few weeks when he fell mortally wounded under a Hun sniper's rifle. He was universally esteemed and respected, and when at home on furlough shortly before Christmas received

the congratulations and expressions of goodwill of hosts of friends and neighbours. He leaves a widow and seven young children. His widowed mother also resides in Tullamore. Great sympathy has been felt by the entire community for the mourning relatives of this brave young Tullamore man, who fell at the post of duty nobly fighting for King and country. Private Hughes was brother-in-law of Mr Patrick Power, the popular Town Inspector of Tullamore.

From the *King's County Chronicle*, May 1916.

Private James Hughes, 2nd Leinsters, was a son of the late Mr J. Hughes, who was for many years employed in Mr Bernard Daly's distillery in Tullamore, and a brother of the Rev. Fr. Hughes P. P., of Australia, and of Mr William Hughes, late Clerk of Tullamore Urban Council – now a member of the Council – and brother-in-law of Mr Patrick Power, Town Inspector of Tullamore. Private Hughes enlisted in Birr in August last, and as killed by a sniper in France on the 29th January. He was a manly, honest, and straightforward man; and was greatly esteemed and respected in Tullamore. His widow and seven young children, and widowed mother reside in Tullamore, and great sympathy was felt by the public for them in the great loss they had sustained when the news of the brave fellows death was received.

He is also listed on the Tullamore Roll of Honour under **James HUITES.** Grave or Memorial Reference: I.F.6. Cemetery: Menin Road South Military Cemetery in Belgium.

**HUGHES, William Sladen:** Rank: Lieutenant. Regiment or Service: Royal Sussex Regiment. Unit: 2nd Battalion. Date of death: 14 September 1914. Age at death: 24. Killed in action.

*Supplementary information*: Son of A.F. Hughes, of Hillbrook, Birr, Co. Offaly. From the *King's County Chronicle*, 1914:

Lieut Wm. S. Hughes, Sussex Regiment, who was reported wounded and missing since 14 October [*sic*], has, we regret to state, now been reported as having died of wounds. Much sympathy will be felt in Birr District for Mr A. F. and Mrs Hughes, who have been very popular since they came to reside in the Birr suburbs at Millbrook. The late Lieut Hughes who was an only son, was nephew of Colonel Hughes, Cameron Highlanders, and Colonel Hughes R.M.C.A. [*sic*].

Grave or Memorial Reference: He has no known grave but is listed on the La Ferte-Sous-Jouarre Memorial in France.

**HYNES, James:** Rank: Pte. Regiment or Service: Royal Army Medical Corps. Date of death: 11 December 1918. Service no: 093956 and T4/093956. Born in Birr. Died of fever in France.

Age at death: 32 ('Ireland's Memorial Records') 35 (Commonwealth War Graves Commission). Worked in the Birr Saw Mills.

*Supplementary information*: Son of Daniel and Margaret Hynes, of Birr. Husband of Bridget Hynes, of Newbridge Street, Birr. From the *King's County Chronicle*, March 1916:

> Mr James Hynes, a respected former employee at the Birr Saw Mills, joined the A.S.C. in May last. He has been engaged in the dangerous work of bringing supplies almost to the firing line, and had many narrow escapes. Some months ago he was granted a short leave home, and looked in first rate health. His wife and family reside in Newbridge Street. There are two more brothers of the above serving viz: Private Daniel Hynes, who was coachman to Sir Francis Synge, Syngefield, Birr, and Private Thomas Hynes, who joined the 6th Leinsters, and is now in Salonika.

From the *King's County Chronicle*, August/September 1918:

> Driver James Hynes, A.S.C., came home on a well earned furlough last week. He has been on very dangerous work in France, and although many of his comrades are on the missing list, he has come through without a scratch. Before enlisting he was a respected and industrious employee at the Saw Mills, and his wife and family reside at Newbridge Street.

Grave or Memorial Reference: IV.J.5. Cemetery: Tournai Communal Cemetery Allied Extension in Belgium.

Advertisements that appeared in Offaly Newspapers during the First World War.

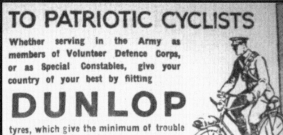

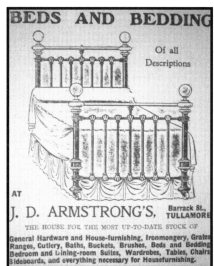

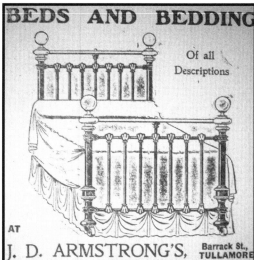

# J

**JAEGERS, John:** Rank: Pte. Regiment or Service: Australian Force. Killed in France in July 1916 (was wounded previously in Gallipoli). He is not in any other War Dead database and there is not one single man named **JAEGERS** in the Australian Military records. He is listed on the Tullamore Roll of Honour. I do not see the Offaly connection but include him for your reference.

**JAMES, Thomas:** Rank: Lance Corporal. Regiment or Service: Royal Dublin Fusiliers. Unit: 8th Battalion. Date of death: 9 September 1916. Service no: 24535. Born in Enniscorthy, Co Wexford. Enlisted in Dublin while living in Ballycumber, Co. Laois. Killed in action. From an article in a Wexford newspaper:

> KILLED IN ACTION.
>
> Much sympathy is felt with Mr and Mrs J. James, Ballinapierce, Enniscorthy, in the loss they have sustained by the death of their third eldest son, Lance Corporal Thomas James who was killed in action on the 9th September last.

Grave or Memorial Reference: He has no known grave but is listed on Pier and Face 16.C. on the Thiepval Memorial in France.

**JONES, Thomas:** Rank: Pte. Regiment or Service: Machine Gun Corps. Unit: Infantry, 56th Battalion. Date of death: 27 September 1918. Service no: 156499. Formerly he was with the Royal Irish Regiment where his number was 25414. Born in Abbeylara, Co. Longford. Enlisted in Dublin while living in Clara, Co. Offaly. Killed in action. Age at death: 27.

*Supplementary information*: Son of David and Kate Jones, of Carrickduff, Granard, Co. Longford. Grave or Memorial Reference: II.G.14. Cemetery: Windmill British Cemetery, Monchy-Le-Preux in Freance.

**JONES, Thomas William:** Rank: Lance Corporal. Regiment or Service: Lancashire Fusiliers. Unit: 2nd Battalion. Date of death: 28 October 1914. Service no: 274. Born in Birr, Co. Offaly. Enlisted in Birmingham. Killed in action. Grave or Memorial Reference: Has no known grave but is commemorated on Panel 4. Memorial: Ploegsteert Memorial in Belgium.

**JOUGHIN, Tom:** Rank: Pte. Regiment or Service: Machine Gun Corps. Unit: Cavalry. 60th Company. Date of death: 20 September 1917. Service no: 105468. Formerly he was with the 6<sup>th</sup> Dragoons where his number was 285. Born in Durrow, Co. Offaly also listed as born in Edenderry, Co. Offaly. Enlisted in Enniskillen while living in Ballyduff. Killed in action. From the *King's County Independent*, October 1917:

Grave or Memorial Reference: He has no known grave but is listed on Panels 159 on the Tyne Cot Memorial in Belgium.

**JOYCE, Edward:** Rank: Pte. Regiment or Service: Connaught Rangers. Unit: 2<sup>nd</sup> Battalion. Date of death: 14 September 1914. Service no: 8471. Born in Tullamore, Co. Offaly also listed as born in Kilbride. Enlisted in Tullamore, Co. Offaly while living in Tullamore, Co. Offaly. Killed in action. Age at death: 26.

*Supplementary information:* Son of John Joseph and Mary Joyce. He is listed in De Ruvigny's Roll of Honour with no additional information. Grave or Memorial Reference: He has no known grave but is listed on the La Ferte-Sous-Jouarre-Memorial in France.

**JULIAN, Ernest Lawrence:** Rank: Lieutenant. Regiment or Service: Royal Dublin Fusiliers Unit: 'D' Coy. 7<sup>th</sup> Battalion. Age at death: 36. Date of death: 8 August 1915. Supplementary information: Son of the late John and Margaret Julian, of Drumbane, Birr, Co. Offaly. Held the Reid Professorship of Criminal Law, Trinity College, Dublin. Educated at Charterhouse, and Trinity College, Dublin. Died of wounds after leading his men during the assault on Chocolate Hill on August 7. He died of his injuries the next day on a hospital ship, aged 36, and was buried at sea. Grave or Memorial Reference: Panel 190 to 196. Memorial: Helles Memorial in Turkey.

# K

**KANE, John:** Rank: Pte. Regiment or Service: Leinster Regiment. Unit: 7th Battalion. Date of death: 7 September 1916. Service no: 3218. Born in Kilbride, Co. Offaly. Enlisted in Tullamore, Co. Offaly. Died of wounds. Age at death: 40.

*Supplementary information:* Husband of Margaret Kane, of Tullamore, Co. Offaly. Served in the South African Campaign. He is also listed on the Tullamore Roll of Honour. Grave or Memorial Reference: II. C. 27. Cemetery: La-Neuville British Cemetery, Corbie in France.

**KAVANAGH, Eugene:** Rank: Sapper. Regiment or Service: Corps of Royal Engineers. Date of death: 28 November 1916. Service no: 139487. Formerly he was with the Leic. Regt. (181st Tunn Coy., R.E.) where his number was 1396. Born in Roscrea, Co. Offaly. Enlisted in Birr, Co. Offaly. Died of wounds. Age at death: 43.

*Supplementary information:* Son of Kate Kavanagh, of Grove Street, Roscrea, Co. Tipperary, and the late Gilbert Kavanagh. From the *Midland Tribune, Tipperary Sentinel* and *King's County Vindicator*, November 1914:

Eugene Kavanagh, who was wounded on the side by a shell splinter at Lille has returned from the front. He relates a very narrow escape by Christopher Keily, a former employee at the Bacon Factory. He was splashed with the blood of his slain comrades as they fell about him from bursting shells, while he escaped uninjured.

Grave or Memorial Reference: XX.D.I. Cemetery: Etaples Military Cemetery in France.

**KAVANAGH, James:** Rank: Gunner. Regiment or Service: Royal Garrison Artillery. Date of death: 15 June 1917. Service no: 62783. Born in Birr, Co. Offaly. Enlisted in Liverpool while living in Boston, U.S.A. Died. From the *King's County Chronicle*, April 1916, 'Gunner James Kavanagh, R.F.A., son of the late Mr James Kavanagh, Pound Street, Birr travelled all the way from America to 'do his bit', and is now in training in England.' Grave or Memorial Reference: I.D.23. Cemetery: Feuchy British Cemetery in France.

**KAVANAGH, Michael:** Rank: Pte. Regiment or Service: Leinster Regiment. Unit: 1st Battalion. Date of death: 15 March 1915. Service no: 2041. Born in Frankford, Co. Offaly. Enlisted in Birr, Co. Offaly. Killed in action. Grave or Memorial Reference:

Has no known grave but is commemorated on Panel 44. Memorial: Ypres (Menin Gate) Memorial in Belgium.

**KEAN, Daniel:** (Alias, correct name is **KEENAN, Daniel**). Rank: Sergeant. Regiment or Service: Royal Dublin Fusiliers. Unit: 8th Battalion. Date of death: 27 April 1916. Service no: 15678. Born in Ballyboy, Co. Offaly. Enlisted in Naas while living in Montreal, Canada. Killed in action. Age at death: 36.

*Supplementary information*: Son of Thomas and Eliza Keenan, of Mount Rath Street, Kilcormac, Co. Offaly. Grave or Memorial Reference: XV.L.28. Cemetery: Cabaret-Rouge British Cemetery, Souchez in France.

**KEARNEY, Thomas:** Rank: Pte. Regiment or Service: Royal Irish Regiment. Unit: 4th Battalion. Date of death: 10 October 1918. Service no: 7875. Born in Birr, Co. Offaly. Enlisted in Clonmel, Co. Tipperary. Died at sea. Grave or Memorial Reference: He has no known grave but is listed on the Hollybrook Memorial, in Southampton, UK.

**KEENAN, Daniel:** (Served under the alias **KEAN, DANIEL**). Rank: Sergeant. Regiment or Service: Royal Dublin Fusiliers. Unit: 8th Battalion. Date of death: 27 April 1916. Service no: 15678. Born in Ballyboy, Co. Offaly. Enlisted in Naas while living in Montreal, Canada. Killed in action. Age at death: 36.

*Supplementary information*: Son of Eliza Keenan, of Mount Rath Street,

Kilcormac, Co. Offaly, and the late Thomas Keenan. From the *King's County Chronicle*, 1916:

> Daniel and Thomas Keenan are sons of Mr Thomas Keenan, of Frankford. The former joined the R.I.F. on mobilisation, and there is no account of him officially or otherwise. Thomas is in Cork in the Leinster Regiment.

Grave or Memorial Reference: XV.L.28. Cemetery: Cabaret-Rouge British Cemetery, Souchez in France.

**KELLY, James:** Rank: Pte. Regiment or Service: Leinster Regiment Unit: 2nd Battalion. Age at death: 30. Date of death: 10 October 1918. Service no: 5365. Born in Mullingar and enlisted in Mullingar. Killed in action.

*Supplementary information*: Son of James Kelly, of William Street, Tullamore. Grave or Memorial Reference: VI.B.27. Cemetery: Dadizeele New British Cemetery in Belgium.

**KELLY, James:** Regiment or Service: Royal Flying Corps. This man does not appear in any of the war dead databases. The only reference to him is a short paragraph in a newspaper. He may not be listed as he died after the end of the war (11 November 1918). From the *King's County Independent*, November 1918:

> MILITARY FUNERAL.
> Private James Kelly, William Street, who joined the Royal Flying Corps a couple of weeks ago and who

contracted influenza while undergoing training in England and died on Friday last, was buried in Clonminch cemetery on Wednesday with military honours. The remains were brought home from England on Tuesday. The coffin was draped in the Union Jack and the hearse containing it was preceeded by a platoon of of the Hants Carabiners, and a guard of honour of six men from the same Corps. Rev. J. Lynam, C.C. officiated at the house and at the graveside.

Grave or memorial reference: Cemetery: Clonminch Catholic Cemetery, Co. Offaly.

**KELLY, Joseph:** Rank: Pte. Regiment or Service: Royal Horse Artillery and Royal Field Artillery. Date of death: 17 August 1918. Service no: 248416. Born in Clara, Co. Offaly. Enlisted in Athlone. Died of wounds. Grave or Memorial Reference: He has no known grave but is listed on the Hollybrook Memorial, in Southampton, UK. From the Commonwealth War Graves Commission:'The Hollybrook Memorial commemorates by name almost 1,900 servicemen and women of the Commonwealth land and air forces whose graves are not known, many of whom were lost in transports or other vessels torpedoed or mined in home waters. The memorial also bears the names of those who were lost or buried at sea, or who died at home but whose bodies could not be recovered for burial.'

**KELLY, Joseph:** Rank: Pte. Regiment or Service: Leinster Regiment. Unit: 2$^{nd}$ Battalion. Date of death: 20 October 1914. Service no: 7894. Formerly he was with the Royal Army Medical Corps where his number was 19940. Born in Banagher, Co. Offaly. Enlisted in Aldershot, Hants. Killed in action. Grave or Memorial Reference: He has no known grave but is listed on Panel 10 on the Ploegsteert Memorial in Belgium.

**KELLY, Patrick:** Rank: Pte. Regiment or Service: Leinster Regiment. Unit: 2$^{nd}$ Battalion. Date of death: 1 August 1917. Service no: 10613. Born in Birr, Co. Offaly. Enlisted in Birr. Died of wounds. Grave or Memorial Reference: XVI. G. 19A. Grave or Memorial Reference: I.A.14. Cemetery: Lijssenthoek Military Cemetery in Belgium.

**KELLY, Patrick:** Rank: Pte. Regiment or Service: Leinster Regiment. Unit: 1$^{st}$ Battalion. Date of death: 14 February 1915. Service No: 3422. Born in Killane, Co. Offaly. Enlisted in Tullamore. Killed in action. Age at death: 23.

*Supplementary information:* Son of William and Rose Kelly, of Edenderry, Co. Offaly. Husband of Sarah Doyle (formerly Kelly), of Edenderry, Co. Offaly. Grave or Memorial Reference: Panel 44. Memorial: Ypres (Menin Gate ) Memorial in Belgium.

**KELLY, Patrick:** Rank: Pte. Regiment or Service: Leinster Regiment. Unit: 2$^{nd}$ Battalion. Date of death: 25 August 1916.

Service no: 3532. Born in Cloghan, Co. Offaly. Enlisted in Birr. Killed in action. From the *King's County Chronicle*, April 1916: 'Cloghan and District. Two brothers, Privates, James and Patrick Kelly, of the Leinsters, are serving in France.' Grave or Memorial Reference: Has no known grave but is commemorated on Pier and Face 16.C. Memorial: Theipval Memorial in France.

**KELLY, Patrick:** Rank: Pte 2nd Class. Regiment or Service: Royal Air Force. Unit: 5th Stores Depot. Age at death: 18. Date of death: 25 October 1918. Service no: 306338.

*Supplementary information:* Son of James and Annie Kelly, of Foley's Lane, Tullamore. Grave or Memorial Reference: Near South-West corner. Cemetery: Mucklagh Catholic Churchyard, Co. Offaly.

**KELLY, Patrick:** Rank: Pte. Regiment or Service: Munster Fusiliers. Unit: 1st Battalion. Date of death: 25 June 1915. Service no: 6302 Born in Tullamore, Co. Offaly. Enlisted in Listowel, Co. Kerry while living in Listowel, Co. Kerry. Killed in action in Gallipoli. Age at death: 22.

*Supplementary information:* Son of John and Mary Kelly, Listowel, Co. Kerry. Grave or Memorial Reference: VII.A.6. Cemetery: Twelve Tree Copse Cemetery in Turkey.

**KELLY, William:** Rank: Pte. Regiment or Service: Leinster Regiment. Unit: 2nd Battalion. Date of death: 20 October 1914. Service

no: 9846. Born in Killane, Co. Offaly. Enlisted in Tullamore. Killed in action. Grave or Memorial Reference: Panel 10. Memorial: Ploegsteert Memorial in Belgium.

**KEMPSTON, James Campbell:** Rank: Sergeant (De Ruvigny's Roll of Honour), Corporal (Commonwealth War Graves Commission). Regiment or Service: Central Ontario Regiment. Unit: 15th Canadians, attached to the 48th Highlanders, Canadian Expeditionary Force. Service no: 77726. Data from enlistment documents: Born: Dublin. Next of kin: Mrs J. Campbell Kempston, Phoenix BC. Date of birth: 15 March 1876. Trade or calling: Miner. Former service: Seaforths, eight years India, 1896, Athora, S.A. 1907, Crete, 1897, Obdurman, 1902, Sudan, 1898. Age: 38. Height: 5ft 9in. Complexion: Fair. Eyes: Grey. Hair: Iron Grey. From De Ruvigny's Roll of Honour:

Son of the late Rev. William Augustus Kempston, rector of Bally, Vurly [*sic*] [Ballyburly?] King's County by his wife, Mary, dau, of Henry Campbell; b. Dublin, 15 March, 1871. educ. Benson's School, Rathmines, Dublin; enlisted in May, 1892, in the Seaforth Highlanders, served in India and the Sudan (Medal) and afterwards in the South African War, 1899-1902 (Medal and clasps); on the outbreak of war re-enlisted; served with the Expeditionary Force in France and Flanders and was killed in action in Ypres, 3 June, 1916.

Capt. Spottiswoode wrote; "I have always liked him, and he has invariably borne an excellent character in the regiment." He married at Fernie, British Columbia, in 1906, Olive Georgina, dau. of William Earls, of Dublin and had three children. Lancelot Campbell, born 4 June, 1911; Vera Agnes, born 4 July, 1907; and Iris Mabel, born 29 August, 1908. The family are on the Kootenay sheet of the 1911 Census on page 1.

Grave or Memorial Reference: Panel 18-24-26-30. Memorial: Ypres (Menin Gate ) Memorial in Belgium.

**KENNEDY, Thomas E.:** Rank: Pte. Regiment or Service: Irish Guards. Unit: 1st Bn. Age at death: 25. Date of death: 9 October 1917. Service no: 10168. Born in Dingle, Co. Kerry. Enlisted in Dublin while living in Derrinlough, Co. Offaly. Killed in action.

*Supplementary information*: Son of Michael Kennedy, of Derrinlough, Fiveally, Birr, Co. Offaly. From the *King's County Chronicle*, November 1915:

> Mr Thomas E. Kennedy, R.I.C., lately stationed at Tullaroan, Co Kilkenny, has joined the Irish Guards. His brother, Michael, is at present in the trenches in France, where he is serving with the Royal Irish Rifles. Both these young volunteers are sons of Ex-Costable Kennedy, Derrinlough, Birr, and nephews of Mrs Murray, Coolanarney N.S, Blueball.

From the *King's County Chronicle*, April 1916, 'Cloghan and District. Private Michael Kennedy, of the Irish Rifles, wounded severely. He was home and has gone back again to the firing line. He is son of Mr Kennedy, ex-R.I.C., Derrinlough.' Grave or Memorial Reference: Panel 10 to 11. Memorial: Tyne Cot Memorial in Belgium.

**KENNY, Cecil John:** Rank: Lieutenant. Regiment or Service: Royal Irish Regiment. Unit: 3rd Bn. Secondary Regiment: Machine Gun Corps (Infantry) Secondary. Age at death: 25. Date of death: 24 March 1918. He worked for the Bank of Ireland.

*Supplementary information*: Son of Harry Briscoe Kenny and Elizabeth Kenny, of Clyduffe House, Roscrea, Co. Tipperary. From the *King's County Chronicle*, April 1916: 'King's County officers. Among the many patriotic families in King's County, who are represented in the firing line by commissioned officers are the following from the Banagher and Shinrone districts. The following gentlemen from the Shinrone district have received commissions.' From De Ruvigny's Roll of Honour.

> *Kenny, Cecil John*, Lieut, 3rd (Reserve) Battn, The Royal Irish Regiment, attached to the Machine Gun Corps. 3rd son of Harry Briscoe Kenny, of Clyduff House, Roscrea, County Tipperary, by his wife, Elizabeth, daughter of the late John Wallace, of

Cecil John Kenny.

Ballincor, Shinrone, King's County. Born 8 May, 1895, educated at the Grammar School, Tipperary, subsequently held an appointment in the Queenstown branch of the Ban of Ireland. Enlisted as a Motor Despatch Rider on the outbreak of war, gazetted 2nd Lieut, in Jan, 1915, Lieut. in Sept, 1917, served with the Expeditionary Force in France and Flanders from Jan 1916, was wounded at Mametz Wood the following July. On recovery was attached to the Machine Gun Corps, and was killed in action at Ham, during the retreat from St Quentin, 24 March, 1918. An officer wrote; "Your son Cecil, who was universally loved by his brother officers and men, died fighting in an endeavour to save his gun. For two days he had bluffed the Boche and held back their attack, persuading the infantry to hold the line with him. Even when the Boche came to handgrips, he could have got away, but scorned to do so without his gun."

Another: 'Lieut. Kenny is sadly missed by his fellow officers and men. He was always so good humoured, a thorough gentleman and an all-round sportsman.' Grave or Memorial Reference: II.C.7. Cemetery: Ham British Cemetery, Muille-Villette in France. He is also listed on the 1914-1918. Bronze War Memorial in the Bank of Ireland in College Green, Dublin 2.

**KENNY, Francis:** Rank: Pte. Regiment or Service: Connaught Rangers. Unit: 1st Battalion. Date of death: 8 November 1914. Service no: 9873. Born in Banagher, Co. Offaly. Enlisted in Ballinasloe, Co. Galway while living in Banagher, Co. Offaly. Killed in action. Age at death: 27.

*Supplementary information:* Son of Patrick and Mary Kenny, of Curraghvama, Banagher, Co. Offaly. From the *Midland Tribune, Tipperary Sentinel* and *King's County Vindicator* 1914:

BANAGHER PARISH.

Private Francis Kenny. The parents of Private Francis Kenny, Connaught Rangers, have received the sad news that he was killed in action on the 8th of November, while serving with the Indian Expeditionary Force. He was of fine athletic appearance, and much sympathy is felt for his parents. The notification was accompanied with the usual note of sympathy from the King and the Queen.

Grave or Memorial Reference: I.A.14. Cemetery: Rue-Du-Bacquerot No.1 Military Cemetery, Laventie in France.

**KENNY, Patrick:** Rank: Pte. Regiment or Service: Irish Guards. Unit: 1st Battalion. Date of death: 26 September 1916. Service no: 8568. Born in Ballinahown, Co. Offaly. Enlisted in Tullamore. Killed in action. Age at death: 23.

*Supplementary information:* Son of Michael and Bridget Kenny, of Ballycumber, Co. Offaly. Grave or Memorial Reference: Pier and Face 7 D. Memorial: Thiepval Memorial in France.

**KEOGH, William:** Rank: Pte. Regiment or Service: Royal Irish Regiment. Unit: 4th Battalion. Date of death: 5 October 1917. Service no: 6106. Born in Kilbride, Co. Offaly. Enlisted in The Curragh, Co Kildare. Age at death: 17. Died at home.

*Supplementary information:* Son of Paul Keogh, of Barrack Street, Tullamore. Grave or Memorial Reference: 2.194. Cemetery: Clonminch Catholic Cemetery, Co. Offaly.

**KERRIGAN, Francis Eugene:** Rank: Company Sergeant Major. Regiment or Service: Leinster Regiment. Unit: 2nd Battalion. Date of death: 25 August 1916. Service no: 5134. Born in Crinkle, Co. Offaly. Enlisted in Birr, Co. Offaly. Died. Age at death: 35/36. He won the Military Medal and is listed in the *London Gazette*. He also won the South African Medal and the Mons Star. Listed in 'Ireland's Memorial Records' under **KERRIGAN, Francis C.**

*Supplementary information*: Son of Christopher and Sarah Kerrigan, of St Kilda Lodge, Birr, Co. Offaly. From the *King's County Chronicle*, January 1915:

CRIMEAN VETERAN DEAD IN BIRR.
One by one the old Crimean veterans in and about Birr are going from us. The last to answer "the call" was Mr Christopher Kerrigan, Military Road, who died on Wednesday, 30th December, at the age of 80, after an illness of about two months. He joined the 3rd East Kents, Buffs, and saw service abroad for 10½ years, gaining the Crimea medal with clasp for Sabastapol, the Turkish medal, and the China medal with clasp for the Taku Forts. He left the army in 1872 and spent 39 of the 42 intervening years in Birr, holding an appointment at the barracks for 24 years. Four of his sons were soldiers but one fell in South Africa; three are on active service at present with the 2nd Leinsters, 2 being Sergeants. The funeral took place on Sunday to Clonoghill Cemetery. The immediate family representatives were his sons, Anthony and Christopher Kerrigan, and his daughter Mrs Sarah Patterson. Military honours were accorded, about a hundred of the troops in charge of Sergeant Callaghan, marching behind the hearse. The coffin was wrapped in the Union Jack and after the last prayers were recited by Rev. E. J. Scanlan, R.C.C, three volleys were fired and the 'last post' sounded.

See the article attached to **MURRAY, George**. Grave or Memorial

Reference: Plot 2. Row B. Grave 86. Cemetery: Corbie Communal Cemetery Extension in France.

**KERSHAW, Michael:** Rank: Pte. Regiment or Service: Leinster Regiment. Unit: C Company, 2nd Battalion. Date of death: 20 October 1914. Service no: 7194. Born in Frankford, Co. Offaly. Enlisted in Birr. Killed in action. Age at death: 22.

*Supplementary information*: Son of the late Michael and Mary Kershaw; husband of Mary E. Kershaw, of Spa, Castleconnell, Co. Limerick. He was reported missing in 1914 and left a family and children in Pound Street. Grave or Memorial Reference: Has no known grave but is commemorated on Panel 10. Memorial: Ploegsteert Memorial in Belgium.

**KEYS, Patrick:** Rank: Pioneer. Regiment or Service: Corps of Royal Engineers. Unit: Inland Waters and Docks Division. Date of death: 15 September 1917. Service no: 296156. Enlisted in Tullamore. Died at home. Grave or Memorial Reference: Screen Wall, War Plot. Cemetery: Bristol (Arnos Vale) Roman Catholic Cemetery, UK. Note: Died at Home usually means that he 'Died' (drowning, suicide, accident or illness) and at home means out of the battle area and back in England; rarely does it actually mean in Offaly. I have found other Irish men buried in this Cemetery and they usually died in Bishop's Knoll Hospital, Bristol. None of the war dead databases available to me give his birth place. I have no fur-

ther information about this man but I would rather include him than take a chance on him not being a Co. Offaly man and left out in the cold.

**KINAHAN/KILAHAN, Daniel:** Rank: Pte. Regiment or Service: Leinster Regiment. Unit: 2nd Battalion. Date of death: 4 November 1915. Service no: 4219. Born in Kilcormac, Co. Offaly. Enlisted in Birr. Killed in action. Listed in 'Ireland's Memorial Records' and 'Soldiers died in the Great War' as Kilahan. Listed in the Commonwealth War Graves Commission as Kinahan. Age at death: 25.

*Supplementary information*: Son of the late David Kinahan and of Anne Kinahan, of Birr Street, Kilcormac, Tullamore, Co. Offaly. Grave or Memorial Reference: IIC.C.I5. Cemetery: Voormezeele Enclosures No 1 and No 2 in Belgium.

**KILLACKEY, Patrick:** Rank: Sergeant. Regiment or Service: Leinster Regiment. Unit: 2nd Battalion. Date of death: 16 June 1917. Service no: 1630. Born in Banagher, Co. Offaly. Enlisted in Birr, Co. Offaly. Killed in action. Age at death: 37.

*Supplementary information:* Husband of Mary Manning (formerly Killackey), of 54 West Craven Street, Salford, Manchester. Grave or Memorial Reference: I.G.II. Cemetery: Divisional Collecting Post Cemetery and Extension in Belgium.

**KILLACKY, Thomas:** Rank: Pte. Regiment or Service: Leinster

Regiment. Unit: Not given. Date of death: 28 July 1916. Service no: 2860. Born in Co. Offaly. Killed in action. Age at death: 34.

*Supplementary information*: Awarded the Mons Star. He only appears in 'Ireland's Memorial Records'. From the *King's County Chronicle*, April 1916: 'Banagher's Record. Sergt. Patrick Killacky, 3rd Leinsters, Private Thomas, do, and Driver, Joseph, A.S.C. (wounded) brothers.' He is not listed in 'Soldiers died in the Great War' and he is not listed with the Commonwealth War Graves Commission. A quick check with the National Archives in Kew shows that there is no Medal Index Card for Serial No 2860, Thomas Killacky/Killackey.

## KILLACKEY/KILLACKY, Thomas: Rank: Pte. Regiment or Service: Household Cavalry and Cavalry of the line including the Yeomanry and Imperial Camel Corps. Unit: 13[rd] Hussars. Date of death: 28 July 1916. Service no: 6850. Born in Cloghan, Co. Offaly. Enlisted in Athlone, Co Westmeath while living in Banagher, Co. Offaly. Died in Mesopotamia. From the *Midland Tribune*, *Tipperary Sentinel* and *King's County Vindicator*, December 1914:

BROTHERS AT THE FRONT.
Lance Corporal Joseph Killacky (3404) R.A.M.C. who was through the battle of Mons, and all engagements or retirement back to Soissons in the Fifth Division, states that he witnessed cruelty to women and children. He accompanied home Lieutenant Herbert, who was wounded severely at Landou _____ and who's leg was amputated on October 9th in ____ Cross Hospital, Netley. The Lieutenant has since succumbed to his injuries. Lance Corporal Killacky is now transferred to guide duty, and escorted Corporal O'Toole, First Leicesters, from Havre to Richmond Asylum, Dublin, having received a bullet wound which effected the head. He states that the Germans keep a close watch of the Red Cross workers, and that they make targets of churches, hospitals and schools. Corporal Killacky, who is home again, is confined to bed suffering from a severe cold.

His brother, Lance Corporal T, Killacky, 11th Hussars, is at present a patient in First Western General Hospital, Fazerkerley, Liverpool, after undergoing an operation to his knee which was fractured at the battle of St Quinten. Another brother, Corporal Patrick Killacky, of the third Battalion, Leinster Regiment, is at present serving in Cork. All three saw active service in the South African War, and are sons of the late Private Thomas Killacky, who went through the Indian Mutiny in 1857, and got injured at the siege of Lucknow, and who was the only representative from the Co. Offaly who attended the banquet in the Albert Hall, London, in 1907. He was then 85 years of age, and the late Lord Roberts congratulated him upon being the youngest looking man by 20 years, and the oldest by 12 years. He died in 1909. Corporal Killacky has brought home several trophies in the shape of German bridles and bits.

Grave or Memorial Reference: V.P.16. Cemetery: Basra War Cemetery in Iraq.

**KINAHAN, Gregory:** Rank: Pte. Regiment or Service: Royal Dublin Fusiliers. Unit: 9th Battalion. Date of death: 9 September 1916. Service no: 5495. Born in Geashill, Co. Offaly. Enlisted in Naas while living in Kildare. Killed in action. Grave or Memorial Reference: Has no known grave but is commemorated on Pier and Face 16C. Memorial: Theipval Memorial in France.

**KING, Thomas Christopher:** Rank: Pte. Regiment or Service: Royal Scots Fusiliers. Unit: 6/7th Battalion. Date of death: 22 July 1917. Service no: 23631. Born in Parsonstown. Enlisted in Glasgow while living in Kilrush, Co. Clare. Died of wounds. Age at death: 39.
*Supplementary information*: Son of George and Alice King, of 7 Black Street, Townhead, Glasgow. Born at Birr, Co. Offaly. Grave or Memorial Reference: II.F.21. Cemetery: Mendinghem Military Cemetery in Belgium.

**KINNARNEY, William:** Rank: Pte. Regiment or Service: Leinster Regiment. Unit: "A" Coy. 2nd Bn. Age at death: 37. Date of death: 9 June 1917. Service no: 6853. Born Balltcommon Co. Offaly and enlisted in Tullamore. Died.

*Supplementary information*: Son of John Kinnarney. Husband of Annie Pender (formerly Kinnarney), of Dublin Road, Roscrea, Co. Tipperary. Grave or Memorial Reference: VI.F.8. Cemetery: Wytschaete Military Cemetery in Belgium.

**KINSELLA, William:** Rank: Pte. Regiment or Service: Canterbury Regiment, New Zealand Expeditionary Force. Unit: 1st Battalion. Date of death: 6 September 1918. Service no: 6/2434. Age at death: 29.
*Supplementary information*: Son of Laurence Kinsella, of Castle Street, Birr, Co. Offaly.

Nominal Ross of the New Zealand Expeditionary Force.
William Surname: Kinsella War: Serial No: 6/2434. First Known Rank: Private Next of Kin: Mrs M.A. Kinsella (mother), Carribirr, Parsons Town, King's County, Ireland. Marital Status: Single. Enlistment Address: C.P.O., Auckland, New Zealand. Military District: Auckland. Body on Embarkation: 6th Reinforcements. Embarkation Unit: Canterbury Infantry Battalion. Embarkation Date: 14 August 1915. Place of Embarkation: Wellington, New Zealand. Transport: Vessel: Willochra or Tofua. Destination: Suez, Egypt. Page on Nominal Roll: 396. Last Unit Served: Canterbury Infantry Regiment. Place of Death: Havrincourt, France. Date of death: 6 September 1918. Year of Death: 1918 Cause of Death: Killed in action.

From the *King's County Chronicle*, September 1918:

Mr Kinsella, farmer, Carrig, has been informed by telegram from the military authorities of the death in action in France of his son, Private William Kinsella, of the New Zealanders. This brave soldier was a brother of Mr John J. Kinsella, of Castle Street, Birr, had over three and a half years service, and was twice home on a visit to his friends. He was well known in Birr and district and the news of his death will be received with very deep regret.

Grave or Memorial Reference: IV.C.II. Cemetery: Lebusquiere Communal Cemetery Extension in France.

# L

**LAING, ST. CLAIR, King Nixon:**
Rank: Second Lieutenant. Regiment
or Service: Royal Munster Fusiliers.
Unit: 7th Battalion. Died. Date of
death: 2 April 1917. Age at death: 42.

*Supplementary information*: Son of
Maria Louisa and James Kerr Laing,
of Overcliffe, Enniscrone, Co. Sligo, of
Knox Street, Ballina, Co. Mayo. At the
time of the 1911 census he was lodging
at 14 Windsor Street, the house of Ezliz
Pearson. He was then a thirty-three-
year-old bank cashier, Presbyterian
and a native of Roscommon. Grave
or Memorial Reference: III.B.59.
Cemetery: Bailleul Communal
Cemetery (Nord) in France. He is
listed on the memorial in Castro Petre
Church of Ireland in Edenderry and
also listed in the Mayo Memorial
Peace Park Garden of Remembrance
in Castlebar, County Mayo.

**LAVELLE, Garrett:** Rank: Lance
Corporal. Regiment or Service:
Leinster Regiment. Unit: 2nd Bn. Date
of death: 1 September 1916. Service
no: 5172. Born in Carrigatroy, Co
Tipperary. Enlisted in Borrisokane
while living in Birr, Co. Offaly.
Killed in action. Grave or Memorial
Reference: He has no known grave
but is listed on Pier and Face 16 C on
the Thiepval Memorial in France.

**LAWLOR, Edward:** Rank:
Pte. Regiment or Service: Royal
Inniskilling Fusiliers. Unit: 8th
Battalion. Date of death: 21 March
1918. Service no: 27615. Formerly
he was with the Leinster Regiment
where his number was 914. Born
in Killeigh, Co. Offaly. Enlisted in
Tullamore, Co. Offaly. Killed in action.
Age at death: 21.

*Supplementary information*: Son of the
late Thomas Lawlor, of Barrack Street,
Tullamore, Offaly. Grave or Memorial
Reference: Panel 38 to 40. Memorial:
Pozieres Memorial in France.

**LAWLOR, T.:** Rank: Pte. Regiment
or Service: 8th (King's Royal Irish)
Hussars. Date of death: 29 November
1918. Service no: 3421.

*Supplementary information*: Son of Mr
Lawlor, of Barrack Street, Tullamore.
From the *King's County Independent*,
March 1917, 'Military item. In con-
nection with the Tullamore roll
of honour which appeared in a
recent issue of the "King's County
Chronicle" the following were inad-
vertently omitted: Pte Denis Lawler,
3rd Connaught Rangers.'
Note: Denis survived the war. Grave
or Memorial Reference: L.32.
Cemetery: Durrow (St. Columbcille)
Catholic Churchyard, Co Offaly.

**LEHANE, Thomas:** Rank: Pte. Regiment or Service: London Regiment. Unit: 5<sup>th</sup> (City of London) Battalion (London Rifle Brigade). Date of death: 28 March 1918. Service no: 303299. Born in Birr, Co. Offaly. Enlisted in London while living in Balham. Killed in action. Age at death: 20.

*Supplementary information:* Son of Garrett Lehane and Mary Teresa Lehane, of 96 Tooting Bec Road, Tooting, London. Grave or Memorial Reference: Bay 9. Memorial: Arras Memorial in France.

**LONGWORTH-DAMES. T D.:** Rank: Lieutenant. Regiment or Service: 6<sup>th</sup> Dragoons (Inniskilling). Date of death: 28 November 1919.

*Supplementary information:* Alternative Commemoration: buried in Ballyburley Church of Ireland Churchyard, Co. Offaly. From the *King's County Independent*, August 1917:

LIEUT DAMES LONGWORTH
The Clerk read the following letters;

1<sup>st</sup> London General Hospital.
Camberwell,
London, E.C.
"Sir,
I should be very much obliged if, at the next meeting of the Athlone Board of Guardians, you would convey to them my thanks for the action they took in receipt of the news of my death, which I very much appreciated. I am glad to say that I am very much better and so far from being dead. I hope in the future to spend many happy days in the neighbourhood of Athlone.
Yours faithfully,
Mrs. Lennon – I hope so.
Travers R. Dames. Longworth."

Clerk – I have another one also from Mrs Dames Longworth as follows;--

Golf Links Hotel,
Rosses Point,
Sligo.
"Dear Mr Donnelly
I hope that you will convey to the Athlone Board of Guardians my best thanks for the message they deputed you to send me of sympathy in the reported loss of my son. They will, I know, share my happiness in knowing that it was only a rumour, as he is alive and nearly well again. After the illness he was invalided home from the front. With renewed thanks,
Believe me, yours faithfully.
Hester Dames Longworth."

Grave or Memorial Reference: Panel 2 (Screen Wall). Memorial: Grangegorman Memorial, Dublin.

**LONGWORTH, Patrick:** Rank: Pte. Regiment or Service: Leinster Regiment. Unit: 2<sup>nd</sup> Battalion. Date of death: 20 October 1914. Service no: 7173. Born in Frankford, Co. Offaly. Enlisted in Birr, Co. Offaly. Killed in action.

*Supplementary information*: Son of John Patrick and Frances Longworth, of Mount Rath Street, Kilcormac, Co. Offaly Grave or Memorial Reference: Has no known grave but is commemorated on Panel 10. Memorial: Ploegsteert Memorial in Belgium.

**LONGWORTH, Robert:** Rank: Pte. Regiment or Service: East Lancashire Regiment. Unit: C Company, 1st Battalion. Date of death: 26 August 1918. Service No: 8802. Born in Frankford, Co. Offaly. Enlisted in Tullamore, Co. Offaly while living in Frankford, Co. Offaly. Killed in action. Age at death: 27.

*Supplementary information:* Son of John Patrick Longworth, D.C.M., and Frances Longworth, of Mount Rath Street, Kilcormac, Co. Offaly. From the *King's County Chronicle*, 1916, 'Frank Longworth, of the Dublins, is also in Greece. He is son of Mr Patrick Lingworth, and ex-army pensioner, who had three sons in the army. Two were called up on mobilisation, being on the Reserve. One son, Robert, was killed in action in France, and a second is a prisoner of war in Germany.' From the *King's County Independent*, March 1917, 'Military item. In connection with the Tullamore roll of honour which appeared in a recent issue of the "King's County Chronicle" the following were inadvertently omitted: Driver, James Longworth, R.F.A."

Note: James survived the war. He is also listed in De Ruvigny's Roll of Honour with no additional information. Grave or Memorial Reference: Memorial: La Ferte-Sous-Jouarre Memorial in France.

**LOUGHNANE, Patrick:** Rank: Stoker, 2nd Class. Regiment or Service: Royal Navy. Unit: HMS *Ettrick*. Date of death: 7 July 1917. Service no: K/32262. Born in Co. Offaly. Torpedoed and drowned. The ship HMS *Ettrick* (a river class destroyer) is a bit of a mystery. She was supposed to have been torpedoed and sunk by the German mine laying submarine UC61 15 miles off Beachy Head. Another report says she hit a mine which blew off her bows and she was sold for scrap in 1919. Whatever the incident that damaged her in 1917, the fact remains that approx 50 of her crew died on that day. See the image below showing her bows blown apart. This is from 'Swept Channels by Traffail'. Age at death: 24.

Patrick Loughnane.

*Supplementary information*: Son of Hubert and Mary Anne Loughnane, of Boherdal, Birr, Co. Offaly. Grave or Memorial Reference: 24 (Commonwealth War Graves Commission) 22 ('Ireland's Memorial Records'). He has no known grave but is listed on the Chatham Naval Memorial, UK.

**LOWRY, Patrick:** Rank: Pte. Regiment or Service: Royal Field Artillery. Unit: D Battery, 56th Brigade. Date of death: 4 March 1919. Service no: 101624. Born in Co. Offaly. Died of pneumonia. Age at death: 25.

*Supplementary information*: Son of Patrick and Ann Lowry, of Raheen, Clara, Co. Offaly Grave or Memorial Reference: Div. 64. VIII.K.4. Cemetery: Ste. Marie Cemetery, Le Havre in France.

**LUCAS, Herbert:** Rank: Pte. Regiment or Service: Dorsetshire Regiment. Unit: 6th Battalion. Date of death: 11 October 1918. Service no: 20183. Formerly he was with the Hampshire Regiment where his number was 38728. Born in Birr, Co. Offaly. Enlisted in Portsmouth, Hants. Killed in action.

*Supplementary information*: Son of William Lucas, of 64 Collins Road, Southsea, Portsmouth. From the *King's County Chronicle*, 14 November 1918:

With deep regret we heard of the death in action of Second Lieut. Bertie Lucas, M.C., 6th Dorset Regiment. In a recent issue we recorded the news

of this brave lad being awarded the M. C. for gallantry. His death coming so soon and so near the end of the war make the news more sad. To his father, Colour Sergt. Lucas, Leinsters, Birr, and Mrs Lucas, we tender our deepest sympathy in the loss of the second brave boy. Also to Quartermaster D. Hayes, Leinsters, Mrs and family, and to George and Mrs Shummacher, junior, Dublin, and other relatives. Colour Sergt. Lucas has a daughter serving in the R.A.F., as well as his three sons, who are in the army.

Grave or Memorial Reference: I.C.17. Cemetery: Montay-Neuvilly Road Cemetery, Montay in France.

**LYNCH, Patrick:** Rank: Rifleman. Regiment or Service: Royal Irish Rifles. Unit: 14th Battalion. Date of death: 13 April 1916. Service no: 5404. Born in Philipstown, Co. Offaly. Enlisted in Tullamore, Co. Offaly while living in Philipstown, Co. Offaly. Killed in action. Age at death: 20.

*Supplementary information*: Son of John and Mary Lynch, of Daingean, Offaly. From the *King's County Independent*, July 1918:

REGRETTED DEATH.

At the Masses in Philipstown Catholic Church on Sunday last, prayers were asked for the repose of the soul of Private Patrick Lynch, who died in France. Officially reported missing some twelve months ago, it is only now that his fate has been ascertained. A mere youth when he joined the army, Patrick Lynch was very popular with all classes, being a most obliging and winning disposition, and his early death fighting for freedom is universally regretted. May he rest in peace.

Grave or Memorial Reference: Pier and Face 15 A and 15 B. Memorial: Thiepval Memorial in France

**LYNCH, Peter:** Rank: Pte. Regiment or Service: Connaught Rangers. Unit: 5<sup>th</sup> Battalion. Date of death: 20 October 1918. Service no: 5209. Born in Philipstown, Co. Offaly. Enlisted in Hamilton while living in Newmains, Lanark. Died of wounds. Age at death: 25.

*Supplementary information:* Son of Patrick and Annie Lynch, of 3 Pillan's Land, Newmains, Lanarkshire. Native of Philipstown, Co. Offaly. Grave or Memorial Reference: I.A.6. Cemetery: Highland Cemetery, Le Chateau in France.

# M

**MACFARLANE, Thomas Morton:** Rank: Engineer Lieutenant. Regiment or Service: Royal Naval Reserve. Unit: HMS *Knight Templar*. Date of death: 7 April 1018. Age at death: 37.

*Supplementary information*: Son of John Russell MacFarlane, of Liverpool. Husband of Charlotte Mary MacFarlane, of 28 Hereford Road, Wavertree, Liverpool. From the *King's County Chronicle*, April 1918, 'Engineer Lieutenant, Thomas Morton MacFarlane, R.N.R., lost at sea through enemy action on April 7th, 1918, was the husband of Charlotte youngest daughter of John Henry Flynn, C.P.S., Ferbane.' Grave or Memorial Reference: 30. Memorial: Plymouth Naval Memorial, UK.

**MADIGAN, William:** Rank: Pte. Regiment or Service: Leinster Regiment. Unit: 1st Battalion. Date of death: 1 March 1915. Service no: 9001. Born in Johnstown, Co. Offaly. Enlisted in Birr, Co. Offaly. Killed in action. Age at death: 22.

*Supplementary information:* Son of John and Margaret Madigan, of Ballyroan, Co. Laois. Grave or Memorial Reference: Panel 44. Memorial: Ypres (Menin Gate ) Memorial in Belgium.

**MAGUIRE, Patrick Joseph:** Rank: Pte. Regiment or Service: Royal Army Service Corps. Date of death: 30 April 1918. Service no: M/341206. Born in Clara, Co. Offaly. Enlisted in Glasgow while living in Bridgeton. Died in East Africa. Grave or Memorial Reference: 6.H.4. Cemetery: Dar Es Salaam War Cemetery in Tanzania.

**MAHER, Patrick:** Rank: Pte. Regiment or Service: Royal Munster Fusiliers. Unit: 2nd Battalion. Date of death: 16 November 1914. Service no: 10019. Born in Shinrone, Co Offaly. the Great War' gives his place of birth as Shinrone, Tipperary. Enlisted in Limerick while living in Roscrea. Killed in action. Grave or Memorial Reference: Panel 44. Memorial: Ypres (Menin Gate) Memorial in Belgium.

**MAHON, William:** Rank: Pte. Regiment or Service: Connaught Rangers. Unit: 1st Battalion. 'Ireland's Memorial Records' and the Commonwealth War Graves Commission give his date of death as 26 April 1915 and 'Soldiers died in the Great War' gives it as 2 November 1914. Service no: 10586. Born in Banagher, Co. Offaly. Enlisted in Manchester while living in Banagher. Killed in action. Age at death: 23. Won the Mons Star. Grave or Memorial Reference: Panel 42. Memorial: Ypres (Menin Gate) Memorial in Belgium.

**MANNING, John:** Rank: Pte. Regiment or Service: Leinster Regiment. Unit: 2nd Battalion. Date of death: 14 March 1915. Service no: 3583. Born in Banagher, Co. Offaly. Enlisted in Athlone. Killed in action.

*Supplementary information:* Son of Mrs B. Manning, of Queen Street, Banagher, Co. Offaly. Grave or Memorial Reference: A.21. Cemetery: Ferme Buterne Military Cemetery, Houplines in France.

**MARKS, Joseph:** Rank: Pte. Regiment or Service: Devonshire Regiment. Unit: 2nd Battalion. Date of death: 18 December 1914. Service no: 5290. Born in Birr, Co. Offaly. Enlisted in London while living in Portsmouth. Killed in action. Grave or Memorial Reference: Has no known grave but is commemorated on Panel 8 and 9. Memorial: Le Touret Memorial in France.

**MARTIN, John:** Rank: Pte. Regiment or Service: Connaught Rangers. Unit: 5th Battalion. Date of death: 8 October 1918. Service no: 15080. Formerly he was with the Leinster Regiment where his number was 4245. Born in Kilbride, Co. Offaly. Enlisted in Tullamore, Co. Offaly while living in Tullamore. Killed in action. Grave or Memorial Reference: A.10. Cemetery: Serain Communal Cemetery Extension in France.

**MARTIN, Michael:** Rank: Pte. Regiment or Service: Leinster Regiment. Unit: 2nd Battalion. Date of death: 1 September 1916. Service no: 10463. Born in Tullamore, Co. Offaly. Enlisted in Tullamore, Co. Offaly. Killed in action. He is also listed on the Tullamore Roll of Honour. Grave or Memorial Reference: Pier and Face 16C. Memorial: Theipval Memorial in France.

**MATHER, Edward William:** Rank: Second Lieutenant. Regiment or Service: Royal Engineers. Unit: 1st (Northumberland) Field Coy, Territorial. Date of death: 13 October 1916. Died of wounds.

*Supplementary information:* Son of E.W. and Ada Mather. Husband

Edward William Mather.

of H.A. Mather, of Brookville, Edenderry, Co. Offaly. From De Ruvigny's Roll of Honour:

> Mather, Edward William, 2nd Lieut. R.E., 2nd son of the late Edward William Mather, Land Owner, by his wife, Charlotte Adelaide (Brookville) Edenderry, Co. Offaly), daughter of Thomas Bor; born Edenderry aforesaid, 6 Oct, 1888. Educated at home; subsequently became an Engineer and held an important position for some years in Mexico; later returned to England to take up a post in Newcastle-on-Tyne, where he was when war broke out; obtained a commission in the R.E. 8 Dec, 1915; trained at Silkstone and Newark-on-Trent; served with the Expeditionary Force in France and Flanders from 17 Aug, 1916, and died on No 22 Ambulance Train, 13th Oct, following, from wounds received in action at Martinpuich. Buried in St Pierre Cemetery, Amiens. He married at St George's Parish Church, Dublin, 16 Aug, 1915, Harriet Amelia (Brookville, Edenderry, Co. Offaly), daughter of Garrett Charles Tyrrell, J.P., F.S.I., and had a daughter, Willa Doreen, born (posthumous) 15 February 1917.

Grave or Memorial Reference:VI.B.5. Cemetery: St Pierre Cemetery, Amiens in France.

**MATHEWS, James:** Rank: Sergeant Major. Regiment or Service: Kings African Rifles. Unit: 3rd Battalion. Date of death: 29 June 1917. Service no: Not given. Born in Tullamore, Co. Offaly. Killed in action in Ikoma, German East Africa, aged 31. Awarded the Cross of Chevalier, Order of Leopold II. He only appears in 'Ireland's Memorial Records'. He is not listed in 'Soldiers died in the Great War' and he is not listed with the Commonwealth War Graves Commission. A quick check with the National Archives in Kew shows that there is no Medal Index Card for him there.

**MATHEWS, Sam:** Rank: Not given but possibly Gunner. Regiment or Service: Royal Field Artillery. Date of death: 25/27 October 1919. Service no: Possibly L/35881. Born in Co. Offaly. Died of wounds.

*Supplementary information:* Won the M.M. and the D.S.M. so he should be listed in the *London Gazette*. He only appears in 'Ireland's Memorial Records'. He is not listed in 'Soldiers died in the Great War' and he is not listed with the Commonwealth War Graves Commission. A quick check with the National Archives in Kew shows that there is a Medal Index Card for Serial No L/35881 Gunner Samuel Mathews.

**MAXWELL, James:** Served under the Alias of **CARPENTER, James,** Rank: Pte. Regiment or Service: Leinster Regiment. Unit: 1st Battalion. Date of death: 12 May 1915. Service no: 9437. Born in Tullamore, Co. Offaly. Enlisted in Tullamore, Co. Offaly. Died of wounds.

*Supplementary information:* Son

of James and Mary Maxwell, of Tullamore, Co. Offaly. From the *King's County Chronicle*, September 1917:

> News has been received my Mr James Maxwell, ex-Sergt, R.I.C., Charleville, Tullamore, of his son, Quartermaster-Sergeant J. Maxwell, R.I.R., having been seriously wounded in action at Lens, by being struck with shrapnel on the head and lower jaw, the injuries extending to the roof of his mouth.
>
> He lies in the Canadian hospital in France. Quartermaster-Sergt, Maxwell served eight years in his regiment in India and Burma and was on the army reserve at the outbreak of the war. He rejoined the colours of his old battalion in which he went in the first British Expeditionary Force, and was wounded in the battle of Mons.

Grave or Memorial Reference: 1.A.9. Cemetery: Brandhoek New Military Cemetery in Belgium.

**McAFEE, Johnston:** Rank: Company Quartermaster Sergeant. Regiment or Service: Royal Irish Fusiliers. Unit: 2nd Bn. Age at death: 36. Date of death: 3 January 1917 Service no: 6717. Born in Portadown, Co. Armagh. Enlisted in Portadown. Died in Salonika.

*Supplementary information:* Son of Mrs McClatchey, of 111 Donegal Road, Belfast. Husband of Elizabeth Jane McAfee, of Portland School House, Birr, Co. Tipperary. Served in the South African Campaign. Grave or Memorial Reference: 760. Cemetery: Salonika (Lembet Road) Military Cemetry in Greece.

**McBRIDE, Alex:** Rank: Pte. Regiment or Service: Royal Dublin Fusiliers. Unit: 9th Bn. Date of death: 29 June 1918. Service no: 12405. Husband of Mrs M. McBride, of Main Street, Edenderry. From the *Leinster Leader* 15 July 1916:

Alex McBride.

177

Edenderry soldiers Private Jack Connolly 9th battalion R. D. Fusiliers and Private Alex McBride have received the parchment cert for the gallant conduct and devotion to duty. Names and deeds entered on the record of each division. Connolly is a mere boy and a native of the Tunnel. McBride is a painting contractor and married a daughter of John Dunne of the Main St. they are both members of the Ancient Order of Hibernian Boys' brigade band. McBride was an accomplished bandmaster.

Grave or Memorial Reference: Near southwest boundary. Cemetery: Monasteroris Old Graveyard, Co. Offaly.

**McCABE, James:** Rank: Rifleman. Regiment or Service: Royal Irish Rifles. Unit: 8th Battalion. Date of death: 7 June 1917. Service no: 5221. Born in Tullamore, Co. Offaly. Enlisted in Tullamore, Co. Offaly. Died of wounds. Grave or Memorial Reference: III.C.235. Cemetery: Bailleul Communal Cemetery Extension (Nord) in France.

**McCABE, Thomas:** Rank: Pte. Regiment or Service: Leinster Regiment. Unit: 7th Battalion. Date of death: 7 June 1917. Service no: 5109. Born in Kilbride, Co. Offaly. Enlisted in Tullamore, Co. Offaly while living in Tullamore, Co. Offaly. Killed in action. Grave or Memorial Reference: He has no known grave but is listed on Panel 44 on the Ypres (Menin Gate) Memorial in Belgium.

**McCANN, John:** Rank: Gunner. Regiment or Service: Royal Horse Artillery and Royal Field Artillery. Date of death: 16 September 1918. Service no: 76461. Born in Edenderry, Co. Offaly. Enlisted in Mullingar, Co. Westmeath. Died. Grave or Memorial Reference: In the northeast quarter near the crucifix. Cemetery: St. Pierre-Le-Moutier Communal Cemetery in France.

**McCARTHY, Joseph:** Rank: Pte. Regiment or Service: Irish Guards. Unit: 1st Battalion. Date of death: 25 April 1916. Service no: 4675. Born in Clare [*sic*], Co. Offaly. Enlisted in Tullamore, Co. Offaly. Killed in action. Age at death: 23.

*Supplementary information:* Son of James and Mary McCarthy, of 125 St Patrick's Terrace, Clara, Offaly. Listed in Ireland's Records under both Joseph and James McCarthy. Grave or Memorial Reference: I.L.4. Cemetery: Menin Road South Military Cemetery in Belgium.

Joseph McCarthy. The image is taken from the *King's County Independent* February 1916.

**McCORMACK/McCORMICK, Bernard:** Rank: Pte. Regiment or Service: Connaught Rangers. Unit: 1st Bn. Age at death: 30. Date of death: 5 November 1914. Service no: 8313. Born in Eyrecourt, Co. Galway. Enlisted in Ballinasloe while living in Galway. Killed in action.

*Supplementary information*: Son of Patrick and Catherine McCormick, of Banagher, Co. Offaly. Grave or Memorial Reference: XVI.AA.36. Cemetery: Cabaret Rouge British Cemetery, Souchez, France.

**McCORMACK, John:** Rank: Pte. Regiment or Service: Connaught Rangers. Unit: 5th Battalion. Date of death: 11 October 1918. Service no: 15210. Formerly he was with the Leinster Regiment where his number was 4290. Enlisted in Birr, Co. Offaly while living in Birr. Killed in action. Age at death: 36.

*Supplementary information*: Son of John and Bridget McCormack, of Birr; husband of Mary McCormack of Mill Street, Birr, Co. Offaly. From the *King's County Chronicle*, February 1916:

> Mr John McCormack, Pound Street, has two sons serving: Private Michael, of the 5th Royal Irish Lancers, who was in the South African War, and had completed his service on the reserve. He re-enlisted at the outbreak of the war, and re-joining his regiment on mobilisation went with them to France, where he was wounded. He has happily recovered, and is again on active service.

> Private John, of the 6th Leinsters, who joined for the duration of the war, is out in the Near East with his regiment.

From the *King's County Chronicle*, August 1917:

> There is at present home on leave at his sister's residence, Pound Street, Private M. McCormick, 5th Royal Irish Lancers, who joined up on the outbreak of war, he being on the reserve. He then went to France and was in many engagements for some months till he was wounded. He was then home, but when he got better he was sent out for the second time. He is looking fine, and is very cheerful, although he has gone through a lot. He is son of Mr John McCormick, gardener, Pound Street.

From the *King's County Chronicle*, November 1918:

> PTE. JOHN MCCORMACK, 6TH LEINSTERS.
>
> This valiant Irish soldier, who was well known, admired and respected in his native town of Birr, has been officially reported killed in action on the 11th October. He fought at the Dardanelles, and in the retreat in Servia, and in Salonika, and Egypt, and was sent thence to the French front. Prior to the war, he was a steady and industrious man, employed in Birr sawmills, and shortly after the outbreak of the war he enlisted on the formation of the 6th Battalion of the Leinsters. His brother, Trooper Michael McCormack, is serving

in the 5ᵗʰ Royal Irish Lancers; and deceased leaves a widow and two little children.

Unofficial news contained in a letter from a comrade stated he had just come back from the trenches when volunteers were asked to perform a dangerous duty in connection with the field kitchen under fire; McCormack and his comrade and a third of the brave stepped forward, but they had advanced only a short distance when an exploding shell fell beside them killing the two and dangerously wounding the third man and thus after the many dangers he had passed he gallantly fell in what might have been a passing incident, and within a few days of peace, and the prospect of a soldiers return, but, though buried far away,.

"After life's fitful fever,
He sleeps, well. "

Grave or Memorial Reference: I.F.22. Cemetery: Montay-Neuvilly Road Cemetery, Montay in France.

**McCORMACK, Joseph:** Rank: Pte. Regiment or Service: Irish Guards. Unit: 1ˢᵗ Battalion. Date of death: 1 November 1914. Service no: 4094. Born in Kilbride, Co. Offaly. Enlisted in Tullamore. Died of wounds. Grave or Memorial Reference: IV.A.20. Cemetery: Perth Cemetery (China Wall) in Belgium.

**McCORMACK, Michael:** Rank: Acting Lance Corporal. Regiment

or Service: Royal Dublin Fusiliers. Unit: 2ⁿᵈ Battalion. Date of death: 24 May 1915. Service no: 9601. Born in Ballinahown. Enlisted in Carlow. Killed in action. Grave or Memorial Reference: He has no known grave but is listed on Panel 33 on the Ypres (Menin Gate) Memorial in Belgium.

**McCORMACK, Michael:** Rank: Pte. Regiment or Service: Leinster Regiment. Unit: B Company, 2ⁿᵈ Battalion. Date of death: 16 August 1915. Service no: 3142. Born in Kilbeggan, Co. Westmeath ('Soldiers died in the Great War') Co. Offaly ('Ireland's Memorial Records'). Enlisted in Tullamore. Killed in action. Age at death: 29.

*Supplementary information:* Son of the late Joseph and Annie McCormack. Husband of Margaret McCormack, of 8 St James' Street, Oldham. Grave or Memorial Reference: He has no known grave but is listed on Panel 33 on the Ypres (Menin Gate) Memorial in Belgium.

**McCORMACK, Patrick:** Rank: Pte. Regiment or Service: Leinster Regiment. Unit: 2ⁿᵈ Bn. Age at death: 22. Date of death: 15 August 1915. Service no: 3340. Born in Kilbeggan. Enlisted in Tullamore. Killed in action.

*Supplementary information:* Son of Mrs M.K. McCormack, of Collinstown, Clara, Co. Offaly. Grave or Memorial Reference: Union St. Graveyard No. 1 Cem. Mem. 14. Cemetery: Birr Cross Roads Cemetery in Belgium.

**McCORMACK/McCORMICK, Thomas:** Rank: Gunner. Regiment or Service: Royal Field Artillery and Royal Horse Artillery. Unit: A Battery, 28th Brigade. Date of death: 5 December 1917. Service no: 6184. Born in Edenderry, Dublin [*sic*]. Enlisted in Falkirk. Killed in action. Age at death: 25.

*Supplementary information*: Son of Darby McCormick, of Killane, Edenderry, Co. Offaly. Grave or Memorial Reference: XIV.F.7. Cemetery: Dozinghem Military Cemetery in Belgium.

**McCORMACK, William:** Rank: Pte. Regiment or Service: Leinster Regiment. Unit: 6th Battalion. Date of death: 11 August 1915. Service no: 71. Born in St Brendan, Birr, Co. Offaly. Enlisted in Birr, Co. Offaly. Killed in action in Gallipoli. Son of Mr James McCormack, Pound Street. Formerly he was in the Connaught Rangers. In the *King's County Chronicle* of 1916 there is a photograph of Private James McCormack, 2nd Leinsters and adds: 'Third son of Mr James McCormack, Pound Street, Birr.' He also served in the South African War. From the *King's County Chronicle*, February 1916:

> Mr James McCormack, Pound Street, well-known as the winner of several old-age pensioner's races, gave three sons to his King and Country – Private Michael, who was killed in the South African War with the Connaughts; Privates William, 6th Leinsters, killed at the Dardanelles; and James, 3rd Leinsters, wounded, and again on active service.

Grave or Memorial Reference: He has no known grave but is listed on Panel 184 to 185 on the Helles Memorial in Turkey.

**McCORMACK, William:** Rank: Pte. Regiment or Service: Leinster Regiment. Date of death: 15 July 1915. Service no: 3576. Born in Birr, Co. Offaly. Died of wounds in the Dardanelles. Age at death: 46.

*Supplementary information:* Won the South African King's and Queen's medals. He only appears in 'Ireland's Memorial Records'. He is not listed in 'Soldiers died in the Great War' and he is not listed with the Commonwealth War Graves Commission. A quick check with the National Archives in Kew shows that there is no Medal Index Card for Serial No 3576, McCormack.

William McCormack.

**McCORMICK/McCORMACK, Bernard:** Rank: Pte. Regiment or Service: Connaught Rangers Unit: 1ˢᵗ Bn. Age at death: 30. Date of death: 5 November 1914. Service no: 8313. Born in Eyrecourt, Co. Galway. Enlisted in Ballinasloe while living in Galway. Killed in action.

*Supplementary information:* Son of Patrick and Catherine McCormick, of Banagher, Co. Offaly. Grave or Memorial Reference: XVI AA. 36. Cemetery: Cabaret Rouge British Cemetery, Souchez, France.

**McCULLA, John:** Rank: Corporal. Regiment or Service: Leinster Regiment. Unit: 2ⁿᵈ Bn. Age at death: 32. Date of death: 14 October 1918. Service no: 7412. Born in Maryborough, Co. Laois. Enlisted in Maryborough. Killed in action.

*Supplementary information*: Son of John and Kate McCulla, of Maryborough, Co. Offaly. Grave or Memorial Reference: II.B.4. Cemetery: Dadizeele New British Cemetery in Belgium.

**McCUTCHEON, George Orr:** Rank: Sergeant. Regiment or Service: Royal Inniskilling Fusiliers. Unit: C Company, 5ᵗʰ Battalion. Date of death: 10 September 1916. Service no: 11382. Born in Edenderry, Co. Offaly. Enlisted in Pollokshaws, Renfrew. Killed in action in the Balkans. Age at death: 22.

*Supplementary information*: Son of Andrew and Rachel McCutcheon, of Bishop Street, Londonderry.

Native of Omagh, Co. Tyrone. Grave or Memorial Reference: IV.J.6. Cemetery: Struma Military Cemetery in Greece.

**McDONALD, Frederick:** Rank: Pte. Regiment or Service: Royal Inniskilling Fusiliers. Unit: 2ⁿᵈ Battalion. Date of death: 16 May 1915. Service no: 10555. Born in Birr, Co. Offaly. Enlisted in Birr, Co. Offaly. Killed in action. *King's County Chronicle*, February 1916: 'The following sons of the late Mr George McDonald, Sandymount, Birr, late of the 3ʳᵈ Leinsters, who had been in the South African War, and was out on pension, are: Privates Harry, of the 2ⁿᵈ Leinsters, missing since early in the war; Fred, of the Inniskillings, reported

Frederick McDonald. The image is taken from the *King's County Chronicle* 1916 and includes the following information, 'Son of the late Mr George McDonald, Sandymount, Birr. He has three other brothers serving, one, Pte Henry, and a brother-in-law, Pte Henry Sheedy, of the Leinsters being missing since 1914'.

missing, and Gunner John, of the R. F. A., on active service.' He has no known grave but is listed on Panels 16 and 17 on the Le Touret Memorial in France.

**McDONALD, Henry:** Rank: Lance Corporal. Regiment or Service: Leinster Regiment. Unit: 2nd Battalion. Date of death: 20 October 1914. Service no: 8401. Born in Birr, Co. Offaly. Enlisted in Birr, Co. Offaly. Killed in action. Age at death: 21.

*Supplementary information:* Son of George and May McDonald. From the *King's County Chronicle*, August 1915:

> Four sons of the late Mr George McDonald, of Birr, and formerly of the Leinster Regiment, are serving in the Army, and two of them who were in the British Expeditionary Force in France have been missing for several months, namely, Private Harry [*sic*], 2nd Leinster Regiment, and Private Fred, 2nd, Inniskilling Fusiliers. Fred who is about 20 years of age, has not communicated with his people since May. Their brothers, John and Edward, are serving with the Artillery and the Royal Irish Rifles respectively.

Grave or Memorial Reference: 2.F.13. Cemetery: Canadian Cemetery No. 2, Neuville-St. Vaast in France.

**McDONALD, Peter:** Rank: Pte. Regiment or Service: Royal Army Service Corps. Unit: 341st Motor Transport Company. Date of death: 21 January 1916. Service no: M2/102018. Born in Rahan, Co. Offaly. Enlisted in Dublin while living in Tullamore, Co. Offaly. Died at Home. Age at death: 20.

*Supplementary information*: Son of Michael and Mary McDonald, of Charleville Road, Tullamore, Co. Offaly. From *King's County Chronicle*, February 1916:

> Private Peter McDonald, A.S.C., a native of Charleville, near Tullamore, who was drafted to Weston, Somerset, for training, while examining a Colt automatic pistol accidentally shot a comrade named Goldsmith in the leg. The latter, observing that McDonald was unaware the weapon was loaded, took it from him, and while removing the cartridges it went off again, the bullet entering McDonald's abdomen, who died in a few hours. Goldsmith's injury is trivial.

Grave or Memorial Reference: 1426. Cemetery: Weston-Super-Mare Cemetery, UK.

**McDONNELL, Edward:** Rank: Pte. Regiment or Service: Australian Pioneers. Unit: 4th. Date of death: 21 April 1917. Service no: 2166. Age at death: 25.

*Supplementary information*: Son of Patrick and Mary Ann McDonnell, of Wooloowin, Queensland. Born in 1891 in Co. Offaly. Data from enlistment documents: Born in Birr, Co. Offaly. Trade or calling: Labourer. Next of kin: Patrick McDonnell (father) c/o Mr W.E. Young, 3 Henry Street, Spring Hill, Brisbane. Age: 26. Height: 5ft 7ins. Weight: 11st. Complexion: Fair.

Eyes: Hazel. Hair: Brown. Embarked overseas per "Lake Manitoba" 1 August 1916 to Tel-el-Kabir. Taken on strength, Pioneer Training Battalion, 20 August 1916. Admitted to Delhi Hospital, Perham Downs 8 October 1916. Marched in from No. 2 Com Depot, 1 December 1916. Charged at Perham Downs with 'Breaking camp and remaining absent without leave on 26 December 1916. Breaking away from escort. Award twenty-eight days detention, total forfeiture thirty-one days pay. Another sheet in his records says he was fined twenty-three days' pay. Marched out to Larkhill, Perham Downs on 26 February 1917. Left Larkhill for Folkestone 9 March 1917. Proceeded overseas to France 20 March 1917. Marched in to Etaples. Killed in action by a High Explosive shell and was buried in a temporary grave, N. E. Bapaume. Pension of 35 shillings per fortnight was awarded to his mother, Mrs Mary McDonnell, 39 Little George Street, S. Hill from 6 July 1917. His memorial plaque was sent to his father in August 1922 and his medals were also sent to him in 1923. Grave or Memorial Reference: I.F.14. Cemetery: Vaulx Hill Cemetery in France.

**McDONNEL, Francis:** Killed in Flanders, 14 August 1915. This man is not in any other war dead database. He is listed on the Tullamore Roll of Honour. I do not see the Offaly connection but include him for your reference.

**McDONNELL, Patrick:** Rank: Pte.

Regiment or Service: Connaught Rangers. Unit: 5th Battalion. Date of death: 20 December 1915. Service no: 5506. Born in Kilbride, Co. Offaly. Enlisted in Tullamore, Co. Offaly while living in Clara, Co. Offaly. Died of wounds in Salonika. Grave or Memorial Reference: He has no known grave but is listed on the Doiran Memorial in Greece.

**McDOWELL, John:** Rank: Pte. Regiment or Service: Royal Inniskilling Fusiliers. Unit: 1st Battalion. Date of death: 21 August 1915. Service no: 20079. Born in Edenderry, Co. Offaly. Enlisted in Derry while living in Belfast. Killed in action in Gallipoli. Grave or Memorial Reference: He has no known grave but is listed on Panel 55 on the Helles Memorial in Turkey.

**McDOWELL, James:** Rank: Rifleman. Regiment or Service: New Zealand Rifle Brigade. Unit: 3rd Battalion. Date of death: 27 October 1918. Service no: 39547. Occupation on enlistment: Farmhand. Next of kin listed as J. B. Collier (friend) Ruanui, New Zealand. Went out with the 21st Reinforcements Wellington Infantry Battalion. B Company on 19 January 1917 from Wellington, New Zealand on the 'Ulimaroa'. From the *King's County Chronicle*, August 1918, 'Mr James McDowell, New Zealand Force, one of the four fighting sons of Mr McDowell, Barnaboy, is home on leave from France.' From the *King's County Chronicle*, November 1918:

**Pte James McDowell, New Zealanders.**

The sad new has reached Mr and Mrs Robert McDowell, of Barnaboy, Frankford, of the death of their sixth son, James from wounds received in action in France. He was in every sense an excellent type of the patriot soldier, all the ardour of whose manly and generous nature had irresistibly drawn him to the service of his country. He had emigrated to New Zealand, and there fortune seemed to favour his enterprise, when the war broke out, and the voice of the Motherland calling her sons to her defence was to him the call of duty. After many months of the hard fortunes of war, borne with all the heroic fortitude of the bravest, he got leave last summer, and was home on a visit to his parents, who, needless to say, were rejoiced beyond measure to receive him; and as at all time he had been a favourite with his friends and the people of the district, he was welcomed back with the heartiest goodwill.

The news came that he was seriously wounded, and in the short interval before the news of his death, his relatives earnestly hoped that he might be spared, and their hearts would have gladdened at his return; but it was not to be; he has given his life for his country. Only a few months ago, we published the news of the death of his sister while engaged in medical work at Salonika. Great sympathy is felt for the bereaved parents.

Grave or Memorial Reference: II.E.18. Cemetery: Delsaux Farm Cemetery, Beugny in France.

**McEVOY, Edward:** Rank: Pte. Regiment or Service: Irish Guards. Unit: 2nd Battalion. Date of death: 21 September 1917. Service no: 11208. Born in Banagher, Co. Offaly. Enlisted in Maryhill, Lanark while living in Garbally, Co. Offaly. Died of wounds. Age at death: 28.

*Supplementary information:* Son of Margaret McEvoy, of Garbally, Co. Offaly. From De Ruvigny's Roll of Honour:

> McEvoy, Edward P., Private, No 11208, Irish Guards. Youngest son of Patrick McEvoy, of Garbally, Birr, King's County, Farmer, by his wife, Margaret. Daughter of Peter Sully, of Moystown; born Garbally, Birr aforesaid, 12 May, 1886. Educated at Garbally Catholic Boys School; was a Farmer; enlisted in the Irish Guards, 11 April 1915; served with the Expeditionary Force in France and Flanders from Aug, 1916, and died at Wimereux General Hospital 21 Sept, 1917, of wounds received in action. Buried in the cemetery there.

Grave or Memorial Reference: VI.B.5. Cemetery: Wimereux Communal Cemetery, Pas de Calais, in France.

**McEVOY, Joseph:** Rank: Private. Regiment or Service: Irish Guards. Unit: 1st Bn. Age at death: 20. Date of death: 17 July 1916 Service no: 9082.

Born in Portarlington, Co. Laois. Enlisted in Portarlington, Co. Laois. Died of wounds.

*Supplementary information:* Son of Michael and Katherine McEvoy, of Gracefield, Portarlington, Co. Offaly. Grave or Memorial Reference: VIII.C.28A. Cemetery: Lijssenthoek Military Cemetery in Belgium.

**McEVOY, Patrick:** Rank: Pte. Regiment or Service: Royal Irish Regiment. Unit: 2nd Battalion. Date of death: 14 September 1914. Service no: 9216. Born in Geashall, Co. Offaly. Enlisted in Tullamore while living in Ballymacarberry, Co. Waterford. Died of wounds. Grave or Memorial Reference: Plot 38, 1914-18, Row A Grave 4. Cemetery: Le Mans West Cemetery in France.

**McEWAN, Patrick:** Rank: Pte. Regiment or Service: Black Watch (Royal Highlanders). Unit: 2nd Battalion. Date of death: 4 November 1914. Service no: 2017. Born in Clara, Co. Offaly. Enlisted in Perth. Killed in action. From the *King's County Chronicle*, January 1915:

WASHED OUT TRENCHES.

In these latter weeks, says the Special Correspondent of the 'Times' in Northern France, no infantry movement has been possible beyond sniping. The incessant rains have converted the trenches into a quagmire. Both sides are at a stand in the mud. By constant purring, life in the trenches is tolerable. Outside the men sink to their knees. In such conditions an assault on a trench, even across the narrow space which separates them, is impossible. A tributary of the little Lounne flooded one of our trenches north of Festubert, and two men were drowned. During a storm the parapets of one of our trenches and one of the Germans were washed away. Friend and foe set to work to repair in full view of each other, as only 60 yards separates them, but not a shot was fired. Getting into and out of the trenches at night is dangerous. Wooden causeways have been constructed from the billets to within a quarter of a mile of the entrance to the trenches. But that quarter of a mile has sometimes taken two hours to traverse.

Grave or Memorial Reference: VII.H.9. Cemetery: Brown's Road Military Cemetery, Festubert in France.

**McGIFF/McGIFT, Joseph:** Rank: Pte. Regiment or Service: Leinster Regiment. Unit: 2nd Battalion. Date of death: 20 October 1914. Service no: 9737. Born in Kilbride, Co. Offaly. Enlisted in Tullamore. Killed in action. Age at death: 19.

*Supplementary information*: Son of Mrs Anne McGiff, of Kevin Street, Tullamore, Co. Offaly. Grave or Memorial Reference: Panel 10. Memorial: Ploegsteert Memorial in Belgium.

**McGIFF, Thomas:** Rank: Pte. Regiment or Service: Highland Light Infantry. Unit: 1st Battalion. Date of death: 2 July 1915. Service no: 11077.

Born in Clare [*sic*], Co. Offaly. Enlisted in Coatbridge, Lanarkshire while living in Glenboig, Lanarkshire. Died of wounds. Has no known grave but is commemorated on Panel 37 and 38. Memorial: Le Touret Memorial in France.

**McGLYNN/McGLVNN, John:** Rank: Lance Corporal. Regiment or Service: East Lancashire Regiment. Unit: 6th Battalion. Date of death: 9 April 1916. Service no: 9244. Born in Tullamore, Co. Offaly. Enlisted in Birr, Co. Offaly while living in Tullamore, Co. Offaly. Killed in action in Mesopotamia. Grave or Memorial Reference: He has no known grave but is listed on Panel 19 on the Basra Memorial in Iraq.

**McGLYNN, John:** Rank: Pte. Regiment or Service: Royal Dublin Fusiliers. Unit: 2nd Battalion. Date of death: 3 May 1917. Service no: 20009. Born in Philipstown, Co. Offaly. Enlisted in Birr, Co. Offaly while living in Philipstown, Co. Offaly. Killed in action. Age at death: 36.

*Supplementary information:* He won the Military Medal and is listed in the *London Gazette*. Son of the late Mr and Mrs Thomas McGlynn. Husband of Easter Mulloy (formerly McGlynn), of Clara, Offaly. From the *King's County Independent*, January 1916:

CAUGHT IN A TRENCH.

John McGlynn, of the Little Island, Philipstown, was an old soldier, having fought through the South African war, and shortly after the outbreak of the present titanic struggle, he again offered himself for service and rejoined his old regiment, the Royal Dublin Fusiliers. Since then he has gone through many a hard engagement, but escaped being hurt until the 8th December last, when a German shell exploded within three yards of the trench where he was. Four of his comrades were killed outright, while McGlynn was caught underneath the falling trench, and not being able to extricate himself from his difficult position he was forced to remain beneath the debris for about seven hours, until relief came. He was then quite exhausted, and was removed to hospital.

From the *King's County Independent*, June 1917:

MISSING.

Private Christopher Brock, of the 5th Lancers, and Private John McGlynn, of the Royal Dublin Fusiliers, both belonging to Philipstown, have been reported 'missing', since an engagement on the 3rd of May. Private Brock, who, before he joined the Army, was part owner of an extensive and flourishing business, was a prominent member of the local Corps of National Volunteers, while McGlynn was an Instructor in the same Corps. Private McGlynn fought through the South African War. He was awarded the Military Medal for bravery in the field.

Note: Private Brock does not appear in any War dead database. Another reference to this missing soldier appears in the King's County Independent in December, 1916, however he did survive the war. Grave or Memorial Reference: Panel 44 and 46. Memorial: Ypres (Menin Gate) Memorial in Belgium.

**McGRATH, John:** Rank: Sergeant. Regiment or Service: Irish Guards. Unit: 1st Battalion. Date of death: 3 October 1915. Service no: 4594. Born in Clara, Co. Offaly. Enlisted in Tullamore, Co. Offaly. Died of wounds.

*Supplementary information:* Son of David and Mary McGrath, of Erry Hills, Clara, Co. Offaly. Born 8 June 1896, 'Soldiers died in the Great War' gives his number as 4594. The Commonwealth War Graves Commission also gives his number as 4594. 'Ireland's Memorial Records' gives his number as 4595. His meal index card shows that his number was 4594 and he first entered the theatre of war in France on 13 February 1915.

He is also listed in *The Irish Guards in the Great War, The first Battalion* by Rudyard Kipling. His number is also given as 4594. Grave or Memorial Reference: I.E.2. Cemetery: Noeux-Les-Mines Communal Cemetery in France.

**McGUINNESS, Joseph:** Rank: Pte. Regiment or Service: Irish Guards. Unit: 1st Battalion. Date of death: 30 November 1917. Service no: 10575. Born in Edenderry, Co. Offaly. Enlisted in Dublin. Died of wounds. Grave or Memorial Reference: II.C.10. Cemetery: Fins New British Cemetery, Somme in France.

**McGUIRE, Hugh:** Rank: Pte. Regiment or Service: Royal Dublin Fusiliers. Unit: 2nd Battalion. Date of death: 21 March 1918. Service no: 10387. Born in Birr, Co. Offaly. Enlisted in Glasgow. Killed in action. From the *King's County Chronicle*, September 1918:

John McGrath's medal index card showing his entry to the French theatre of War 13 February 1915 and his medal entitlements.

Official notification has been received of the death, in action, in France, of Hugh McGuire, aged 30, of the Royal Dublin Fusiliers. His father, Mr Michael McGuire, who now resides at Ballina, was formerly in the R.I.C., and was stationed for some years at Killyon, Birr, where the deceased was born. Sergeant McGuire R.I.C., Shannonbridge, and Sergeant P McGuire, Army Pay Corps, are brothers of the deceased.

Grave or Memorial Reference: He has no known grave but is listed on Panel 79 and 80 on the Pozieres Memorial in France.

**McKENNA, John:** Rank: Pte. Regiment or Service: Connaught Rangers. Unit: 6th Battalion. Date of death: 26 June 1916. Service no: 6912. Born in Killeigh, Co. Offaly. Enlisted in Glasgow while living in Glasgow. Killed in action. Age at death: 39.

*Supplementary information*: Husband of Catherine McKenna, of Distillery Cottages, Garnkirk, Glasgow. Grave or Memorial Reference: I.B.10. Cemetery: St Patricks Cemetery, Loos in France. He is also listed on panel 124 of the Loos memorial.

**McKEON/McKEOWN, Patrick:** Rank: Lance Corporal. Regiment or Service: Connaught Rangers. Unit: 1st Battalion. Date of death: 24 May 1916. Service no: 9734. Born in Clara, Co. Offaly. Enlisted in Tullamore while living in Clara, Co. Offaly. Died of wounds in Amara, Mesopotamia.

Killed in action. From the *King's County Independent*, November 1914:

CLARA RANGER'S STORY.

Frank Hill and Paddy McKeon, privates in the 2nd Connaught Rangers, have just returned to Clara suffering from wounds which they received at the battle of the Aisne. The former was wounded by a portion of the casing of a shell in the leg and also in the neck, while the latter received a bullet wound in the back. According to Private Hill, the battle of the Aisne was a veritable hell on earth. It began on the morning of the 14th September. When a small party of sharp-shooters were selected from each company to pick out the German commanders. The main body of the Connaughts began the advance half and hour afterwards.

"We had to fight our way to a small canal branching off the River Aisne and when we got to the canal the Uhlans commenced sniping us. We succeeded in crossing the canal and when we got to a big bridge across the Aisne we had to sling our rifles and get down one side and got through the water to the other side. After crossing the river we advanced for about 8 miles when we came in contact with the Germans who were about 2, 000 strong. We opened fire at about 550 yards and continued to advance up to within about 200 yards of them when they commenced a deadly fire on us. Every now and again five or six of our fellows would be knocked down. The Germans showed a white flag and even turned the butts of the rifles towards us and we continued to approach them. They seemed as if they were about to surrender but when within fifty yards of them they again opened fire and knocked us clean out in fact. We then got the order to retire, but some of our chaps refused to retire and continued banging away with their rifles. All of a sudden I felt myself hit in the back, under the right shoulder bone."

A NARROW ESCAPE.

Private Hill then related that he was afterwards brought to a building adjacent where there were several other wounded soldiers. It was a kind of old stable he said and he was left there until 2 o'clock the following morning. "When I got shot," he continued, "I was put on a stretcher and just as the stretcher-bearers were about to bear me away, one of them was hit with shrapnel and flattened out. The other dropped the handles of the stretcher and fled. When a lull came in the firing I was carried away to the stable referred to. We had not left it three quarters of an hour next morning, when the Germans started shelling the whole place. They had the range from the day before and they did not leave as much as a stone upon a stone in the building. We were then shifted to a big farm house and put to lie in about three feet of corn and where

we were treated for our injuries by Lady Dudley's hospital corps. We remained about three weeks there when we were sent home."

Private Hill mentioned that in the advance at the battle of the Aisne the Connaught Rangers had to advance through a mangled field on their hands and knees. The magazine of his own rifle got clogged with clay and he had to throw it away and get a dead comrade's. It also got clogged and became useless, when he had to get another with which he continued to fire away. It was while he was on his knees that he was wounded.

Grave or Memorial Reference:VII.F.9. Cemetery: Amara War Cemetery in Iraq.

**McKEON/McKEOWN, William:** Rank: Pte. Regiment or Service: Irish Guards. Unit: 2$^{nd}$ Battalion. Date of death: 17 April 1918. Service no: 6607(SDGW and 'Ireland's Memorial Records') and 6507 (CWGC). Born in Bannagher, Co. Offaly. Enlisted in Dublin. Died of wounds. Age at death: 22.

*Supplementary information:* Son of Thomas McKeon. Native of Banagher, Co. Offaly. From the *Midland Tribune*, *Tipperary Sentinel* and *King's County Vindicator*, November 1915, 'Wounded: Private William McKeon, who volunteered from Banagher for the Irish Guards at the outbreak of the war, has been wounded with shrapnel, and is in hospital.' From the *Midland Tribune*, May 1918:

Private Willie McKeon, Irish Guards, has succumbed in the Base Hospital, France, as a result of abdominal wounds received in action. The news of his being wounded was notified by wire, and the gravity of his condition was such that no permission would be given to his parents to visit him. Having lingered for almost three weeks, and having himself written to his parents describing his wounds, hopes were entertained of his recovery, but a relapse took place, and pneumonia set in with fatal results. He was previously twice wounded at Cambrai and the Somme. He was the youngest son of the late Mr Thomas McKeon and Mrs J. A. McKeon, The Square, Banager, and 69 Cabra Road, Dublin.

From the *King's County Chronicle*, May 1918:

Deep sympathy with the grief-stricken parents was the prevailing feeling in Banagher when the news was received that Private Willie McKeon, of the 2nd Batt, Irish Guards, had succumbed in the Base Hospital, France as a result of abdominal wounds received in action. The news of his being wounded was notified by wire and the gravity of his condition was such that no permission would be given to his parents to visit him. Having lingered on for almost three weeks, and having himself written to his parents describing his wounds, hopes were entertained of his recovery, but a relapse took place and bronchitis set in with fatal results.

He was previously twice wounded at Cambrai and the Somme. Shortly after the outbreak of war he voluntarily joined up, his fine physique and appearance being favourably commented on. Of a quiet and unassuming disposition, and cheery and pleasant nature, he was beloved by all, both by his comrades in the trenches and those acquainted with him in civil life. He was the youngest son of the late Mr Thomas McKeon, the Square, Banagher, and 69 Cabra Road, Dublin, and to his bereaved mother, brothers and sisters and deepest sympathy is extended at the loss of a brave young son and soldier.

Grave or Memorial Reference: XXIX.F.7A. Cemetery: Etaples Military Cemetery in France.

**McLOUGHLIN, Patrick:** Rank: Acting Corporal. Regiment or Service: Royal Munster Fusiliers. Unit: 9th Battalion. Date of death: 22 September 1916(SDGW), 22 September 1915 ('Ireland's Memorial Records' and the Commonwealth War Graves Commission). Service no: 3353. Born in Cloghan, Co. Offaly. Enlisted in Coatbridge while living in Cloghan, Co. Offaly. Died at Home. Grave or Memorial Reference: About 13 Yards south west of the ruin. Cemetery: Banagher Old Graveyard, Co Offaly.

**McLOUGHLIN, William:** Rank: Pte. Regiment or Service: Leinster Regiment. Unit: 1st Battalion. Date of death: 14 January 1915. Service no:

9679. Born in Cloughan, Co. Offaly. Enlisted in Birr, Co. Offaly. Killed in action. 'Ireland's Memorial Records' state that he died of wounds in Germany. Age at death: 35.

*Supplementary information*: Son of John and Mary McLoughlin, of Banagher Street, Cloghan, Co. Offaly. From the *King's County Chronicle*, April 1916, 'Cloghan and District. Three sons of John McLoughlan, himself an old soldier, viz: Patrick, of the 6th Leinsters; Willie, of the Irish Guards, killed in action in France; and Joseph, of the 3rd Leinsters, in France for twelve months.' Grave or Memorial Reference: He has no known grave but is listed on Panel 44 on the Ypres (Menin Gate) Memorial in Belgium.

**McMAHON, James:** Rank: Pte. Regiment or Service: Royal Dublin Fusiliers. Unit: 6th Battalion. Date of death: 8 October 1918. Service no: 43680. Formerly he was with the Leinster Regiment where his number was 1852. Born in Kilbride, Co. Offaly. Enlisted in Tullamore, Co. Offaly while living in Clara, Co. Offaly. Killed in action. Age at death: 20.

*Supplementary information*: Son of Robert and Maggie McMahon, of 104 High Tullamore, Clara, Co. Offaly. Grave or Memorial Reference: C.II. Cemetery: Beaurevoir British Cemetery in France.

**McMULLEN, Alexander Percival:** Rank: Lieutenant. Regiment or Service: Royal Navy Unit: HMS *Invincible*. HMS *Invincible* was sunk during the battle of Jutland. Age at death: 24. Date of death: 31 May 1916.

*Supplementary information:* Son of Alex. R. and Frances E. McMullen, of Dixie, Ontario, Canada. Native of Tullamore. Grave or Memorial Reference: 11. Memorial: Portsmouth Naval Memorial, UK.

**McNAMARA, John:** Rank: Pte. Regiment or Service: Leinster Regiment. Unit: 2nd Battalion. Date of death: 15 August 1915. Service no: 3572. Born in Kilbride, Co. Offaly. Enlisted in Tullamore, Co. Offaly. Killed in action. From the *King's County Independent*, March 1917, 'Military item. In connection with the Tullamore roll of honour which appeared in a recent issue of the "King's County Chronicle" the following were inadvertently omitted: Driver, William McNamara, R.F.A.' Note: William survived the war. Grave or Memorial Reference: III.C.18. Cemetery: Birr Cross Roads Cemetery in Belgium.

**McNAMEE, Lawrence/Laurence:** Rank: Pte. Regiment or Service: South Wales Borderers. Unit: 5th Battalion. Date of death: 25 March 1918. Service no: 18121. Born in Edenderry, Co. Offaly, ('Ireland's Memorial Records') Aidenderry, Kingscourt. ('Soldiers died in the Great War'). Enlisted in Haverfordwest, Glam. Killed in action. Grave or Memorial Reference: He has no known grave but is listed in Bay 6 on the Arras Memorial in France.

ERECTED
TO THE GLORY OF GOD
AND IN PROUD AND LOVING MEMORY OF
J. C. McNEILL,
2ND LIEUT 2ND ESSEX REGT
WHO FELL AT ARRAS ON MAY 3RD 1917
IN THE GREAT WAR OF 1914-1919
GREATER LOVE HATH NO MAN THAN THIS

John Charles McNeill.

**McNEILL, John Charles:** Rank: Second Lieutenant. Regiment or Service: Essex Regiment. Unit: 2nd Bn. Age at death: 20. Date of death: 3 May 1917. The image above forms part of the War Memorial in Tullamore Presbyterian Church courtesy of Rev. William Hayes. The memorial also contains the names of men from the Tullamore Presbyterian Church congregation who served and survived the war.

*Supplementary information*: Son of J. and Mary Anne McNeill, of Tullamore, Offaly. Grave or Memorial Reference: Bay 7. Memorial: Arras Memorial in France.

**McNULTY, Michael Anthony:** Rank: Pte. Regiment or Service: Leinster Regiment. Unit: 7th Battalion. Date of death: 16 April 1916. Service no: 2718. Born in Birr, Co. Offaly. Enlisted in Birr, Co. Offaly while living in Birr, Co. Offaly. Killed in action. Age at death: 19.

*Supplementary information*: Son of Patrick and Abina McNulty, of Crinkle, Birr, Co. Offaly From the *Midland Tribune*, *Tipperary Sentinel* and *King's County Vindicator* April 1917, 'Pte McNulty, of the 1st Irish Guards, has come home on a visit to his people at Crinkle. He is stationed in Bradford with three late members of the Birr R.I.C., now in the Irish Guards, Ptes Hempenstall, Conway and Duffy, all of whom expect to be soon well enough to return to the front.' From *King's County Chronicle*, April 1916:

BRAVE YOUNG CRINKLE SOLDIER KILLED.

The sad intelligence has been received of the death, in action, of Pte Michael Anthony McNulty, of the 7th Leinsters, son of Const. McNulty, Crinkle, Birr. This brave young soldier, who was only 19 years of age, was killed near Ypres on the 16th April. The melancholy news was conveyed to his bereaved father in the following letter from Company Quarter-Master Sergt. R. Nixon, of the same regiment:

In the field,
17th April, 1916.
'Dear Mr McNulty,
I take this very painful opportunity of writing the sad news of the death of your noble son (Michael), who was killed in action on the night of the 16th inst. He was one of the bravest grenadiers who was engaged in the bloody fight of that night. Very few men have ever worked harder than he did that night. He died the death of a true Irish soldier. Thank God he got Absolution a very short time before the attack. Dear Mr McNulty, break the news very gently to his poor mother and sisters; I

know it will break their poor hearts. Convey to Mrs McNulty and the girls my very deepest sympathy in their sad bereavement. I can assure you it is a very painful task for me to have to write you the sad tidings. But rest happy with the knowledge that the noble boy died doing his duty, and his last few moments were spent in prayer.

Dear Mr McNulty, poor Michael was buried in the military cemetery behind our line. I hope you will excuse this poor sad note as I am a bit shook up after our awful night's work

I am, dear Mr McNulty, your very sympathetic friend,
Bob Nixon.'

The greatest sympathy is felt for the Constable and Mrs McNulty and family on the death of their promising boy. Another son, John Joseph, who served for four years in the R.I.C. is with the Irish Guards in France.

From the *King's County Chronicle*, November 1918:

Birr.
Private J.J. McNulty, Irish Guards, of Crinkle, who was awarded the Military Medal for bravery in the field, by attending and dressing wounded comrades under heavy shell fire on 27th September last, has been again recommended for a similar award for like gallantry [sic] on

22nd October, when he was himself wounded the fourth time during the present war. He is now progressing favourably in a base hospital in France. His brother, Michael AS, who was killed in France on 16th April, 1916, at the age of 19 years, while engaged in a bombing expedition. In a letter of condolence sent to his father, the colonel of his regiment described Michael as a brave soldier, and a loss to his battalion.

Grave or Memorial Reference: II.K.29. Cemetery: Harlebeke New British Cemetery in Belgium.

**McVICAR, Frederick:** Rank: listed as Acting Sergeant and Sergeant. Regiment or Service: Royal Army Medical Corps. Secondary Unit: E.E.F. Date of death: 19 October 1918. Service no: T1SR/92. Born in Birr, Co. Offaly. Enlisted in Fulham while living in Pimlico. Died in Egypt. Grave or Memorial Reference: E.27. Cemetery: Alexandria (Hadra) War Memorial Cemetery in Egypt.

**MEAGHER, John:** Rank: Pte. Regiment or Service: Irish Guards. Unit: 1st Bn. Date of death: 4 September 1914. Service no: 3243. Born in Rathdowney, Co. Laois. Enlisted in Dublin. Killed in action.
*Supplementary information*: Son of Mr T. Meagher, of Rathdowney, Co. Offaly. Grave or Memorial Reference: 25. Cemetery: Guards Grave, Villers Cotterets Forest in France.

**MEARA, Martin:** Rank: Sapper. Regiment or Service: Corps of Royal Engineers. Unit: 432nd Field Company, Royal Engineers. Date of death: 22 March 1918. Service no: 204181. Formerly he was with the Royal Irish Rifles where his number was 7/3719. Born in Tipperary. Enlisted in the Curragh while living in Birr, Co. Offaly. Killed in action. Age at death: 30.

*Supplementary information*: Son of Martin (Gardner) and Mary Meara, of Townsend Street, Birr, Co. Offaly. From the *Midland Tribune*, May 1918, 'Sapper Martin Meara, of the Royal Engineers, is reported missing since the middle of March. He is son of Mr Martin Meara, gardener, Birr.' From the *King's County Chronicle*, March 1916, 'Mr Martin Meara, a well known Birr carpenter, who worked for local contractors, decided to take a Government contract on his own account, and is at present engaged in carrying it out in France with the 7th Royal Irish Rifles. His father was the late Mr Martin Meara, Gardener.' From *King's County Chronicle*, March 1916, 'Mr Francis Meagher, plasterer, Townsend Street, has one son, Martin, in the South Irish Horse, and is training in Cahir, Co. Tipperary. This fine specimen of a soldier was a Clerk in Mr Henry Frend's office.' Grave or Memorial Reference: He has no known grave but is listed on Panel 10 and 13 on the Pozieres Memorial in France.

**MEIGH, Arthur:** Rank: Pte. Regiment or Service: Household Cavalry and Cavalry of the line including the Yeomanry and Imperial Camel Corps. Unit: 4th (Queens Own) Hussars. Date of death: 30 May 1915. Service no: 9970. Born in Kilbride, Tullamore. Enlisted in Tullamore while living in Tullamore. Died of wounds. Age at death: 19.

*Supplementary information*: Son of Arthur J. and Annie Meigh, of 221 Percy Road, Sparkhill, Birmingham. Native of Tullamore, Co. Offaly. From *King's County Chronicle*, May 1916:

> Private Arthur Meigh, 4th Hussars, was killed in action in France on 30th May, 1915. He was a native of Tullamore, and the son of Mr Joseph Meigh, late porter of the King's County Infirmary, and formerly of the York and Lancaster Regiment, who had many years service with his battalion, and fought in the Egyptian campaign of 1884. Like many of the sons of British soldiers, Arthur Meigh wished to follow in the footsteps of his father; and being a spirited and well-developed youth endeavoured to enlist at the age of sixteen, at Athlone, but he was rejected on account of being under age. A short time afterwards, however, he succeeded in joining the militia reserve and on completion of training passed into the Hussars, in which he served at Dublin and the Curragh, so that although only nineteen at the time of his death he had been over two years in the regiment.
>
> On the fatal morning the gallant young fellow was in the trenches near the enemy position, and, as his party

was being relieved by fresh troops, he was in the act of leaving, when-just as he appeared above the trench – he was shot in the head by a German sniper. Mr Meigh, in the course of his duties at the Co. Infirmary, met with a very serious accident, breaking his leg so badly that it became necessary to amputate it, and this entailed the resignation of his position. But he is, of course, in receipt of an army pension. He is also listed on the Tullamore Roll of Honour as **MEAGH.**

Grave or Memorial Reference: II.A.16. Cemetery: Hazebrouck Communal Cemetery Nord, in France.

**MELSOP, Joseph:** Rank: Sergeant. Regiment or Service: Leinster Regiment. Unit: 2nd Battalion. Date of death: 11 March 1917. Service no: 7103. Born in Birr, Co. Offaly. Enlisted in Birr, Co. Offaly. Killed in action. From the *King's County Chronicle*, March 1917:

SERGEANT JOSEPH MELSOP.

We are sure we may speak for Mr and Mrs Patrick Melsop, Birr, the sincere sympathy of the inhabitants on the sad death of their third son, Sergeant Joseph Melsop, Leinster Regiment, who fell in action on 11th March. The deceased young soldier, who leaves a widow and child, was killed instantaneously while gallantly leading his section out of a trench. He had been wounded in May, 1915, and was five months in France when he lost his life. His death is much regretted by his officers, by whom he was much esteemed for his fine soldierly qualities, and also by his comrades. His death adds another sorrow to the already heavily stricken parents, as a very short time ago their daughter, Mrs Margaret Mullins, wife of Sergt Mullins, Leinster Regiment, died, leaving a large young family.

Grave or Memorial Reference: II.D.2. Cemetery: Bois-De-Noulette British Cemetery, Aiz-Noulette in France.

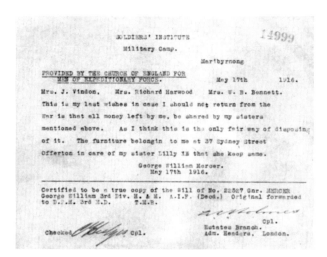

George William Mercer.

**MERCER, George William:**
Rank: Driver/Gunner. Regiment or Service: Australian Field Artillery. Unit: 3ʳᵈ Heavy and medium Trench Mortar Battery. Date of death: 29 September 1918. Service no: 22527. The image above is Gunner Mercers last will and testament. Born in Birr. Attested on 1 May 1916. Enlisted in Melbourne on 24 December 1915. Died of wounds at the 53ʳᵈ Casualty Clearing Station. Data from enlistment documents: Next of kin: Mrs Lillian Vindon, 37 Sydney Street, Offerton, Stockport, England. Trade or calling: Orchardist. Age: 21. Height: 5ft 7ins. Weight: 119lbs. Complexion: Fresh. Eyes: Hazel. Hair: Light brown. Grave or Memorial Reference: V.F. 15. Cemetery: Tincourt New British Cemetery in France.

**MIDDLETON, Patrick:** Rank: Sergeant. Regiment or Service: Royal Irish Regiment. Unit: 6ᵗʰ Battalion. Date of death: 12 August 1917. Service no: 9573. Born in Kilcolman, Birr, Co. Offaly. Enlisted in Birr. Killed in action. Age at death: 28.

*Supplementary information*: Son of John and Mary Middleton, of Ballyegan, Birr. Husband of Sarah Middleton, of Oakley Park, Fortel, Birr, Co. Offaly. Was gassed in France and sent back again. From the *King's County Chronicle*, 1916, 'Sergeant Patrick Middleton, aged 28. The Royal Irish Regiment, son of Mr John Middleton, Ballyeighan, killed in action in France on 12ᵗʰ August. R.I.P. If we were near to raise his head, or hear his last farewell. The blow

The image above is taken *King's County Chronicle* 1916.

would have been so hard to those he loved so well. Inserted by his wife and loving children.' Grave or Memorial Reference: Panel 33. Memorial: Ypres (Menin Gate) Memorial in Belgium.

**MILLS, George:** Rank: Pte. Regiment or Service: Leinster Regiment. Unit: 2ⁿᵈ Battalion. Date of death: 4 July 1915. Service no: 3337. Born in Kilbride, Co. Offaly. Enlisted in Tullamore. Killed in action. He is also listed on the Tullamore Roll of Honour. Grave or Memorial Reference: Z. 23. Cemetery: Potijze Chateau Lawn Cemetery in Belgium.

**MILLS, Joseph:** Rank: Pte. Regiment or Service: Leinster Regiment. Unit: 2ⁿᵈ Battalion. Date of death: 26 March 1918. Service no: 8620. Born in Kilbride, Co. Offaly. Enlisted in Tullamore, Co. Offaly. Killed in action. Age at death: 23.

*Supplementary information:* Son of the late Mr and Mrs William Mills. Grave or Memorial Reference: Has no known grave but is commemorated on Panel 78. Memorial: Pozieres Memorial in France.

**MILLS, William Thomas:** Rank: Captain. Regiment or Service: Royal Army Medical Corps. Date of death: 25 October 1915.

*Supplementary information*: Husband of E.E. Mills, of 'Elm Bank, Pirbright Surrey. Alternative Commemoration: He is buried in Ballyburley Church of Ireland Churchyard, Co. Offaly. Grave or Memorial Reference: Panel 9 (Screen Wall). Memorial: Grangegorman Memorial, Dublin.

**MITCHELL, Henry Theophilus Michael:** Rank: Lieutenant. Regiment or Service: Royal Sussex Regiment. Unit: 1st Battalion. Date of death: 11 November 1915. Age at death: 24. Supplementary information: Son of Thomas and Fanny Mitchell, of Walcot, Parsonstown, Co. Offaly (Buried Peshawar (Right) B. C. XXVI. 755). From the *Midland Tribune, Tipperary Sentinel* and *King's County Vindicator*, November 1915, 'In South King's Co; Fatal Accident. It is announced that Lieutenant H. T. K. Mitchell, son of the late Mr T. Mitchell, Birr, met with a fatal accident while riding at Peshawar, India, where he was stationed with his regiment, the First Royal Sussex.' From the *King's County Chronicle*, August 1915:

> It rouses a feeling of admiration to the sublime cause of the Allies to hear of the sacrifices made by some of the best sons of the old and respected residents of the Birr district. This is so when we hear of the home-coming

of Mr Francis Mitchell from far away Australia, where he was manfully forging ahead in his profession as an electrical engineer. With the patriotic spirit of his family hearing the call from afar, he at once responded. He has come home to pass presumably on to the fighting line. He is one of seven brothers, all of whom are a credit to their native Birr, as their late father and ancestors were in the past.

Grave or Memorial Reference: Face 1-23. Cemetery: Delhi Memorial (India Gate) in India.

**MITCHELL, Joseph:** Rank: Pte. Regiment or Service: North Staffordshire Regiment. Unit: 8th Battalion. Date of death: 19 November 1916. Service no: 43032. Formerly he was with the Royal Dublin Fusiliers where his number was 25210. Born in Mount Bowles, Co. Offaly. Enlisted in Dublin while living in Tullamore, Co. Offaly. Killed in action. Age at death: 33.

*Supplementary information*: Awarded the Distinguished Service Medal. Son of Mrs Mary Mitchell, of Pallace, Blue Ball, Tullamore, Co. Offaly. Grave or Memorial Reference: IX.L.14. Cemetery: Regina Trench Cemetery, Grandcourt in France.

**MITCHELL, Thomas:** Rank: Major. Regiment or Service: 1st Battalion, Royal Sussex Regiment, attached to the 8th battalion, Cheshire Regiment. Date of death: 12 April 1917. Age at death: 35. Died of wounds.

*Supplementary information*: Son of Thomas and Fanny Mitchell, of Parsonstown, Co. Offaly. Husband of Elizabeth Violet Mitchell (*née* Harold), of 15 Goldington Avenue, Bedford. From the *Midland Tribune*, *Tipperary Sentinel* and *King's County Vindicator*, May 1917, 'The death from wounds received in action has taken place of Major Thomas Mitchell, Royal Sussex Regiment, (attached to the Cheshires) second son of the late Mr Thomas Mitchell, Solicitor, Birr.' Grave or Memorial Reference: X.H.9. Cemetery: Baghdad (North Gate) Cemetery in Iraq.

**MOLLOY, Arthur B.:** Rank: Pte. Regiment or Service: Irish Guards. Unit: 1st Battalion. Date of death: 1 November 1914. Service no: 3595. Born in Athlone, Co. Westmeath. Enlisted in Liverpool, Lancs while living in Charlestown, Co. Offaly. Killed in action. Age at death: 25.

*Supplementary information:* Brother of Edward Molloy, of Kilcoursey, Clara, Co. Laois. Grave or Memorial Reference: He has no known grave but is listed on Panel 11 on the Ypres (Menin Gate) Memorial in Belgium.

**MOLLOY, Arthur Michael:** Rank: Sapper. Regiment or Service: Corps of Royal Engineers. Unit: B.T. Cable Section, Royal Engineers. Date of death: 15 August 1918. Service no: 56761. Born in Phillipstown, Co. Offaly. Enlisted in Cork while living in Portarlington, Co. Offaly. Died. Age at death: 24.

*Supplementary information*: Son of Arthur and Henrietta S. Molloy, of Bridge House, Portarlington, Co. Offaly. Late of Post Office Staff Portarlington. Grave or Memorial Reference: II.C.2. Cemetery: Vauxbuin French National Cemetery in France.

**MOLLOY, Denis:** Rank: Pte. Regiment or Service: Irish Guards. Unit: 1st Battalion. Date of death: 6 November 1914. Service no: 1604. Born in Kinnitty, Co. Offaly. Enlisted in Birr, Co. Offaly. Killed in action. Grave or Memorial Reference: He has no known grave but is listed on Panel 11 on the Ypres (Menin Gate) Memorial in Belgium.

**MOLLOY, John:** Rank: Pre. Regiment or Service: Australian Infantry. Unit: 25th Battalion. Date of death: 11 January 1917. Service no: 184. Age at death: 26.

*Supplementary information:* Son of Joseph and Mary J. Molloy, of 'Wycliff', Irving Street, Auchenflower, Brisbane, Queensland. Born in Birr, Co. Offaly. Buried on 15 January 1917. Data from enlistment documents: Born in Offaly. Age: 24. Trade: Labourer. Next of kin: Joseph Francis, (father) Molloy, 'Wycliff', Irving Street, Auchenflower, Brisbane. Age: 24. Height: 5ft 9¾in. Weight: 168lbs. Complexion: Fair. Eyes: Gray. Hair: Light Brown. Date of birth: 18 February 1915 in Melbourne. Victory medal sent to Joseph Molloy on 20 January 1923. Admitted to Northumberland War Hospital, Gosforth, Newcastle-Upon-Tyne on 15 October 1916 suffering from mild pleurisy. He suffered with dysentery/pneumonia in Cairo while serving in Gallipoli and this seemed to aggravate the condition that finally killed him. He died from multiple abscesses on his liver 20 days after initial diagnosis (Dysentheric Abscess on Liver). He spent 89 days in hospital. From letter in his records:

C/o Miss Jagoe,
Glebe Street,
Alberton,
S Australia.

"To Officer in charge.
Could you please give me any information on Private J. Molloy, 25 Battalion, No 184 nearest relative. I work for the Red Cross in Adelaide and they told me to write to you in Melbourne. The reason I want to know who his nearest relative is because my Father sent me an English newspaper from home and there was a photograph of Private Molloy's grave and I know that his friends would like it. It is covered with flowers and a beautiful cross put up in the noble fellow's memory and as the grave is in the village I lived at home. I am leaving shortly for England so would you please oblige me with a reply.
Obliged.
D. Humble"

Served in Cairo, Gallipoli, Anzac, Mudros, Helouan, Abbassia, Montazah, Tel-el-Kabir, Alexandria, Rollestone, France, England and finally Gosforth.

From *King's County Chronicle*, February 1916, 'Mr Joseph Molloy, ex-Head-const., Moorpark Street, has two sons serving with the colours – Private John, of the Australian contingent, who was severely wounded at the Dardanelles, and Private Richard, of the South African contingent.' Grave or Memorial Reference: C.384. Cemetery: Ashburton Roman Catholic Cemetery, Gosforth, UK.

**MOLLOY, Michael:** Rank: Lance Corporal. Regiment or Service: Royal Irish Rifles. Unit: 1st Garrison Battalion. Date of death: 26 October 1919. Service no: 521 and G/521. Born in Kilbridge, Tullamore, Co. Offaly. Enlisted in Birr, Co. Offaly while living in Tullamore, Co. Offaly. Died in India. Age at death: 49.

*Supplementary information:* Son of Michael and Ellen Molloy, of Harbour Street, Tullamore. Grave or Memorial Reference: Face 10. Memorial: Kirkee 1914-1918 Memorial in India.

**MOLLOY, Michael:** Rank: Pte. Regiment or Service: Royal Inniskilling Fusiliers. Unit: 2nd Battalion. Date of death: 3 April 1917. Service no: 26185. Formerly he was with the Royal Irish Rifles where his number was 1635. Born in Kilbridge, Co. Offaly. Enlisted in Tullamore. Died of wounds. Age at death: 18.

*Supplementary information*: Son of Mrs Anne Molloy, of Wheelwright Lane, Tullamore, Co. Offaly. From the *King's County Chronicle*, June 1916:

Private Michael Molloy, 8th Inniskilling Fusiliers is the younger son of Mr Michael Molloy, of Wheelright Lane, Tullamore. He enlisted in Kitchener's Army at the age of 18, and has served in the war in France. He is at present in hospital at Blackpool suffering from gas poisoning.

Private John Molloy, 6th Leinsters, was in his second year of service in another battalion at the outbreak of the war. He is 21 years of age, and the elder son of Mr Michael Molloy. He was sent to France with the first Expeditionary Force in August, 1914, and fought in many of the great battles in the early stages of the war. He was wounded at Ypres, and on recovery in hospital was granted leave for a few weeks. While at home he consummated a cherished desire by taking in matrimony the young lady of his affection, and the happy event was the occasion of many felicitations and encomiums on the soldier hero and his bride. He was afterwards engaged in the sanguinary battles at the Dardanelles from whence he went with the battalion to Salonika, where he is now.

Grave or Memorial Reference: I.A.14. Cemetery: Cayeux Military Cemetery in France.

**MOLONEY, Patrick:** Rank: Pte. Regiment or Service: Connaught Rangers. Unit: 2nd Battalion. Date of death: 29 October 1914. Service no: 8973. Born in Tullamore, Co. Offaly. Enlisted in Boyle, Co. Roscommon while living in Tullamore, Co. Offaly. Killed in action. Grave or Memorial Reference: IV. E. 4/6. Cemetery: Santuary Wood Cemetery in Belgium.

**MONAGHAN, Andrew:** Rank: Private. Regiment or Service: Leinster Regiment. Unit: 2nd Bn. Date of death: 20 October 1914. Service no: 7886. Born in Stradbally, Co Laois. Enlisted in Birr.

*Supplementary information*: Grandson of Mrs Ann Tracey, of Freegh, Kilcormac, Co. Offaly. Grave or Memorial Reference: Panel 10. Memorial: Ploegsteert Memorial in Belgium.

**MONKS, John:** Rank: Sergeant. Regiment or Service: Royal Irish Rifles. Unit: 7th Bn. Age at death: 33. Date of death: 16 August 1917. Service no: 6339.

*Supplementary information*: Son of Frank and Margaret Monks. Husband of Annie Monks, of Croghan, Daingean, Co. Offaly. Grave or Memorial Reference: Panel 138 to 140 and 162 to 162A and 163A. Memorial: Tyne Cot Memorial in Belgium.

**MOONEY, James:** Rank: Pte. Regiment or Service: Leinster Regiment. Unit: 2nd Battalion. Date of death: 17 January 1916. Service no: 4941. Born in Birr, Co. Offaly. Enlisted in Birr, Co. Offaly. Killed in action. From the *King's County Chronicle*, January 1916:

The Chaplain of the 2nd Battalion Leinsters has informed Mrs Mooney,

Mountsally, Birr, that her son, Private James Mooney, was killed in action on 17th January. He was only seventeen years of age, answered his country's call five months ago, was in France for a month before he was sent up to the trenches, and was killed the very night he was sent to the firing line. His father, Patrick Mooney, is on active service in Egypt, and another brother, Private Patrick, is serving in France with the Royal Dublin Fusiliers.

From the *King's County Chronicle*, February 1916:

BIRR SOLDIER'S DEATH.
Mrs Mooney, Mount Sally, Birr, has received the following letter: 20th January, 1916, France.

"Dear Mrs Mooney,
My heart breaks to write and tell you the sad news of the death of your son, James, who was killed on the 17th inst. He was young to give his life, but gave it willingly, and when I saw him in death he had a brave smile on his face and looked peaceful. He did not suffer, but was killed outright, and will see a cross is put over his grave. Mother of God, who also lost her son, and she will give you comfort in your sorrow.
With deep sympathy
Yours truly,
Denis Doyle, Chaplain."

From the *King's County Chronicle*, February 1916, 'Private Patrick Mooney, of Mount Sally, Birr, serving in Egypt, has given three sons to his King and Country, viz: Private Patrick, of the Dublins, in France; Private James, 2nd Leinsters, killed in action in France; Private Christopher, of the same regiment, being under age was claimed out.' Grave or Memorial Reference: I.D.6. Cemetery: Menin Road South Military Cemetery in Belgium.

**MOONEY, Martin:** Rank: Pte. Regiment or Service: Royal Irish Fusiliers. Unit: 1st Battalion. Date of death: 1 October 1918. Service no: 42402. Formerly he was with the Royal Irish Rifles where his number was 5471. Born in Philipstown, Co. Offaly. Enlisted in Tullamore while living in Philipstown. Killed in action. Age at death: 20.

*Supplementary information:* Son of Martin and Mary Mooney, of Clonadd, Philipstown, Co. Offaly. From the *King's County Independent*, November 1918:

PHILIPSTOWN NOTES.
Died in Action.
The parents of Private Martin Mooney, late of Clonadd, Philipstown, who belonged to the Royal Irish Rifles, but was transferred to the Royal Irish Fusiliers, recently received the sad news on Wednesday morning of the death in action in France on the 1st October of their son, who was but a mere youth when he enlisted, and had only been in France a few months when he met his death. His brother, John Mooney, who joined the Dublin Fusiliers some months ago,

was severely wounded at Cambrai, and is at present in a convalescent home. Of an obliging disposition, the deceased soldier was popular amongst all classes, and his untimely death at the hands of the Germans, is deeply regretted. He was a member of the Philipstown Corps of National Volunteers before his enlistment, and acted as bugler to the Corps for some time. May he rest in peace.

Grave or Memorial Reference: IV.A.27. Cemetery: Dadizeele New British Cemetery in Belgium.

**MOONEY, Partick/Patrick:** Rank: Pte. Regiment or Service: Royal Dublin Fusiliers. Unit: 8th Battalion. Date of death: 6 April 1916. Service no: 15813, ('Soldiers died in the Great War'), 25183 ('Ireland's Memorial Records'). Born: St Brendan, Co. Offaly. Enlisted in Birr, Co. Offaly. Killed in action. Age at death: 24. He has no known grave but is listed on Panel 127 and 129 on the Loos Memorial in France.

**MORAN, E.P.:** Rank: Pte. Regiment or Service: Connaught Rangers. Unit: 1st Bn. Attached to the Labour Corps where his number was 621730. Date of death: 29 September 1919. Service no: 6101.

*Supplementary information:* Son of Mrs Mary Moran, of Orchard House, Ballycumber, Co. Offaly. Grave or Memorial Reference: About 11 yards East of Church. Cemetery: Ballycumber (Liss) Churchyard, Co.

Offaly.

**MORAN, John:** Rank: Pte. Regiment or Service: Connaught Rangers. Unit: 5th Battalion. Date of death: 6 July 1917. Service no: 6960. Born in Leomonaghan, Co. Offaly. Enlisted in Athlone while living in Ballycumber, Co. Offaly. Died of dysentery in Salonika. Age at death: 29.

*Supplementary information:* Son of William and Margaret Moran, of Wineport, Ballykeeran, Athlone. Husband of Georgina Moran, of Ballycumber, Co. Offaly. Grave or Memorial Reference: II.B.3. Cemetery: Lahana Military Cemetery in Greece.

**MORRIS, John:** Rank: Farrier Sergeant. Regiment or Service: Royal Field Artillery and Royal Horse Artillery. Unit: B Battery, 179th Brigade. Date of death: 15 November 1916. Service no: 51533. Born in Tullamore. Enlisted in Tullamore. Died. Age at death: 27.

*Supplementary information:* Son of John and Bridget Morris, of Crow Street, Tullamore, Co. Offaly. From *King's County Independent*, December 1916:

TULLAMORE SOLDIER'S DEATH.
Mr John Morris, blacksmith, in the employment of Messrs. T.P. and R. Goodbody, Tullamore, received the sad intelligence a few days ago of the death of his son, Farrier Sergeant J. Morris, R.F.A., in France, from pneumonia. Deceased, who was only 27 years of age, was the second son of Mr Morris, and had 9 years military service, being for several years in

India. He was wounded at the landing at the Dardanelles, by a shell, and was for several months in hospital, when he returned to England. He afterwards got a short furlough, and visited Tullamore to see his parents.

While at home he suffered considerably from the effects of the wound, and though a medical certificate as to his condition was obtained, an application for an extension of his leave was not acceded to, and a Red Cross Ambulance arrived from the Curragh one morning, in which he was conveyed to camp. He was subsequently sent on a draft to France, where he had been in several of the recent big engagements. On the 15th Nov, his parents were officially informed that he was suffering from pneumonia, and a later communication announced his death. Deep sympathy is felt for the parents and relatives of the deceased soldier in their bereavement.

Grave or Memorial Reference: XII.E.18. Cemetery: Etaples Military Cemetery in France.

**MORRIS, Thomas:** Rank: Pte. Regiment or Service: Royal Irish Regiment. Unit: 1st Bn. Age at death: 19. Date of death: 26 February 1915. Service no: 4410. Born in Ballingarry and enlisted in Kilkenny while living in Ballingarry. Killed in action.

*Supplementary information*: Son of Mr P. and Annie Morris, of 38 Clashawaun, Clara, Co. Offaly. Native of Co. Tipperary. Grave or Memorial Reference: I.C.3. Cemetery: Elzenwalle Brasserie in Belgium.

**MOSSMAN, Harry:** Rank: Sapper. Regiment or Service: Royal Engineers. Unit: 97th Company. Date of death: 2 January 1916. Age at death: 28. Service no: 16942. Died of wounds. Born in Athlone. Enlisted in Athlone while living in Tullamore. From the *King's County Independent*, January 1916:

Sapper H. Mossman, R. E.
On Thursday morning last the death occurred, to the deep regret of his relatives and friends, of Sapper Harry Mossman, of the Royal Engineers, at King Street, after a rather protracted illness, caused by wounds received in France in December, 1914. Deceased was 28 years of age and was well and favourably known by all classes. He was of a quiet and friendly disposition. He served his time to the blacksmith trade in Messrs Sloane's factory, and turned out a first-class tradesman. He then enlisted in the Royal Engineers for three years service and nine years on the reserve. At the time of the outbreak of the war he was employed at Messrs P. and H. Egan's, Ltd., Tullamore. He was sent out to France at the beginning of hostilities. He was wounded in December and afterwards treated in Gravesend hospital. During his time there bombs were dropped on the hospital by Zeppelins, but, fortunately, the damage done was slight.

Since then he had been in delicate health and had the attendance of local doctors frequently. He also had the tender care of a loving mother and sisters with whom deep sympathy is felt in their sad bereavement. The funeral took place on Saturday afternoon, with military honours. The remains were placed on the gun carriage drawn by four horses, after which a member of the local men of the R.F.A. marched two deep.

The chief mourners were: Mr Armstrong, Galway (brother-in-law); Mrs Mossman (mother); and Miss Ethel Mossman (sister). He was one of the original 'Old Contemptible' and qualified for his 1914 Star (often referred to as the 'Mons Star') on the 23 August 1914. This medal was awarded to men who were within the sound of the guns between August and September 1914. He also qualified for the Victory medal and the War medal.

He is not listed in any of the war dead databases. The following information is taken from his records: Entitled to the 1914 star, the Victory medal and the British war medal. His 1914 Star was signed for by his Mother in 1919 and the Victory and War medals were delivered to, and signed for by, his Mother also, Mary Mossman, on New years eve 1921. Enlisted on the 11 November 1907 in Athlone. Occupation on enlistment, Blacksmith. Age: 20. Height: 5 ft 11¾ ins. Weight: 147lbs. Born in the parish of St Peter's, Athlone where his parents were caretakers until his father's death. Served his apprenticeship with Mr Sloan, Athlone for five years and was fully qualified in September 1907. Transferred to the Army Reserve in

1910 and was re-engaged in 1910 for one year. Mobilised in August 1914 and went to France on the 8 August 1914. Next of kin listed as Father, John Mossman, Mother, Mary Mossman, Brother, Fred. Intended place of residence on discharge, King Street, Athlone. In December 1914, he was admitted to a No 8 Casualty Clearing Station on Service and transferred by the hospital ship, *Oxfordshire* to England. Discharged in Chatham, 22 June 1915. Four weeks after he was diagnosed with the illness. Cause of discharge: no longer physically fit for military service, *Kings Regulations*, Para 392 (XVI). From his medical documents it seems that he suffered with a type of T. B. which was aggravated by military service. Grave or Memorial Reference: No burial information other than he was buried in a cemetery in Tullamore.

**MULCAHY, Patrick:** Rank: Sergeant. Regiment or Service: South Lancashire Regiment. Unit: 1$^{st}$ Battalion. Date of death: 12 August 1917. Service no: 6887. Born in Newmarket, Co. Clare. Enlisted in Birr, Co. Offaly. Died of fever in Quetta ('Soldiers died in the Great War' gives his place of death as India). Age at death: 33.

*Supplementary information*: Son of John and Julia Mulcahy, of 4 Pound Street, Birr, Co. Offaly. (Buried Quetta Govt. Cem. 2304). From the *Midland Tribune*, August 1917:

Sergeant Mulcahy, son of Mr J. Mulcahy, Pound Street, Birr, has died of fever in India. A brother has been invalided having lost his leg on active service. In all there were seven brothers in the army.

Patrick had five other brothers who served and survived the war. They were John, Peter, and Daniel all in the 2nd Leinsters. Stephen, Leinsters and Michael in the South Lancashire Regiment. They were all sons of John Mulcahy, painter, Pound Street.

Grave or Memorial Reference: Panel 44. Cemetery: Delhi (India Gate) Memorial in India.

**MULCAHY, Stephen:** Rank: Pte. Regiment or Service: Kings Own Scottish Borderers. Unit: 1/5th Battalion. Date of death: 13 November 1917. Service no: 31182, ('Soldiers died in the Great War'), 311182, ('Ireland's Memorial Records'). Formerly he was with the Leinster Regiment where his number was 4841. Born in Birr, Co. Offaly. Enlisted in Birr, Co. Offaly while living in Birr, Co. Offaly. Killed in action, ('Soldiers died in the Great War'). Died of Wounds in Egypt, ('Ireland's Memorial Records'). Age at death: 23 in 'Ireland's Memorial Records' and 27 in Commonwealth War Graves Commission.

*Supplementary information:* Son of John Mulcahy, of 4 Pound Street, Birr, Co. Offaly. From *King's County Chronicle*, June 1915, 'Interesting local military news. In at least one respect it is given to very few to rank with Mr John Mulcahy, painter, of pound Street, Birr. This respected citizen having no fewer than half-dozen sons

in the Army – one in the Royal Irish Regt, two in the South Lancashires, two in the Leinsters, and one in the Irish Guards.' From the *King's County Chronicle*, February 1916:

Six soldier sons. Mr John Mulcahy, painter, Pound Street, has also six sons serving in the army:

Sergt. Patrick and Private Michael of the South Lancashires; Privates Stephen, Peter, John and Daniel, all of the Leinsters, and on active service. A letter from the R. C. Chaplain to the regiment last week stated that Peter had been wounded below the knee and that he would soon be sent to England. A later account from a Nurse in France states that he is severely wounded, and had to go under an operation. His brother, Jack, was home for a short rest from the trenches a few weeks ago, and is back in the firing line again.

From the *King's County Chronicle*, December 1917:

Mr John Mulcahy, painter, Pound Street, Birr, received the sad news on Monday last that his son, Pte Christopher [*sic*], of the Leinster Regiment (attached Scottish Borderers) had been killed in action in Egypt on 13th November. The deceased young soldier was only in his 20th year, and what makes the present sad news all the more sad is the fact that only three months ago Mr Mulcahy lost another son, Sergt. Patrick of the South Lancashire

Regt., who died of fever in India.

There are three more sons serving in the army, and another is home on pension, having lost a leg in action in France.

From the *King's County Chronicle*, December 1915:

The following sympathetic letter has been received by Mrs Mulcahy, Pound Street, Birr, in connection with the death of her son, Private Stephen Mulcahy, who was killed in action, and a reference to which appeared in our last issue;

"Dear Mrs Mulcahy

As officer commanding the K.O.S.B., I am writing on behalf of the battalion to send you our very sincere sympathy on the death in action of your very gallant son. I can assure you that we mourn your loss and ours, not only as we have lost a comrade, who cannot be replaced, but as a soldier, whose courage and endurance has been admired and respected by us all.

Believe me to be, yours very sincerely,

A. Kearsey, Lt. - Col. K.O.S.B."

Grave or Memorial Reference: O.34. Cemetery: Ramleh War Cemetery in Israel.

**MULOCK, Edward Ross:** Rank: Second Lieutenant. Regiment or Service: Royal Irish Regiment. Gordon Highlanders. Unit: 2<sup>nd</sup>

Battalion. Date of death: 11 March 1915. Age at death: 24. Killed in action.

*Supplementary information:* Son of Edward Ross Mulock, Staff-Surgeon, R.N., and Georgina A. Mulock. From the *Midland Tribune*, *Tipperary Sentinel* and *King's County Vindicator*, the same article appeared in the *King's County Chronicle*, April 1915, 'Sec-Lieut Edward Ross Mulock, aged 25, was killed in action on March 13<sup>th</sup>. He was the only son of the late Staff Surgeon E.R. Mulock, R.N., of Kilnagarna, Co. Offaly. He served for several years in the Artists Rifles, and was gazetted to the Gordon Highlanders in December last.' Grave or Memorial Reference: VIII.H.17. Cemetery: Guards Cemetery, Windy Corner, Cuinchy in France.

**MULRIEN/MULRANEY, Bernard:** Rank: Sergeant. Regiment or Service: Bedfordshire Regiment. Unit: C Company, 7<sup>th</sup> Battalion. Date of death: 15 March 1917. Service no: 12702. Born in Edenderry, Co. Offaly. Enlisted in Hertford while living in Hertford. Killed in action. Age at death: 28.

*Supplementary information*: He won the Military Medal and is listed in the *London Gazette*. Son of John and Kate Mulraney, of Carrick, Co. Kildare. Bernard's brother Bill was killed in the 1916 Rising. Grave or Memorial Reference: III.J.20. Cemetery: Achiet-Le-Grand Communal Cemetery Extension in France.

**MURDON, John:** Rank: Pte. Regiment or Service: Royal Dublin Fusiliers. Unit: C Company, 10th

Battalion. Date of death: 13 November 1916. Service no: 26167. Formerly he was with the Leinster Regiment where his number was 3563. Born in Birr, Co. Offaly. Enlisted in Galway while living in Birr, Co. Offaly. Killed in action. Age at death: 26.

*Supplementary information:* Son of the late Joseph and Elizabeth Murdon. Enlisted from R.I.C. From the *Midland Tribune, Tipperary Sentinel* and *King's County Vindicator.* December 1916:

> Official intimation was received in Birr, on Saturday last of the death in action of John Murdon, Connaught Street. The late soldier was a member of the R.I.C. stationed at Galway, and joined the army about twelve months ago. The encounter in which he was killed took place on the 13th of November. Much sympathy is felt with his relatives in Birr. He is son of the late Mr John Murdon, shoemaker, Birr and precious to joining the army was in the Royal Irish Constabulary.
>
> He was formerly in the R.I.C., and was stationed in Galway. His father, the late Mr Joseph Murdon, boot-maker, resided at Bridge Street Birr.

From the *King's County Chronicle,* February 1916, 'Mrs Murdon, Bridge Street, has given two sons to the army, viz: Private Christopher, of the A.O.C., at present on active service in France, and Private John, of the Leinsters, at present in training in Mullingar. Private John, who was in the R.I.C., offered his services, which were accepted.' Grave or Memorial Reference: Pier

John Murdon. Image taken from the *King's County Chronicle* and includes the following information, 'He joined the army from the R.I.C. and was son of the late Mr John Murdon, Birr.'

and Face 16C. Memorial: Theipval Memorial in France.

**MURPHY, Charles:** Rank: Sergeant. Regiment or Service: Royal Garrison Artillery. Unit: 41st Siege Battery. Date of death: 4 June 1917. Service no: 17825. Born in Clara, Co. Offaly. Enlisted in Dublin. Died of wounds. Grave or Memorial Reference: I.Q.I. Cemetery: Trois Arbres Cemetery, Steenerck in France.

**MURPHY, Michael:** Rank: Lance Corporal. Regiment or Service: London Regiment (Post Office Rifles). Unit: 8th Bn. Age at death: 34. Date of death: 25 July 1918 Service no: 372301. Born in Portarlington, Co. Offaly. Enlisted in Portarlington while living in Portarlington. Killed in action. Awarded the Military Medal and listed in the *London Gazette.*

*Supplementary information:* Husband of M. Murphy, of Chaple Street, Portarlington, Co. Offaly. Grave or Memorial Reference: IX.B.5. Cemetery: Contay British Cemetery, Contay in France.

**MURPHY, William John:** Rank: Guardsman. Regiment or Service: Scots Guards. Date of death: 26 October 1914. Service no: 9213. Born in Ballyought, Wexford. Enlisted in Maryburgh, Aberdeen while living in Mount Wilson, Edenderry. Killed in action. Brother of Mrs Mary Walsh of Mount Wilison, Edenderry, Co. Offaly. Age at death: 38. Has no known grave but is commemorated on Panel 11. Memorial: Ypres (Menin Gate) Memorial in Belgium.

**MURRAY, Cornelius:** Rank: Lance Corporal. Regiment or Service: Royal Irish Regiment. Unit: 2nd Bn. Date of death: 13 June 1917. Service no: 8692. Born in Crumlin, Co. Tipperary and enlisted in Roscrea while living in Crumlin. Died of wounds.

*Supplementary information*: Son of Mary Murray, of Crumlin, Moneygill, Co. Tipperary. Alternative Commemoration: buried in Castletown Old Graveyard, Co. Offaly. Grave or Memorial Reference: Has no known grave but is commemorated on Panel 5 (Screen Wall). Memorial: Grangegorman Memorial in Dublin.

**MURRAY, George:** Rank: Captain. Regiment or Service: Leinster Regiment. Unit: 2nd Bn. Age at death: 25. Date of death: 4 June 1916. Killed in action.

*Supplementary information:* Son of Mr and Mrs G. Murray, of Crickle, Birr, Co. Offaly. From the *King's County Chronicle*, June 1916:

BIRR OFFICER KILLED.

We regret to learn that Captain George Murray, Leinster Regiment, son of Mr George Murray, Crinkle, has been killed in action in France on Sunday morning. Captain Murray was a born soldier and his marked ability gained him rapid promotion. He was wounded and had been home only a few weeks ago. Much sympathy is felt for his parents at the cutting short of the very promising career of their eldest boy.

From the *King's County Chronicle*, June 1916:

THE LATE CAPTAIN GEORGE MURRAY.

Some details of the circumstances attendant on the death of this gallant young officer, and many expressions of appreciation of his worth, and regret at his having fallen so early in life, when his career as an officer, which gave so much promise of brilliancy, was but opening before him, have been received by his father, Mr George Murray, of Crinkle, since the announcement of the casualty in our

George Murray. Image from the *King's County Chronicle* 1916.

issue of the 10<sup>th</sup> June. The manner of his death was thus; On the night of the 3<sup>rd</sup> and 4<sup>th</sup> June a heavy bombardment had been taking place from the British lines in retaliation against the Germans, when it ceased and after the usual stand-to in the British trenches. Captain Murray was looking over the parapet trying to locate a German machine-gun, when he was hit by a bullet below the right ear. He fell mortally wounded; his men bandaged the wound, and the doctor was present in a very short time, but the brave Captain was already gone beyond all hope, and passed peacefully away at 3.10a.m without regaining consciousness.

He was buried next evening in the Brigade cemetery not far from the trenches, where many of the men of his own company, who loved him as well, are laid. The Brigardier-General commanding the Brigade, and very many of all ranks, both officers and men, were present to testify to the esteem in which he was held.

Capt. George Murray, was mentioned in Sir Douglas Haig's despatch for gallantry and distinguished service in the field. He had nine years service, 7½ of which he was in the ranks of the 1<sup>st</sup> battalion of the Leinster Regiment. He was transferred to the 2<sup>nd</sup> Battalion on being commissioned in January, 1915.

The Keeper of the Privy Purse, Buckingham Palace, telegraphed; "The King and Queen deeply regret the loss you and the army

have sustained by the death of your son in the service of his country. Their Majesties truly sympathise with you in your sorrow."

General Capper, commanding the Division, wrote to Lieut-Col. Orpen-Palmer, commanding the Battalion: "I am deeply grieved to hear that Murray has been killed. Will you and the Battalion accept my sympathy in your loss? A good and gallant soldier, he will be a great loss not only to the regiment but to the whole division. Lieut-Col. R. Orpen-Palmer: "He was a gallant soldier, and a fine fellow, beloved and respected by us all, and he would have risen high in the service. I have lost a friend and my best company commander."

The Adjutant of the Battalion: "He was a splendid officer and one of our very best, with a great future before him. The regiment will miss him. He died a gallant and noble death, and it is a fine end of which we may all be proud."

Lieut-Col. Murphy, late of the 2<sup>nd</sup> Batt: "He died the honourable death of a true soldier, but his loss to the battalion is very great. The Rev. Edward Evitt, chaplain to the 73<sup>rd</sup> Infantry Brigade, wrote: "May I add a word of sympathy and appreciation for your gallant son; he was a fine man and a splendid soldier, and we can ill afford his loss." Captain Murray was shortly to have been married to Miss Edith Bagnall of Birr.

Mr George Murray received the sorrowful news of the death of his distinguished son while under treatment in hospital in Dublin after a severe operation; and the most earnest sympathy has been felt and expressed to his by all within the wide circle of his friends and acquaintances. A letter of great sympathy and solace reached him from the Rev. Samuel Hemphill, D. D. formerly of Birr. Mr Murray devoted his own life to the service of his country, and also gave three other sons to its cause; Sergt. R. Murray, 21st Leinsters, severely wounded at Armentiers, June, 1915; ten months in King's Hospital, London, and now barrack warden at Strensall Camp, Yorkshire. Bombardier Frederick and Trumpeter Richard Murray, both of the R.F.A. His eldest daughter, wife of Regimental Qr. Mr–Sergt. Kerrigan, Leinster Regiment, while passing through the street to visit him in hospital, was wounded in the Sinn Féin rebellion, and is at present a patient under treatment in Richmond Hospital, Dublin.

Grave or Memorial Reference: II.B.16. Cemetery: Ration Farm (La Plus Douve) Annexe in Belgium.

**MURRAY, John:** Rank: Pte. Regiment or Service: Leinster Regiment. Unit: 1st Battalion. Date of death: 15 March 1915. Service no: 9900. Born in Clara, Co. Offaly. Enlisted in Athlone, Co. Westmeath. Killed in action. Age at death: 22.

*Supplementary information*: Son of Edward and Charlotte Murray, of 109 Erryarmstrong, Clara, Co. Offaly. From the *King's County Independent*, June 1915:

CLARA CAPTURE.

Two Clara Constables, Ryan and Cox, effected a smart capture at the river Brosna, a few evenings ago, and the persons, whose name are John Minnock and Fred Murray, were presented at Clara Petty Sessions on Wednesday, the former being fined a guinea, and the latter half a guinea, for each of the offences under the Fisheries Act. Murray, who is only a youth, was the only one to put in an appearance, and the Chairman, Mr Callan, inquired if he had offered to join the army. Sergeant Brady struck a tender chord when he informed the magistrates that Murray's brother was recently killed in action at the front fighting for King and Country. Mr Callas took this into consideration, and only imposed the fine mentioned above. At the same time he gave Murray a sharp lecture as to damage he and the like of him were doing to the salmon fishing industry in this country. The poor chap had nothing to say, and before the court rose he came forward and intimated his willingness to join the army and to thus serve his King and Country.

Grave or Memorial Reference: He has no known grave but is listed on Panel 44 on the Ypres (Menin Gate) Memorial in Belgium.

**MURRAY, John:** Rank: Pte. Regiment or Service: Kings Own Scottish Borderers. Unit: 1st Battalion. Date of death: 1 July 1916. Service no: 18927. Formerly he was with the Highland Light Infantry where his number was 7629. Born in Kilbride, Tullamore, Co. Offaly. Enlisted in Glasgow, Lanarkshire while living in Glasgow, Lanarkshire. Killed in action. Grave or Memorial Reference: He has no known grave but is listed on Panel and Face 4A and 4D of the Theipval memorial in France.

**MURRAY, Patrick:** Rank: Acting Corporal. Regiment or Service: Connaught Rangers. Unit: 2$^{nd}$ Battalion. Date of death: 30 October 1914. Service no: 8408. Born in Clara, Co. Offaly. Enlisted in Tullamore, Co. Offaly while living in Clara, Co. Offaly. Killed in action. Age at death: 29.

*Supplementary information:* Son of Maurice and Mary Murray, of River Street, Clara, Co. Offaly. Grave or Memorial Reference: He has no known grave but is listed on Panel 42 on the Ypres (Menin Gate) Memorial in Belgium.

**MURRAY, Peter:** Rank: Pte. Regiment or Service: Leinster Regiment. Unit: 7$^{th}$ Battalion. Date of death: 3 September 1916. Service no: 1435, ('Soldiers died in the Great War' and Commonwealth War Graves Commission), 1437, ('Ireland's Memorial Records'). Born in Kilbride, Co. Offaly. Enlisted in Tullamore, Co. Offaly. Killed in action. Age at death: 25. This man may be in 'Ireland's Memorial Records' twice both as No 1435 and as 1437 and date of death as 3 September 1916 and 4 September 1914. Murray No 1437 is not In 'Soldiers died in the Great War'.

*Supplementary information:* Son of Bartholomew and Margaret Murray, of Church Street, Clara, Co. Offaly. Grave or Memorial Reference: Pier and Face 16 C. Memorial: Thiepval Memorial in France.

**MURTAGH, William:** Rank: Pte. Regiment or Service: Irish Guards. Unit: 1$^{st}$ Battalion. Service no: 4411. Born in Clara, Co. Offaly. Enlisted in Tullamore, Co. Offaly. Killed in action. Age at death: 23.

*Supplementary information:* Son of Mrs Kate Murtagh, of Clara, Co. Offaly. Grave or Memorial Reference: Panel 2 and 3. Memorial: Cambrai Memorial in Louveral in France.

**MYLES, Charles William Chester:** Rank: Major also listed as Captain (Acting Major). Regiment or Service: Royal Army Medical Corps. Date of death: 19 October 1918. Died. From the *King's County Chronicle*, October 1918:

OBITUARY.

Major Charles W.C. Myles, M.C.

We deeply regret to announce the death, from pneumonia, of Major Charles William Chester Myles, M.C., M.B.T.C.D., R.A.M.C. (T.F), while on active service in Palestine on October 19$^{th}$. Born Nov, 5$^{th}$, 1885, he was younger son of the late Dr James Peacocke Myles, late of Duke Street, Birr. He was educated at Galway Grammar School, and Dublin University and Richmond Hospital, and graduated M.B., B.Ch, B.A.O, 1912.

Before the outbreak of war he was in colliery practice, being assistant to Dr. C. Richardson White, M. B., Merthyr Vale, Glam.

Always keen on military work, he had been a member of the D.U.O.T.C. from its inception, and shortly after coming to South Wales he was gazetted Lieutenant in the 2nd Welsh Field Ambulance (T.F.), in which his principal, Dr, White, then held the rank of Captain.

When the Territorial Force was mobilised in August, 1914, he immediately joined his unit, and after undergoing training in England, embarked for the Dardanelles in July, 1915, having been promoted Captain a month or two previously.

He served in the Peninsula until the evacuation; and since that time had been continuously in Egypt and Palestine with the exception of a short leave home in Nov, 1916.

For his work at the first battle of Gaza he was mentioned in despatches, and awarded the Military Cross in January, 1918, Lieutenant Colonel C. Richardson White being gazetted a Companion of the Distinguished Service Order at the same time.

Described by all as a most zealous and hard-working officer, his promotion to the rank of major was well deserved. Overwork had within the past 12 months twice caused a breakdown in health, and he only returned to duty for the last time about the middle of September, after six weeks in hospital. Never sparing himself at his work – (the official record awarding him the Military Cross describes him as "untiring in his efforts to get the wounded away," and also that "he worked unceasingly during the night, March 26-27, 1917, to recover wounded left on the battlefield – a most difficult task in the pitch darkness" – he had evidently over-estimated his strength, and in consequence was not in a fit state to resist the attack of pneumonia, to which he succumbed on Oct, 19th, when a most promising career was brought to a premature end.

A born athlete he played every game well, but more especially cricket. An excellent bat and field, and also a useful wicket keeper, he captained his school eleven, and afterwards played for Birr and Corolanty Clubs. His worth as a player was quickly recognised when he came to South Wales, and he soon became a member of Hill's Plymouth C. C. 1st XI, which at that time was one of the strongest sides in the principality

Awarded the Military Cross. Grave or Memorial Reference: Z.5. Cemetery: Ramleh War Cemetery in Israel.

# N

**NAYLOR, John:** Rank: Pte. Regiment or Service: Leinster Regiment. Unit: 1st Battalion. Date of death: 7 February 1915. Service no: 3269. Born in Birr, Co. Offaly. Enlisted in Birr, Co. Offaly. Killed in action. From the *Midland Tribune*, *Tipperary Sentinel* and *King's County Vindicator* 1914:

> Birr Wounded.
>
> Private C. Naylor, who was severely wounded and who is now in hospital in Cardiff, writes to his mother, Mrs Naylor, Moorpark, that he is improving. He states that Mr and Mrs Whitehead, parents of Mr Whitehead, Birr, have been to see him, and have been very kind to him.

From the *King's County Chronicle*, June 1915:

> We understand that the crowd of Birr men who joined the Leinsters on Whit Monday are making progress in their training at the Victoria Barracks, Cprl. Mr W. O'Meara, became suddenly ill on the square a couple of days after his arrival, but he has so improved in hospital that he will be back at drill prior to joining the Royal Engineers. Private Michael Gleeson, also on the sick list, will soon resume duties. It is of interest to note that there are now just a hundred Birr men in the above Barracks, which also have a section of the Dublin Fusiliers and a battery of the Artillery. Privates Loftus, Naylor, and Mullins have taken up musketry, and probably will be leaving soon for the range at Youghal to complete their course.

From the *King's County Chronicle*, December 1915:

> Private Henry Naylor, Moorpark Street, Birr, who has been here on four days leave, has again returned to the front. He went out to France with the Leinsters in the original Expeditionary Force, and came through all his trying experiences absolutely unscathed. That he may continue to enjoy such luck is the sincere wish of his friends in the Model Town.
>
> There is a picture of Henry Naylor in the King's County Chronicle in 1916. He looks very like Michael Collins. It also states that Henry is the son of Private William Naylor.

From the *King's County Chronicle*, February 1916:

> Father's unique distinction. Mr Thomas Naylor, Moorpark Street,

Birr, employed at the Maltings, has the unique distinction of having at present serving in the army six sons, namely: Private William of the 2nd Connaught Rangers, who did his bit in France, and is at present in Berehaven. Private Thomas, 2nd East Lancashires, who went to France with the original Expeditionary Force, and is back again at the front. Private Christopher, of the 2nd Leinsters, who also went out with the first Expeditionary Force, was wounded at the Aisne, and is again on active service. Private Henry, of the same regiment, who had been in the trenches for 15 months and escaped without a scratch. He was home and has gone back once more to the firing line. Private Michael, of the 6th Leinsters, is at present in the Near East, and last but not least.

Private John, of the same regiment, is also in the Balkans. We may mention that the father of all these gallant soldiers was himself over thirty years in the 3rd Leinsters, saw service in the South African War, and was awarded the King's and Queen's Medals and also the good conduct and long service medals.

From the *King's County Chronicle*, February 1916:

Mr William Naylor, Moorpark Street, who was through the whole South African campaign, offered his services, which were accepted for the 3rd Leinsters. He is stationed at Queenstown. His son, Private Henry, formerly employed with Messrs. Williams, is now in France with the Irish Guards.

(Private Henry Naylor was awarded the D.C.M.).

Grave or Memorial Reference: He has no known grave but is listed on Panel 44 on the Ypres (Menin Gate) Memorial in Belgium.

**NEALE, Arthur Hill:** Rank: Lieutenant. Regiment or Service: 1st Brahmans, Attached to the 6th Jat Light Infantry. Date of death: 21 January 1916. Age at death: 26. From De Ruvigny's Roll of Honour:

Neale, Arthur Hill, Lieut, 2nd Brahams Infantry, Indian Army, youngest son of William Neale, M.D., of Mountymellick, Queen's County, Ireland, by his wife Jessie. Born (25 Ormond Road, Rathmines, Dublin), daughter of T.B. Forwood, of Thornton Manor, Chester. Born Queen's County, Ireland, 15 May, 1880. Educated at St Columba's College, Dublin (B.A. 1906); was a keen sportsman and represented his college at football and cricket; obtained one of the two commissions offered annually to the University; attached to the Royal Irish Regiment, for a year's training; gazetted 2nd Lieut., unattached, 17 Jan, 1911; appointed to the Indian Army 24 March, 1913; promoted Lieut, 17 April following; went to France in Oct, 1914 with the Lahore Division of the Indian Expeditionary Force, being

Arthur Hill Neale.

attached to the 9th Bhopal Infantry and took part in the operations of the Division after five months service in France, went to Egypt in Dec, 1915, and was attached to the 6th Jat Light Infantry, and joined General Aylmer's Force in the Persian Gulf; killed in action at El Hanna, Mesopotamia, 21 July, 1916, being one of the first to enter the Turkish trench. A officer wrote that; "it quite beat him how he managed to reach the Turkish trench; he felt he had lost a very true friend, and all the regiment regretted him; he never wished to meet a finer fellow, always so cheery." And his Colonel wrote "He was very proud of him, as he was as capable, hard-working and pains-taking as any he ever had had under him."

Grave or Memorial Reference: He has no known grave but is listed on Panel 47 of the Basra memorial in Iraq.

**NELSON, George William:** Rank: Pte. Regiment or Service: Royal Inniskilling Fusiliers. Unit: 9th Battalion. Date of death: 1 July 1916. Service no: 18092. Born in Edenderry, Co. Offaly. Enlisted in Boyle while living in Edenderry, Co. Offaly. Killed in action. Age at death: 28.

*Supplementary information*: Son of Henry and Alice Nelson, of Edenderry, Co. Offaly. A.C.P. A National School Teacher. Grave or Memorial Reference: Pier and Face 4 D and 5 B. Memorial: Thiepval Memorial in France.

**NESTOR, Patrick:** Rank: Pte. Regiment or Service: Machien Gun Corps. Unit: Infantry 17th Company. Date of death: 18 March 1916. Service no: 20603. Formerly he was with the Leinster Regiment where his number was 9841. Born in Killanc/Killane, Edenderry, Co. Offaly. Enlisted in Tullamore while living in Edenderry, Co. Offaly. Died of wounds. Age at death: 28.

*Supplementary information*: Son of Patrick and Julia Nestor, of Blundell Street, Edenderry, Co. Offaly. Grave or Memorial Reference: V.C.16. Cemetery: Lijssenthoek Military Cemetery in Belgium.

**NEW, Denis:** Rank: Pte. Regiment or Service: Leinster Regiment. Unit: 2nd Battalion. Date of death: 20 March 1915. Service no: 3230. Born in Shinrone, Co. Offaly. Enlisted in Birr, Co. Offaly. Died of wounds. Killed in action. Age at death: 27.

*Supplementary information:* Son of Martin and Bessie New, of Shinrone, Co. Offaly. Grave or Memorial Reference: IX.B.15. Cemetery: Cite Bonjean Military Cemetery, Armentaires in France.

**NEWELL, John:** Rank: Pte. Regiment or Service: Leinster Regiment. Unit: 1st Battalion. Date of death: 20 June 1915. Service no: 3431. Born in Philipstown, Co. Offaly. Enlisted in Maryborough, Co. Laois. Killed in action. Grave or Memorial Reference: X.F.2. Cemetery: Strand Military Cemetery in Belgium.

**NIXON, James:** Rank: Lance Corporal. Regiment or Service: Leinster Regiment. Unit: 'D' Company, 1st Bn. Date of death: 19 April 1915. Service no: 9146. Age at death: 25. Born in Birr, Co. Offaly. Enlisted in Maryborough, Co. Laois. Died of wounds.

*Supplementary information:* Son of John and Jane Nixon of Parkmore, Roscrea. He had five brothers who also served with the British Army in WW1. Grave or Memorial Reference: Enclosure No 2. V. A. 9. Cemetery: Bedford House Cemetery in Belgium.

**NIXON-ECKERSALL, Frederic Eckersall:** Rank: Captain. Regiment or Service: Royal Garrison Artillery. Unit: 157th Siege Battery. Date of death: 10 November 1917. Age at death: 48. Died of wounds. Killed in action.

*Supplementary information*: Son of the Rev. Canon Eckersall Nixon and Mrs C.M. Nixon. Husband of Florence Eleanor Nixon-Eckersall, of 'Gainsborough' College Road, Cheltenham. From the *King's County Chronicle*, 1916, 'Killed in action, Major Frederic Eckersall Nixon-Eckersall, Royal Garrison Artillery, eldest son of the late Rev. Eckersall-Nixon, of Ettagh rectory, King's County.' From the *King's County Chronicle*, December 1915, 'Major Frederic Eckersall Nixon-Eckersall, Royal Garrison Artillery, whose death, in action, was recently announced, was a brother of Mrs C.W. Eckersall-Nixon, of Ettagh Rectory, King's County. He was 48.' Grave or Memorial Reference: I.A.40. Cemetery: Ypres Reservoir Cemetery in Belgium.

**NOLAN, John:** Rank: Pte. Regiment or Service: Irish Guards. Unit: 1st Battalion. Date of death: 9 November 1914. Service no: 3649. Born in Dunkerrin, Co. Offaly. Died of wounds. Age at death: 26.

*Supplementary information:* Son of Mr and Mrs Nolan, of Main Street, Crinkle. Husband of Annie Nolan, of Main Street, Crinkle, Birr, Co. Offaly. Grave or Memorial Reference: C.I Cemetery: Messines Ridge British Cemetery in Belgium

**NOLAN, Patrick:** Rank: Corporal. Regiment or Service: Leinster Regiment. Unit: 2nd Battalion. Date of death: 10 February 1916. Service no: 56. Born in Kilbride, Co. Offaly. Enlisted in Birr, Co. Offaly. Killed in action. Grave or Memorial Reference: I.G.6. Cemetery: Menin Road South Military Cemetery in Belgium.

**NOONAN, Bernard:** Rank: Pte. Regiment or Service: Leinster Regiment. Unit: 2nd Battalion. Date of death: 1 September 1916. Service no: 3363. Born in Kilbride, Co. Offaly. Enlisted in Tullamore, Co. Offaly. Killed in action. From the *Midland Tribune, Tipperary Sentinel* and *King's County Vindicator*, May 1917, 'At the Birr Court, Rose Ward was sent to jail for 14 days for assaulting Patrick Noonan, a discharged soldier. Defendant was stated to be a native of Tullamore and has two sons in the army. It appeared that there had been previous trouble between the parties.' He is also listed on the Tullamore Roll of Honour. Grave or Memorial Reference: Pier and Face 16C. Memorial: Theipval Memorial in France.

**NORRIS, Patrick:** Rank: Pte. Regiment or Service: Connaught Rangers. Unit: 2nd Battalion. Date of death: 26 August 1914. Service no: 4244. Born in Birr, Co. Offaly. Enlisted in Birr, Co. Offaly while living in London. Killed in action. From the *King's County Chronicle*, February 1916, 'The late Mr Thomas Norris, Moorpark Street, had three sons: Private Patrick, of the Connaughts, who went through the South African campaign, unofficially reported missing; Private John, A.S.C., in France; and Private Thomas, Leinster regiment, killed in action.' Grave or Memorial Reference: Commonwealth War Dead. Cemetery: La Ferte-Sous-Jouarre-Memorial in France.

**NORRIS, Thomas:** Rank: Pte. Regiment or Service: Leinster Regiment. Unit: 2nd Battalion. Date of death: 27 April 1915. Service no: 2112. Born in Birr, Co. Offaly. Enlisted in Birr, Co. Offaly. Died of wounds. Age at death: 30.

*Supplementary information:* Son of the late John and Mary Norris, of Birr, Co. Offaly. From the *King's County Chronicle*, May 1915, 'His many friends in Birr will learn with regret that Thomas Norris who was in the 3rd Leinsters and had seen a good deal of active service, has died in England from wounds received in the engagement at Hill 60. Jack Norris, a brother of the deceased, joined the A.S.C. a few weeks ago. His name was John Norris and had worked at the Maltings.' Grave or Memorial Reference: I.A.173. Cemetery: Bailleul Communal Cemetery Extension (Nord) in France.

# O

**OAKLEY, John:** Rank: Pte. Regiment or Service: Australian Infantry. Unit: 2<sup>nd</sup> Bn. Date of death: 20 September 1914. Service no: 7078. Killed in action in Belgium. Data from enlistment documents: Born in Birr. Age: 32. Trade: Slater. Next of kin: Eliza Oakley (mother), Burkes Street, Birr, Co. Offaly. Height: 5ft 8½in. Weight: 159lbs. Complexion: Florid. Eyes: Blue. Hair: Dark Brown. Date: 25 July 1916. According to his charge sheet the only 'crime' he committed was taking double rations at breakfast in May 1917 at Larkhill. He was confined to Barracks for a week. Embarked the *Benalle* in Sydney on 9 November 1917, disembarked in Davenport on 9 January 1917. Hospitalised with scabies in April 1917 for twelve days and discharged to Depot. Proceeded overseas via Folkestone on 22 May 1917. Marched in to Etaples on 25 May 1917. Commanding Officer of the 2<sup>nd</sup> Battalion takes him on strength on 8 September 1917 and is reported missing in action in Belgium on 22 September 1917. A.A.G. Australian Section, 3<sup>rd</sup> Echelon, G.H.Q, reports (7 January 1918) that he was killed in action on 20 September 1917. Statement made by No 7094 Pte Edwards J. 2<sup>nd</sup> Battalion, re: No 7078 Pte Oakley J. 2<sup>nd</sup> Battalion, missing 20 September 1917:

On or about September 18<sup>th</sup>, 1917. I was at Clapham Junction near Ypres on duty with a fatigue party. A shell came over and killed four men including No 7078, Pte Oakley J. 2<sup>nd</sup> Battalion. His remains were searched for and could not be found. I am certain he was there at the time of the explosion. Dated at Monte Video this 13<sup>th</sup> day of December 1917.

Statement made by No 7215 Private Burnett, J.R. 2<sup>nd</sup> Battalion. Re: No 7078 Pte Oakley J. 2<sup>nd</sup> Battalion, missing 20 September 1917;

"On 3<sup>rd</sup> September 1917. I was told by several men in my unit that Private Oakley J was killed while going up to the front line out of the support trenches. I myself know nothing about it." Dated at King Georges Hospital this day 11<sup>th</sup> December, 1917.

His sister Mrs Katie Woods (23 Railway Parade, Sydenham, Sydney, N.S.W.) had been receiving some of his pay and when he was killed it stopped. She contacted a Senator Pierce who made representations to the Army to clarify the matter. Acknowledging the Senators letter they informed her that Pte Oakley had nominated his Mother as his next of kin and that was why it was stopped. She replied saying that she had no problem with it. A letter from his Mother to the army records;

Burke's Hill. Birr. King's County. Ireland. 1st Feb, 1919.
"Sir

Will you be so kind as to the above address the personal effects (if any) of my late son, No 7078 Private John Oakley, A.I.F. attached to the 2nd Battalion. He was killed in action last year but I have not yet received anything that he may have had in his possession when he fell. An early reply will greatly oblige a sorrowing Mother.
Yours faithfully,
Eliza Oakley."

His medals and death plaque were sent to his Mother in Burke's Hill in October 1922. From the *King's County Chronicle*, October 1914:

Their acquaintances were glad to see troopers Kerrison, Oakley and Woods looking so fit and happy in the smart uniform of the South Irish Horse, a detachment of which is now in training in Limerick. These gallant young Birrmen, who are in the best of spirits, had availed of a weekend leave. They returned on Monday and the same 4. 50 p. m. train which brought them out of Birr had Major Wright. 1st Batt, Royal Irish Rifles, en route for the seat of war. As an instance of the exigencies of war, he had scarcely disembarked from one of the fifty troop ships which brought the second contingent of the Expeditionary Force from India last week, when he was granted 48 hours leave, which, owing to travelling from his regiment and back allowed him a bare five hours to see what is left of the family circle.

Grave or Memorial Reference: Panel 7-17-23-25-27-29-31. Memorial: Ypres (Menin Gate) Memorial in Belgium.

**O'BRIEN, Patrick:** Rank: Pte. Regiment or Service: London Regiment. Unit: 3rd (City of London) Battalion (Royal Fusiliers). Unit also listed as B Company, 2nd/4th Battalion. Date of death: 11 August 1918. Service no: 279265. Formerly he was with the 7th London Regiment where his number was 6297. Posted 2/4th London Regiment. Born in Birr, Co. Offaly. Enlisted in Finsbury Barracks while living in Stoke Newington. Died of wounds. Age at death: 33.

*Supplementary information:* Son of Michael and Lucy O'Brien, of Birr, Co. Offaly. Husband of Amy Hester O'Brien, of 91 Carysfort Road, Stoke Newington, London. Grave or Memorial Reference: III.D.4. Cemetery: Pernois British Cametery, Halloy-Les-Pernois in France.

**O'BRIEN, Patrick:** Rank: Corporal. Regiment or Service: Leinster Regiment. Unit: E Company, 1st Battalion. Date of death: 14 February 1915. Service no: 8695. Born in Tullamore, Co. Offaly. Enlisted in Navan, Co. Meath. Killed in action. Age at death: 27.

*Supplementary information:* Son of James and Ann Scally, of Rhode, Co. Offaly. Grave or Memorial Reference: Panel 44. Memorial: Ypres (Menin Gate) Memorial in Belgium.

**O'CONNELL, Patrick J.:** Rank: Lance Sergeant. Regiment or Service: Irish Guards. Unit: 1st Battalion. Date of death: 1 November 1914. Service no: 2434. Born in Cordal, Co. Kerry. Enlisted in Whitehall, Middlesex while living in Birr, Co. Offaly. Originally listed as missing in action in November later changed to killed in action. His family are listed in the newspaper as living in Newbridge Street, Birr. Age at death: 32.

*Supplementary information:* Son of Mrs David O'Connell, of Castleisland, Co. Kerry. Husband of Mary O'Connell, of 95 Bird-in-Bush Road, Peckham, London. He has no known grave but is listed on Panel 11 on the Ypres (Menin Gate) Memorial in Belgium.

**O'CONNOR, Walter:** Rank: Pte. Regiment or Service: Royal Army Service Corps. Date of death: 11 July 1917. Service no: 4094201. Born in Birr, Co. Offaly. Died of fever in London. Age at death: 32. He appears as above in 'Ireland's Memorial Records'. He is not listed in 'Soldiers died in the Great War' and he is not listed with the Commonwealth War Graves Commission under this name and number. The National Archives in Kew shows that there is no medal index card for Pte Walter O'Connor, No 4094201.

He may in fact be this man listed with the Commonwealth War Graves Commission.

**O'CONNOR, Walter** Rank: Driver. Regiment or Service: Army Service Corps. Date of death: 11 July 1917. Service no: T4/094201. A quick check with the National Archives in Kew shows there exists a medal index card for Driver, Walter O'Connor, T4/094201, Army Service Corps.

*Supplementary information:* Husband of Elizabeth O'Connor, of Chapel Street, Birr. From the *King's County Chronicle*, July 1917:

MILITARY FUNERAL IN BIRR.

On Friday last, with full military hon-ours, three were consigned to their last resting place in Clonoghill cem-etery, the remains of Private Walter O'Connor, A.S.C., who died in Tooting Military Hospital from pneu-monia following wounds received in France. The deceased, who leaves a wife and two children, was 32 years of age, and previous to volunteering two years ago, was employed if the Birr Maltings, where, by his sober and industrious habits, he earned the esteem of his employers and the respect of his fellow workers. A large number of sympathisers followed the remains, while the Leinster Depot band, playing Chopin's funeral march, also attended. The chief mourners were Mrs O'Connor, wife; and also the sisters and brothers of deceased from Kilmallock and Dublin. The Rev. E.J. Scanlan, C.C. officiated at the graveside and the solemn obsequies concluded by the sounding of the "Last Post" and the firing of three volleys over the grave.

Grave or Memorial Reference: 2.5. Cemetery: Birr (Clonoghill) Cemetery, Co. Offaly.

**O'DEA, William:** Rank: Pte. Regiment or Service: Leinster Regiment. Unit: 2nd Battalion. Date of death: 2 November 1918. Service no: 10032. Born in Birr, Co. Offaly. Enlisted in Birr, Co. Offaly. Died. Age at death: 21.

*Supplementary information:* Son of Daniel and Mary O'Dea, of Bridge Street, Birr, Co. Offaly. From the *King's County Chronicle*, September 1916:

> Corporal Michael O'Dea, Connaught Rangers, son of Mrs O'Dea, Bridge Street, Birr, writing to his mother from 4th Scottish General Hospital Glasgow, describes how he had the calf of his leg blown off whilst he was finishing off a third German with his bayonet and he lay for a day and a night in a shell hole. He was able to tie himself up. Another son of Mrs O'Dea's was killed in May, and a third son wounded a short time ago, namely, Willie O'Dea, in the 2nd Leinsters. These three brave young Birr men have been out since the beginning of the war.

Grave or Memorial Reference: V.E.39. Cemetery: Longuenesse (St Omer) Souvenir Cemetery in France.

**ODLUM, John:** Rank: Pte. Regiment or Service: Royal Irish Regiment. Unit: 'C' Coy. 1st Garrison Bn. Age at death: 26. Date of death: 13 January 1919. Service no: 5896.

*Supplementary information:* Son of Mrs Mary Odlum, of 13 Anerley Grove, Norwood, London. Born at Tullamore, Co. Offaly. Grave or Memorial Reference: M. 223. Cemetery: Cairo War Memorial Cemetery in Egypt.

**ODLUM, Martin:** Rank: Rifleman. Regiment or Service: Royal Irish Rifles. Unit: 1st Battalion. Date of death: 10 March 1917. Service no: 7857. Born in Clara, Co. Offaly. Enlisted in Dublin. Died at Home. From the *King's County Chronicle*, April 1916: 'Banagher's Record. Private Patrick Odlum, Curraghvarna, Irish Guards (Killed).' Note: This man, Patrick, does not appear in any war dead database. Grave or Memorial Reference: Screen Wall 89, 32729. Cemetery: Nunhead, (All Saints) Cemetery, UK.

**ODLUM, William:** Rank: Pte. Regiment or Service: Irish Guards. Unit: 2nd Battalion. Date of death: 9 October 1917. Service no: 6378. Born in Birr, Co. Offaly. Enlisted in Birr, Co. Offaly. Killed in action. Age at death: 22.

*Supplementary information:* Son of John and Farmy Odlum, of Newbridge Street, Birr, Co. Offaly From the *Midland Tribune, Tipperary Sentinel* and *King's County Vindicator*, November 1916:

Corporal William Odlum, Newbridge Street, is at present at home on leave, in order that he may recuperate, having been wounded in the back and hand some weeks ago.

## From the *King's County Chronicle*, March 1916.

Mrs Odlum, Newbridge Street, gave two fine sons to the army viz: Sergt. John, of the Dublin Fusiliers, who saw a great deal of active service in France, and was home suffering from the effects of the severe winter of 1914. He has since recovered, and is now at the Depot. Private William, of the Irish Guards, was sent to the French front a few months after enlisting. Although he has been in the thick of the fighting for over a year he has, so far, escaped uninjured.

## From the *King's County Chronicle*, October 1917:

YOUNG BIRR SOLDIER.

Killed in action.

Yet another young Birr man has made the great sacrifice. This week the news was received unofficially, that Corpl. William Odlum, Irish Guards, had been killed in action. Sincere regret is felt with the widowed mother, Mrs Odlum, Newbridge Street, in her bereavement. The late Corporal Odlum was a splendid specimen of young manhood, and was of a most unassuming disposition. He joined after the outbreak of war and was, some months ago, severely wounded. A brother, Sergt.

John Odlum, is also at the front. To the bereaved mother and other relatives we tender our sympathy in their great loss.

## From the *King's County Chronicle*, April 1918:

The brave action for which Company Sergt: Major John Odlum, M.G.C., was awarded the Distinguished Conduct Medal is in the official report: "For conspicuous gallantry and devotion to duty during an enemy attack. He took charge of two guns of another company when no officers were available, and held the bridges over a canal against the enemy's advance. Later, he took up a position with two other guns and covered the digging of a new line. His fine example of cheerfulness and determination was the greatest encouragement to his men."

Grave or Memorial Reference: X.E.7. Cemetery: Artillery Wood Cemetery in Belgium.

**O'DONOHUE, John:** Rank: Pte. Regiment or Service: Irish Guards. Unit: 2nd Battalion. Date of death: 13 April 1918. Service No: 11158. Born in Cloughan, Co. Offaly. Enlisted in Dublin, while living in Clennoneymore, Co. Offaly. Killed in action. Age at death: 21.

*Supplementary information:* Son of Thomas and Johanna O'Donohue, of Clennoneymore, Cloghan, Co. Offaly. Has no known grave but is commemorated on Panel 1. Memorial: Ploegsteert Memorial in Belgium.

**O'DOWD, Robert:** Rank: Corporal. Regiment or Service: Royal Horse Artillery and Royal Field Artillery. Unit: C Battery, 94th Brigade. Date of death: 8 October 1917. Service no: 100910. Born in Tullamore. Enlisted in Maryborough. Died of wounds. Age at death: 19.

*Supplementary information:* Son of Patrick and Annie O'Dowd, of Charleville Parade, Tullamore, Co. Offaly. Grave or Memorial Reference: I.H.3. Cemetery: Godewaersvelde British Cemetery in France.

**O'GRADY, Patrick:** Rank: Pte. Regiment or Service: Leinster Regiment. Unit: 6th Battalion. Date of death: 11 August 1915. Service no: 1183. Born in Clara, Co. Offaly. Enlisted in Birr, Co. Offaly. Killed in action in Gallipoli, February 1916. Grave or Memorial Reference: He has no known grave but is listed on Panel 184 to 185 on the Helles Memorial in Turkey.

**O'HIGGINS, James:** Rank: Sergeant. Regiment or Service: Royal Dublin Fusiliers. Unit: 8th Battalion. Date of death: 10 October 1915. Service no: 15172. Born in Birr, Co. Offaly. Enlisted in Dublin. Died at home. Grave or Memorial Reference: St Bridget's. OJ.303. Cemetery: Glasnevin (or Prospect) Cemetery in Dublin.

Patrick O'Houlihan.

**O'HOULIHAN, Patrick:** Rank: Pte. Regiment or Service: Australian Army Medical Corps. Unit: 1st Field Ambulance. Date of death: 18 September 1917. Service no: 1256. From Abbeyville, Lorrha. Co Tipperary. Brother of **HOULIHAN. Thomas** who died with the Newzealenders. According to his records he enlisted in Perth on the 10th of October 1914. Place of birth: Lorrha, Birr. He was 22½ years old, 5 foot 8 inches tall and worked as a farmhand. His wife's name was Ruby and she was born in Australia but lived in London. He had blue eyes, brown hair, a ruddy complexion, and weighed 12 stone.

During his training and service he was in Tidworth, Folkstone and London. He was also in Boulogne, Alexandria, Egypt, Tel-El-Kabir, Abbassia, Rouen, Belgium, and also trained in the famous Bull Ring in Etaples. He had some illnesses during his service including Mumps and Myalgia, which was common in those days in the trenches. On the 18 September he received two bullet wounds; the first fractured his left thigh and the second hit him in the head. He was brought by a field ambulance to a Canadian Casualty Clearing Station, where he later died. Two months later his widow began to receive a pension of 40 shillings every two weeks. Grave or Memorial Reference: XIX. D.15A. Cemetery: Lijssenthoek Military Cemetery in Belgium.

**O'KEEFE, Patrick:** Rank: Pte. Regiment or Service: Royal Irish Regiment. Unit: 6th Battalion. Date of death: 1 September 1916. Service no: 2110. Born in Clare, Co. Offaly. Enlisted in Kilkenny while living in Clifton, Co. Kilkenny. Killed in action. Age at death: 22.

*Supplementary information*: Son of John and Mary O'Keefe, of Ballysalla, Kilderry, Co. Kilkenny. Born Clifden, Co. Kilkenny. Grave or Memorial Reference: III.M.4. Cemetery: Quarry Cemetery, Montauban in France.

**O'ROURKE, Michael:** Rank: Sergeant. Regiment or Service: Cameronians (Scottish Rifles). Unit: 5/6th Battalion. Date of death: 8 May 1918. Service no: A/8009. Born in Rhode, Co. Offaly. Enlisted in Lochgelly. Killed in action. He has no known grave but is listed on Panels 68 to 70 and 162 to 162A on the Tyne Cot Memorial in Belgium.

**O'SHEA, MICHAEL,** See **SHEA, Michael:**

# P

**PALMER, James:** Rank: Pte. Regiment or Service: Leinster Regiment. Unit: 3rd Battalion. Date of death: 3 July 1917. Service no: 10493. Born in Kilbride, Co. Offaly. Enlisted in Tullamore, Co. Offaly. Died at Home. Grave or Memorial Reference: 2.393. Cemetery: Clonminch Catholic Cemetery, Co. Offaly.

**PALMER, Joseph M.:** Rank: Lance Corporal. Regiment or Service: Irish Guards. Unit: 2nd Battalion. Date of death: 13 September 1916. Service no: 6922. Born in Kilbride, Co. Offaly. Enlisted in Tullamore, Co. Offaly. Killed in action. *King's County Independent*, April 1917, 'Tullamore Soldier's Death. The friends of Corporal Joseph Palmer, Irish Guards, received news during the week of his having been killed in action in France. Corporal Palmer, who is a Tullamore man, and who has a brother serving with the Leinsters, was reported missing in September of last year.' He has no known grave but is listed on Pier and Face 7D on the Theipval Memorial in France.

**PARKER, Thomas:** Rank: Pte. Regiment or Service: Irish Guards. Unit: 2nd Battalion. Date of death: 13 April 1918. Service no: 4595. Born in Clara, Co. Offaly. Enlisted in Tullamore, Co. Offaly while living in Purley in Surrey. Killed in action. An account of the action is given on page 174 and 175 of 'The Irish Guards in the Great War, Second Battalion'. His brother John Parker was also in the Irish Guards where his number was 14336 and he survived the war. Grave or Memorial Reference: He has no known grave but is listed on Panel 1 on the Ploegsteert Memorial in Belgium.

**PARSONS, Patrick:** Rank: Pte. Regiment or Service: Leinster Regiment. Unit: B Company, 1st Battalion. Date of death: 14 February 1915. Service no: 10145. Born in Birr, Co. Offaly. Enlisted in Birr while living in Birr, Co. Offaly. Killed in action at St Eloi. Age at death: 18.

*Supplementary information:* Son of William and Lizzie Parsons, of Moorpark Street, Birr, Co. Offaly. Grave or Memorial Reference: He has no known grave but is listed on Panel 44 on the Ypres (Menin Gate) Memorial in Belgium.

**PARSONS, William Edward:** Rank: Major (recorded in 'Officers Died in the Great War' as Earl of Major, Rosse, William Edward) Regiment or Service: Irish Guards.

William
Edward
Parsons.

Age at death: 44. Date of death: 10 June 1918. Died of wounds.

*Supplementary information:* 5th Earl of Rosse. Son of Laurence Parsons, 4th Earl of Rosse. Husband of Countess of Rosse (*née* Frances Lois Listerkaye). From the *King's County Chronicle*, 29 October 1914:

> The Earl of Rosse having made a remarkably rapid recovery from a serious illness which necessitated surgical treatment, has left Birr Castle to rejoin a part of the Irish Guards, the main body of which has been in the front since the beginning of hostilities and suffered heavily in casualties in all ranks. In these uncertain times when every soldier is needed, it may soon be his Lordships turn to go out with a reinforcement. He served in the South African campaign in 1900 under Lord Metheun and took part in some of the conflicts in the region of the Modder River, for which he has the Queens Medal.

From the *King's County Chronicle*, 1 April 1915:

> One of the officers is the Earl of Rosse who has been for some time at the front. His Lordship, we understand, received just a week's leave, most of which, as in similar brief respites, was used up by travelling home and back. In these circumstances where time was so precious he was met on Monday morning at Roscrea station on the arrival there of the train from Dublin, and was motored to Birr by his agent, Mr T. Robert Garvey, thus arriving at Birr Castle about an hour earlier than if brought to Birr by train. We are glad to know the hard experience of life in the trenches had, so far as could be judged by his looks, no ill effects on his health; and we are informed that he is in fine form. He could only remain till Tuesday evening, being due to report himself this Thursday morning.

From the *King's County Chronicle*, June 1915:

> The Earl of Rosse, who was wounded last month, celebrated his 42nd birthday on the 14th June. He is happily recovering steadily, and the Countess of Rosse was able to return from London to Birr Castle on the 14th June. The public concern has been so genial about his lordship's condition that we may be sure that the above favourable news will elicit the sincerest pleasure over the community at large.

From the *Midland Tribune*, June 1918:

> Death of Lord Rosse. The funeral obsequies at Birr.

Totally unexpected was the announcement that the death of Lord Rosse had taken place at Birr Castle on Monday morning. Lord Rosse, who was a Major in the Irish Guards, was severely wounded in the head near La-Basse, in May 1915. As a result of the wounds that he then received, he had been subject to attacks, which, however, to a large extent, had passed away, and it was felt the he was on the way towards full recovery. On Monday morning, after an interval of almost a year, he had another of these attacks, with the result that he was discovered at about 9 o'clock in his bath in a collapsed condition by the butler. Mr Morton, of Birr, was at once summoned, and on arrival pronounced life extinct. Lord Rosse appears to have been but a short while dead when the butler found him.

William Edward Parsons, fifth Earl of Rosse, was born on the 14th of June, 1873. He was the son of the fourth Earl and of the Hon Frances Casandra Harvey Hawke. He married in 1908, Lois, daughter of Cecil and Lady Beatrice Lister-Kaye, and succeeded to the title on the death of his father in 1908. He leaves two sons and a daughter. He was educated at Eton and Oxford University. He served in the South African War with the 1st Battalion, Coldstream Guards, for which he held the Queen's Medal and three clasps. In 1915 he was wounded in the head while serving in France with the Irish Guards, of which he was a Major, and he retired from the army. He was his Majesty's Lieutenant for King's Co., and a Representative Peer for Ireland. He was prominently connected with the Royal Dublin Society, and was a member of several of its committees.

Lord Rosse was also a vice-president of the Irish Forestry Society. Locally he was a member of the Birr Urban Council and of the Birr Technical Committee. He was deeply interested in scientific farming, and at its inception was made president of the King's Co. Farmer's Association. He was also keenly interested in projects of industrial development, and recently interested himself in a scheme of electrical lighting for the town of Birr. Amongst other projects which were carried through under his auspices was one for the supply of pure milk at reasonable rates to the people of Birr. This scheme has proved of immense benefit, especially since the start of the war, and particularly during last winter. His death is sincerely deplored in Birr.

On Wednesday evening, the remains were removed from Birr Castle to St Brendan's Parish Church at Birr, where they remained during the night. On Thursday, the funeral, which was a military one, took place. The order of the funeral procession was as follows;--Band of the Leinster Depot; firing party from Leinster Depot, with arms reversed; other troops; clergy; coffin, carried by the estate employees, and escorted on either side by the military officers; family; immediate friends; police; general public.

The Burial Office in St Brendan's Church was read at 2o/c, Rev. H.E. Patten, B.D. Rector, and Rev. C.W. Thompson officiating. Miss Byrne presided at the organ. After leaving the church the procession wended its way down Oxmantown Mall, and by Rose Row, fronting the Castle walls, to the gates of the Churchyard attached to the Old-----.

There in the family vault the remains were interred. The band of the Leinster Depot played the Dead March (Chopin) and the Last Post. The other soldiers present lined the nave of the church.

The chief mourners were: Countess of Rosse and her son, the Earl of Rosse; Hon Geoffrey Parsons, uncle; Mr Cecil Lister-Kaye, father-in-law; Lady Beatrice Lister-Kaye, mother-in-law.

Amongst the wreaths were – With deepest sympathy from all ranks from the Irish Guards (tied with Guards colours); From Betty and Geoffrey; With loving sympathy, from uncle Clere and Aunt Agnes; With deepest sympathy from Viscount and Viscountess Powerscourt; Mrs and Captain Cowan, with sincere sympathy; With Colonel and Margaret Proby's sincere sympathy; With deep regret from Brigadier General and Mrs Lloyd; With deep sympathy from Earl and Countess of Huntingdon; With our love, from Johnnie and Alice (Mr and Mrs J. R. Parsons).

Messages of sympathy were received from – Duke and Duchess of Newcastle; Lord Francis Hope, Cassandra Countess of Rosse (mother); Theodesia Countess of Cottenham; Colonel Hall, Com. Irish Guards, Colonel and Lady Powerscourt, The Hon. Sir Charles Parsons, The Hon. and Rev Randal Parsons, Captain and Mrs J.R. Parsons.

The officers of the Leinster Depot present were – Colonel Duggan, Major Finch, Captain Trench, Captain Lister, Captain Howes. Officers in charge of other troops were: Captain Munroe, Captain Morrisson, Lieutenant Fayle. Mr Knox, D.I. was in charge of the police.

Amongst those present were: Very Rev Canon Ryan, P.P. V.F. Birr; Rev Father Martin, C.C., Birr; Rev E.J. Scanlan, C.C. Birr; Dr Hemphill, D.D.; Rev Mr Richardson, Rev Mr Wilson, Lord Dunally. H.M.L.; Sir Francis Synge, Bart; Banon D.L.; J.C. Darby, D.L.; Allen, High Sherriff; Durnford. J.P.; Bailey, Secretary North Tipp Co. C; Dr Morton, Dr Fleury, Dr Houlihan, J. C. Willington, J.P.; Wright, National Bank, Birr; Croke O'Brien, Roscrea; J.P. Fagan, Clerk Crown and Peace; Drew, Manager Hobernian Bank, Birr; St George, Manager Provincial Bank, Birr; T.R. Garvey, J.P.; J.R. Simpson, I.R.; Major Bredin, R.M; T. O'Reid, J.P. Surgeon-Col Woods; Major Bennett, E.H. Browne, J.P. etc.

At a special meeting of the Birr

Urban Co on Tuesday evening, on the motion of the chairman, Mr J. Dooley, J.P., seconded by Mr Fayle, J.P., a resolution of sympathy was adopted with the relatives.

Grave or Memorial Reference: In large family vault. Cemetery: Birr Old Graveyard, Co. Offaly.

**PEARCE/PEARSE, Joseph:** Rank: Pte. Regiment or Service: Leinster Regiment. Unit: 4th Battalion. Date of death: 14 October 1916. Service no: 4307. Born in Birr, Co. Offaly. Enlisted in Bonnybridge, Stirling while living in Bonnybridge. Died at Home. Age at death: 36.

*Supplementary information:* Grave or Memorial Reference: 30872. Cemetery: Limerick (St Lawrence's) Catholic Cemetery, located at the mouth of the Shannon Estuary, Republic of Ireland.

**PEARCE, William Ernest Prewitt:** Rank: Acting Corporal. Regiment or Service: Hampshire Regiment. Unit: 2nd Battalion. Date of death: 4 October 1915. Service no: 8634. Born in Crinkle, Birr, Co. Offaly. Enlisted in Southampton while living in Millbrook, Hants. Killed in action in Gallipoli. Age at death: 19.

*Supplementary information:* Son of Lucy Mary Pearce, of 16 Foundry Lane, Millbrook, Southampton, and the late Ernest George Pearce (Q.M.S., Hampshire Regt). Born in the Regiment. Grave or Memorial Reference: I.A.8. Cemetery: Azmk Cemetery, Suvla, Turkey.

**PERRY, John:** Rank: Pte. Regiment or Service: Canadian Infantry (Alberta Regiment). Unit: 49th Battalion. Date of death: 9 June 1917. Age at death: 33. Service no: 811572. Born in Birr. Enlisted in Edmonton while living in Edmonton.

*Supplementary information:* Son of the late John Perry, of Birr, Co. Offaly. Husband of Thomasina M. Address: 11237-72nd Street, Edmonton, Alta. Born in Birr, Co. Offaly. Date of birth: 27 December 1881. Trade or calling: Survey work. Age: 34 years. Height: 5ft 9ins. Complexion: Clear. Eyes: Grey. Hair: Brown. From the *King's County Chronicle*, July 1917:

> The news was heard with much regret of the death in action of Private Jack Perry, Canadian Infantry, second surviving son of the late John and Ellen Perry, Ross Row, Birr, at the early age of 35 years.
>
> Deceased, who was well known in Birr, and who only joined about a year ago in Canada, was a brother-in-law of Mr T. Powys Love, Professor of Music, Oxmanstown Mall, Birr.

Grave or Memorial Reference: He has no known grave but is listed on the Vimy Memorial in France.

**PIERCE, Joseph:** Rank: Pte. Regiment or Service: Leinster Regiment. Unit: 4th Battalion. Date of death: 5 May 1916. Service no: 44103. Born in Birr. Died of fever in Limerick. Age at death: 40. Awarded the 1914 Star.

He only appears in 'Ireland's Memorial Records'. He is not listed in 'Soldiers died in the Great War' and he is not listed with the Commonwealth War Graves Commission. A quick check with the National Archives in Kew shows that there is no medal index card for Pte Joseph Pierce, No 44103 even though he is supposed to have won the 1914 Star.

**PIKE, John:** Rank: Acting Corporal. Regiment or Service: Royal Dublin Fusiliers. Unit: 2nd Battalion. Date of death: 21 March 1918. Service no: 21051. Born in Kilbride, Co. Offaly. Enlisted in Dublin while living in Kilbride, Co. Offaly. Killed in action. From the *King's County Independent*, June 1918:

> PRIVATE PIKE.
>
> Private John Pike, formerly of the South Irish Horse, and transferred some time ago to the Dublin Fusiliers has been reported missing since the 21st March, when the first big German offensive took place. His mother would be glad to hear from any comrade living who was present and who may have seen her son. That he is a prisoner in Germany she has not yet received any information.

From the *King's County Independent*, July 1918:

> MISSING TULLAMORE SOLDIER.
>
> In our paragraph in Tullamore Notes last week in reference to a Tullamore soldier named Corporal Pike, R.D.

Fusiliers, who is reported missing since March, we gave the rank as 'Private.' No communication has yet been received by Corporal Pike's mother, who is very anxious about him as to whether he is a prisoner of war or otherwise. Possibly some chums of the 21st March engagement and who are still in the firing line might be able to assist Corporal Pike's friends in ascertaining whether he fell or became a prisoner of war.

Grave or Memorial Reference: He has no known grave but is listed on Panel 79 and 80 on the Pozieres Memorial in France.

**PIPER, George:** Rank: Pte. Regiment or Service: London Regiment. Unit: 23rd (County of London) Battalion, also listed as 2nd/23rd Battalion. Date of death: 5 October 1915. ('Soldiers died in the Great War' and 'Ireland's Memorial Records') 5 October 1918 (Commonwealth War Graves Commission). Service no: 701542, ('Soldiers died in the Great War'), 107542, ('Ireland's Memorial Records'). Born in Birr. Enlisted in Clapham Junction while living in Lambeth. Killed in action. Age at death: 32.

*Supplementary information:* Son of the late Alfred and Margaret Piper. Husband of Ethel Piper, of 126 Vauxhall Walk, Lambeth, London. Grave or Memorial Reference: Has no known grave but is commemorated on Panel 150 to 153. Memorial;

Tyne Cot Memorial in Belgium.

**POLLOCK, William:** Rank: Pte. Regiment or Service: Gordon Highlanders. Unit: 2nd Battalion. Date of death: 20 July 1916. Service no: 3/6258. Born in Birr, Co. Offaly. Enlisted in Glasgow. Died of wounds. Grave or Memorial Reference: II.C.14. Cemetery: Heilly Station Cemetery, Mericourt-L'Abbe in France.

**POWER, Frederick:** Rank: Pte. Regiment or Service: Canreronians (Scottish Rifles). Unit: D Company, 10th Battalion. Date of death: 7 April 1917. Service no: 28175. Born in Clara. Enlisted in Hamilton while living in Motherwell. Died of wounds. Age at death: 19. Frederick died of shrapnel wounds to the right lung at a casualty clearing station in France on 7 April 1917, his wounds being received while in the trenches east of Arras. He was 19 years of age and was part of 46th Brigade 15th Scottish Division. Prior to enlistment he was employed by the Tramway Company. His father was also serving in the Argyll and Sutherland Highlanders.

*Supplementary information:* Son of Patrick and Norah Power, of 10 Cadzow View, Ladywell, Motherwell. Born in Ireland. Grave or Memorial Reference: I.J.3. Cemetery: Duisans British Cemetery,

**POWER, Patrick:** Rank: Pte. Regiment or Service: Connaught Rangers. Unit: 1st Battalion. Date of death: 13 April 1916. Service no:

6858. Born in Athlone. Enlisted in Athlone while living in Athlone. Killed in action in France, also listed as Mesopotamia. I include this man in the Offaly War Dead as he is listed on the Tullamore Roll of Honour published in the *King's County Independent* in February 1917 and also because of the article in the same paper in November 1916 which shows his wife, Annie Power, living in Wellington Barracks in Tullamore with her five children, sister Margaret Keena, and his brother-in-law Joseph Gavan. He is also listed on the Tullamore Roll of Honour. He has no known grave but is listed on the Basra Memorial in Iraq.

**PRETTY, Albert Edward:** Rank: Pte. Regiment or Service: Canadian Infantry (British Columbia Regiment). Unit: 1st Reserve Battalion. Date of death: 17 October 1918. Service no: 2140944. Age at death: 34. Data from enlistment documents: Address: C/o John Y Smith, 114 East 57th Street, Seattle, Washington, USA. Frankford, Co. Offaly. Next of kin: James Pretty, brother, Anchorage, Alaska. Date of birth: 11 September 1884. Trade: Farmer and Horseman. Age: 34. Height: 5ft 8½ins. Complexion: Fair. Eyes: Brown. Hair: Brown. Private Pretty died within the first five weeks of his service.

*Supplementary information*: Son of John and Sarah Pretty, of Garbally Rape Mills, Birr, Co. Offaly. Grave or Memorial Reference: Church C. 4800. Cemetery: Plymouth (Efford) Cemetery, UK.

**PURCELL, Edward:** Rank: Pte. Regiment or Service: Royal Irish Regiment. Unit: 1st Bn. Date of death: 27 March 1915. Service no: 8939. Born in Moyne, Co Tipperary. Enlisted in Kilkenny while living in Templemore. Died of wounds. Age at death 29.

*Supplementary information:* Son of Robert and Ellen Purcell, of Monamondra, Errill, Ballybrophy, Co. Offaly. Ten years' service. Grave or Memorial Reference: J. 49. Cemetery: Bailleu Communal Cemetery (Nord) in France.

**PYKE, Joseph Kilbride:** Rank: Pte. Regiment or Service: Leinster Regiment. Unit: 1st Battalion. Date of death: 12 May 1915. Service no: 10291. Born in, Co. Offaly, 'Ireland's Memorial Records' have his birth as Kilbride, Co. Offaly. Enlisted in Tullamore, Co. Offaly. Killed in action.

*Supplementary information:* 'Ireland's Memorial Records' state that Kilbride is his place of birth whereas 'Soldiers died in the Great War' and the Commonwealth War Graves Commission have **KILBRIDE** as part of his name. He is also listed on the Tullamore Roll of Honour as **JOSEPH PYKE.** Grave or Memorial Reference: He has no known grave but is listed on Panel 44 on the Ypres (Menin Gate) Memorial in Belgium.

# Q

**QUADE, Frank:** Rank: Greaser. Regiment or Service: Mercantile Marine. Unit: SS *Huntstrick* (London). Age at death: 58. Date of death: 8 June 1917.

*Supplementary information:* Son of the late William and Eliza Quade. Husband of Norah Quade (*née* Sullivan), of 13 Brunel Street, Canning Town, London. Born in Co. Offaly. The Steamship *Huntstrick* was torpedoed and sunk by a German torpedo while it was 80 miles off Cape Spartel, 14 men and the Captain died. Grave or Memorial Reference: Has no known grave but is commemorated on the Tower Hill Memorial, London.

**QUEGAN, John:** Rank: Pte. Regiment or Service: Australian Infantry. Unit: 11th Battalion. Date of death: 6 August 1915. Service no: 2009. Killed in action. Age at death: 26.

*Supplementary information:* Son of William and Mary Quegan, of Kinnitty, Co. Offaly. Born: Kinnitty, Co. Offaly. Age: 24 years. Trade or calling: Labourer. Worked as an apprentice harnessmaker. Next of kin: William Quegan (father) Kinnitty, Co. Offaly. Height: 5ft 4ins. Weight: 140lbs. Eyes: Brown. Hair: Brown. Distinctive marks: Large mark over left collar bone, 3 inch

John Quegan.

by 1 inch. A small scar on left side of skin. Mark on left side of neck due to burn. Records: Went out with the 5th Reinforcements (11th Battalion) on 8 February 1915. Embarked at Freemantle on H.M.A.T. A20 *Hororata* 26 April 1916. While on board H.M.H.S. *Gascon* he became ill. He disembarked in Alexandria and was admitted to hospital in Lemnos. Was detained in the Barracks Isolation Hospital and discharged to duty seven days later. Re-admitted to hospital from the 1st Australian Casualty Clearing Station and admitted again to hospital. Rejoined his unit (11th Battalion) on 31 July 1916 in the Dardanelles and was wounded in action two weeks later with a bullet wound to the stomach, taken to the 1st Australian Casualty Clearing Station, admitted to

Hospital, transferred from the hospital to a H.M.H.S. *Sicilla* hospital ship where he died at 8.20pm from, 'Gun shot wound penetrating abdomen. He was buried at sea by Chaplain E Teele. His pension of 20 shillings per fortnight was awarded to his father William Quegan in Kinnitty from 26 June 1917.' From De Ruvigny's Roll of Honour:

> Quegan, John, Private, No 2009, 11th Battn, Australian Imperial Force, 2nd son of William Quegan, of Kinnitty, King's County, Labourer, by his wife, Mary, daughter of Terence Higgins; born, Kinnitty aforesaid, 20 Oct, 1890. Educated in Kinnitty national School; went to Australia in April, 1912 and worked on the Trans-Australian Railway. Volunteered after the outbreak of war and joined the Commonwealth Expeditionary Force in Dec, and died on board H.M. hospital ship Sicilia, 6 Aug, 1915 from wounds received in action at Lone Pine, Gallipoli.

Grave or Memorial Reference: 34. Memorial: Lone Pine Memorial in Turkey.

**QUINN, John:** Rank: Pte. Regiment or Service: Royal Inniskilling Fusiliers. Unit: 6th Bn. Date of death: 3 October 1918. Service no: 8096. Born in Edenderry. Enlisted in Dublin. Killed in action.

*Supplementary information:* Son of Mrs S. Quinn, of Blundell Street, Edenderry, Co. Offaly. Grave or Memorial Reference: I.C.1. Cemetery: Prospect Hill Cemetery in France.

**QUINN, John Peter:** Rank: Acting Corporal. Regiment or Service: Essex Regiment. Unit: 10th Battalion. Date of death: 6 March 1917. Service no: 10239. Born in Killeigh, Tullamore, Co. Offaly. Enlisted in Warley, Essex while living in Dovercourt, Essex. Died of wounds. Age at death: 24.

*Supplementary information:* Husband of Nellie Elizabeth Quinn, of 6 Woodside, Llwyn Road, Oswestry, Salop. Grave or Memorial Reference: VI.C.17. Cemetery: Dernancourt Communal Cemetery Extension in France.

**QUINN, Michael:** Rank: Pte. Regiment or Service: Irish Guards. Unit: 1st Battalion. Date of death: 24 February 1919. Service no: 1810. Born in Edenderry, Co. Offaly. Enlisted in Edenderry. Died. Grave or Memorial Reference: I.G.10. Buried in Charmes Military Cemetery, Essegney in France.

**QUINN, Patrick:** Rank: Pte. Regiment or Service: Machine Gun Corps. Unit: Infantry. Date of death: 12 August 1918. Service no: 124679. Formerly he was with the North Staffordshire Regiment where his number was 37155. Enlisted in Dundee while living in Edenderry, Co. Offaly. Killed in action. Grave or Memorial Reference: VI.A.4. Cemetery: Klein-Vierstraat British Cemetery in Belgium.

**QUIRKE, John:** Rank: Pte. Regiment or Service: Leinster Regiment. Unit: 2nd Battalion. Date of death: 4 September 1918. Service no: 4532. Born in Birr, Co Offaly. Enlisted in Birr, while living in Birr. Killed in action. Age at death: 19.

*Supplementary information:* Son of James and Anne Quirke, of Hospital Lane, Birr, Co. Offaly. Grave or Memorial Reference: Has no known grave but is commemorated on Panel 10. Memorial: Ploegsteert Memorial in Belgium.

# R

**RAIT-KERR, Sylvester Cecil:**
Rank: Captain. Regiment or Service: Royal Field Artillery. Age at death: 27. Date of death: 13 May 1915. Killed in action.

*Supplementary information:* Second son of Sylvester and Mary Isabel Rait Kerr, D.L., of Rathmoyle, Edenderry, Co. Offaly. From *The Times* 21 May 1915:

Sylvester Cecil Rait-Kerr.

Capt S. Rait Kerr RFA who fell on 13 May 27 yrs was the eldest surviving son of Mr Rait Kerr. He was educated at Rugby and Royal military Academy Woolwich, 2nd Lieutenant in the RFA in December 1907, lieutenant in Dec 1910, Capt in November last. Served in South Africa, India and was on home leave when the war broke out. Went to the front with the G battery RHA in early November 1914 and put in charge of a Howitzer battery in April. Eldest brother Capt William Charles Rait Kerr D.S.O RFA was killed at Ypres on November 10.

From the *King's County Chronicle*, 1915:

CO. OFFALY BROTHERS KILLED.
Captain Sylvester Cecil Rait Kerr, R.F.A., who fell in action on May 30th, aged 27, was eldest son of Mr Rait Lerr, of Rathmoyle, Edenderry. He was home on leave from India when war broke out, and he went to the front early in November. He was given command of a French Howitzer battery in April, and was with his guns at the time of his death. His older brother, Captain William Charles, D.S.O., R.F.A., was killed near Ypres in November, 1914.

From De Ruvigny's Roll of Honour:

*Rait-Kerr, Sylvester Cecil,* Capt, 22nd Trench Howitzer Battery, Royal Field Artillery, 2nd son of Sylvester Rait-Kerr, of Rathmoyle, Edenderry, King's County, Ireland, by his wife, Mary, daughter of the late Major-General Charles Scrope Hutchinson, C.B., R.E. Born in Rathmoyle, afsd., 14 Oct, 1887. Educated at Arnold House Llandulas, Rugby School, and the Royal Military Academy, Woolwich.

Gazetted Lieut, 18 Dec, 1910. Went to South Africa in Oct, 1910 with the 100th Barrety, R.F.A. and afterwards preceeded to India and was home on leave from India when war broke out. He was employed for some weeks in training men in various places, being promoted Capt, 30 Oct, 1914, and on 6 Nov, left for France with "G" Battery, T.H.A., but was subsequently transferred to the 41st Battery, R.F.A. In April, 1915, he was given the command of a Trench Howitzer Battery, with which he went into the trenches near Wieltje on 6 May, and was killed in action on the 13th, being shot through the head by a German sniper whilst carrying bombs to his guns.

Buried in the trenches close to the spot where he fell. The General Officer Commanding the 11th Infantry Brigade, wrote; "I have been informed that you would like to know a few particulars of the gallant work done by your son and the 22nd Trench Mortar Battery while they were under me in the hard fighting of May 9 to 13, during the 2nd Battle of Ypres. Your son was posted in the trenches to the left of a building, named by the troops 'Shelltrap Farm', which was about the hottest part of the line, and his duty was to assist the infantry in keeping back the enemy from sapping up to the farm buildings, and to endeavour to blow their saps. The enemy's shelling was so intense at that time after the trench mortars were silenced and the crews buried, but they were dug out and started on again, and they refused to be relieved. Cooke, the Subaltern, was hit and his shoulder dislocated, but he refused to go to hospital, and the whole battery displayed a similar spirit all through the fighting, the severity of which may be judged from the fact that Shelltrap Farm was lost and re-taken with the bayonet three times in twenty-four hours."

And the General Officer Commanding the 4th Division; "I remember Rait-Kerr and his 22nd Trench Mortar Battery well. It was the best battery of that sort that we ever had with the 4th Division, and under him it did invaluable service in the front trenches during the fighting from the 6th to the 13th of May (1915) which was some of the worst we had in France. I know he was a great loss to the Division and to the Service." The officer in charge of the Trench Howitzer School, 2nd Army Corps, wrote; "He had done magnificently with his trench battery and had received the congratulations of the divisional and Brigade commanders to whom his battery was attached. He was a great friend of mine, and without doubt the finest officer who had passed through the Trench Howitzer School. There was no officer in the British Army who could have done it better. He was a gallant fellow. He was the ideal British officer, a real tiger with his men, but loved and admired by them. In this Army (the 2nd) he *made* trench Howitzers.

He was, of course, recommended for a decoration, and he richly deserved it," and the Subaltern under him in his battery wrote, "His death was a great blow to all of us in the battery. He was a splendid fellow, and did no know what fear was. He was recommended to General Commanding 4th Division for gallantry during the action by officer commanding the 2nd Monmouths, who told me he had upheld the best traditions of the Royal Artillery." His brother, Capt. W.C. Rait-Kerr, was killed in action at Veldhoek, 10 Nov, 1914.

Grave or Memorial Reference: Has no known grave but is commemorated on Panel 5 and 9 on the Ypres (Menin Gate) Memorial in Belgium.

## RAIT-KERR/RAIT KERR, William Charles: Rank: Captain.
Regiment or Service: Royal Field Artillery. Unit: 57th Battery. Date of death: 14 November 1914. Age at death: 28. Killed in action.

*Supplementary information:* Eldest son of the late Sylvester and Mary Isabel Rait Kerr, D.L., of Rathmoyle, Edenderry, Co. Offaly. He won the D.S.O. and was mentioned in Despatches.

*King's County Chronicle*, November 1914:

King's County Officer Killed: Mr Sylvester Rait Kerr, Rathmoyle, Edenderry, has received a telegram from the War Office announcing that his eldest son, Captain Charles

William
Charles
Rait-Kerr.

Rait Kerr, R. A., was killed in action on Tuesday last, the 10th November. Captain Kerr was 27 years of age, had about 10 years service, and was only promoted to his Captaincy last month.

From De Ruvigny's Roll of Honour:

*Rait-Kerr, William Charles*, D.S.O. Capt., 57th Howitzer Battery, R.F.A., eldest son of Sylvester Rait-Kerr, of Rathmoyle, Edenderry, King's County, Ireland, by his wife, Mary, daughter of the late Major-General Charles Scrope Hutchinson, C.B., R.E. Born in Rathmoyle, afsd, 6 Aug, 1886. Educated at Arnold House, Llandulas, Rugby School and the Royal Military Academy, Woolwich. Gazetted 2nd Lieut. R.F.A. 23 July, 1907; and promoted Lieut. 23 July, 1910, and Capt. 30 Oct, 1914. Went to France 16 Aug, 1914 with the 1st Division commanded by Sir Douglas Haig, as Lieut. in the 57th Howitzer Battery, 43rd Brigade, R.F.A. Took part in the Battle of, and retreat from Mons, the Battles of the Marne and the Aisne, and the 1st battle of Ypres, and was killed in action at Veldhoek, near Ypres 10 Nov, following, whilst in charge of an advanced gun 250 yards from the enemy, being shot through the head by a German sniper. The rest of his battery had gone to the rear to rest and refit, having been out since the beginning of the war.

Buried at Veldhoek, beside the gun "he had commanded so well". He was awarded the D.S.O. "for gallant conduct in bringing up a gun to within 250 yards of the enemy in a wood, and blowing down a house in which the enemy were working a machine-gun" (*London Gazette*, 1 Dec, 1914); and was mentioned in F. M. Sir John (now Lord) French's Despatch of 14 Jan, 1915. His Colonel wrote; "He was in charge of a gun which had for some days been placed in a forward position for a special purpose, to destroy some houses from which some German snipers were causing heavy losses in our trenches. He had been doing splendid work, which had been specially noticed by the General, and only the day before his death the Commander of the French troops on our left had sent a letter of thanks for one particularly useful lot of shooting which he had put in and destroyed some German trenches in front of them. He was a brave and excellent officer and man. He had just appeared in the Gazette as Capt. and was so delighted that I had been able to get him posted to one of my batteries."

Another officer wrote; "He was up in the infantry trenches with one gun close behind, in communication by telephone with him. He was there about a fortnight, and in that time did very fine work, knocking houses down with Germans and machine-guns in them, and various other jobs. He was highly praised by all the people up there, and by the General in command of the Infantry Brigade. He had a very rough time from both shell and rifle fire, but had done great execution in spite of it." His brother, Capt. S.C. Rait-Kerr, was killed in action 13 May, 1915.

Grave or Memorial Reference: Has no known grave but is commemorated on Panel 5 and 9 on the Ypres (Menin Gate) Memorial in Belgium.

**RALPH, Michael:** Rank: Pte. Regiment or Service: Irish Guards. Unit: 1st Battalion. Date of death: 25 October 1914. Service no: 3777. Born in Killeshin, Co. Offaly. Enlisted in Carlow, Co. Carlow. Killed in action. Age at death: 21.

*Supplementary information:* Son of John and Annie Ralph, of Chapel Street, Carlow Graigue, Carlow. Grave or Memorial Reference: He has no known grave but is listed on Panel 11 on the Ypres (Menin Gate) Memorial in Belgium.

**REARDON, Edward:** Rank: Pte. Regiment or Service: Irish Guards. Unit: 1st Battalion. Date of death: 1 November 1914. Service no: 2403. Born in Birr, Co. Offaly. Enlisted in Birr. Killed in action. Age at death: 30.

*Supplementary information:* Son of Joseph Reardon, of Kilcormac, Tullamore, Offaly, and the late Kate Reardon. From the *King's County Chronicle*, Thursday, 15 October 1914, 'Rumours having reached him that his son in the Irish Guards had been killed at the front, Mr Joseph Reardon, Fivealley, sent an inquiry, and has had his mind set at rest by the reply from the War Office to the effect that the report is groundless.' From the *King's County Chronicle*, Thursday, 22 October 1914, 'Mr Joseph Reardon, Fivealley, has received word from the War Office that his son, Edward, in the Irish Guards, received a gun shot wound on the 14th September. From the *King's County Chronicle*, July 1915, 'We are sorry to hear that there is no word of Mr Riordan, of Frankford. It is supposed that he was a prisoner of war since last November by replies now leave little hope except that he was killed in action. The poor father has the satisfaction of knowning that his son died a noble and honourable death.' Grave or Memorial Reference: Panel 11. Memorial: Ypres (Menin Gate) Memorial in Belgium.

**REID, John:** Rank: Lance Corporal. Regiment or Service: Royal Irish Regiment. Unit: B Company, 9th Battalion. Date of death: 16 August 1915. Age at death: 24. Service no: 20083. Born in Limerick. Enlisted in Birr. Killed in action.

*Supplementary information:* Son of James and Mary Reid, of High Street, Birr, Co. Offaly. From the *Midland Tribune*, November 1917, 'It has been officially notified that Lance Corporal J. Reid, R.D.F., son of Mr J. Reid, High Street Birr, is missing.' From *King's County Chronicle*, May 1915, 'Birr men and the call. John Reid kept the life in a number of people while he was delivering bread for Mr W. Griffin, and now as a Dublin Fusilier, he intends to take the lives of a number of Germans before her returns.' From the *King's County Chronicle*, November 1917:

YOUNG BIRR SOLDIER MISSING.

The official news has been received by Mr James Reid, High Street, Birr that his son, Lance-Corporal, J. Reid, of the Royal Dublin Fusiliers, is missing since 16th August, on which date there was severe fighting, in which this young soldier's regiment took part. The news was heard with much regret by a large number of friends, and all hope that at the worst it means that he is a prisoner. Enlisting in 1914, his first experience of war was at the Dardanelles and he afterwards went to France. In civil life he was an industrious young fellow and was a hardworking employee of Mr Griffin's, Main Street.

He showed much promise as a soldier, and earned the praise of his superiors, which was official recognised by his parents receiving this week the Parchment Certificate of the Irish Brigade, signed by Major-General W. B. Hickie, Commanding the 16th

(Irish) Division, and which stated; "I have read with much pleasure the reports of your regimental commander regarding your gallant conduct and devotion to duty in the field on June 7th, 1917, and have ordered your name and deed to be entered in the record of the Irish Division."

Grave or Memorial Reference: He has no known grave but is listed on Panels 144 to 145 on the Tyne Cot Memorial in Belgium.

**REILLY, John Joseph:** Rank: Pte. Regiment or Service: Household Cavalry and Cavalry of the line including the Yeomanry and Imperial Camel Corps, South Irish Horse. Date of death: 13 March 1916. Age at death: 30. Service no: 1702. Died at Home. Born in Lea, Co. Laois. Enlisted in Naas while living in Portarlington. Grave or Memorial Reference: In south-west part. Cemetery: Ballintemple Old Graveyard, Co. Offaly.

**REILLY, Joseph:** Rank: Pte. Leinster Regiment. Unit: 2nd Battalion. Date of death: 31 July 1917. Service no: 3513. Born in Kilbridge, Co. Offaly. Enlisted in Birr, Co. Offaly. Killed in action. Age at death: 31/32.
*Supplementary information*: Brother of Miss B. Reilly, of The Square, Clara, Co. Offaly. Grave or Memorial Reference: Panel 44. Memorial: Ypres (Menin Gate) Memorial in Belgium.

**REYNOLDS, Michael:** Rank: Pte. Regiment or Service: Leinster Regiment. Unit: 2nd Battalion. Date of death: 1 December 1914. Service no: 2067. Born in Banagher, Co. Offaly. Enlisted in Birr, Co. Offaly. Killed in action. Grave or Memorial Reference: Has no known grave but is commemorated on Panel 10. Memorial: Ploegsteert Memorial in Belgium.

**REYNOLDS, Patrick:** Rank: Pte. Regiment or Service: Leinster Regiment. Unit: 2nd Battalion. Date of death: 20 August 1915. Service no: 3503. Born in Banagher, Co. Offaly. Enlisted in Birr, Co. Offaly. Killed in action. Age at death: 30.
*Supplementary information*: Son of James and Mary Reynolds, of Feigh's Cottage, Banagher, Co. Offaly. Patrick and Michael above both of the Leinsters are brothers. Grave or Memorial Reference: H. 4. Cemetery: Ramparts, Cemetery, Lille Gate in Belgium.

**REYNOLDS, Patrick:** Rank: Pte. Regiment or Service: Royal Munster Fusiliers. Unit: Y Company, 1st Battalion. Date of death: 22 March 1918. Service no: 6309. Born in Philipstown, Co. Offaly. Enlisted in Clydebank, Dunbarton while living in Glasgow. Killed in action. Age at death: 22.
*Supplementary information:* Son of John Reynolds, of 51 Ronald Street, Coatbridge, Lanarkshire. Grave or Memorial Reference: He has no known grave but is commemorated

on the Poziers memorial on panel 78 and 79 in France.

**RICE, Thomas:** Rank: Pte. Regiment or Service: Leinster Regiment. Unit: 2nd Battalion. Date of death: 5 July 1918. Service no: 3512. Born in Birr, Co. Offaly. Enlisted in Birr, Co. Offaly while living in Birr, Co. Offaly. Died. From the *King's County Chronicle*, 29 October 1914:

> On Monday 26th October, Mr Thomas Rice, High Street, Birr, succumbed to a brief illness, and we understand that a few hours before his death he was informed that a couple of his sons in the Leinster Regiment at the front were wounded. He also had the distinction of having a third son in the same Regiment. He was formerly a tenant farmer on the Myshall Estate at Tinlough, Riverstown, but falling into depressing conditions he came to reside in Birr, where that kind hearted man, Mr J. J. Byrne, seeing his worth gave him constant employment. For the past few months he worked for the Presentation Brothers by whom he was greatly respected. The funeral to Pallas testified to the respect in which he was held.

From the *Midland Tribune*, July 1918, 'Private T. Rice, of the Leinsters, has died in hospital in France. Previous to the war he was employed by the Birr Presentation Brothers in Birr.' From the *King's County Chronicle*, February 1916, 'Three sons of the late Mr Thomas Rice, High Street, are serving with the Leinsters, viz: Privates Thomas, with the 2nd Batt. In France for 15 months and never got a scratch; Albert, at present in hospital for the second time; John, wounded, and sent out again, and is at present stationed at Birr Barracks.' From the *King's County Chronicle*, July 1918:

> The news of the death of Private Thomas Rice, of the Leinster Regiment, in an hospital in France, was heard with great regret. He was on the reserve on the outbreak of war, and had been in innumerable engagements. In civil life he was of a quiet disposition, an industrious worker, sober and reliable, and was fast employed by the Presentation Brothers, who had a high opinion of him. Two other brothers were also in the army.

Grave or Memorial Reference: V.C.47. Cemetery: Longuenesse (St Omer) Souvenir Cemetery in France.

**RIVERS, Michael:** Rank: Sergeant. Regiment or Service: Leinster Regiment. Unit: 2nd Battalion. Date of death: 7 June 1917. Service no: 8020. Born in Kilbride, Co. Offaly. Enlisted in Athlone, Co. Westmeath. Killed in action. Grave or Memorial Reference: Has no known grave but is commemorated on Panel 44. Memorial; Ypres (Menin Gate) Memorial in Belgium.

**ROBBINS, George:** Rank: Gunner. Regiment or Service: Royal Field Artillery. Unit: 21st Bty. 2nd Bde. Age at death: 36. Date of death: 18 May 1918. Service no: 238820. Born in Clare [*sic*],

Co. Offaly. Enlisted in Seaforth in Lancs. Killed in action.

*Supplementary information:* Son of Michael and the late Teresa Robbins, of Co. Offaly. Husband of Elizabeth Robbins, of 203/5, Derby Road, Bootle, Liverpool. Grave or Memorial Reference: I. D. 8. Cemetery: Hagle Dump Cemetery in Belgium.

**ROBBINS, James:** Rank: Pte. Regiment or Service: Leinster Regiment. Unit: 2nd Battalion. Date of death: 20 October 1914. Service no: 8034. Born in Birr, Co. Offaly. Enlisted in Birr, Co. Offaly. Killed in action. Age at death: 24.

*Supplementary information:* Son of Thomas and Maria Robbins. Husband of Teresa Robbins, of 15 Burns Street, Bradford, Manchester. From the *King's County Chronicle*, February 1916, 'Mr Thomas Robbins, late of Pound Street, has tree sons serving, viz: Corpl. Thomas of the East Lancashires; and Privates Patrick and James of the Leinsters.' Grave or Memorial Reference: Has no known grave but is commemorated on Panel 10. Memorial: Ploegsteert Memorial in Belgium.

**ROBBINS, James:** Rank: Pte. Regiment or Service: Royal Army Service Corps. Unit: Remount Depot, Ormskirk. Date of death: 21 January 1919. Service no: R/359/369, R/359369. Born in Co. Offaly. Died under an operation in Liverpool. Age at death: 49 in Commonwealth War Graves Commission and 46 in 'Ireland's Memorial Records'. Grave or Memorial Reference: In the North West part. Cemetery: Clara Monastery Old Graveyard, Co. Offaly.

**ROBBINS, John George:** (also listed as **ROBBINS, George).** Rank: Gunner. Regiment or Service: Royal Field Artillery and Royal Field Artillery. Unit: 21 Battery, 2nd Brigade. Date of death: 18 May 1918. Service no: 238820. Born in Clare [*sic*], Co. Offaly. Enlisted in Seaforth, Lancs. Killed in action. Age at death: 36.

*Supplementary information:* Son of Michael and Teresa Robbins, of Co. Offaly. Husband of Elizabeth Robbins, of 203/5 Derby Road, Bootle, Liverpool. Grave or Memorial Reference: I.D.8. Cemetery: Hagle Dump Cemetery in Belgium.

**ROBINSON, George Whalley:** Rank: Captain. Regiment or Service: Leinster Regiment. Unit: 1st Bn. Age at death: 38. Date of death: 14 February 1915. Killed in action.

*Supplementary information:* Only son of Robert and Eliza Frances Robinson, of Fairy Hill, Shinrone, Co. Offaly. From De Ruvigny's Roll of Honour:

*Robinson, George Whalley,* Capt., 3rd (Reserve), attd, 1st (100th Foot), Battn, The Prince of Wales's Leinster Regt. (Royal Canadians), only child of the late Robert Robinson, of Fairy Hill, County Tipperary, Tea Planter in Ceylon, by his wife, Eliza Frances, daughter of the late Joseph Griffith, of Aglismear, County Tipperary.

George Whalley Robinson.

Born in Ceylon, 15 March, 1877, joined the Tipperary Artillery as 2nd Lieut. March, 1914. Was promoted Lieut. June, 1905, and capt, May, 1906. Transferred to the 3rd Battn, The Leinster Regt, 5 May, 1909, but after the outbreak of war in Aug, 1914, applied to be attached to the 2nd Battn, then proceeding to France; this request was not granted, and he remained with the Reserve Battn, until Jan, 1915, when he was attached to the 1st Battn, then in Flanders, and was killed in action at St Eloi, 14 Feb, following, while leading his platoon to the support of the first fire trench. Buried at Vermozelle.

Grave or Memorial Reference: XIII.B.23. Cemetery: Voormezeele Enclosures No3 in Belgium.

**ROBINSON, Henry T.:** Rank: Lance Corporal. Regiment or Service: Household Cavalry and Cavalry of the line including the Yeomanry and Imperial Camel Corps. Unit: 12th Lancers. Date of death: 19 March 1915. Age at death: 26. Service no: 1668. Born in St Paul's in Dublin. Enlisted in Dublin while living in Dolphins Barn. Died.

*Supplementary information:* Son of John and Mary Robinson, of 34 Rectory Road, West Bridgeford, Nottingham. He is listed on the Tullamore Roll of Honour under **ROBINSON H.V,.** (National Health Insurance Inspector) and the rank of Sergeant. It also states that he was killed (not died). I do not see the Offaly connection but include him for your reference. Grave or Memorial Reference: II.J.7. Cemetery: Merville Communal Cemetery in France.

**ROBINSON, Richard Arthur Wynne:** Rank: Sub-Lieutenant. Regiment or Service: Royal Naval Volunteer Reserve. Unit: Drake Battalion, Royal Naval Division. Date of death: 5 February 1917. Age at death: 32. From De Ruvigny's Roll of Honour:

*Robinson, Richard Arthur Wynne,* Sub Lieut., R.N,V. R., 3rd surv son of the Rev Andrew Craig Robinson, M. A., Rector of Ballymoney, Ballineen, County Cork, by his wife, Emily Anna, daughter of the late Thomas Jones of Donnybrook, Douglas, County Cork, Barrister-at-Law. Born in Cork, 6 Aug 1884. Educated there and the Bandon Grammar School. Entered the service of the Bank of

Ireland in April, 1904, serving successively in the offices at Tullamore, Mountmellick, Clonakilty and Fermoy. Joined the Royal Naval Division in Aug, 1915 and after a period of training at the Crystal Palace, obtained a commission in the R.N.V.R., 31 Jan, 1916. Served with the Expeditionary Force in France and Flanders from 1 Dec, following, being attached to the Drake Battalion of the Royal Naval Division, and died in hospital at or near Albert, Picardy, 5 Feb, 1917, from wounds received in action the same day, while he was responsible for the carrying of ammunition up to the firing line of one of the Royal Naval Division Battns.

Buried in Avelny Wood Cemetery, two miles north of Albert. One of his brother officers, who was wounded about the same time, wrote from No 1 London General Hospital, St Gabriel's College, Camberwell, S.E. "I thought you might like to know that I worked with him the whole of the night before until daybreak the next day, when we had breakfast together. I can't tell you how grieved I was to see that he had died of wounds, for until I saw it in the paper I did not know he had been wounded. The night that he and I worked together he behaved magnificently. He was responsible for the carrying of ammunition up to the firing line of one of our battalions – a very important thing – and it was work full of danger, but I know he worked absolutely regardless of his own personal safety. It will, I know, be a consolation to you to know that whatever happened to him, he met it like a man. He is a great loss to the battalion, because he was one of the most manly officers we had, and we all loved him, and I know that he was very popular indeed with his men." And another; "Like all who knew him, I shall always have the recollection of a brave officer and a noble hearted gentleman."

The Secretary of the Bank of Ireland also wrote; "His duty to the bank was at all times faithfully discharged, and my directors wish to place on record their appreciation of services so efficiently rendered both to them and to his country. It gives me pleasure to add that his name is inscribed on the Roll of Honour of the bank." And the agent of the bank at Fermoy; "He was a great favourite with everybody in Fermoy … He died a noble death for his King and his country. He was a most capable and efficient banker, and had he lived would easily have attained a prominent post in the Bank of Ireland." He married at Christ Church, Bray, County Wicklow, 8 October, 1908, Clemena Mary Elizabeth (Tullamore, Co. Offaly), only child of the late George Peiree Ridley, M. D., and had a son, Arthur George, born Posthumous, 17th April, 1917 (died 18 April, 1917).

Grave or Memorial Reference: I.C.3. Cemetery: Aveluy Wood Cemetery,

Mesnil-Martinsart in France

**ROBINSON, Samuel:** Rank: Pte. Regiment or Service: Household Cavalry and Cavalry of the line including the Yeomanry and Imperial Camel Corps. Unit: North Irish Horse. Date of death: 9 August 1917. Service no: 850. Born in Seagoe. Enlisted in Portadown while living in Edenderry, Co. Offaly. Died. Grave or Memorial Reference: IV.B.23. Cemetery: Mendinghem Military Cemetery in Belgium.

**ROCK, Christopher:** Rank: Pte. Regiment or Service: Leinster Regiment. Unit: 2nd Battalion. Date of death: 1 September 1916. Service no: 4919. Born in Clara, Co. Offaly. Enlisted in Mullingar, Co. Westmeath while living in Clara, Co. Offaly. Killed in action. Grave or Memorial Reference: He has no known grave but is listed on Pier and Face 16C and 16C on the Thiepval Memorial in France.

**ROGERS, Joseph:** Rank: Pte. Regiment or Service: Connaught Rangers. Unit: 1st Battalion. Date of death: 18 April 1916. Service no: 9865. Born in Banagher, Co. Offaly. Enlisted in Ballinasloe, Co. Galway while living in Banagher, Co. Offaly. Killed in action in Mesopotamia. Age at death: 28 in Ireland's Memorial Records and 26 in Commonwealth War Graves Commission.

*Supplementary information:* Awarded the Mons Star. Son of Thomas Rogers, of Cuba Cottage, Banagher, Co. Offaly. From the *Midland Tribune*, *Tipperary Sentinel* and *King's County*

*Vindicator*, November 1915:

A BANAGHER SOLDIER'S BRAVERY.

Private Joseph Rogers, a Banagher man belonging to the Second Battalion, Connaught Rangers, has performed a conspicuous act of bravery on the battlefield by going to the rescue of Major Muir, Fourth Black Watch. The story is told in a letter which Private Rogers has received as follows; Holmshead, Craigie, Broughty Ferry, 24th September, 1915.

"Dear Rogers,
I am sending you along this silver cigarette case and cheque for two pounds, which I hope you will accept as a small recognition of the way you came to my assistance after my fight with the "Hun" shell. In my dazed condition of mind it is more than likely I would have run into some others had it not been for your assistance.

I shall retain grateful remembrance of your conduct, and tender you my sincere thanks, and all the best wishes for your personal safety and good luck throughout the war. Yours sincerely,
John B. Muir, Major, Fourth Black Watch."

The accompanying massive cigarette case is thus inscribed: To Private Rogers, of the Connaught Rangers, for conspicuous bravery, and in recognition for the services rendered to me on the field of war, 14th July,

1915, from J. B. Muir, Major, Fourth Black Watch. Private Rogers joined the Expeditionary Force in France at the outbreak of the war, having previously serving in India. He was wounded by shrapnel at the battle of Ypres, and was invalided home, and is again back in the trenches.

Note: Major John B. Muir survived the war. Grave or Memorial Reference: He has no known grave but is listed on Panel 40 and 64 on the Basra Memorial in Iraq.

**ROHAN, Patrick Bernard:** Rank: Second Lieutenant. Regiment or Service: King's Own Yorkshire Light Infantry. Unit: 2nd Bn. Age at death: 33. Date of death: 16 March 1915. Killed in action.

*Supplementary information:* Son of Keiran and Mary Rohan, of Ballinahown, Athlone, Co. Westmeath. Husband of Gertrude Amy Crickmar (formerly Rohan), of 'Woodside' The Haye, Fingringhoe, Colchester, Essex. From the *King's County Chronicle*, March 1915, 'Quartermaster-Sergeant Rohan, Irish Guards, of Ballinahown, has received a commission in the Yorkshire Infantry. He was well known ten years ago as an athlete in the King's County and Midlands.' Grave or Memorial Reference: Has no known grave but is commemorated on Panel 47 on the Ypres (Menin Gate) Memorial in Belgium.

**ROONEY, Thomas:** (listed in Commonwealth War Graves Commission as **ROONEY, J**). Rank: Sergeant. Regiment or Service: Royal Dublin Fusiliers. Unit: 8th Battalion. Date of death: 11 September 1916. Service no: 16279. Born in Kilbrae [*sic*], Co. Offaly. Enlisted in London while living in Tullamore, Co. Offaly. Died of wounds. Age at death: 25.

*Supplementary information:* Son of Michael and Bridget Rooney (*née* Durley). Grave or Memorial Reference: II.C.65. Cemetery: La-Neuville British Cemetery, Corbie in France.

**ROONEY, Patrick:** Rank: Pte. Regiment or Service: Leinster Regiment. Unit: 2nd Battalion. Date of death: 25 August 1916. Service no: 10603. Born in Kilbride, Co. Offaly. Enlisted in Tullamore, Co. Offaly. Killed in action. From the *King's County Chronicle*, 1915, 'Mr H. Coldwell, Connaught Rangers (from Cavan, died of wounds in 1916) with the Expeditionary Force in France, writes to say, he has found a postal order payable to P. Rooney.' Grave or Memorial Reference: He has no known grave but is listed on Pier and Face 16C on the Thiepval Memorial in France.

**ROSA, Herbert Charles:** Rank: Second Lieutenant. Regiment or Service: Royal Field Artillery. Unit: 8th Div. Ammunition Col. Age at death: 33. Date of death: 31 July 1917. Killed in action.

*Supplementary information:* Eldest son of Mr and Mrs Carl Rosa, of 17

Herbert Charles Rosa.

Westbourne Street, London. Husband of Marie Rosa, of Drumbawn, Birr, Co. Offaly. From the *King's County Chronicle*, August 1917:

### LIEUT H. C. ROSA, R.F.A.

Deep and gloomy regret settled in the hearts of his many friends when they heard on Monday morning of the death in action of Lieut H.C. Rosa, R.F.A. Mr Rosa was the second son of the late Mr Carl Rosa and Mrs Rosa, the founders of the Carl Rosa Opera Company, and he married a few years ago Miss Marie O'Meara, eldest daughter of Mr William, O'Meara, Drumbane, Birr. Quite recently he purchased the lands and mansion house of Killavilla, Borrisokane, and settles there to live a country life, little dreaming of the tragic fate in store for him. He was a man of fine physique, full of youthful life and vigour, and his death in the early thirties is most painful and depressing to think about. An enthusiastic sportsman, he was keen on every form of outdoor sport – football, tennis, golf, cricket – game for anything. Horses and dogs he couldn't do without, and in pre-war days hail, rain and snow wouldn't keep him from a hunt anywhere in North Tipperary.

As a boy he joined the Yeomanry, and used to look forward to his yearly training as eagerly as a schoolboy does his Xmas vacation. He then joined the H.A.C. in London, where he was a partner in a lucrative business. The bustle of city life was not in his line, and as above stated he came back to Ireland. When war broke out he promptly volunteered for active service, and went to Egypt with the H.A.C. Later he transferred to the R.F.A., and a few short weeks ago left here for France with a light heart and the good wishes of every man that ever met him. Frank and open in disposition, full of fun and good humour, he was the best of company. Straight and sincere as they make 'em, and honour bright, poor "Erb," as they called him, is sadly missed by his many friends. The details of his death to hand are meagre, but we understand his death was instantaneous, and beside his gun he died like a soldier and a man. To his sorrowing widow and little daughter, and the other members of his family we tender our sincere sympathy.

From the *King's County Chronicle*, August 1917:

Late Lieutenant Rosa.

Fate of a Gallant Officer.

Further particulars are now to hand concerning the death in action of Sec. Lieut, Herbert C. Rosa, Royal Field Artiller, of Killavalla, Borrisokane, Co Tipperary, who met his fate on August 1st, 1917. He was the eldest son of the late Carl Rosa, and Mrs Carl Rosa, of 17 Westbourne, Hyde Park, London. He was educated at Clifden College.

After leaving college he joined the Honorable Artillery Company, which he resigned on coming to live in Ireland. At the outbreak of the war he rejoined his old battery and served with the H.A.C. in Egypt, from whence he returned in 1916 to take a commission in the Special Reserve, R.F.A. His officer commanding, writing to announce his death after expressing his profound sympathy at the loss of a gallant and cheerful comrade – "a gentleman of unfailing courtesy who always had a smile for everyone"– he states that he suffered no pain. He was struck by a shell and death was instantaneous.

He was buried at Poperinghe. Major Cowan, also a King's County officer, who was wounded, writing from King Edward VII, Hospital, Cardiff, gives the following additional details; "Lieut, Rosa very pluckily volunteered to take the place of another officer who was not feeling fit, on what turned out to be a rather hazardous enterprise and he showed a very fine example to the men of both courage and resource. We were detailed to form a dump for the infantry attack. The journey was half completed without incident, but on coming to a newly-made track which had evidently been spotted by aeroplanes we encountered very heavy fire and found it necessary to take out the teams and take shelter where we could until conditions had bettered.

After waiting an hour and as several men and animals had been hit and the fire had slackened somewhat it was decided to push on. We reached our destination and had unloaded and sent off several wagons when a shell burst on the road a few yards from where Lieutenant Rosa stood, directing operations. He suffered no pain and was killed instantaneously. He was brought back to our lines so that he might be buried. He was an excellent officer and exceedingly popular with everybody.

Grave or Memorial Reference: II.G.1. Cemetery: Poperinghe New Military Cemetery in Belgium.

**ROSBOROUGH, Henry:** Rank: Pte. Regiment or Service: Royal Inniskilling Fusiliers. Unit: 10th Battalion. Date of death: 1 September 1916. Service no: 15981. Born in Banagher, Co. Offaly. Enlisted in Donegal. Killed in action. Age at death: 30.

*Supplementary information:* Brother of Miss J. Rosborough, of Banagher Rectory, Derrychrier, Co. Londonderry. Grave or Memorial Reference:I.H.19. Cemetery: Berks Cemetery Extension in Belgium.

**ROSE, James:** Rank: Lance Sergeant and Sergeant. Regiment or Service: Irish Guards. Unit: 1st Bn. Date of death: 27 July 1916. Service no: 2880. Born in Clonmel. Enlisted in Mullingar. Killed in action. Age at death: 31.

*Supplementary information:* Son of the late Joshua Rose and the late Elizabeth Rose, of Kilduff House, (Barnane), Philipstown, Co. Offaly. Husband of Sarah Rose, of Bandon, Co. Cork. Grave or Memorial Reference: I.X.2. Cemetery: La Brique Military Cemetery, No 2 in Belgium.

**ROSSE, 5th Earl of.:** Rank: Major. Regiment or Service; ALIAS. Served as **PARSONS, William Edward:** Date of death: 10 June 1918.

*Supplementary information:* See **PARSONS**, the true family name. Grave or Memorial Reference: Cemetery: Birr Old Graveyard, Co. Offaly.

**RUTTLEGE/RUTTLEDGE, John Forrest:** Rank: Temporary Captain. Regiment or Service: West Yorkshire Regiment. Unit: A Company, 2nd Battalion. Date of death: 1 July 1916. Age at death: 21. Killed in action.

John Forrest Ruttledge.

*Supplementary information*: Awarded the Military Cross. Son of Lt. Col. Alfred Ruttledge, of the Woodlands, Castleconnell, Co. Limerick. From the *King's County Chronicle*, March 1915, 'Lieut, J.F. Ruttlege, West York Regiment, son of Col Ruttlege, Castleconnel, late of Birr, has been awarded the Military Cross for meritorious conduct in the battle of Neuve Chapelle.' Grave or Memorial Reference: He has no known grave but is listed on Pier and Face 2a, 2C and 2D on the Thiepval Memorial in France.

**RUXTON, George Percy:** Rank: Staff Sergeant. Regiment or Service: Royal Army Veterinary Corps, Depot. Date of death: 29 December 1915. Service no: SE/5731. Born in Kilbride, Co. Offaly. Enlisted in Woolwich. Died at Home. Grave or Memorial Reference: D.T.52. Cemetery: South Ealing Cemetery, UK.

**RUXTON, Joseph:** Rank: Rifleman. Regiment or Service: Royal Irish Rifles. Unit: B Company, 2nd Battalion. Date of death: 9 July 1916. Service no:

10394. Born in Tullamore, Co. Offaly. Enlisted in Dublin. Killed in action. Age at death: 21.

*Supplementary information:* Son of Joseph and Mary Ruxton, of 2 Newport Street, Dublin. Grave or Memorial Reference: He has no known grave but is listed on Pier and Face 15 A and 15 B on the Theipval Memorial in France.

**RYALL, George:** Rank: Corporal. Regiment or Service: Royal Munster Fusiliers. Unit: 1st Battalion. Date of death: 21 March 1918. Service no: 3410. Born in Aghacon, Co. Offaly. Enlisted in Birr, Co. Offaly while living in Fortel, Co. Offaly. Killed in action. From the *Midland Tribune*, May 1918, 'Mr Gerald Ryall, Glencurra, Birr, has the unofficial news of the death of his only son George, confirmed by the War Office. He was 23 years of age.' From *King's County Chronicle*, May 1918, 'Much sympathy is felt for Mr Gerland Ryall, Glencurra, Birr, who has had the unofficial news of the death of his only son, George, con-firmed by the War Office. Early in the war young Ryall answered the call, and served in the Munster Fusiliers until the 21st March when he was killed in his hut by a shell. He was 23 years of age.' Grave or Memorial Reference: Has no known grave but is commem-orated on Panel 78 and 79. Memorial: Pozieres Memorial in France.

**RYAN, John Joseph:** Rank: Pte. Regiment or Service: Sherwood Foresters. Unit: 1st Battalion. Date of

John Joseph Ryan.

death: 1 April 1915. Service no: 12187. Born in Birr. Enlisted in Birr, Co. Offaly while living in Co. Offaly. Died of wounds. From the *King's County Chronicle*, 8 April 1915:

Mr John Ryan coach smith, Mill Street, Birr, has received a telegram from the War Office announcing the death of his son, John, aged 18, at the battle of Neuve Chapelle. The young soldier, who was popular in his native town, was a grandson to Mr Patrick Melsop, and belonged to the Notts and Derby Regiment. His family here received much sympathy since the news of his death became known, and in addition Mrs Ryan has had a letter from one of the officers in the regi-ment stating that her son was a good boy and died like a soldier.

Grave or Memorial Reference: III.A.49. Cemetery: Houplines Communal Cemetery Extension in France.

**RYAN, John Patrick:** Rank: Pte. Regiment or Service: Labour Corps. Date of death: 9 May 1918. Service no: 336134 and listed in the Commonwealth

War Graves Commission as G/309 and listed as transferred to the Eastern Command Labour Section under the number 336134. Formerly he was with the Royal Dublin Fusiliers where his number was 4619. Born in Tullow, Co. Carlow. Enlisted in Carlow while living in Crinkle, Co. Offaly. Died of wounds.

*Supplementary information:* Husband of Katherine Ryan, of School Street, Crinkle, Birr, Co. Offaly. Born in Limerick. Grave or Memorial Reference: Screen Wall O1. 359. Cemetery: Leicester (Welford Road) Cemetery, UK.

**RYAN, Michael Joseph:** Rank: Pte. Regiment or Service: Australian Infantry, A.I.F. Unit: 12th Bn. Age at death: 39. Date of death: 28 April 1915. Service no: 1427.

*Supplementary information*: Son of Michael and Catherine Ryan. Husband of Agnes Ryan, of 3 Charlemont Square, Claremont Street, Dublin. Native of Tullamore. From the *King's County Independent*, June 1915:

TULLAMORE MAN KILLED.

Intelligence of the death of Mr Michael Ryan, brother-in-law to Mr Patrick Smyth, U.D.C., in action in the Dardanelles, has just reached Tullamore. Deceased, who belonged to the Twelfth Australian Battalion, was a son of the late Mr Michael Ryan, a well known and popular figure in the commercial life of Tullamore. He joined the South African Yeomanry during the Boer War, and when the campaign was over he settled down in that country where he remained until a few years ago, when he went to Australia. When the European War broke out he volunteered for active service again. Deceased, who was about 30 years of age, has two brothers at present with the Colours, one serving under General Botha in South Africa and the other in England. We desire to tender our sympathy to Mr and Mrs Smyth in their bereavement.

Grave or Memorial Reference: I.B.3. Cemetery: Beach Cemetery, Anzac in Turkey.

**RYAN, Patrick:** Rank: Pte. Regiment or Service: Irish Guards. Unit: 2nd Battalion. Date of death: 2 May 1916. Service no: 7326. Born in Doon, Co. Limerick. Enlisted in Dublin, while living in Crinkle, Co. Offaly. Killed in action. Grave or Memorial Reference: I.G.4. Cemetery: White House Cemetery, St Jean-Les-Ypres in Belgium.

**RYAN, Patrick:** Rank: Pte. Regiment or Service: Irish Guards. Unit: 1st Battalion. Date of death: 1 November 1914. Service no: 3385. Born in Banagher, Co. Offaly. Enlisted in Birr, Co. Offaly. Killed in action. Age at death: 23.

*Supplementary information:* Son of Edward and Mary Ryan, of Clongowney, Banagher, Co. Offaly. Grave or Memorial Reference: Panel 11. Memorial: Ypres (Menin Gate) Memorial in Belgium.

# S

Daniel Sammon. Image from *King's County Chronicle* 1916.

**SAMMON, Daniel:** Rank: Pte. Regiment or Service: Leinster Regiment. Unit: 2nd Battalion. Date of death: 1 September 1916. Service no: 1103. Born in Birr, Co. Offaly. Enlisted in Birr while living in Birr. Killed in action. Age at death: 20 (Ireland's Memorial Records), 45 (Commonwealth War Graves Commission).

*Supplementary information:* Husband of Bridget Sammon, of Eden Road, Birr, Co. Offaly. This man is listed in Memorial Records under Sammon, Daniel (1103) and Sammon, William (10095). From the *King's County Chronicle*, February 1916, 'Mr James Sammon, boot maker, Castle Street, has given two sons to the colours, viz: Private James, of the 2nd Leinsters, who was wounded early in the war, and Private Patrick, of the same regiment, also on active service.' Grave or Memorial Reference: Pier and Face 16 C. Memorial: Thiepval Memorial in France.

**SCALLY, Christopher:** Rank: Pte. Regiment or Service: Leinster Regiment. Unit: 1st Battalion. Date of death: 20 May 1915. Service no: 2958. Born in Tullamore, Co. Offaly. Enlisted in Mullingar, Co. Westmeath. Died of wounds during the fighting at Armentieres. He is also listed on the Tullamore Roll of Honour as **SCALLY, Christy.** Grave or Memorial Reference: I.A.46. Cemetery: Bailleul Communal Cemetery Extension (Nord) in France.

**SCANLON, John:** Rank: Sergeant. Regiment or Service: Royal Dublin Fusiliers. Unit: W Company, 1st Battalion. Date of death: 21 March 1918. Service no: 9115. Born in Birr, Co. Offaly. Enlisted in Dublin. Killed in action. Age at death: 29.

*Supplementary information*: Husband of Q. Elizabeth Scanlon, of 74 Clarendon Road, Shirley, Southampton. Grave or Memorial Reference: Has no known grave but is commemorated on Panel 79 and 80. Memorial: Pozieres Memorial in France.

**SCANLON, Thomas:** Rank: Pte. Regiment or Service: Royal Dublin Fusiliers. Unit: 1st Battalion. Date of death: 30 April 1915. Service no: 9966. Born in Birr, Co. Offaly. Enlisted in

Dublin. Killed in action in Gallipoli. Grave or Memorial Reference: He has no known grave but is listed on the Special Memorial, B, 97. Cemetery, V Beach Cemetery in Turkey.

**SCHOALES, George:** Rank: Sergeant. Regiment or Service: East Lancashire Regiment. Unit: 2nd Battalion. Date of death: 9 May 1915. Service no: 9694. Born in Clara, Co. Offaly. Enlisted in Tullamore, Co. Offaly while living in Clara, Co. Offaly. Killed in action. Grave or Memorial Reference: He has no known grave but is listed on Panel 5 and 6 on the Ploegsteert Memorial in Belgium.

**SHANAHAN, John:** Rank: Pte. Regiment or Service: Machine Gun Corps. Unit: Infantry. 47th Company. Date of death: 17 August 1917. Service no: 12614. Formerly he was with the Royal Irish Regiment where his number was 9767. Born in Shinrone, Co. Offaly. Enlisted in Dublin while living in Johnstown, Co. Kilkenny. Died of wounds. Grave or Memorial Reference: III.F.14. Cemetery: Mendingham Military Cemetery in Belgium.

George Schoales.

**SHANAHAN, Patrick:** Rank: Lance Bombardier. Regiment or Service: Royal Horse Artillery and Royal Field Artillery. Unit: D Battery, 95th Brigade. Date of death: 24 March 1918. Service no: 43606. Born in Shinrone, Co. Offaly. Enlisted in Nenagh. Killed in action. Grave or Memorial Reference: Has no known grave but is commemorated on Panel 7 to 10. Memorial: Pozieres Memorial in France.

**SHAUGHNESSY, James:** Rank: Pte. Regiment or Service: Royal Dublin Fusiliers. Unit: 10th Battalion. Date of death: 5 February 1917. Service no: 25423. Born in Clonbullogue, Co. Offaly. Enlisted in Carlow while living in Clonbullogue. Died. Grave or Memorial Reference: XXI. E. 14. Cemetery: Etaples Military Cemetery in France.

**SHAUGHNESSY, Thomas:** Rank: Pte. Regiment or Service: Royal Dublin Fusiliers. Unit: 8/9th Battalion. Date of death: 25 March 1918. Service no: 15737. Born in Rathangan, Co. Kildare. Enlisted in Naas while living in Edenderry, Co. Offaly. Killed in action. Grave or Memorial Reference: He has no known grave but is listed on Panel 79 and 80 on the Pozieres Memorial in France.

**SHEA, Michael:** Listed in the Commonwealth War Graves Commission under **O'SHEA, Michael:** Rank: Pte. Regiment or Service: Leinster Regiment. Unit:

2nd Battalion. Date of death: 14 October 1916. Service no: 3306. Born in Kilbride, Co. Offaly. Enlisted in Tullamore, Co. Offaly. Died. Age at death: 21.

*Supplementary information:* Son of John and Mrs E. O'Shea, of Rapp, Tullamore, Co. Offaly From the *King's County Independent*, October 1916:

TULLAMORE SOLDIER'S DEATH

The details of Private O'Shea's death in a French hospital contained in a paragraph appearing elsewhere were but meagre at the time of writing. The deceased soldier who was a popular young Tullamore man, joined the 2nd Leinster Regiment in 1914, and having completed his training was soon sent to the West front, where with the exception of a brief period of ten days when he came home to visit his parents, he had been serving up to the time of his death. He contracted a severe illness in the trenches which developed into cerebro-spinal meningitis during the strenuous days which followed in the summer of the present year when the Leinsters took part in many fierce conflicts with the enemy, the deceased having been wounded during the campaign. He was admitted to the base hospital on the 9th October, being then very ill. The good sister in charge at once communicated with Private O'Shea's mother informing her that everything possible would be done for her son.

Two days later a further note from the sister informed Mrs O'Shea that her son's condition was lightly improved but was dangerously ill. Some days later on the 15th inst, Mrs O'Shea was grieved as only a mother can be on receipt of the following letter from the Sister-conveying the sad news

"Dear Mrs O'Shea,

I am sorry to tell you that you dear son, Private O'Shea died yesterday afternoon. His condition was slightly improved until yesterday morning when he lapsed into unconsciousness and passed peacefully away at 5.10 p.m. It will comfort you to know that he did not suffer any pain. The priest visited him several times and ministered to him the last rites of the Church. His funeral was the afternoon. He was laid to rest in the little cemetery close to here with full military honours. I am sure his thoughts were with you, but he left no last message,

Yours in sympathy,
H. Craig, Sister."

The deepest sympathy is felt for the parents of the deceased in the great loss they have sustained.

From the *King's County Independent*, March 1917:

MILITARY ITEM.

In connection with the Tullmore roll of honour which appeared in a recent issue of the "King's County

Chronicle" the following were inadvertently omitted: Sergt Charles O'Shea, Irish Guards, who was home on a short furlough to see his parents returned to England on Thursday

Note: Charles survived the war. He is also listed on the Tullamore Roll of Honour under **O'SHEA.** From the *King's County Independent*, February 1916:

MRS SHEA'S MAINTENANCE

Mrs. F.H. Fitzgerald-Beale, Hon. Sec. Soldiers and Sailors association, Mountmellick, sent the following letter;

"I have just seen a letter supposed to be from a son of Mrs Kate Shea. I say "supposed," for I believe her son, Jack Shea, enlisted under his brother's name and is Cornelius Shea (not O'Shea). Mrs Shea is drawing 13s 10d at the post office weekly. I do not know what sons are making her allowances, but she is drawing that sum. If Jack Shea, otherwise Con Shea, has not written this letter it is unfair towards him. I can scarcely believe he did for he was very illiterate."

Mr. Phelan: What was the purport of his letter!

Clerk: He complained of his mother having to pay for her maintenance while here in the hospital. There was no such thing because no bill was sent to the woman.

Mr. Brady: Will there be a bill sent to her!

Clerk: The Master can tell you that. The Guardians were in favour last week of sending no bill to her.

Master: I saw John Shea on Sunday last and he must be in the army, for he was wearing khaki. He said he wrote the letter himself.

(Illegible): Is she a big strong woman, Mr (Illegible)

Clerk: (Illegible)

Mr. Phelan: And she has no one but these four sons to provide for, and she is getting 13s 10d a week?

Mr. Geoghagan: What does she cost the rates?

Master: At least 4s or 5s a week.

Mr. Phelan: He only wanted to have an accumulated sum for a spree when he returns.

Mr. Pattison: I think she ought to be charged something.

Master: If the Guardians make an order I will apply for it.

Chairman: She ought to pay something for her maintenance in the house. What would it be?

Master: I don't charge less than 1s a day at any time: 7s a week. That would be little enough.

Mr. Bailey: We passed a resolution last Saturday that she be charged nothing for her maintenance while she is here. I have interviewed the woman in the hospital. I have been informed by Mr Delaney (relieving officer) that the amount the woman should get would be 13s 10d a week. She informed me in the presence of the Sister in charge that one week she got 12s, one week 4s; one week, 1s 5d; and one week 4s 4d. There is a leakage some place.

Mr. Pattison: It is not in the Post Office.

Mr. Brady: And it is not the fault of the Guardians.

Mr. Delaney, R. O.: That could not be possible at all, because what she gets one week she should get every week.

Mr. Bailey: She informs she is only three weeks in hospital.

Master: She has been in on several occasions.

Mr. Bailey: The last time is three weeks anyhow. She informs me that her niece draws this money and she has every confidence in her niece. I asked her did she think that her niece would appropriate any of this money and not give it all to her, and she states, no, that she believes she would not keep a penny. I asked her did she draw any of her money from Mr Burns, postmaster, herself and she says, yes, she goes there herself and the money always varies. Her statement is that Mr Burns gives her the money, not in even sums: it varies very much. Sometimes small sums and then sometimes larger. I intend also seeing Mrs Beale and seeing Mr Burns to see how this money is paid, because I am not in a position to criticise, but there is a leakage somewhere.

Chairman: To put the whole thing in a nutshell, I propose she pays 7s a week.

Mr. Pattison: I second it. I would not go behind Mrs Beale's letter at all.

Mr. Bailey: Well, as far as I can I will oppose strongly a penny being taken from the woman. I think it a monstrous thing that we, standing here under the protection of her sons who are giving their lives for us on the battlefields of Flanders, should come here and stop her money and not leave her anything to give her a decent burial.

Mr. Brady: What will you do with the money?

Mr. Bailey: Let her save it for her sons when they come home wounded. I will see that it is accumulated.

Mr. Brady: To have a spree or what?

Mr. Bailey: To have it for her children when they come home, and have a sum saved to give her a decent burial.

Chairman: Didn't you say the last day that two of her sons were killed? She could only have two songs then, not four.

Mr. Bailey: Well, all the more credit to her.

Mr. Brady: We are here in the interests of the ratepayers.

Mr. Bailey: I protest against it most strongly. You, farmers, here are protected by her sons, and you are coming here to victimise her.

Mr. Keating: There is no victimising at all.

Several members protested against

Mr Bailey's statement.

Mr. Bailey: You would feel the pinch if the Huns were devastating your country. You would cry aloud for such men to come to your assistance then.

Mr. Geoghegan: The ratepayers are paying for her sons and every one of them that are fighting.

Master: There is another case from Maryborough: Margaret Costigan; and another case from Mountmellick: Annie Campbell, a maternity case. Margaret Costigan can hire a car to come here whenever she likes.

Mr. Bailey proposed that "Mrs Shea be not charged for her maintenance in consequence of the sacrifices she has made."

Mr. Thomas Cushion seconded.

Mr. Phelan suggested that Mr Delaney go to the Post Office and ascertain what Mrs Shea was paid.

Mr. Bailey again asked for an adjournment, but the Board decided to go to a division on the question, when the result was: for the Chairman's motion: Messrs Loughlin, Pattison, Keating, Mooney, McGee, Brady, Fitzpatrick, Phelan, Devoy, and the Chairman-10.

Against: Messrs Bailey and Cushion 2.

The motion was therefore carried, and the Master was ordered to apply to the army paymaster in payment of the cost of the maintenance in hospital of Mrs O'Shea.

In the case of Margaret Costigan the Master said she had gone out of the house, but he supposed she would be back in a few days' time. She had been in several times since the war commenced and he could get out the number of days for her.

Clerk: Is it to herself you will send the bill?

Master: No; to the paymaster at Cork.

The Master was instructed to apply accordingly for payment.

In reference to Annie Campbell, the Master said that she was getting an allowance from her brother.

A similar order was made in this case.

Mr. Bailey: She is getting it from her brother, not from the Government. You are trying to rob those people. I will try and get those people's sons and brothers to stop the allowances.

After transacting some routine business the meeting adjourned.

In another article in the same month:

The following letter was read:

No. 1 Ward, Military Hospital, Curragh Camp. Sir, I consider the treatment of my mother in hospital as only small recompense for the sacrifice she has given to this country in its hour of need. She has given four sons to help in the great struggle to beat back the would-be invading Hun, two being killed while performing that sacred duty, another at present engaged in the same struggle, whilst the fourth awaits the call at a moment's notice. Can such a woman in no way be shown a little gratitude by those who have given nothing, nor done nothing for the Empire, and still enjoy the same security as the patriotic people of Ireland? She has been a ratepayer for more than 30 years, and, considering that in the sacrifice of her four sons to the country, and the loss of as (illegible)d relief from the Guardians, they are not satisfied - they must make her pay still more. Her brave sons left her half their pay, which amounts to 7s per week; then the big sum of 5s, added by the Government, makes the grand total up to 12s per week. They take the liberty of existing payments from this poor widow, who, in the event of the remaining two sons being killed, would be left destitute, and the Guardians would have to keep her, or, if the sons viewed the situation as the Poor Law Guardians do, they would say we are fighting for the ratepayers' safety, the least they can do is to look after my mother, and pocket the money they are earning so hard, instead of saving the Guardians £6 10s per year by their patriotic action. Such claims for payment in this woman's case from the District Paymaster of our regiment by your Board is absurd, and should be viewed as such by any patriotic members that may have the privilege or the pluck of bringing up same for the consideration of your honourable Board. If this does not have the desired effect which we expect, we will resort to the one and only means left to us to gain our gaol, and that is to keep our money, and let the ratepayers keep my mother. All we want is that the Guardians make no claim on our money for my mother's keep in hospital. How is it that they think so bad of giving her four shillings' worth of poor sons' fighting and they can give half-pay to any official who joins the army? Why is there no protest against this waste of public money on a man that is only doing his duty as me and my brothers are doing for one shilling a day? Our pay won't run two sheets of paper, so you must turn paper-war time economy.

Respectfully yours,
Private J. O'Shea, 3693,
4th Leinster Regiment."

Chairman: a brother of his was an employee of the Union. He was in charge of the ambulance, and he was killed at the front, and another brother was killed, and two others are there.

Mr. Bailey: What is she being charged?

Master: Nothing.

Mr. Bailey: Then this letter is a libel on the charity of the Guardians.

Master: She is in hospital at present, and I have furnished no account at all yet.

Mr. Duane: Has any application been made?

Master: No, sir; not one. I was not in a position to furnish an account, because I did not know whether the Guardians would get the money or not.

Mr. Bailey: I propose the account be not furnished, and that she get the best care while she is in the house.

Master: There is another: Margaret Costigan. She is in hospital, and she is getting money from the army. I suppose I will send an account.

Mr. Bailey: Certainly not. Not while she has a son in the army protecting us.

I have not been able to locate the other brother referred to in the above article as having died at the front. He is not referred to in later articles or war dead databases and so may not have been a casualty. Grave or Memorial Reference: I.R.12. Cemetery: Wimereux Communal Cemetery, Pas de Calais in France.

**SHEEHAN, Charles:** Rank: Sergeant. Regiment or Service: Leinster Regiment. Unit: 2nd Battalion. Date of death: 15 March 1916. Service no: 7182. Born in Birr, Co. Offaly. Enlisted in Birr, Co. Offaly. Died of wounds. Listed in 'Ireland's Memorial Records' as Sheehan, George C. Date of death: 16 March 1916. From the *Midland Tribune, Tipperary Sentinel* and *King's County Vindicator*, July 1916, 'Corporal P Sheehan, 1st Batt, Irish Guards, son of Mr P. Sheehan, of Birr, went to France in the first British Expeditionary Force shortly after the outbreak of war, and has been mentioned by Sir Douglas Haig for gallantry and distinguished conduct in the field. From the *King's County Chronicle*, March 1916:

Sergt. C. Sheehan's death. Officer's tribute to a gallant soldier. News reached Birr some days ago that Sergeant Charles Sheehan, 2nd Leinsters, was killed in action on March 16. The gallant Sergeant was the third son of Mr Denis Sheehan, Crinkle, himself an old soldier, who has re-enlisted and is now serving at the Birr Barracks. Although only 27 years of age, the late Sergeant Sheehan had twelve years service to his credit, and was wounded in October, 1914. A brother of his, Private George, is now with the 1st Batt, Leinsters in Serbia, and the two other brothers went through the South African War. Much sympathy will be felt for the relatives of the deceased sergeant in their great bereavement, but they will be consoled in knowing that he was highly esteemed by the officers and men of his regiment, and that he died the death of a hero.

What his superior officers and his comrades thought of him can best be seen by the following extracts which we take from letters received by his mother and wife.

Revd Denis Doyle, Chaplain of the Battalion, writes on March 16:

I am heart broken to write such sad news to you, but God's will be done. Your son, Sergeant Sheehan, was very badly wounded through the head early yesterday morning, and died about quarter to eight. I was with him from six a. m. till he died, and did all I could for him, but there was no hope. He was sadly missed in the regiment by the young officers and men, for he was a fine man and a good catholic. I shall lay him to rest to-day, and tomorrow he will celebrate St Patricks Day in heaven with our King Christ and His Holy Mother, and may they both comfort you and his poor wife. Tell you daughter Florrie that I have the harp from his pocket, I shall wear it tomorrow as a token from a good brave Irishman. God bless you. "

Sec. -Lieut. Archibald E. Nye, writing on March 17 to Mrs Sheehan, wife of the late Sergeant, says:

"I am writing to console with you on the death of your husband. He was hit in the head at 3.45 a.m. on March 16 whilst on duty in the front line trenches. He was taken to the dressing station at once, but died at 7.45 a.m. only regaining consciousness for a moment; his death was painless. He was buried by the R.C. Chaplain just before midnight on March 16th. I am not allowed to say where he was buried, but I know, and in due time I will see that you are informed. I am afraid that nothing I can say can help you in your loss, but I simply must tell you what we thought of him. He was my platoon Sergeant, and I have been with him for the past four months.

He was held in the greatest respect by officers and men, and I don't think I have ever met a man of such sound reliability and high principals before. The men worshipped him, he never knew what fear was, and he will be sadly missed by all. In him the regiment has lost an excellent non-commissioned officer and a very brave man, and I have lost a personal friend. Please accept my deepest sympathy in you sad loss."

From the *King's County Chronicle*, July 1916:

THE LATE CORPORAL SHEEHAN. MILITARY FUNERAL.

On Sunday, the 16th inst., the remains of the late Corpl. Denis Sheehan, 2nd Leinsters, were interred at Clonoghill cemetery with full military honours. His father, Mr Denis Sheehan, was a veteran of life-long service, on pension, re-joined since the outbreak of war, and is now attached to the military headquarters depot at Crinkle, Birr. The deceased corporal was 34 years of age, had 14 years service, three of which were in the South African War, and was retired on pension, and in ill health. The family is essentially a military one, the father and three sons being soldiers; of the two brothers of the deceased Sergt. Charles, of the 2nd Leinsters, was killed in action in France on 15th March last, and Private George is now in the 1st Batt. At Salonika.

During his period of invalid retirement, which has ended with his demise, Corporal Sheehan was a highly respected resident of Crinkle, and very greatly esteemed by his many friends and acquaintances, both civil and military. He was of a true military type, with a certain manly bearing and calm cheerfulness during the days of weakness and broken health, which he bore without complaint, or thought of it. The funeral cortege was attended by the regimental band, and a firing party, and a large concourse of soldiers and civilians. Major O'Connor was in command of the military. The chief mourners were; Mr Denis Sheehan, father; Mary Agnes and Florence Beatrice, sisters.

Mr and Mrs Sheehan and family wish to return their sincere thanks to the officers, non-commissioned officers and men of the Depot of the Leinster Regiment for their kindness, and also their thanks to their many civilian friends who attended the funeral.

From the *King's County Chronicle*, March 1918:

SECOND ANNIVERSARY.

In loving memory of Sergt. Charles Sheehan, 2nd Batt, Leinster Regiment, dearly-beloved son of Mr and Mrs Denis Sheehan, Crinkle, Birr, killed at Ypres on 15th March 1915.

Jesus have mercy on his dear soul.
One of the millions who forward
   went
With joy to the great adavance;
One who for freedom has died
   content
In the Sunny land of France

A small white cross on a lonely
   grave,
Where no kith or kin may pray,
And a heart that was bravest of all
   the brave
Lies cold in the grave today.
Inserted by his loving mother, father,
   sisters and brother.

Grave or Memorial Reference: I.J.16. Cemetery: Menin Road South Military Cemetery in Belgium.

**SHEPPARD, Robert:** Rank: Lance Corporal. Regiment or Service: Irish Guards. Unit: 1st Bn. Age at death: 32. Date of death: 18 May 1915. Service no: 1262. Born in Kilcolman in Co. Offaly and enlisted in Birr while living in Portland, Co. Tipperary, Killed in action. Supplementary information: Son of Benjamin and Hester Sheppard, of Portland, Birr, Co. Offaly. From the *King's County Chronicle*, June 1915:

A BIRR MAN'S BATTLE EXPERIENCE.
A friend of his in Birr has sent the following interesting extract from a letter which he has just received from Private Wm. Cleary, 1st Battalion, Irish Guards, son of the late Mr Patrick Cleary, of Castle Street, and in which we are sure many readers of the "*King's County Chronicle*" will take a lively interest.

"I had some narrow escapes since I saw you last Christmas, having come out of three big battles without a scratch, the last being on 18th May, at Reichburg. Out of 1, 100 men we only had 464 left at the roll call, and

4 officers out of 19 were left to take charge that night. Bob Sheppeard, of Cree, and Willie Dunne, of Mill Street were killed, and Lord Rosse was severely wounded. He went into action a brave man, and I hope he will pull through. The men on my right and left were killed, so I am lucky. The "Jack Johnsons" were flying all over the place, but in spite of everything we took the German trenches and a farm-house. What do you think of the Huns using gas? I was knocked out yesterday, but I am alright again. It's not bad when a fellow wants to sleep (moryah)!"

The Bob Sheppard referred to was son of the late Mr Ben. Sheppard, Fortal, Birr, and looked the picture of a splendid soldier when on furlough recently. Willie Dunne was son of the late Mr Matthew Dunne, Mill Street, served his time to the cabinet making in Mr John Dooly's works, and was on the Reserve when war broke out.

Grave or Memorial Reference: Has no known grave but is commemorated on Panel 4. Memorial: Le Touret Memorial in France.

**SHERIDAN, James:** Rank: Pte. Regiment or Service: Leinster Regiment. Unit: B Company, 1ˢᵗ Battalion. Date of death: 5 May 1915. Service no: 3645. Born in Cloghan, Co. Offaly. Enlisted in Birr, Co. Offaly. Killed in action. Age at death: 47. Supplementary information: Son of Patrick and Anne Sheridan, of Cloghan. Husband of Bridget Sheridan, of Ballyloughan, Cloghan, Belmont, Offaly. From the *King's County Chronicle*, April 1916, 'Cloghan and District. James Sheridan, an old soldier, of the Leinsters, who served in the Boer War, was killed at Lille, after being at the front for ten months. His son, Private Thomas, of the 3ʳᵈ Leinsters is in France.' Grave or Memorial Reference: Panel 44. Memorial: Ypres (Menin Gate) Memorial in Belgium.

**SHERLOCK, Gerrard Loundes Edward:** Rank: Captain. Regiment or Service: 3ʳᵈ (King's Own) Hussars Secondary. Regiment: Nigeria Regiment, W.A.F.F. Secondary. Unit: attd. 5ᵗʰ Bn. Age at death: 30. Date of death: 25 August 1914. From the *King's County Chronicle*, November 1914:

HOW A BRAVE YOUNG KING'S COUNTY MAN DIED.

We previously informed our readers of the death of Lieut. G.L.E. Sherlock, 3ʳᵈ Hussars. He had been seconded for duty in Africa, and immediately after the outbreak of the war his detachment was engaged. A brother officer belonging to the Yola Column of the Nigerian Field Force, has sent home an account from the Cameroons. As the letter gives some details of the manner in which Lieut Sherlock upheld the best traditions of the British Army and his native land, the appended abstract will, we doubt not, be considered with special interest by the subscribers of the "*King's County Chronicle*" The writer says:

"We reached Yola by forced marches on the 14th September, six days march, averaging 26 miles a day, good going for an ordinary infantry column with scratch carriers. Our mounted infantry turned up on the 21st, and at once crossed the river. We reached the border on Monday. We had not been over half an hour before heavy fighting took place. Col. Maclear had ordered them to clear the Germans out, and within half an hour of crossing the Teil were heavily engaged at Tepe. The Germans let through the scouts, and the advanced guard and the main body got somewhat bunched. The German soldiers evidently had orders to pick the white men. Wickham and Sherlock were killed, and Lord M. Seymour dangerously, and McDonald severely wounded-four out of the six white officers. Only two rank and file were wounded.

It was very sad about poor Sherlock. The action was practically over and he had just come up in time to save a German officer's life. He turned away and the officer's orderly let drive, and got Sherlock through the throat. Needless to say, both officer and orderly didn't survive half a minute.

I don't know how the mounted infantry took the place, as they hadn't more than sixty men, and the Germans had between fifty and a hundred, under five officers."

The readers of this brief narrative may well note with national pride that their young countryman sacrificed his life in chivalrously saving a defeated footman in the hour of victory.

*Supplementary information:* Son of David Sherlock, of Rahan Lodge, Tullamore. From De Ruvigny's Roll of Honour: '*Sherlock, Gerard L. E.*, Capt. 3rd. (King's Own) Hussars, 2nd son of David Sherlock, of Rahan, King's County. Served with the Expeditionary Force in France and Flanders and was killed in action 25 Aug, 1914.' Grave or Memorial Reference: Zaria in Nigeria.

**SHORTT, Vere Dawson.** Rank: Captain. Regiment or Service: Northamptonshire Regiment. Unit:7th Battalion. Date of death: 25 September 1915. Died of wounds. Killed in action. Grave or Memorial Reference: Panel 91 to 93. He has no known grave but is listed on Panel 60 on the Loos Memorial in France. From the *King's County Chronicle*, November 1915:

LOCAL HERO'S NOBLE END

In the last "King's County Chronicle" we recorded the death of Captain Vere Dawson Shortt. By his death Ireland is the poorer of a capable wielder of the word and pen. We are now able to give the following further facts, which will doubtless be read with keen interest all over King's County, Queen's County and County Tipperary.

Captain Shortt, who was killed in action on the 27th September, was born in 1874. He was the only son of the late Mr James Fitzmaurice

Shortt, of Moorfield, Mountrath, and grand-nephew of the late Vere Shortt, Larch Hall, Queen's County, and of the late Mr William Woods, J.P., Oxmanstown Mall. He was educated at the Preparatory College of his uncle, Dr William Ewing, Chesterfield, Birr, and afterwards at the Galway Grammar School, of which the late Dr Biggs was headmaster. He joined the Cape Mounted Rifles in 1890, and was in it for five years, taking part in the Pondoland campaign, where he received an assegai wound. He also served through the Boer War in Steinaecker's Horse, and has the South African medal with two clasps. Captain Shortt also fought on the Carlist side in Spain, receiving a wound in the leg. He was the author of "Lost Sheep," one of the best viewed novels of last year, and also published numerous short stories in various magazines. He was engaged on another novel at the outbreak of the war, which, however, is unfinished, as he was gazetted Captain in the 7th Northamptonshire regiment shortly afterwards. He went with the regiment to France at the end of August, and was killed leading a charge on Monday, 27th September, last (1915). His Adjutant writes – "He was a brave and experienced soldier, fearless in the execution of his duty, and most capable in carrying it through. Such men are invaluable and cannot be replaced again. He has done his work now, and died the death he would have preferred above all others. I am very proud of him."

Among the flattering references to his novel, "Lost Sheep," the "London Opinion" said: "Captain Vere Shortt is another khaki-clad author, whose recently published novel, "Lost Sheep," is probably the best work of fiction (not excepting 2Under Two Flags"), that has been written of France's Foreign Legion, of which he was a member for a year or more. He also fought in the South African War, and has a decoration to show for it. He is now a Captain in Kitchener's Army."

Before joining for the present war he was staying in Drogheda on a visit with his sister, Mrs Stafford Matthews, and was then full of his novel, but keen to take up soldiering again.

**SKERRITT, Joseph Henry:** Rank: Pte. Regiment or Service: Royal Dublin Fusiliers. Unit: 1st Battalion. Date of death: 29 April 1915. Service no: 9844. Born in Birr, Co. Offaly. Enlisted in Dublin while living in Birr, Co. Offaly. Killed in action in Gallipoli. From the *King's County Chronicle*, May 1915, 'Sergeant Joseph Henry Skerritt, 1st Dublin Fusiliers, aged 26, eldest son of the late Mr Daniel Skerritt, Birr, killed in action while serving with the Mediterranean Expeditionary Force.' From the *King's County Chronicle*, March 1916, 'Among the many brave young Irishmen who lost their lives at one of the terrible landings at the Dardanelles, was Sergeant Joseph Skerritt, of the

Royal Dublin Fusiliers. His widowed mother resides at Riverside Cottage, Birr.' Grave or Memorial Reference: He has no known grave but is listed on Panel 190 to 196 on the Helles Memorial in Turkey.

**SLAMMON, James:** Rank: Pte. Regiment or Service: Royal Inniskilling Fusiliers. Unit: 13th Battalion. Date of death: 29 October 1918. Service no: 48238. Formerly he was with the Leinster Regiment where his number was 3388. Born in Kilcormack, Co. Offaly. Enlisted in Birr while living in Kilcormack. Died. A relation of his, Thomas Slavin, was in the Leinster Regiment and stationed in Cork. Grave or Memorial Reference: II.H 2. Cemetery: Pont-De-Nieppe Cemetery in France.

**SLEVIN, William:** Listed in the Commonwealth War Graves Commission under **SLAVIN, W.** Rank: Sergeant. Regiment or Service: Seaforth Highlanders. Unit: 2nd Battalion. Date of death: 4 May 1915. Service no: 9455. Born in Shannon Harbour, Co. Offaly. Enlisted in Birr, Co. Offaly. Died of wounds. Grave or Memorial Reference: II.A.166. Cemetery: Bailleul Communal Cemetery Extension (Nord) in France.

**SMITH, Ernest Frederick William:** Rank: Second Lieutenant. Regiment or Service: Royal Flying Corps Secondary. Regiment: Leinster Regiment. Unit: and 1st Bn. Age at

Ernest Frederick William Smith.

death: 20. Date of death: 27 December 1916. Died of wounds.

*Supplementary information:* Son of Annie Ryall (formerly Smith), of Camcor, Birr, Co. Offaly, and the late Ernest Palmer Smith. From the *King's County Chronicle*, January 1917:

YOUNG AIRMAN KILLED IN FLYING ACTION.

Lieut Smith's Career

Pulpit References at Kinnitty.

Lieut Ernest Frederick William Smith, whose sad death in action occurred on the 28th of December, was educated at Bishop Foy's School, Waterford. He entered Trinity College before his seventeenth year. After passing his Little-Go he joined the Medical School and passed the examinations of the first year with credit.

He belonged to the O.T.C. of Trinity College and at the outbreak of the war volunteered in the 7th Leinsters in September, 1914. He went to France with his regiment in December, 1915, spending Christmas in the trenches. In May, 1916, his ankle was injured by the fall off a parapet after shelling and he had to return. He went out again in August to rejoin his regiment and took part in the severe fighting in the battle of the Somme, where his regiment greatly distinguished itself. He then received his orders for the Flying Corps, which he entered in September. He worked as an observation officer for some time and died from injuries received in a flying action. He was the only child of the late Ernest Palmer Smith, of Camcor, Kinnitty, and grandson of the late George William Smith, of Dove Hill. His widowed mother, Mrs Smith, of Camcor, has been the recipient of innumerable messages of sympathy in the loss of her gallant son, who was held in very high regard by everyone who knew him.

The Rector, Dr Montgomery Hitchcock, alluded to the death of this gallant young officer in his sermon on Sunday last. He said: "It was with great distress and genuine grief that we heard on Saturday of the death in action of Lieutenant Ernest Smith, of the Royal Flying Corps. He was a gallant and brave officer, of whom we all may be justly proud. He died in battle. He gave his life for his country. He could do no more. In the battle on the Somme he fought bravely with his regiment – the 7th Leinsters. He then entered the Flying Corps, and was greatly interested in his work, for which he had a natural aptitude. From his youth he had always been keen on flying; and when he was given his chance he took it. His death removes a very promising airman, and a courageous and efficient officer at a time when such can ill be spared. Our hearts go out in sympathy to his poor widowed mother, who has lost her only hope, her only joy in life. May God comfort her and the friends who mourn his loss with her in a common grief. And may the memory and example of this youthful hero encourage and inspire others to show a like enthusiasm for their country's cause. We are sure that the Lord who said "weep not" to the widowed mother and gave her back her only son will restore to the bereaved mother in our midst her son, in His own good time and in a more real, spiritual and lasting hope. Many people have said 'don't cry' and many will say it so long as women may weep; but no one ever said it in such a way, giving the power to bear the blow with the sympathy that went forth from his soul, to heal the broken-hearted and comfort those that mourn. May those words, eternal in value and spirit, alleviate the sorrow that lies upon his mother's heart.

From the *King's County Chronicle*, January 1917:

Late Lieut Smith.

His fine Air Feats.

Commander's Letter.

How he met his death.

In connection with the death in a flying action of the brilliant young King's County man. Lieut Smith (reported in our last issue) the following letter received by his relatives from the commander of his flying squadron give the additional particulars of the manner in which he met his death.

No 9 Squadron, R.F.C.
"28th December, 1916.
Dear Mrs Smith,

I very much regret having to give you some very bad news. It is with feelings of the greatest sympathy that I have to inform you that your son, Ernest, was yesterday involved in an aeroplane smash which resulted in his death whilst in hospital last night. I got to the scene of the accident only a few minutes after it occurred when he was quite unconscious and did not regain consciousness before he died. A doctor attended him almost immediately and he was removed to hospital where he was operated on last night, but died shortly after. The bone of his skull was fractured in the fall, but it will console you to know that he could have suffered no pain. I have only commanded the squadron for a short time and did not, therefore know your son at all well, but the day before his accident he distinguished himself in a flight with a hostile machine which attacked him, by bringing it down, a thing rarely done from the type of machine in which he was flying at the time.

All the officers speak of him as a most capable and promising officer, and from the result of his work I thoroughly endorse their opinion. At the time of his accident he was returning from a very successful photographic flight and the accident occurred just prior to landing on the aerodrome. He will be buried this afternoon at two p.m., when several of his brother officers and men will attend. Please accept my very deepest sympathy with you in your great bereavement.
I am yours sincerely
E. Edwards."

Grave or Memorial Reference:VI.A.5. Cemetery: Heilly Station Cemetry, Mericourt-l'Abbe in France.

**SMITH, James:** Listed in the Commonwealth War Graves Commission under **SMITH, James Joseph:** Rank: Acting Sergeant. Regiment or Service: Royal Army Veterinary Corps. Unit: attached to D Battery, 155th Brigade. Date of death: 19 October 1918. Service no: SE/494. Born in Edenderry, Co. Offaly. Enlisted in Colchester. Died. Age at death: 34.

*Supplementary information:* Son of James and Alice Smith, of Edenderry, Co. Offaly. Husband of M.B. Smith, of 21 South Street, Colchester, Essex. Grave or Memorial Reference: VIII.L.1B. Cemetery: Mont Huon Military Cemetery, Le-Treport in France.

**STANLEY, Edward:** Rank: Pte. Regiment or Service: Irish Guards. Unit: 1st Battalion. Date of death: 23 March 1918. Service no: 10441. Born in Tullamore, Co. Offaly. Enlisted in Dartford, Kent while living in Tullamore, Co. Offaly. Killed in action. Grave or Memorial Reference: Bay 1. Memorial: Arras Memorial in France.

**STANNAGE, Thomas:** Rank: Pte. Regiment or Service: Household Cavalry and Cavalry of the line including the Yeomanry and Imperial Camel Corps. Unit: 10th (Prince of Wales Own) Hussars. Date of death: 9 October 1918. Service no: 74010. Born in Rathdowney. Enlisted in Dublin while living in Philipstown. Killed in action. Age at death: 26.

*Supplementary information:* Son of the late Thomas and M. J. Stannage, of Philipstown, Co. Offaly. Grave or Memorial Reference: He has no known grave but is listed on Panel 5 on the Vis-En-Artois Memorial in France.

**STUDHOLME, Lancelot Joseph Moore:** Rank: Captain. Regiment or Service: Leinster Regiment. Unit: 7th Battalion. Date of death: 9 September 1916. Age at death: 31. Killed in action.

*Supplementary information:* Born in 1884. Won the Military Cross and was a member of the Peerage. Son of the late Joseph Studholme, of Ballyeighan, Birr, Co. Offaly, and of Mrs Mary Hastings Studholme (*née* Davis). Mentioned in Despatches. A poem *King's County Chronicle*, December 1914:

Lancelot Joseph Moore Studholme.

Most respectfully dedicated to Mr Lancelot Studholme, of Ballyeighan, Birr, on his leaving the comforts of his home and enlisting as a private in the Leinsters, November, 1914. Written by Miss Mary Brown, 10 Newbridge Street, Birr;

All honour your hero heart
Young soldier of the line;
A man alone couldn't act your part;
Then bear that grand ensign.

A Man! A Man! The noblest work,
E'en God himself that made –
Not yours one duty path to shirk
On life's sublime parade.

In this dark hour of havoc dread,
'Tis but a hero soul,
Could'st march where fate's red
   wings are spread,
O'er death or glory's roll.

Then go young scion of your race,
If God so wills it go;
His love shall fill your vacant place,
To hearts now steeped in woe

While blood of Dylan Thomas flows,
From your maternal side;

'Tis meet your heart's high courage
    shows,
'Twas fed from that rich side.

The same undying, undauntless nerve,
Long live such noble deed,
Who left your rose strewn home
    to serve
Your country in her need.

A Private in the Leinster corps,
There proudly take your stand,
No truer heart nor had e'er bore,
A sword for native land.

Oh! we shall watch with prayerful eyes,
To heaven, your young career,
No doubt that honour's sacred prize,
Shall crown you year by year.

Then go! – God's speed you on your
    way;
The shield of strength divine,
May nerve and guard you day by day,
Young soldier of the line.

Note: Mrs Studholme's father was brother of the celebrated Irish Protestant patriot and poet, Davis, who took a prominent but most unselfish part for the cause of the Young Ireland Party who mourned his premature death, and not less was the grief of his political opponents.

## From the *King's County Chronicle*, November 1914.

Mr Lancelot Studholme, J.P., Ballyeighan, Birr, has left the comforts of his home life, and with a patriotic zeal beyond the power of tongue to express he has joined as a Private the 7th Service Battalion of the Leinster Regiment at Fermoy. Undoubtedly he could have got a commission, but chose the lowest place. It is needless to say he bears away the heartiest of good wishes and prayers of thousands amongst us.

## From the *King's County Chronicle*, January 1915:

The many friends of Lieut. L. Studholme were rejoiced to see him back again at Ballyeighan House. Although he had scarcely a week's leave he visited the school where he so often bestowed generous gifts on teachers and pupils. He is continuing the Ballyeighan Bank for their benefit, and so advantageous is it that at Christmas he had upwards of £20 distributed amongst them, including the pupils weekly savings with a bonus of 2d to every shilling. Our correspondent adds that parents, teachers and pupils could not too highly appreciate his goodness, and it is their earnest prayer and wish that in the near future the brave and noble gentleman will return safely with highest honours.

## From the *Midland Tribune, Tipperary Sentinel* and *King's County Vindicator*, October 1916:

THE LATE CAPTAIN STUDHOLME.
Mrs Studholme, writing in connection with the death of her son, the late Captain Studholme, says that after the battle of Quillemont

his Commanding Officer recommended him for the Military Cross on account of his great gallantry, and 'most particularly for his personal and daring reconnaissance up to the outskirts of Ginchy on the night of Sunday, 3rd September'. Mrs Studholme has received the following letter from an officer of the 7th Leinster Regiment, under date 16th September

"Dear Mrs Studholme,
It is as great a grief to myself as it is to the whole regiment, officers and men alike, to think of Lancelots death, but I think perhaps you would like to hear something from an eye witness of how it happened.

He had led the whole company over 600 yards of open ground under the heaviest fire from artillery and machine guns that I have yet seen, when his servant, young Harte, was hit by a bullet. Lancelot stopped at once, knelt beside him, and with the assistance of a couple of other men, began to dress the wound. It was at that moment that a bullet from one of the German Machine Guns, which were sweeping the whole field, struck him in the head, and he fell without a sound. Death I know was instantaneous, and this is the one small consolation that we have. It is my belief that there is not one man, serving in the company, from the Sergeant Major to the latest-joined recruit, who would not willingly have given his life to prevent what happened. The former when he heard of it, threw down his only weapon in the trench, and, to use his own words, 'cried like a child'.

The affection the men had for Lancelot was something beyond ordinary words. Not only has the regiment lost its most valuable officer, I myself have lost a friendship whose value it is not easy to estimate. There was a bond between us from the start. In that we were both Christ Church men. We enlisted as cadets on the same day and were gazetted in the same week. Since then our intimacy was unbroken. Such associations are not easily broken. Will you forgive me for dwelling so long upon a sorrowful subject? Perhaps the words of a heart broken private strike deeper at the root of the matter. – 'He was a grand officer, and a brave man; we cried when we buried him.' In deepest sympathy, very sincerely yours."

## From the *King's County Chronicle*, December 1914:

Among the list of officers returned on 20th December as wounded is Major C. Vivian. The gallant gentleman is son-in-law of Mrs Studholme, Ballyegan, Birr; and we are sure it will afford the greatest pleasure to be assured that the wound was slight. Like their fellow native units the Major's gallant corps, the 15th Sikhs, have fought with all the dash of their race since they arrived in France.

Brevet-Lieutenant Colonel Charles Augustus Vivian was killed in action on 27 April 1915. He has no known grave but is commemorated on the Ypres (Menin Gate) Memorial, Panel 1 in Belgium. Author). From the *King's County Chronicle*, September 1916:

DIED LIKE A HERO.

Captain Studholme's Deed.

Killed to save a man.

Glorious act of popular young King's County Gentleman.

This has been a sad week for several families in the King's County. Perhaps the saddest news of all was the intelligence of the death of Captain Launcelot Joseph Moore Studholme, who was killed whilst performing a most heroic deed in action. The news is all the most pathetic by reason of the fact that he was the only son of one of the most esteemed families in the King's County. The manner of his death, too, was one that should never be forgotten, revealing as it did a self-sacrificing devotion to a fellow human being. Captain Studholme was shot through the head whilst he was attempting to bring in his servant Private Thomas Harte, a native of Crinkle, who was employed by the deceased before enlisting and who was wounded. His last act, therefore, was a thought for the man who had served him and to try and save that man's life he lost his own.

HIS BOYHOOD DAYS.

The manner of Captain Studholme's death did not come as a surprise to those who knew him from childhood. As a boy he was gentle, quiet, and rather reserved. Physically he was not over robust, and consequently he did not take a very prominent part in more strenuous sports. Gardening was the work which he loved most. He devoted a good deal of his time to this branch of work and won many prizes. He also was most attentive to his lands and to the care and comforts of the workmen on those lands. By his neighbours and by his men he was indeed beloved, not alone for his many generous acts but also for his kind and pleasing disposition. Probably he would have continued to lead such a quiet and useful domestic life amidst scenes familiar to him from infancy were it not for the outbreak of the world war with all its dreadful consequences.

THE OUTBREAK OF THE WAR.

When the war did break out he took action swiftly. He inaugurated a shooting range and encouraged his men to enlist. He himself felt he could not stay at home and he joined the 7th Leinsters as a private with the cadet Corps. He made himself so efficient in such a short time that he received a commission. He was a keen soldier and was beloved by his men just as at home he was beloved by his workmen. He looked after the soldiers under him in the same paternal and kindly way that he had looked after the labourers who were under him on his lands, and the news of his death caused a deep pang to many hearts both at the front as well as in his home in the King's County

HIS FAMILY.

He was the only son of the late Joseph Studholme, J.P., and Mrs Studholme, of Ballyegan. On his maternal side he was a grand nephew of Thomas Moore, the Irish poet. He was a Justice of the Peace for the King's County, and filled the position of high Sheriff for the county for 1914. He was only about 31 years of age. An additional feature that renders the occurrence very sad is that a brother-in-law of his, Colonel Vivian, was recently killed, so that his sister has within a very brief time, lost both a husband and a brother. It is only a short time since Captain Studholme was home on leave looking the very picture of health. Life in the army seemed to agree with him. The news of his death, therefore came with all the greater sadness. To his bereaved mother the sincere condolence of everyone in King's County, who knew her heroic son, will go forth. Her chief consolation is that he could not die a more gallant death. The sympathy conveyed to Mrs Studholme by Mr John Dooly, J.P., Chairman of the Birr Urban Council, on behalf of the town of Birr, will be re-echoed by the whole county. After the evening service in St Brendan's Church on Sunday the Dead March was played, the congregation standing, and a few appropriate references were made by the Rector, the Rev. Mr Patton, to the sad event.

Grave or Memorial Reference: He has no known grave but is listed on Pier and Face 16C on the Thiepval Memorial in France.

**SULLIVAN, James:** Rank: Pte. Regiment or Service: Irish Guards Unit: 2nd Bn. Date of death: 26 August 1917. Service no: 6176. Born in Lusmagh, Co. Offaly and enlisted in Dublin. Died at home.

*Supplementary information: King's County Chronicle*, April 1916 gives his address as Corgrave North and adds that he joined from the R.I.C. From the *King's County Chronicle*, September 1917:

> Much sympathy is extended to his father, Mr Patrick Sullivan, Lusmagh, and his family in their sad bereavement. Amongst the letters of sympathy are Major Lord de Vesey and the House Physician General Hospital.
>
> The remains were conveyed with full military honours from Nottingham hospital to the Midland station and were conveyed via Holyhead and Dublin and arrived in Banagher on Thursday, 30th August, where they were met at the railway station by a large concourse of people from town and districts.
>
> The internment took place in the family burial ground, Kilmachanna, amidst many manifestations of sorrow and regret. Rev. T. Nohilly, P. P., officiating.
>
> The chief mourners were; Mr Patrick Sullivan, father; Michael

Sullivan, brother; J. Loughnane, Clontusker, uncle; Curley, Bros, Kiltormer, P. Brien, Killimore; J. Treacy, do; Thomas Hynes, cousins; K. Gallagher, brother-in-law.

His sister, Miss May Sullivan, Queen Alexandria Imperial Nursing Service Reserve, who is at present in France and unable to attend, wired her heartfelt sympathy.

Grave or Memorial Reference: Panel 4 (Screen Wall). Memorial: Grangegorman Memorial, Dublin. Alternative Commemoration - buried in Kilmachunna Graveyard, Co. Offaly.

**SULLIVAN, Timothy Christopher:** Rank: Pte. Regiment or Service: Leinster Regiment. Unit: D Company, 2$^{nd}$ Battalion. Date of death: 4 September 1918. Service no: 10600. Born in Birr, Co. Offaly. Enlisted in Birr. Killed in action. Age at death: 18.

*Supplementary information:* Son of Timothy and Mary Ellen Sullivan, of New Cottages, Crinkle, Birr, Co. Offaly. Grave or Memorial Reference: V.B.16. Cemetery: Wulverghem–Lindenhoek Road Military Cemetery in Belgium.

**SWEENEY, John:** Rank: Pte. Regiment or Service: Connaught Rangers. Unit: 2$^{nd}$ Battalion. Date of death: 24 October 1914. Service no: 7851. Born in Ferbane, Co. Offaly. Enlisted in Tullamore, Co. Offaly while living in Clara, Co. Offaly. Died of wounds. Age at death: 33.

*Supplementary information:* Son of Patrick and Mary Sweeney, of Kilcoursey, Clara, Co. Offaly. Served in the South African War. See the article under **GORMAN, James**: Grave or Memorial Reference: A3. 5. Cemetery: Ypres Town Cemetery in Belgium.

# T

**TAGGART, James:** Rank: Pte. Regiment or Service: Royal army Service Corps. Unit: Clearing Office. Date of death: 7 July 1918. Service no: T4/124354, listed in the Commonwealth War Graves as T4/12354. Born in Boyle, Co. Antrim. Enlisted in Tullamore while living in Tullamore. Died at Home. Age at death: 49.

*Supplementary information:* Husband of Mary Taggart of Bushy Park Lodge, Templeogue Road, Terenure, Dublin. Grave or Memorial Reference: CE. 686. Cemetery: Grangegorman Military Cemetery, Dublin.

**TENNANT, Philip Eyre:** Rank: Second Lieutenant. Regiment or Service: Connaught Rangers. Unit: 3rd Battalion. Date of death: 31 October 1917. Killed in action. From the *King's County Chronicle*, April 1916, 'King's County officers. Among the many patriotic families in King's County, who are represented in the firing line by commissioned officers are the following from the Banagher and Shinrone districts … Lieut. Philip E. Tennant, Inns of Court, Cadet Corps. Banagher.' Grave or Memorial Reference: Has no known grave but is commemorated on Panel 42 on the Ypres (Menin Gate) Memorial in Belgium.

**TIERNAN, Michael:** Rank: Pte. Regiment or Service: Connaught Rangers. Unit: 5th Battalion. Date of death: 21 August 1915. Service no: 20. Born in Kilbeggan, Co. Westmeath. Enlisted in Galway while living in Clara, Co. Offaly. Killed in action in Gallipoli. Grave or Memorial Reference: He has no known grave but is listed on Panel 181 to 183 on the Helles Memorial in Turkey.

**TIQUIN/TINQUINN, Daniel:** Rank: Pte. Regiment or Service: Leinster Regiment. Unit: 2nd Battalion. Date of death: 16 June 1918. Service no: 4074. Born in Killoughey, Co. Offaly. Enlisted in Tullamore, Co. Offaly while living in Tullamore, Co. Offaly. Died of wounds. Grave or Memorial Reference: II.D.39. Cemetery: Ebblinghem Military Cemetery in France.

**TOOHER, Patrick:** Rank: Pte. Regiment or Service: Leinster Regiment. Unit: 3rd Battalion ('Soldiers died in the Great War' and 'Ireland's Memorial Records') 6th Battalion (Commonwealth War Graves Commission). Date of death: 16 April 1917. Service no: 6852. Born in Coolderragh, Co. Offaly. Enlisted in Birr, Co. Offaly. Died at home.

*Supplementary information:* Husband of Bridget McDonald (formerly Tooher), of Dromakeenan, Brosna. From the *King's County Chronicle*, March 1916, 'Private Patrick Tooher, Pound Street, of the Leinsters, saw active service in South Africa. He rejoined and is now stationed in Birr.' Grave or Memorial Reference: In southwest part. Cemetery: Ettagh (St Mark) Churchyard, Co. Offaly.

**TORMEY, Patrick:** Rank: Pte. Regiment or Service: Leinster Regiment. Unit: 2nd Battalion. Date of death: 20 October 1914. Service no: 7683. Born in Tyrrell's Pass, Co. Westmeath. Enlisted in Tullamore, Co. Offaly. Killed in action. Age at death: 26.

*Supplementary information:* Son of Edward Tormey, of Toor, Tyrrell's Pass, Co. Westmeath. Grave or Memorial Reference: He has no known grave but is listed on Panel 10 on the Ploegsteert Memorial in Belgium.

**TRAYNOR, Christopher:** Rank: Pte. Regiment or Service: Leinster Regiment. Unit: 2nd Battalion. Date of death: 22 October 1918. Service no: 2622. Born in Edenderry, Co. Offaly. Enlisted in Birr, Co. Offaly. Died of wounds. Age at death: 29.

*Supplementary information:* Husband of Bessie Traynor, of 3 Mortland Square, Bonnybridge, Stirlingshire. Grave or Memorial Reference: VI.A.58. Cemetery: Terlincthun British Cemetery, Wimille, in France.

**TRAYNOR, Edward:** Rank: Pte. Regiment or Service: Royal Dublin Fusiliers. Unit: 1st Battalion. Date of death: 30 June 1915. Service no: 18146. Born in Edenderry, Co. Offaly. Enlisted in Stenhousemuir while living in Camelon, Falkirk. Killed in action in Gallipoli. Age at death: 28.

*Supplementary information:* Son of Mrs B. Traynor, of 22A Dorrator Road, Camelon, Falkirk, Stirlingshire. Grave or Memorial Reference: He has no known grave but is listed on Panel 190 to 196 on the Helles Memorial in Turkey.

**TREACY, William:** Rank: Pte. Regiment or Service: Royal Irish Regiment. Unit: 6th Bn. Date of death: 3 September 1917. Service no: 9113. Formerly he was with the Royal Field Artillery where his number was 134399. Born in Moneygall, Co. Offaly. Enlisted in Roscrea while living in Moneygall. Died of wounds. Age at death: 42.

*Supplementary information:* Son of Michael Treacy, of Moneygall. Husband of Norah Treacy, of Moneygall, Co. Offaly. Grave or Memorial Reference: I.L.3. Cemetery: Bucquoy Road Cemetery, Ficheux in France.

**TRENCH, Frederick Charles:** (Alias, true name is **BLOOMFIELD**). Rank: Pte. Regiment or Service: London Regiment (London Scottish). Unit: 1st/14th Bn, also listed as 14th Bn. Age at death: 38. Date of death: 1 July 1916. Service no: 5746. Enlisted in London while living in Tipperary. Killed in action.

*Supplementary information:* Son of Henry Bloomfield Trench, of Huntington, Portarlington, Co. Offaly. Husband of Catherine Anne Swetenham MacManaway (formerly Trench), M.B.E., of Greystone Hall, Limavady, Co. Derry. Grave or Memorial Reference: He has no known grave but is listed on Pier and Face 9C and 13C on the Thiepval Memorial in France.

**TYRRELL, John:** Rank: Pte. Regiment or Service: Connaught Rangers. Unit: 4th Battalion. Date of death: 8 February 1916. Service no: 6012 ('Soldiers died in the Great War' and 'Ireland's Memorial Records'), 41612 (Commonwealth War Graves Commission). Born in Kilbride, Co. Offaly. Enlisted in Tullamore while living in Tullamore. Died at Home. Age at death: 19.

*Supplementary information:* Son of Patrick Tyrrell, of Barrack Street, Tullamore. From the *King's County Chronicle*, February 1916:

> DEATH OF PTE JOHN TYRRELL.
>
> General regret was expressed in Tullamore at the death of Private John Tyrrell, of the Leinster Regiment. His parents reside here, and are much respected by their friends and neighbours. Private Tyrrell was 22 years of age, and at the time of enlistment, in October last, was employed in the brewery of Messrs. P. and H. Egan. He was a very steady and respectable young fellow, of an obliging and kindly disposition, and was very greatly liked by his employers, fellow workers, and neighbours, and, in fact, by everyone who knew him. He was in training in County Cork, and caught cold, which developed into a severe illness and resulted in his death. The remains were brought to Tullamore for internment. The funeral took place on the arrival of the 11 a.m. train on Friday. Father Daly was present, accompanied the funeral to Durrow cemetery, and performed the burial service. The sorrowing father and other relatives were the chief mourners, and many prominent citizens were in the cortege, which was very large and representative of all classes.

From the *King's County Independent*, March 1917, 'Military item. In connection with the Tullmore roll of honour which appeared in a recent issue of the "*King's County Chronicle*," the following were inadvertently omitted: Sapper, John Tyrell, R.E.' He is also listed on the Tullamore Roll of Honour. Grave or Memorial Reference: Z. 31. Cemetery: Durrow (St Columbcille) Catholic Churchyard, Co Offaly.

# V

**VIVIAN, Charles Augustus:** Rank: Brevet Lieut-Colonel. Regiment or Service: 15th Ludhiana Sikhs. Date of death: 27 April 1915. Age at death: 41.

*Supplementary information:* Mentioned in Despatches. Son of the late Col. and Mrs MacIver Campbell, of Asknish. Husband of Mary Hastings Vivian, of Asknish, Lochgair, Argyll. Served Malakand, 1897 and Tirah Expeditions 1897-1898. From the *King's County Chronicle*, December 1914:

Among the list of officers returned on 20th December as wounded is Major C. Vivian. The gallant gentleman is son-in-law of Mrs Studholme, Ballyegan, Birr; and we are sure it will afford the greatest pleasure to be assured that the wound was slight. Like their fellow native units the Major's gallant corps, the 15th Sikhs, have fought with all the dash of their race since they arrived in France. Brevet-Lieutenat Colonel Charles Augustus Vivian was killed in action on 27 April 1915.

Charles Augustus Vivian.

From the *King's County Chronicle*, September 1916:

DIED LIKE A HERO.
Captain Studholme's Deed.
Killed to save his man.
An additional feature that renders the occurrence very sad is that a brother-in-law of his, Colonel Vivian, was recently killed, so that his sister has within a very brief time, lost both a husband and a brother.

See also **STUDHOLME, Lancelot Joseph Moore.** From De Ruvigny's Roll of Honour.

*Vivian, Charles Augustus,* Brevet Lieut Col., 15th (Ludhiana) Sikhs, Indian Army, 3rd and youngest son of the late Col, Aylmer MacIver-Campbell, formerly Vivian, of Asknish, C.B., D.L., J.P., Bengal S.C., by his wife, Margaret Agnes (Asknish House, Lochgair, Co. Argyle), elder daughter and co. h. of Col. James Duff MacIver-Campbell, of Asknish. Born at Dalhousie, India, 28th July, 1874. Educated at Clifton College and Sandhurst. Gazetted 2nd Lieut (unattd. List) Indian Army, 30 Aug, 1893; was attached to the Gordon Highlanders for his first year; joined the Indian Staff Corps, 27 Jan, 1895, and was promoted Lieut, 30 Aug, 1911.

Served (1) with the Chitral Relief Force, 1895 (medal with clasp); (2) on the N. W. Frontier of India, 1897-8, including operations on the Samana and in the Kurrain Valley during Aug and Sept, 1897, and those of the Flying Column in the Kurrain Valley, under Col. Richardson, 20 Aug to 1 Oct, 1897 (two clasps); (3) in the Tirah Expedition, 1897-8; including actions of Chagree Kotal and dargai; the capture of the Sampagha and Arhanga Passes; reconnaissance of the Saran Sar and action of 9 Nov, 1897; and operations of the Waran Valley; and action of 16 Nov, 1897 (clasp); and (4) with the Expeditionary Force in France and Flanders, Oct, 1914 to 27 April, 1915. Delayed by illness in Egypt, he did not join his regiment at the front until Oct, and was wounded in Dec. He returned to duty in Jan, and was mentioned in Sir John (now Lord) French's Despatch of 14 Jan, 1915, and promoted Brevet Lieut-Col, 19 Feb, following, for service in the field. In the Battle of Neuve Chapelle, where his regiment took a leading part, he was again wounded, but refused to leave his men and remained in the trenches under very heavy fire. He was killed in action near St Julien, during the 2nd Battle of Ypres, 27 April, 1915. About 5.30p.m., under cover of bombardment of the Sirhind Brigade, the 1st Highland Light Infantry, and the 15th Sikhs were ordered to advance, but were met with such a terrific fire that a check ensued. Col. Vivian had

to rush with his company over a fire swept zone to join the remainder of his regiment.

Just as he arrived he was shot through the body. An officer wrote; "I think that Col. Vivian was the bravest man I ever met – he seemed absolutely fearless of bullets, and his patrol work in front of our trenches at night was really wonderful. He inspired the Sikh officers and men of his company with the greatest confidence, and made them nearly as fearless as himself. Once there was a house 30 yards in front of our trenches and it obscured our field of fire. The regt, who occupied the trenches before we did, said that they had tried to pull down the house, but had to give up the attempt, because the enemy fired on them. Col. Vivian called for volunteers of his company to assist him to demolish the house. The whole company to a man volunteered – he chose the requisite number and in two days the house was flat; although they worked in daylight, not a single man was hit. I shall never forget the thrill of admiration I had for him when he volunteered to go behind the German line for two or three nights and reconnoitre the German position at La Bassee, but I was very relieved when the General would not allow him to go. Each time that he was wounded he insisted on going on with his work; any ordinary man would have been very shaken.

We have lost a very dear friend and England on of her bravest soldiers." Col. Abbott, writing to *The*

*Pioneer* about the Tirah Campaign, said; "Your report, moreover, makes no mention of the very gallant and prompt manner in which, when Capt, Lewarne's party was rushed from the wood, the next one was brought up to his aid by Lieut Vivian. The second party also got to close quarters with the enemy and to them must be accredited a large proportion of the Afridi losses on that occasion." He married at Portsmouth, 30 Aug, 1906, Mary Hastings, eldest surviving daughter of the late Joseph Studholme, of Ballyegan, Co. Offaly, J.P., and had three children; Aylmer Studholme, born 17 Aug, 1909, John, born 30 Aug, 1913 and Margaret Ruth, born 25 June 1907.

Grave or Memorial Reference: Has no known grave but is commemorated on Panel 1 on the Ypres (Menin Gate) Memorial in Belgium.

# W

**WALKER, George:** Rank: Pte. Regiment or Service: Royal Inniskilling Fusiliers. Unit: 2ⁿᵈ Battalion. Date of death: 7 November 1914. Service no: 8091. Born in Edenderry, Co. Offaly. Enlisted in Dublin while living in Co. Offaly. Killed in action. Age at death: 20.

*Supplementary information:* Son of Pat Walker, of Blundel Street, Edenderry, Co. Offaly. Grave or Memorial Reference: Panel 5. Memorial: Ploegsteert Memorial in Belgium.

**WALLACE, James:** Rank: Pte. Regiment or Service: Irish Guards. Unit: 1ˢᵗ Bn. Date of death: 4 September 1914. Service no: 1605. Born in Abbeyleix, Co. Laois. Enlisted in Maryborough, Co. Laois while living in Liverpool, Lancs. Killed in action.

*Supplementary information:* Son of Mrs Mary Wallace, of Abbeyleix, Co. Laois. Grave or Memorial Reference: 23. Cemetery: Guards Grave, Villers Cotterets Forest in France.

**WALSH, Daniel:** Rank: Pte. Regiment or Service: Irish Guards. Unit: 1ˢᵗ Battalion. Date of death: 1 November 1914. Service no: 3030. Born in Birr, Co. Offaly. Enlisted in Birr, Co. Offaly. Killed in action. Age at death: 27.

Pte Daniel Walsh.

*Supplementary information:* Son of Elizabeth Walsh, of Seffin, Birr, Co. Offaly, and the late James Walsh. *Midland Tribune, Tipperary Sentinel* and *King's County Vindicator,* 1914:

WOUNDED IRISH GUARDSMAN RETURNS TO BIRR.

His experiences at Mons and Landrecies.

Private Benjamin Walsh of the first Battalion Irish Guards, arrived in Birr on Friday evening, having been wounded at the front. He tells an interesting story of the severe fighting in Belgium and France, between Mons and Laundrecies, having taken part in the now famous retreat of the latter position. The graphic descriptions of the bursting shrapnel and the heavy rifle fire to which the Guards were subjected. 'The German maxims and shrapnel fire he describes as deadly. The rifle fire of the Germans was not so accurate, and to him they seemed to fire mostly from the knee or hip, not sighting their rifles as the British soldiers do. The Guards of the first Battalion, left Wellington Barracks one morning early, and were despatched for France.

From the Havre base they were sent by train, and arrived at a town, the name of which our informant does not now remember. Here they rested for about half an hour. They arrived there at 3.30. From this they marched to Longville, which is about 4 miles from Mons. When about two miles from their destination they saw the artillery fire. They continued on, were formed into platoons and were ordered to load their rifles. He belonged to the twelfth platoon of the third company, and his officer was Lord Guernsey. It was explained that there were four platoons to the company. When going into action the village, with the farmhouse around were on fire. They got an object to march on, and on arriving there they were ordered to lie down in extended order. Here the German artillery shots and shrapnel were passing over their heads and bursting behind them. At this point the firing was over their heads, so at that time no one was injured.

They then passed up along the German left flank, all the time the shrapnel shrieking over them. They arrived at what he thought were castle grounds, and passed up a long avenue. Captain Bernard was in charge of his Company, No 3. They were now for two and a half hours under fire, and got the order to fix bayonets, and to reinforce other regiments which he believed were the Scottish Borderers, Irish Rifles and Coldstream Guards. Several men were now falling around him, and the German rifle men were but 400 yards away, that being the sighting ordered for the rifles. They concentrated their fire on the German Infantry. The Maxims of the British did deadly execution in their opponent's ranks. The German attack drew off, and his company had about three hours rest. It was now Monday, and the men were in an exhausted condition. They then fell back for about 30 miles to Landrecies where he formed one of the Fourth Brigade of Guards. They marched this 30 miles, and were not under fire at the time.

At Landrecies the Irish Guards were on the right flank, the Coldstreams being on outpost duty. The Germans came on to the attack, and passed outposts by speaking French to the officers. When it was discovered that they were Germans a very heavy fire was opened on them. He believes that there were a thousand Germans killed at Landrecies, and at about 4 o'clock on Tuesday morning the Irish Guards were ordered to relieve the Coldstreams. It was at Landrecies, that he was hurt. He got a severe sprain, and a bullet also grazed his knee. He was taken by members of the Fourth Brigade Field Ambulance Transport to Leon, where he was entrained for Rouen where the Base Hospital was situated. After about a day and a half the Base Hospital at Rouen was broken up, the Germans coming within about 30 miles of it. At Rouen he was taken down the Seine on the St Patrick, a steamer belonging to the Great Western Railway. They left Roeun at about 11 o' clock on Monday, and landed at Southampton at about 8, 45 on Tuesday morning. From thence he was taken to Brighton where he remained until he joined the second Battalion of Guards at Brentwood, and was recommended for sick furlough. The Commanding Officer of the Guards was wounded.

Private Walsh speaks very highly of the treatment given to the British soldier by the people of France and Belgium. On the march they supplied them with food, milk, and other necessaries. Part of the time the Guards were not in touch with the convoys. Their army rations were biscuits and bully beef. He shows a piece of French biscuit which appears not to be quite as hard as the English stuff. On the way down from the front the French were also very kind to the wandering Britishers, meeting them at the station, and supplying them with hot coffee, cheese, bread, cigarettes, etc. In the party who returned home with him were 64 wounded Coldstream Guards. Before the war broke out he was on the railway with his brother Daniel [Killed in action a few weeks

after this article was written], who also belonged to the Irish Guard Reserve, and who was also called up to the Regiment. The last he saw of his brother was at Landrecies. When he was wounded, his brother was still uninjured in the fighting line. Nothing has been heard of Daniel since.

Some very pathetic incidents were told to our representative. Two brothers of an English regiment were in the firing line. One was killed and the other brother went over to see him, and received a bullet, and fell dead across the corpse. The time was a very rough one. "I could not describe all my experiences; the din was terrible." Private Walsh showed our representative his jacket, and pointed out where the buttons had been cut off it as souvenirs. He also showed a medal which he had received in Belgium from some people there, as well as a tobacco pouch belonging to a Belgian farmer. On his uniform cap he wears the Belgium colours which had also been presented to him. After being wounded he lost his puttees and other articles, and said that the great coat he had at present was not his own which had also been lost. The wounded man is at present at home in Seffin. He is brother of Mr William Walsh the popular Guard between Birr and Roscrea."

From the *King's County Chronicle*, September 1918:

After a long spell in Salonika, Company Sergeant-Major Joseph

Walsh paid a visit to his relatives last week. He is son of the late Mr James Walsh, the esteemed late guard of the G. S. and W. Railway at Birr, and had other brothers serving, one of whom was killed in action in the early stages of the war.

Grave or Memorial Reference: He has no known grave but is listed on Panel 11 on the Ypres (Menin Gate) Memorial in Belgium.

**WALSH, John:** Rank: Pte. Regiment or Service: Connaught Rangers. Unit: 2nd Battalion. Date of death: 25 February 1915. Service no: 6594. Born in Tullamore, Co. Offaly. Enlisted in Tullamore while living in Tullamore. Killed in action. Age at death: 33.

*Supplementary information:* Son of Mrs Mary Ann Walsh, of Barrack Street., Tullamore, Co. Offaly. From the *King's County Independent*, January 1915:

TULLAMORE UNION.

Application for Relief.

From Woman with three sons at the Front.

A woman named Mary Anne Walsh, Barrack Street, Tullamore, wrote as follows: Gentlemen. – I am compelled to seek some relief as I am destitute. I have no one to earn anything for me, and I cannot get anything to earn myself at the present time. I hope you will consider my case.

Mr Duffy said Mrs Walsh had three sons at the front fighting for the Empire.

Mrs Walsh – One of them is married, and the other two are single.

Mr Duffy – And she never got a half-penny from either the Government or anyone else. All she gets is two shillings worth of provisions from some ladies in the town and she has nothing to pay rent.

Mrs Walsh said she had a letter from the War Office to the effect that one of her sons could not be found, and it was surmised he was a prisoner of war.

Clerk – What regiments are they in?

Mrs Walsh – One is in the Connaughts, and the other is in Kitchener's new Army.

Chairman – There is no difference. Will you write to the War Office, Mr Kelly, about it?

Mr Duffy – They promised they would give some support to fathers and mothers who had sons at the front.

Mrs Walsh – Whenever the sons leave their father and mother the War Office won't give them anything.

Mrs Walsh – No, Sir; I have his number and Company.

Chairman – If he is in the army they should not deny you some support. Mr Kelly will write to the War Office about it. It is capital encouragement to young fellows to join the army to leave their mothers starving.

It was decided to give Mrs Walsh relief for a time.

Another snippet on the same page:

The case of Mrs Mary Anne Walsh, from Barrack Street, Tullamore, who applied for out-door relief to the Tullamore Guardians, and who has three sons at the front is only one of the many which we hear about in Ireland. The British War Office knows the value of Irishmen as soldiers, and they are using every means to induce young Irishmen to join the Army in this trying circumstances, but they seem to care very little about what becomes of the mothers and fathers of these Irish boys who are in the brunt of the fight against the German foe in the far away fields of Flanders. Mrs Walsh, according to her story, has been refused aid from the War Department which should certainly give her some monetary assistance. The Clerk was directed to communicate with the War Office on the subject.

## From the *King's County Chronicle*, June 1916:

A BRAVE MAN.

Private John Walsh, 2nd Connaughts, served with the battalion two years in South Africa, was on the reserve when the war broke out, and called up, rejoining the colours on 5th August, 1914. He fought in the battle of Mons, in which the Connaughts suffered so heavily, and has been missing since the, inquiries having failed to trace him. Sorrow and anxiety regarding his fate which was thus shrouded in doubt and mystery, filled the mind of his mother, who resides in Barrack Street, Tullamore, when, one day, her thoughts, as usual fixed on her son (Mrs Walsh has three other sons serving their King and Country) a Dublin evening newspaper was brought to her joyously by a neighbour, which contained a notice of John's career, in the list of Irish heroes, and the glad intelligence that he was a prisoner of war in Germany. The long pent-up feelings of the mother found vent in tears of joy, as hope returned that she would yet welcome again her favourite son; and with her own hand she wrote him a true mother's letter, saying "Oh, John, John, I am still your mother, as I ever will be even unto death!" and asking him to write and she would send him anything he asked for.

But it was not to be. That reply was anxiously awaited from day to day and, at length, a post-card was delivered, bearing the mark of the German Eagle. It was from Sergt. Hogan, detained at the prison camp to which she had written – a kind-hearted Irish soldier, who expressed his regret to have to inform her that the only soldier in camp of the name of Walsh was a native of Listowel, Co Kerry. Tears well up in her eyes, and blot out from her the vision of the resolute yet kindly face of a brave man which smiles from the photo in the poor woman's hand, as a mother's heart is moved with its strongest emotion.

## From the *King's County Chronicle*, June 1916:

ONE FOR THE SENTRY.

Private Joseph Walsh, A.M.C., is Mrs Walsh's second son. He had completed his service with the Connaughts, and was on reserve when called up on general mobilisation at the outbreak of the war. He was drafted into the Medical Corps, served with it in France, and was taken prisoner of war. After fourteen months in Germany he was sent back to the British on exchange of prisoners, and was afterwards sent out to an hospital in Port Said, where he is on duty at present. Joe, when at home on leave, amused his mother by recounting humorous experiences of the Irish soldiers where massed together in an enemy camp. This is one; The German soldier on sentry over the prisoners stood at attention with rifle and bayonet; he spoke to him in a commanding English accent, which at once surprised and tickled the ear of a big private of the Connaughts known as "Maginnis, of Dublin."

He had a very respectable reputation for being handy with his fists; and passed some humorous jibe to the sentry, who retorted with scornful smile and tilted nose; "You d----d English swine." The humour of "Maginnis, of Dublin," shifted and touched the button of the hydraulic pressure of his great arm, driving his fist under the sentry's chin. The stroke was a bit of magic; up went the sentry still at attention at an angle of 45, just like a wooden soldier; down he came on the flat of his back and lay at attention on the floor, effectually "put to sleep, " as boxers say, and moving not even so much as an eyelash. Then the rumpus came; the guard rushed out, over-powered and marched off poor "Maginnis, of Dublin" – he was court-martialled, and sent into German penal servitude for ten years. But his chums of the Connaughts, with whom he was a great favourite, console themselves by saying that "Maginnis, of Dublin," will be a free man again when the war is over.

From the *King's County Chronicle*, June 1916:

A NARROW SHAVE.

Private James Walsh, Connaught Rangers, is the third son. He was a time-expired man, and in September, 1914, re-joined by enlisting in Kitchener's Army. He was seriously wounded in the Dardanelles, and invalided home. On the passage, on board the S.S. *Neuralia*, he was so far gone that he was believed to have actually crossed the borderland and was reported dead; his kit being labelled with his name and the note; "Died on the S.S. *Neuralia* on the 11th August, 1915"; and the party who came round to prepare his body for burial in the deep, were starting to hear him speak, asking for a drink for God's sake. It was a narrow shave; and that label is retained by the family as a memento.

After arrival in port, James was sent to Aberdeen hospital, where two bullets were extracted from his head. These are also among the treasures of the family. The brave fellow is again in the fighting line in France.

Grave or Memorial Reference: Coll. Grave. Cemetery: Guise Communal Cemetery in France.

**WALSH, Luke:** Rank: Pte. Regiment or Service: Leinster Regiment. Unit: 2nd Battalion. Date of death: 1 May 1915. Service no: 1497. Born in Kilbride, Co. Offaly. Enlisted in Birr, Co. Offaly. Killed in action. Age at death: 40.

*Supplementary information:* Won the 1914 Star. Husband of E. Walsh, of Arden Road, Tullamore, Co. Offaly. From the *King's County Chronicle*, May 1915:

Information reached Tullamore last week of the death in action of Private Luke Walsh, of Third Battalion Leinster Regiment, who was a married man, and who leaves a wife and family. He left in August last on the mobilisation order, and for some months did duty at the concentration camp at Templemore. He was amongst a number of Leinsters and men of other regiments who were treated for frostbite at the base hospital. As soon as he was sufficiently recovered he was sent into the firing line again. He was present at Neuve Chapelle and at the battle of Ypres. Walsh was a son-in-law of Mr Patrick Boland, of Puttaghaun, Tullamore, and a son of Mr Walsh, Ballycowen, and was an excellent rifle shot, and held a medal for efficiency in marksmanship.

From the *King's County Independent*, May 1915:

HILL 60. TULLAMORE MAN KILLED.
Sad news reached Tullamore on Thursday morning of the death in action of Private Luke Walsh, of the Third Battalion, Leinster Regiment. Private Walsh, who was a married man, and who leaves a wife and children, left home in August last under the mobilisation order, and for some months did duty at the concentration camp at Templemore. He was then, with several others of the battalion, selected for the front, whither he and a number of his comrades were drafted some time in the end of October. He has been in several engagements, and since the day he left Tullamore, he was never granted a day's furlough. He was amongst a great number of the Leinsters and men of other regiments who were treated for frost bite at the base hospital. As soon as he was sufficiently recovered he was sent up into the firing line again. He was present at the Neuve Chapelle carnage and at the battle of Ypres.

On Saturday last, the 1st May, he apparently was shot dead, a bullet having pierced his heart. Some comrades who were fortunate to survive the battle, who had saw him fall, afterwards recovered his body and interred it.

Deceased is a son-in-law of Mr Patrick Boland, of Puttaghaun, Tullamore, and a son of Mr Walsh, Ballycowen. He was an industrious, hard-working young man, who was extremely popular, and when the Volunteer movement was started in Tullamore he was about one of the first of the army reserve men to come forward and join it, and to give his services to the corps as instructor. Deceased was an excellent rifle shot, and held a medal for efficiency in marksmanship. Several other Tullamore men, also belonging to the Leinsters, are rumoured as having been wounded at the fight for Hill 60.

He is also listed on the Tullamore Roll of Honour. Grave or Memorial Reference: C.3. Cemetery: Ferme Buterne Military Cemetery, Houplines in France.

**WALSH, Matthew:** Rank: Gunner. Regiment or Service: Royal Garrison Artillery. Unit: 241ˢᵗ Siege Battery. Date of death: 23 April 1917. Service no: 110638. Born in Co. Offaly. Enlisted in Lochgelly, Fife. Died of wounds. Age at death: 36.

*Supplementary information*: Husband of Margaret Kelly (formerly Walsh), of 1243 Cathcart Road, Langside, Glasgow. Grave or Memorial Reference: V.B.10. Cemetery; Faubourg D'Amiens Cemetery, Arras in France.

**WALSH P.:** Rank: Pte. Regiment or Service: The King's (Liverpool Regiment). Unit: Depot. Date of death: 5 April 1919. Service no: 33628. Grave or Memorial Reference: Free ground. 334. Cemetery: Clonminch Catholic Cemetery, Co. Offaly.

**WALSH, William:** Rank: Pte. Regiment or Service: Leinster Regiment. Unit: 2ⁿᵈ Battalion. Date of death: 12 April 1917. Service no: 10542. Born in Birr, Co. Offaly. Enlisted in Birr, Co. Offaly. Killed in action. Age at death: 19.

*Supplementary information*: Son of the late Patrick Walsh, of Townsend Street, Birr, Co. Offaly. Grave or Memorial Reference: He has no known grave but is listed in Bay 9 on the Arras Memorial in France.

**WALSH/WALSHE, Patrick J.:** Rank: Pte. Regiment or Service: Irish Guards. Unit: 1ˢᵗ Battalion. Date of death: 26 July 1917. Service no: 10900. Enlisted in Mountmellick, Co. Laois. Born in Mullingar, however his birth certificate states he was born on 16 September 1892 and was baptised in Tullamore. His parents were Patrick Walsh and Mary Owens, Sponsors were Dan Connolly and Margaret Wynne):

Dear Mrs Walshe. I wanted to write to you long ago, but, while in the fighting area it was impossible, and then I was away for some time and had not your address, but, now that I am back, though it's a long time after, I must write and say how dreadfully sorry I was at the death of your son. He was such a cheery and good-hearted fellow and there is no-one in the company that I would have been sorrier to lose. Everybody loved him and we miss him very much. I never thought of him being killed somehow, and had meant to make him one of my orderlies, because I liked him so much and thought so well of him … It is awful to think of one so full of life, who always had a smile or a song on his lips-like being dead; and I can only imagine how dear he must have been to you and what his death must mean to you. We were carrying up some material that night and came under very heavy shell-fire. I heard that some men had been hit and ran to the place.

There were two men lying dead; but, it was too dark to see who they were at the time. All I knew was that they had been killed absolutely at once, as I got there very soon after it happened. A short time afterwards, a stretcher-bearer brought me the pay books of the two men and by the light of a torch I read your son's regimental number in one of them and knew he had been killed… We could not bury him that night, as we had a hard enough job to get the wounded away; but, next night some of his friends in the platoon went up and brought down his body, and the Priest, up and buried him. He is buried at BLEUET FARM near BOESINGHE which is a few from Ypres. I have not had the chance of seeing his grave, but, I shall try to go and see it if we are near again and I know it will be well looked after.

Yours Faithfully,

R. Rodakowske. (Captain).

Killed in action. He is also listed on the Tullamore Roll of Honour and adds that he is a brother of Luke Walsh listed above. Grave or Memorial Reference: I. B. II. Cemetery: Bleuet Farm Cemetery in Belgium.

**WALSHE, John:** Rank: Pte. Regiment or Service: Leinster Regiment. Unit: 2nd Battalion. Date of death: 20 October 1914. Service no: 8022. Born in Kilbride, Co. Offaly. Enlisted in Athlone, County Westmeath. Killed in action. Grave or Memorial Reference: Has no known grave but is commemorated on Panel 10. Memorial: Ploegsteert Memorial in Belgium.

**WARD, J.:** Rank: Gunner. Regiment or Service: Royal Garrison Artillery. Date of death: 26 February 1920. Service no: 221666. Supplementary information: Son of Mrs R. Ward, of Crinkle, Birr. Grave or Memorial Reference: 4. 743A. Cemetery: Birr (Clonoghill) Cemetery, Co. Offaly.

**WARD, Patrick:** Rank: Staff Sergeant. Regiment or Service: Cheshire Regiment. Unit: 2nd Battalion. Date of death: 28 December 1917. Service no: 7180. Born in Jordanstown, Enfield Co. Meath. Enlisted in Birkenhead, Cheshire while living in Clare, Co. Offaly. Died in East Africa.

*Supplementary information*: Won the Meritorious Service Medal. Grave or Memorial Reference:6. A. 10. Cemetery: Dar Es Salaam War Cemetery in Tanzania.

**WARLING, George William:** Rank: Corporal. Regiment or Service: Royal Field Artillery. Unit: 54th Bty. 39th Bde. Age at death: 21. Date of death: 24 July 1916. Service no: 65594 Awards: Mentioned in Despatches.

William George Warling. Image from the *King's County Chronicle* 1916.

*Supplementary information*: Son of James and Mary Warling of Whiteford, Crinkle, Birr, Co. Offaly. From the *Midland Tribune*, *Tipperary Sentinel* and *King's County Vindicator*, August 1916: From the *King's County Chronicle*, August 1916:

### GALLANT YOUNG BIRR MAN. KILLED IN THE BIG PUSH.

News reached Birr this week of the death in action of Corpl. Warling, of the 54th Battery, 39th Brigade, Royal Field Artillery. He was a son of Mr and Mrs Warling, Military Barracks, Birr, and lived in Birr for about eight years before he joined the army. He was only 21 years of age when he was killed. The sad news was conveyed to the parents in a letter from Lieut, Cocherton. The loss of Corpl. Warling, he stated, was felt by the whole battery, as he was liked by everybody. He was killed instantly by shell-fire on July 24, whilst in action. He was an exceptionally good signaller, and it would be extremely difficult to replace him.

Young Corpl. Warling, was at the front from the very beginning of the war. His Battery, the 54th R.F.A., had the honour of being one of the very first in action, having fought at Mons on August 23, 1914, about 5pm. This battery also fought rearguard actions at Le Chateau, and was at the Aisne, Neuve Chapelle, Richebourg, La Basse, Festubert, Laventie, Guinchy, and at Vermelles, as well as Loos.

In a letter written in January 1915, young Corpl. Warling wrote cheerfully and modestly of these stirring events. He was at Ypres with his battery when the Germans were stopped on the road to Calais. This was a month of fierce fighting. "I have a thousand little incidents to relate to you when I get home," wrote the poor lad to his parents, and undoubtedly he had, for from the first he was in the thickest of the fighting. He only had three days leave since the beginning of the war. His last letter was dated 22nd July, 1916, two days before he was killed. This letter was very cheerful. "Everything is A1," he wrote "It is Somme fight." On the 24th he was killed.

His brother, James Patrick Warling, a Gunner in the same battery, is in hospital with a wound in the leg, which he received four days before Corpl. Warling was killed. It is satisfactory to learn that Gunner Warling is progressing favourably. The greatest sympathy will be felt with Mr and Mrs Warling in the loss sustained by the death of their gallant son, Corporal Warling.

Grave or Memorial Reference: IV.A.13. Cemetery: Quarry Cemetery, Montauban in France.

**WARLING, James Patrick:** Rank: Bombardier, also listed as Gunner. Regiment or Service: Royal Field Artillery. Unit: "A" Bty. 180th Bde. Age at death: 19. Date of death: 31 July 1917. Service no: listed as 694856 and 69485. Born in Deesa, India. Enlisted in Birr. Killed in action.

*Supplementary information:* Son of James and Mary Warling, of Birr, Co. Offaly, *King's County Chronicle*, August 1917:

ROLL OF HONOUR.
JAMES P. WARLING.

The death in action on the 1st August is reported of James Patrick Warling, "A" Battery, R. F. A., 180th Brigade, 16th (Irish) Division, in France, aged 20 years. Before the war he had been in the army and saw active service from the start to his death. He was in action with the 54th Battery, at Mons. His brother, George William Warling, who was in the same battery, was killed on the 24th July, 1916. After being wounded, James was transferred from the 54th to "A" Battery, 180th Brigade, in which he was serving when he was killed.

Deep sympathy is felt for the father and mother, Mr and Mrs Warling. The Barracks, Crinkle, in the loss of their two fine boys. In connection with the 54th battery, to which both these boys were attached so long, the following letter written by "one who knows" is of interest; "I should like to say in connection with the many claims to the first shot of the war that the 54th battery ("Bloodsuckers of the Aisne") of the 39th Brigade consisting of the 46th, 51st, and 54th Batteries were in action at Mons on August 23rd, 1914, about five p.m. We fought rearguard actions at le Chateau, and then were side by side with the French on the Marne. After that the Aisne, Neuve Chapelle, Bichabourg, La Bassee, Festubert, Laventie, Guinchy, and Vermelles and advance to the German first line at Lone Pine (Battle of Loos). At Ypres in October and November, 1914, we were the most forward battery in action and our officers received the D.S.O. for their work. We have been in action at 400 yards without gun pits, and we are still fighting in France as game as ever."

Grave or Memorial Reference: VII.B.22. Cemetery: Vlamertinghe Military Cemetery in Belgium.

**WARNER, Archibald:** Rank: Second Lieutenant. Regiment or Service: London Regiment. Unit: 5th Battalion. Date of death: 1 July 1916. Age at death: 32. Killed in action.

*Supplementary information:* Son of John Warner, of Waddon House, Croydon; husband of Norah E. Marriage (formerly Warner), of The Parsonage, Broomfield, Essex. Served as Pte. in 3rd Bn. Artists' Rifles. From the *King's County Chronicle*, July 1916, 'Second Lieut Archibald Warner, London Regiment, a member of the Society of Friends, fell on July 1. In

September 1916, he married Norah E. Goodbody, youngest daughter of Mr and Mrs J Perry-Goodbody, Clara. He was a solicitor by profession and a keen all round sportsman.' Grave or Memorial Reference: IV.D.7. Cemetery: Hebuterne Military Cemetery in France.

**WATKINS, George:** Rank: Corporal. Regiment or Service: Leinster Regiment. Unit: 1<sup>st</sup> Bn. Date of death: 15 March 1915. Service no: 8975. Born in Roscrea. Enlisted in Birr. Killed in action. Age at death: 23.

*Supplementary information*: Son of John S. and Margaret Watkins, of Ettagh, Brosna, Roscrea, Co. Offaly. Grave or Memorial Reference: He has no known grave but is listed on Panel 44 on the Ypres (Menin Gate) Memorial in Belgium

**WATKINS, John:** Rank: Pte. Regiment or Service: Household Cavalry and Cavalry of the line including the Yeomanry and Imperial Camel Corps. Unit: 17<sup>th</sup> Lancers (Duke of Cambridge's Own) attached to the 5<sup>th</sup> Royal Irish Lancers. Date of death: 1 July 1917. Service no: 16092 and GS/16092. Born in Birr, Co. Offaly. Enlisted in Dublin while living in Dublin. Died of wounds.

*Supplementary information*: Husband of M.K. Watkins, of River Street, Clara, Co. Offaly. Grave or Memorial Reference: II.H.32. Cemetery: Templeux-Le-Guerard British Cemetery Extension in France.

**WATSON, James Norman:** Rank: Second Lieutenant. Regiment or Service: Royal Inniskilling Fusiliers. Unit: 3<sup>rd</sup> Battalion, attached to A Company, 1<sup>st</sup> Battalion. Date of death: 10 August 1916. Age at death: 22. Died of wounds.

*Supplementary information:* Son of Frances Watson, of Avon Lodge, Armagh, and the late James A. Watson. He is listed on the Tullamore Roll of Honour. I do not see the Offaly connection but include him for your reference. Grave or Memorial Reference: IX.B.1. Cemetery: Lijssenthoek Military Cemetery in Belgium.

**WATSON, Thomas:** Rank: Pte. Regiment or Service: Leinster Regiment. Unit: 2<sup>nd</sup> Battalion. Date of death: 13 July 1915. Service no: 3155. Born in Birr. Enlisted in Birr, Co. Offaly while living in Birr, Co. Offaly. Killed in action. From the *King's County Chronicle*, July 1915:

> It will be heard with regret, especially by his comrade compositors in the "King's County Chronicle" that Private Thomas Watson, 3<sup>rd</sup> Battalion, Leinster Regiment, was killed in action; and much sympathy is felt for his young wife and little children, and also his father, Mr James Watson, bootbuilder, Church Lane, Birr. The deceased was very quiet and amiable, and a favourite among all who knew him. During his apprenticeship in this office, and subsequent as a journeyman printer, his conduct was most praiseworthy.

Thomas Watson. Image from *King's County Chronicle* 1916.

Grave or Memorial Reference: Has no known grave but is commemorated on Panel 44. Memorial: Ypres (Menin Gate) Memorial in Belgium.

**WEBSTER, Arthur:** Rank: Lance Corporal. Regiment or Service: Connaught Rangers. Unit: 5<sup>th</sup> Battalion. Date of death: 7 December 1915. Service no: 10897. Born in Birr, Co. Offaly. Enlisted in Galway while living in Blackpool. Killed in action in Salonika. Age at death: 19.

*Supplementary information:* Son of Arthur and Susan Webster. Grave or Memorial Reference: He has no known grave but is listed on the Doiran Memorial in Greece.

**WEIR, James:** Rank: Lance Corporal. Regiment or Service: Royal Dublin Fusiliers. Unit: 2<sup>nd</sup> Battalion. Date of death: 21 July 1915. Service no: 9345. Born in Tullamore, Co. Offaly. Enlisted in Naas while living in Tullamore. Died of wounds. Age at death: 28.

*Supplementary information:* Son of Martin Weir, of Henry Street, Tullamore. He is also listed on the Tullamore Roll of Honour as **James WYER,**

and adds that he died as a prisoner of war in Germany. Grave or Memorial Reference: III.L.16. Cemetery: Niederzwehren Cemetery in Germany.

**WHELAN, Martin:** Rank: Pte. Regiment or Service: Irish Guards. Unit: 2<sup>nd</sup> Battalion. Date of death: 20 January 1915. Service no: 3323. Born in Banagher, Co. Offaly. Enlisted in Tullamore. Died of wounds. Grave or Memorial Reference: III.C.60. Cemetery: Boulogne Eastern Cemetery in France.

**WHELAN, Peter:** Rank: Sergeant. Regiment or Service: Leinster Regiment. Unit: 2<sup>nd</sup> Battalion. Date of death: 13 March 1916. Service no: 2402. Born in Kilbride, Co. Offaly. Enlisted in Birr, Co. Offaly. *Killed in action. From the King's County Independent,* January 1915, 'Midland Notes. Tullmore. Sergeant Peter Whelan of the 3<sup>rd</sup> Leinsters, who had been also invalided home from the front, returned to his headquarters on Monday afternoon.' He is also listed on the Tullamore Roll of Honour. Grave or Memorial Reference: I.J.11. Cemetery: Menin Road South Military Cemetery in Belgium.

**WHELEHAN, Patrick:** Rank: Pte. Regiment or Service: Irish Guards. Unit: 2<sup>nd</sup> Battalion. Date of death: 10 March 1917. Service no: 10078. Born in Geashill, Co. Offaly. Enlisted in Maryborough, Co. Laois. Killed in action. There is a Pte John Whelehan, Irish Guards, son of Mr Whelehan, ex-R.I.C. from the Banagher district mentioned in the *King's County Chronicle*, April 1916. They may be related. Grave or Memorial Reference: V.I.2. Cemetery: Sailly-Saillisel British Cemetery in France.

**WHITE, Christopher:** Rank: Pte. Regiment or Service: Leinster Regiment. Unit: 6th Battalion. Date of death: 23 February 1915. Service no: 131. Born in Birr, Co. Offaly. 'Ireland's Memorial Records' says he was born, St Brendan's, Birr. Enlisted in Birr, Co. Offaly. Died at Home. From the *King's County Chronicle*, 1915:

> A military burial was accorded to Private Christopher White, of the 6th Leinsters, who died on the Curragh from pneumonia on the 24th February. For the consolation of his parents the remains were brought to Birr. On reaching the station they were carried to the hearse by six comrades who happened to be on leave. The intern-ment on Friday was largely attended, and the prayers were recited by the Very Rev. Dean Scanlan, P.P., V.G. A party of the 11th Hampshires fired three volleys over the grave and 'the Last Post' was sounded. The deceased's brother, who is in the 3rd Leinsters, is now home wounded, was one of the chief mourners, and another brother is on active service with the R.A.M.C.

From the *King's County Chronicle*, February 1916:

> Mr John White, Mill Street, at present in the 3rd Leinsters, has three sons in the army – Private John, of the R.A.M.C., in France since the outbreak of hostilities; Private Christopher, 6th Leinsters, died while in training; and Private Michael, who is with the 1st Leinsters in the Balkans.

Grave or Memorial Reference: 4. 748A. Cemetery: Birr (Clonoghill) Cemetery, Co. Offaly.

**WHITE, Patrick:** Rank: Pte. Regiment or Service: Leinster Regiment. Unit: 7th Battalion. Date of death: 21 March 1918. Service No: 3282. Born in Rahan, Co. Offaly. Enlisted in Heath Camp, Maryborough, Co. Laois. Killed in action. From the *King's County Chronicle*, June 1915:

> LOCAL NINE WARRIOR SONS. "BANGS BANAGHER."
>
> Mr John White, mason, Banagher, who served 23 years in the Co. Offaly Militia, and received a congratulatory letter from the King last September, when he had eight sons with the colours, has that fine record further improved by the addition of another son and a grand-son joining, as well as two sons-in-law. Though every member of this military family has not yet been to the "front" four or five have been wounded. The "fighting Whites are represented in the Dublins by Mike, the Leinsters by Pat, Joe, John, and Mart; the Connaughts by Kieran, Bill, Jim, Tom, and Tommie, junior. It will be readily conceded that the father is a proud man and is entitled to every praise. It is a matter for regret

that he is in needy circumstances, but now the readers of the *King's County Chronicle* it is natural enough to suppose that some charitably disposed will give him assistance.

From the *King's County Chronicle*, April 1918:

BANAGHER SOLDIER.
AWARDED D.C.M.

His Majesty the King has been graciously pleased to award the Distinguished Medal to the under mentioned for gallantry and distinguished service in the field;

8006 Private K. White, Connaught Rangers (Banagher).
For conspicuous gallantry and devotion to duty during an attack and an enemy counter-attack. His portion of the trench was heavily bombed by the enemy, but he stationed himself as near to the enemy as possible and continually caught their bombs in mid-air and threw them back. His courage and daring during several critical hours contributed materially to the final defeat of the enemy.

From the *King's County Chronicle*, April 1918:

Private Kieran White, Connaught rangers, Banagher, has been awarded the D.C.M. His mother resides at Banagher, and gave nine sons, two son-in-laws and one grandson to the colours. Private Kieran was himself once wounded, as well as two of his brothers and nephew.

Two are prisoners of war in Germany, and one is invalided.

Grave or Memorial Reference: Has no known grave but is commemorated on Panel 78. Memorial: Pozieres Memorial in France

**WHITFORD, Edward:** Rank: Pte. Regiment or Service: Gloucestershire Regiment. Unit: 2/5th Battalion. Date of death: 24 October 1918. Service no: 203524. Born in Agancon. Enlisted in Bristol. Killed in action. From *King's County Chronicle*, April 1916:

Trooper George Whitford, of the South Irish Horse, is fighting for King and Country on the battlefields of Flanders. He formerly resided at Aghancon, Co. Offaly, and is a first cousin to Trooper Michael and Pte Edward Whitford, of Derry, Brosna, who are also serving their country, and whose names have been recorded in this column.

Grave or Memorial Reference: VII.E.2. Cemetery: Roneries Communal Cemetery Extension in France.

**WHITFORD, George:** Rank: Pte. Regiment or Service: Household Cavalry and Cavalry of the line including the Yeomanry and Imperial Camel Corps. Also listed as the Royal Irish regiment. Unit: South Irish Horse. Date of death: 18 September 1917. Service no: 927. Born in Agancon. Enlisted in Portarlington while living in Mountmellick. Killed in action. Age at death: 25.

*Supplementary information*: Son of the late William and Catherine Whitford, of Rock Farm, Mountmellick, Co. Laois. *King's County Chronicle*, April 1916:

Trooper George Whitford, of the South Irish Horse, is fighting for King and Country on the battlefields of Flanders. He formerly resided at Aghancon, Co. Offaly, and is a first cousin to Trooper Michael and Pte Edward Whitford, of Derry, Brosna, who are also serving their country, and whose names have been recorded in this column.

Grave or Memorial Reference: III.J.11. Cemetery: Coxyde Military Hospital in Belgium.

**WHYTE, H.:** Rank: Sergeant. Regiment or Service: Leinster Regiment. Date of death: 13 August 1914. Service no: 6432. Grave or Memorial Reference: 43. Cemetery: Birr Military Cemetery, Co. Offaly.

**WILLIAMS, Laurence:** Rank: Pte. Regiment or Service: Manchester Regiment. Unit: 18th Battalion. Date of death: 9 July 1916. Service no: 11043. Born in Tullamore, Co. Offaly. Enlisted in Manchester while living in Salford, Lancs. Killed in action. Grave or Memorial Reference: He has no known grave but is listed on Pier and Face 13 A and 14 C on the Thiepval Memorial in France.

**WILLIAMS, Rupert:** Rank: Pte. Regiment or Service: Cheshire Regiment. Unit: 16th Battalion also listed as 12th Entrenching Battalion, late 16th Battalion. Date of death: 23 March 1918. Service no: 63367. Formerly he was with the South Wales Borderers where his number was 10598. Born in Birr, Co. Offaly. Enlisted in Dublin while living in Chatham. Killed in action. Grave or Memorial Reference: He has no known grave but is listed on Panel 35 and 36 on the Pozieres Memorial in France.

**WILLINGTON, James Vernon Yates:** Rank: 2lt (TP). Regiment or Service: Prince of Wales Leinster Regiment (Royal Canadians). Killed in action in Gallipoli aged 20.

*Supplementary information:* Son of James T. C. and Alice Willington of St Kieran's (Lorrha), Birr, Co. Offaly. From the *King's County Chronicle*, August 1915:

We very correctly expressed the all pervading feeling of the community when in the last "*King's County Chronicle*" we stated that the news of the bereavement which had suddenly overtaken Mr and Mrs Willington and family, produced very sincere regret indeed. The first intimation was a War Office telegram received in Birr by the father last week that his son, Sec. Lieut J. V. Y. Willington, 6th Leinsters, fell in action at the Dardanelles, where the battalion was heavily engaged, and suffered, the officers lists numbering four killed and two wounded. At the last meeting of the North Tipp. Agricultural Committee, of which Mr Willington is a valued member, a vote of sympathy was unanimously passed on the motion of Mr Duggan, J.P.

Grave or Memorial Reference: He has no known grave but is listed on the Helles Memorial on Panel 184 and 185.

**WILSON, Gordon Chesney:** Rank: Lieutenant Colonel. Regiment or Service: Household Cavalry and Cavalry of the line including the Yeomanry and Imperial Camel Corps. Unit: Royal Horse Guards. Date of death: 6 November 1914. Age at death: 49. Awards: M.V.O. Killed in action. Supplementary information: Eldest son of Sir Samuel Wilson, Kt. Husband of Lady Sarah I.A. Wilson, R.R.C., of 23c Bruton Street, London. From the *King's County Chronicle*, November 1914:

The late Colonel Wilson: A service was held on the 12th November, at Christ Church, Mayfair. In memory of Lieut, Col. Chesney Gordon Wilson, M.V.O., Commanding Officer, Royal Horse Guards, who was killed on Friday, the 6th of November. This distinguished soldier was brother of the Countess of Huntington and Mrs Hardress Lloyd, of Gloster, King's County, and husband of Lady Sarah Churchill, aunt of the Duke of Marlborough. These ladies, with the deceased's son, Randolf, were present of the solemn occasion. Canon Sheppard, of Chapels Royal, officiated, and the hymns were "Fight a good fight" and the Russian national anthem "God the all terrible" and the anthem was Tennyson's "Crossing the Bar."

The chancel was decorated with white lilies. A hundred troopers of the Guards were present, also the band. The place the deceased held among the highest social ranks was reflected by the large congregation of the nobility and other leading families, for which our space only admits these comparatively few names: Queen Alexandra, represented by General Sir D. Probyn; Field Marshal, Sir E. Wood, Grand Duke Michael and Countess Torby, Lady Norah Spencer Churchill, Dowager Duchess Roxburghe, Lady Randolf Churchill, Priness de Polignac, the Marquesses of Lincoln, Northampton, and de Soveral, the Marquess and Marchioness of Londonderry, the Countess of Huntington, and Lady Kathleen and Lady Norah Hastings, Col. Sir G. Holford and officers of the 1st Life Guards, Col. Ames, representing the 2nd Life Guards; General Sir A. Paget, Sir Starr Jameson, Sir John and Lady Lister-Kaye, Mr and Mrs Alan Campbell, Mr and Hon, Mrs Maguire, Mr Otto Beit. The Earl of Huntingdon being laid up with an attach of colitis, was unable to be present.

Grave or Memorial Reference: B.2. Cemetery: Zillebeke Churchyard, in Belgium.

**WILTON, William Frank:** Rank: Sergeant. Regiment or Service: Royal Welsh Fusiliers. Unit: 2nd Battalion. Date of death: 26 December 1915 ('Soldiers died in the Great War') 26

December 1916 ('Ireland's Memorial Records' and the Commonwealth War Graves Commission). Service no: 4602. Born in Adderbury, Banbury. Enlisted in Dublin while living in Clara, Co. Offaly. Died. Age at death: 39.

*Supplementary information:* Son of Charles and Sarah Wilton. Husband of Jane Wilton, of Adderbury, Oxon. Born at Adderbury. Grave or Memorial Reference: I.B.23. Cemetery: Peronne Road Cemetery, Maricourt in France.

**WOODS, Frederick James:** Rank: Corporal. Regiment or Service: Royal Fusiliers (City of London Regiment). Unit: 2nd Battalion. Date of death: 28 February 1917. Service no: 13873 and L/13873. Born in Birr, Co. Offaly. Enlisted in Stratford while living in Victoria Park. Killed in action. From the *King's County Chronicle*, October 1914:

> Their acquaintances were glad to see troopers Kerrison, Oakley and Woods looking so fit and happy in the smart uniform of the South Irish Horse, a detachment of which is now in training in Limerick. These gallant young Birrmen, who are in the best of spirits, had availed of a weekend leave. They returned on Monday and the same 4.50pm train which brought them out of Birr had Major Wright. 1st Batt, Royal Irish Rifles, en route for the seat of war. As an instance of the exigencies of war, he had scarcely disembarked from one of the fifty troop ships which brought the second contingent of the Expeditionary Force

from India last week, when he was granted 48 hours leave, which, owing to travelling from his regiment and back allowed him a bare five hours to see what is left of the family circle.

From the *King's County Chronicle*, February 1916, 'The many friends, which include all Birr and district, of Mr William Lucas Woods were glad to see him during his few days leave from hospital. Mr Woods, who is in the 31st Canadian Infantry, was severely wounded last October in France, and still carries the bullet in his leg. May his complete recovery be rapid.' Grave or Memorial Reference: II.B.4. Cemetery: Sailly-Saillisel British Cemetery in France.

**WRIGHT, John:** Rank: Lance Sergeant. Regiment or Service: Oxfordshire and Buckinghamshire Light Infantry. Unit: 1st Battalion. Date of death: 29 September 1915. Service no: 8985. Born in Shinrone. Enlisted in Witney, Oxon while living in Gt Barrington, Oxon. Killed in action in the Persian Gulf. Grave or Memorial Reference: He has no known grave but is listed on Panel 26 and 63 on the Basra Memorial in Iraq.

**WRIGHT, John Edenderry:** Also listed as **WRIGHT, T.** Rank: Pte. Regiment or Service: Royal Dublin Fusiliers. Unit: D Company, 2nd Battalion. Date of death: 19 March 1916. Service no: 9487. Born in Co. Offaly. Enlisted in Naas while living in Edenderry. Killed in action. Age at death: 28. 'Ireland's Memorial Records' gives his name as **John WRIGHT**, 'Soldiers died in the Great War' give his name as **John Edenderry WRIGHT** and the Commonwealth Wargraves Commission give his name as T. Wright. Son of James and Mary Wright, of Main Street, Edenderry, Co. Offaly. From the *Leinster Leader* 4 March 1916:

> The relatives of Private 'Jack' Wright have received a letter from Corporal W. Glen on behalf of the 2nd Dublin fusiliers Stretcher Bearers enclosed with the deceased shoulder straps;
>
> "Jack had been in my section since April last year, and was one of the oldest stretcher bearers we had. I can assure you he was very much missed, he was such a good soldier. He was respected by all who knew him. We saw to his funeral and are looking after his grave. We had two beautiful crosses placed on it, also some small crucifixes. Everything was done just as you would have wished."
>
> Private Joe Judge an Edenderry man writing to the brother of the deceased said;
>
> "Jack lived about two hours and was buried in a very nice graveyard. The boys put a cross over his grave".

From the *King's County Chronicle*, July 1915:

> A GALLANT KING'S COUNTY MAN.
> Letters from the front relate the gallant deed of an Edenderry man.

Private John Webb, 2nd Batt. Dublin Fusiliers, in a letter, Private P. Ryan, also of that Battalion, says: "On April 25th at Ypres we paid a heavy penalty, losing 15 officers and over 700 men. But we made the Germans pay too. There were piles of their dead, but still they came on, driven up like sheep into flocks by dogs. It was on that day that John Webb made his name carrying Captain Wheeler on his back under heavy fire. The following morning at three o'clock, I said nothing, but thought the more to see only 15 left out of 900 men the day before. Think of that in Ireland, and of how the Germans poisoned our men. Murder was no name for it. The men of Edenderry are extraordinarily lucky. Not alone Jack Webb for bravery, but Jack Wright; no man would believe his bravery. He is the talk of the regiment."

Grave or Memorial Reference: XIVA.I. Cemetery: Bienvillers Military Cemetery in France.

**WYNNE, Francis:** Rank: Pte. Regiment or Service: Royal Dublin Fusiliers. Unit: 1st Battalion. Date of death: 20 August 1917. Service no: 26973. Born in Kilcormac, Co. Offaly. Enlisted in Tullamore while living in Kilcormac. Killed in action. From the *King's County Chronicle*, September 1917, 'Private Wynne, son of Const. Wynne, of Kilcormac, is reported killed. Only a short time ago another son of Const. Wynne was wounded.' Grave or Memorial Reference: He has no known grave but is listed on Panels 144 to 145 on the Tyne Cot Memorial in Belgium.

**WYNYARD, Damer:** Rank: Captain. Regiment or Service: East Surrey Regiment. Unit: Adjutant, 1st Battalion. Date of death: 20 April 1915. Age at death: 25. Killed in action.

*Supplementary information*: Mentioned in Despatches. Son of Lt. Col. Richard Damer Wynyard (late East Surrey Regt.) and Mrs Wynyard, of 2 South Belfield, Weymouth. Husband of Olive Wakely (now wife of Lieutenant Commander Brind, Royal Navy). Previously wounded at Mons, 23 August 1914. From the *King's County Chronicle*, May 1915:

> Capt. Damer Wynyard, East Surrey Regiment, killed in action on April 20, was previously wounded at Mons, but rejoined his battalion in December, in which month he married Olive, youngest daughter of His Honour Judge Wakely, D.L., of Ballyburley, Co. Offaly. Capt. Wynyard was the sixth in direct succession from father to son of a family of soldiers. He was a keen sportsman, and a well known follower of the Cattistock, the Meaths, the Kildares and the Edenderry and District Harriers.

From the *King's County Independent*, June 1915:

LATE CAPTAIN WYNYARD.

County Court Judge Wakely wrote Mr Heberin as follows; "Please convey to the members of the Roscommon Co. Council my sincere thanks for the kind resolution of sympathy on the death of my son-in-law, Captain Wynyard, and for the kind thoughts which prompted the passing of the resolution. It is only another instance of the many kindnesses I have received since I first came to Roscommon county, and I assure the County Council that it helps to bear this sorrow, which to us is a great one, as Captain Wynyard had won all out hearts as well as the heart of his wife. My daughter is writing to you also. I thank you for kind words in which you have conveyed the resolution to me."

Mrs Olive Wynyard wrote expressing sincere appreciation of the Council's kind sympathy in her great loss.

Grave or Memorial Reference: Has no known grave but is commemorated on Panel 34 on the Ypres (Menin Gate) Memorial in Belgium.

# Y

**YOUNGE, Anthony:** Rank: Pte. Regiment or Service: Irish Guards. Unit: 1st Battalion. Date of death: 20 June 1916. Service no: 4182. Born in Raheen, Co. Offaly. Enlisted in Maryborough, Co Laois. Died of wounds. Killed in action. Age at death: 22.

*Supplementary information*: Awarded the D.C.M. Son of James and M.A. Young, of Dereen, Cloneygowan, Portarlington. Grave or Memorial Reference: I.P.26. Cemetery: Essex Farm Cemetery in Belgium.

**YOUNGE, Frederick George Patrick:** Rank: Lieutenant. Regiment or Service: Leinster Regiment. Unit: 2nd Bn. Age at death: 22. Date of death: 14 February 1915.

*Supplementary information*: Son of Mr J.M. and Mrs J. Younge, of Oldtown, Rathdowney, Co. Offaly. Grave or Memorial Reference: F.7. Cemetery: Bailleul Communal Cemetery (Nord) in France.

**YOUNGER, Harry:** Rank: Pte. Regiment or Service: (Queens) Royal West Surrey Regiment. Unit: 7th Battalion. Date of death: 1 July 1916. Service no: G/1562. Born in Birr, Co. Offaly. Enlisted in Guildford, Surrey while living in Aldershot, Hants. Killed in action. Grave or Memorial Reference: VII.P.6. Cemetery: Danzig Alley British Cemetery Mametz in France.